Sex in College

Recent Titles in
Sex, Love, and Psychology
Judy Kuriansky, Series Editor

In the Company of Men: Inside the Lives of Male Prostitutes
Michael D. Smith and Christian Grov

Sixty, Sexy, and Successful: A Guide for Aging Male Baby Boomers
Robert Schwalbe, PhD

Managing Menopause Beautifully: Physically, Emotionally, and Sexually
Dona Caine-Francis

New Frontiers in Men's Sexual Health: Understanding Erectile Dysfunction and the Revolutionary New Treatments
Kamal A. Hanash, MD

Sexuality Education: Past, Present, and Future (4 volumes)
Elizabeth Schroeder, EdD, MSW, and Judy Kuriansky, PhD, editors

Sex When You're Sick: Reclaiming Sexual Health after Illness or Injury
Anne Katz

Secret Suffering: How Women's Sexual and Pelvic Pain Affects Their Relationships
Susan Bilheimer and Robert J. Echenberg, MD

Teenage Sex and Pregnancy: Modern Myths, Unsexy Realities
Mike Males

Monogamy: The Untold Story
Marianne Brandon

Sex, Love, and Mental Illness: A Couple's Guide to Staying Connected
Stephanie Buehler

Coming Home to Passion: Restoring Loving Sexuality in Couples with Histories of Childhood Trauma and Neglect
Ruth Cohn

Losing the Bond with God: Sexual Addiction and Evangelical Men
Kailla Edger, PhD

SEX IN COLLEGE

The Things They Don't Write Home About

Richard D. McAnulty, Editor

Sex, Love, and Psychology
Judy Kuriansky, Series Editor

AN IMPRINT OF ABC-CLIO, LLC
Santa Barbara, California • Denver, Colorado • Oxford, England

Library of Congress Cataloging-in-Publication Data

Sex in college : the things they don't write home about / Richard D. McAnulty, editor.
p. cm. — (Sex, love, and psychology)
Includes bibliographical references and index.
ISBN 978-0-313-38383-0 (hardcopy : alk. paper) — ISBN 978-0-313-38384-7 (ebook)
1. College students—Sexual behavior. I. McAnulty, Richard D.
HQ35.2.S39 2012
306.7084'2—dc23 2011053512

ISBN: 978-0-313-38383-0
EISBN: 978-0-313-38384-7

16 15 14 13 12 1 2 3 4 5

This book is also available on the World Wide Web as an eBook.
Visit www.abc-clio.com for details.

Praeger
An Imprint of ABC-CLIO, LLC

ABC-CLIO, LLC
130 Cremona Drive, P.O. Box 1911
Santa Barbara, California 93116-1911

This book is printed on acid-free paper ∞

Manufactured in the United States of America

CONTENTS

SERIES FOREWORD

College is one of the most stressful times in life, made more complicated by transitions in relationships and temptations of sexuality. From the many years I spent answering young people's questions about relationships and sexuality, particularly on the radio, I know how troubling the issues and decisions regarding this important aspect of life are for youth. The problems young people have asked me about cover such a wide range—from changes in their body, to dating, dysfunctions, sexual identity, and depression. So many stories distressed me, like those about betrayal, and others were shocking, including experimenting with dangerous activities like bloodletting and asphyxiation for sexual highs. I hoped over time that the sexuality information many sexual experts like myself had worked so hard to spread would have educated generations, and that many of those problems would be solved and dangerous behaviors would die out. Yet, as I combed the pages of my book *Generation Sex* where I documented thousands of those questions and my answers, and reviewed the comprehensive and impressive articles in the Praeger series I coedited about "Sexuality Education: Past, Present, and Future," I realized that we have to continue to address these issues, as youth still struggle in this technological, fast-paced, and challenging world today.

For these reasons, I was supportive of Richard McAnulty editing this book about college students and sex. As a researcher, journal editor, and college teacher of courses on human sexuality for over 20 years, he is well versed in the issues faced by young people. This resulting volume is a valuable resource on what is facing young people at that crucial crossroads today, from developmental theories about college students and sex, to issues like dating and infidelity, sexual harassment, sexual identity, sexual risk taking, and the climate about sexuality on campuses today—all of which professionals, parents, and policy makers alike need to know.

PREFACE

Misconceptions and stereotypes about college students' sexual activities abound. For example, some social critics have concluded that college students have abandoned dating in favor of casual sexual encounters. While it is true that the courtship approach to dating has largely fallen out of favor, most students still dream of finding their soul mates and eventually becoming involved in long-term committed relationships. Clearly, some things have changed, including the terminology that students use in reference to sex and dating (such as "hook-ups," "sexting" over the cell phone, and being "sexiled" by an inconsiderate roommate). Yet many things have not changed. There is, however, no single source on the sexual attitudes and practices of college student. This volume intends to fill the void.

The vast majority of sex research continues to rely on college student samples. For example, in one recent issue of the *Journal of Sex Research*, five of the nine empirical studies relied on college student samples. Yet no single book has attempted to organize the relevant research findings. This edited volume offers reviews of the essential topics related to college students' sexuality. Drawing on contributors with expertise in the topics, the volume provides an up-to-date summary of the research on sexuality in college. As a reference, the volume is aimed at a broad audience. Anyone interested in the topic of sex in college should find it useful and timely. Sexologists, health educators, college teachers, and administrators, in addition to graduate and undergraduate students in a wide range of disciplines, should appreciate the research reviews on topics ranging from dating patterns and romantic relationships to such problems as homophobia and sexual assault. Coverage includes the brighter side of college relationships, including love, and the darker side, such as rape and sexually transmitted infections.

The contributors were selected on the basis of their expertise or promise of future contributions in the area. Preference was given to contributors who have worked in college settings and those who have studied college sexuality and related topics. Some contributors truly offer an insider's perspective on the topic: several are graduate students who are budding professionals in their field. The authors include seasoned educators at such institutions of higher learning as the University of Georgia, DePaul University, Florida State University, and the University of Ottawa.

Chapter One

COLLEGE STUDENT DATING IN PERSPECTIVE: "HANGING OUT," "HOOKING UP," AND FRIENDLY BENEFITS

Richard D. McAnulty and Arnie Cann

In recent years, some commentators and social critics have lamented the apparent demise of dating among young adults in favor of informal and uncommitted arrangements (DeGenova, 2006). Some have suggested that "hanging out" and "hooking up" have become the norm among teens and college students (Bogle, 2008; Freitas, 2008; Penhollow, Young, & Bailey, 2007; Wallace, 2007). Stepp (2007) concluded that "young people have virtually abandoned dating and replaced it with group get-togethers and sexual behaviors that are detached from love and commitment—and sometimes even from liking" (p. 5). These practices have introduced new terminology, including "friends with benefits" relationships, which involve friends who are sexually but not romantically involved (Lehmiller, VanderDrift, & Kelly, 2011). As B. L. Bailey (1988) noted, popular culture seems "rife with nostalgia for the old ways" (p. 3), and this seems especially obvious in the context of dating and intimacy. These critics, however, ignore several important trends in the intimate lives of college students in the United States. First, dating, as it is usually defined, is actually a fairly recent social phenomenon. Prior to the 1920s, dating took the form of courtship, which was practiced according to specific guidelines (it was rather formal and closely supervised by a chaperone). In parallel with dramatic changes in societal norms and out of necessity, the practice of courtship gradually fell out of favor and was replaced by dating, which afforded more freedom and opportunities for young women and men to experiment with sex and intimacy. Ongoing changes in social roles, including more equitable gender roles, have permitted further relaxing of rules in intimate relationships. Men are no longer expected to initiate. Women are more willing and able to pursue their romantic interests than in the past. Second, like the institution of marriage (Amato, Booth, Johnson, & Rogers, 2007), the practice of dating is likely to continue evolving. Alternatives to marriage, such as cohabitation or "living together" in a trial relationship, are increasingly accepted. Young adults are postponing the age of marriage, and a growing number are choosing not to marry at all. Rates of marital breakups remain high, hovering near 50 percent of all first marriages. It is not surprising, then, that dating patterns have followed similar changes in practice. Perhaps young adults are more cautious of commitment. Regardless, it is apparent that most close relationships in Western cultures have become less formal and more variable than in previous generations. Intimate relationships are no exception.

This chapter offers a brief overview of college dating trends over the past century. We will consider some of the major and often dramatic societal and cultural shifts that made these changes either possible or essential. Try to imagine dating without automobiles and telephones! Advances and developments in industry, commerce, and technology have had a major impact on dating relationships. Technological advances, such as the introduction of the cellular telephone and the Internet, transformed patterns of communication and introduced new practices, such as so-called sexting (using the phone to transmit messages or photographs that are sexually explicit) and the posting of intimate personal information on online social networks (J. D. Brown, Keller, & Stern, 2009; Rich, 2008). Accompanying changes in gender roles and attitudes toward "premarital sex" over the past century also contributed in significant ways (Regnerus & Uecker, 2011). We conclude, as Cavan did over 50 years ago, that dating is a "recent American innovation and not a traditional or universal custom" (1969, p. 125). Therefore dating trends among young adults, including college students, are very likely to continue evolving in the coming years.

MATE SELECTION: THE TRADITION OF COURTSHIP

In the nineteenth century, for middle-class Caucasian young adults courtship consisted of a formal prearrangement in which a young man "called upon" a young woman. During this visit, he could expect to be received in her family's parlor or on the front porch, and perhaps to meet her mother and have refreshments (B. L. Bailey, 1988). With parental consent, she might subsequently expect to be taken on a "date" to some community event, such as a church function. In most cases, opportunities to get to know potential mates were closely supervised, by either parents (usually hers) or members of the community (B. L. Bailey, 1988; Bogle, 2008). These formal encounters were closely supervised for at least two reasons: (1) to ensure that the suitor was suitable as a prospective husband and provider, and (2) to reduce the chances of premarital sexual activity and associated problems, such as unwanted pregnancies (Bogle, 2008). Romantic attractions were afforded secondary importance in this era.

Through the second half of the nineteenth century and into the twentieth, Western culture witnessed developments that dramatically changed most people's lives. Changes in economic realities, in social customs, and in gender roles were transforming life in Western Europe and in the United States. European immigrants, numbering as many as 10 million in the first 10 years of the century, imported their own values and customs to the country (J. S. Turner, 2003). Urban populations swelled as a growing number of people moved from rural areas and farming communities to the cities in search of an easier and more prosperous life (Beaudoin, 2003). Rapid economic growth was fueled by major discoveries and by industrialization, which also provided new employment opportunities (D'Emilio & Freedman, 1997) and more disposable income than ever before (B. L. Bailey, 1988).

Increased opportunities for education permitted young women and young men to interact on an unprecedented scale. Between 1900 and 1960, the number of adolescents attending public school grew from 7 percent to 90 percent (B. L. Bailey, 1988)! The war of 1914–1918, World War I, created a need for a workforce to replace the men who served in the military, and growing numbers of women welcomed this opportunity to fill a new role outside of the home and away from parental control. For the first time, large numbers of women were going to work in factories, offices, and stores or attending college to pursue professional careers. In various settings, women were afforded more freedom and autonomy than ever before. For example, voting rights were granted to women in 1920.

These departures from tradition also brought changes in sex norms and gender roles. Increasingly, dance halls drew a "predominantly young, unmarried crowd of both genders, without the chaperonage of adults" (D'Emilio & Freedman, 1997, p. 195). Dance halls and clubs provided a forum for dating and close physical contact. Sex was discussed more openly, young people were relatively free from parental control, men and women could interact openly in public settings, love became a legitimate pursuit, and leisure became an acceptable goal for hardworking adults. By the 1920s, many of these changes were well established in North America.

A growing popular media disseminated updates on the changing norms and roles. Advice columns were widely read by audiences of eager young adults. The circulation of the media reports helped shape a peer culture on an unmatched scale. More than ever before, young women and young men could read about what their age-mates were doing, including what they were reportedly doing in private with members of the "opposite sex." Advice columns offered information on the ideal of "going steady" while also warning young women of the dangers to their reputation resulting from breaking the rules of courtship (B. L. Bailey, 1988). For these reasons, young women usually restricted sexual intercourse to one partner, the man they expected to marry (D'Emilio & Freedman, 1997). At least that was what the cultural script called for. "Going all the way" by having sexual intercourse was permissible only in the context of a committed romantic relationship that would culminate in marriage.

These trends toward more openness in dating relationships and greater opportunities for sexual intimacy, however, were put on hold by the Great Depression of 1929. Struggling to survive in a time of economic austerity, the ideals of romance and love were luxuries few people could afford (J. S. Turner, 2003).

THE ERA OF DATING

Following World War II (1939–1945), dating became a popular pursuit for young adults from the middle class. Owing to a shortage of eligible men due to the war, exclusive dating or "going steady" was a significant goal for many young adults. On college campuses, dating became a popularity contest (Bogle, 2008; Peril, 2006). Postwar economic prosperity restored the earlier ideals of romantic love and commitment (J. S. Turner, 2003).

Institutions of higher learning were originally intended to educate young men in preparation for their careers and their traditional role of "breadwinner." The social lives of college students, especially women, were regulated by rules and guidelines. Coeducational campuses imposed curfews and restricted opposite-sex visitors in dormitories. These rules were intended to help monitor female students' activities and to protect their "reputations" (Peril, 2006). Many colleges prohibited female students from leaving campus unsupervised; others required a sign-out procedure.

The practice of dating favored young adults who had disposable income and access to an automobile, and whose educational or work setting provided opportunities to meet potential dating partners (B. L. Bailey, 1988; D'Emilio & Freedman, 1997). Yet a double standard still prevailed: young women, as the gatekeepers of sex, were expected to live up to a higher moral standard than men (Reiss, 1967). "Boys pushed, while girls set the limit" (D'Emilio & Freedman, 1997, p. 262). "Going steady" became the leading pattern of dating for young adults (B. L. Bailey, 1988), providing the preferred context for sexual exploration, usually in the form of "necking" or intimate kissing, "petting" or fondling, or even "going further" (B. L. Bailey, 1988; D'Emilio & Freedman, 1997). Indeed, Alfred Kinsey's landmark surveys (Kinsey, Pomeroy, & Martin, 1948; Kinsey, Pomeroy, Martin, & Gebhardt, 1953) suggested that 20 percent of women and 40 percent of men had experienced sexual intercourse by age 20. These estimates, which were probably quite conservative, were nonetheless quite sensational at the time.

Not everyone enthusiastically supported these changes, however. The unprecedented freedom of middle-class youth was a threatening development to an older generation largely accustomed to traditional values (B. L. Bailey, 1988). The improvement in and consequent increased use of birth control methods were most controversial, because these developments signaled a shift away from sex for procreation toward sex for pleasure (D'Emilio & Freedman, 1997). Older generations lamented what they perceived as assaults on traditional values and on such institutions as marriage, the family, and religion. Prostitution, which flourished in large cities, was partly blamed for the breakdown of traditional moral values "because so many evils seemed related to it: exploitation of children, pornography, disease, and crime" (Bullough, 1994, p. 97). Prostitutes became a symbol of degradation and sinfulness, an association that was only strengthened by advances in medical understanding of sexually transmissible infections, or "social diseases," as they were euphemistically called. All of these changes challenged existing sexual norms and signaled the beginning of a new era—the rise of "sexual liberalism" (D'Emilio & Freedman, 1997, p. 241). This trend culminated in the "sexual revolution" of the 1960s.

By the mid-1960s, cultural views of sex in the United States were characterized by a growing emphasis on openness, freedom, and experimentation. "Free love" became a rallying call for a generation of young adults disenchanted with traditional views. They challenged the existing rules and the government's authority and proclaimed the importance of love. Along with love, they heralded uninhibited sexual experimentation—which was made possible by advances in birth control methods after World War II. The growing accessibility and effectiveness of contraception reinforced the view that sex could be fun instead of just for creating a family. Other cultural trends, such as the greater freedom and independence of women, the increased availability of automobiles, and the improvement of economic conditions, also played a part in shifting sexual norms (D'Emilio & Freedman, 1997).

The 1960s are best remembered as spawning the birth of the "hippie" movement. Opposing materialism and the government, the "flower children" espoused an uninhibited, drug-oriented, and pleasure-seeking lifestyle. They protested the Vietnam War and dreamed of changing cultural values. Analysis of the media of that time, especially films, novels, and plays, reveals that for the first time "sex became a daily staple of American popular culture" (D'Emilio & Freedman, 1997, p. 288). On college campuses, students campaigned for an end to visiting hours in dormitories and against college policies that withheld contraceptives from unmarried students and that prohibited female students from living off-campus with males. Most universities eventually gave in, and it was during this time that coeducational or "coed" dormitories were introduced (the earliest experiment with coed dormitories was at the University of Kansas in 1959; Harvard's dorms went coed in 1970). The double standard about acceptable sexual behavior for men and women began to shift toward equality. Surely, what was acceptable for men should be acceptable for women, too. Sexual standards were clearly changing (Reiss, 1967). A 1967 editorial in *Newsweek* concluded, "The old taboos are dead or dying. A new, more permissive society is taking shape."

Again, not everybody welcomed these changes with open arms (Heidenry, 1997). Conservative-minded groups deplored the disintegration of moral values and warned of the impending breakdown of society as a whole (Mathewes-Green, 1997). Coed dorms gave cause for concern to many parents. Media reports of these trends on college campuses were sensational, "predicting that sex in the streets would surely follow the advent of coed toilets" (Peril, 2006, p. 173). Reality, of course, was nothing nearly so dramatic.

THE "HOOKUP" CULTURE?

One trend that has been discussed extensively in recent years is the declining formality in dating practices over the past century (J. S. Turner, 2003). Indeed, it seems that "the dating system has lost its coherence" (B. L. Bailey, 1988, p. 141). Some critics have concluded that casual or uncommitted sexual interactions void of any emotional bond have become normative on college campuses. For example, N. Glenn and Marquardt (2001) reported that "one of the most well-defined forms of male-female interaction on campus today, shaped by relatively clear and widely shared rules and expectations, is hooking up. Hookups usually occur between persons who do not know one another well, with little if any expectation that either person will follow through and try to continue the relationship" (p. 13). The authors cautioned that the practice of hooking up is detrimental to meaningful committed relationships, marriage in particular.

Clearly, dating patterns continue to change. Dating is less formal and more spontaneous, and the guidelines seem more ambiguous than in the past. These changes reflect broader cultural trends over the past 50 years, especially the growing acceptance of sex in unmarried relationships and the changing gender roles, particularly for women. However, other patterns have not changed much during the past decades: the vast majority of young adults hope to be in a romantic relationship characterized by mutual love and commitment. They generally expect that the relationship will involve sexual activity and that it will be exclusive. Sex with someone other than one's romantic partner, including casual sex, still meets with disapproval. Most young adults will be involved in a series of such monogamous relationships before "settling down," which means marrying for most, but not prematurely. Today's young adults, or "emerging adults," do not want to rush into a committed long-term relationship, only to later regret missed opportunities (Arnett, 2004). Most do eventually "settle down" and marry (Regnerus & Uecker, 2011).

Most sex in the United States still occurs in the context of some type of relationship, and this is especially true for college students (Furman & Shaffer, 2011; Regnerus & Uecker, 2011). Contrary to what some critics claim (see Bogle, 2008; N. Glenn & Marquardt, 2001; Stepp, 2007), young adults have not abandoned intimate relationships. Those relationships simply look different than in the past (Arnett, 2004; Regnerus & Uecker, 2011). Serial monogamy is the primary sexual script for young adults: a pattern of consecutive and relatively exclusive relationships involving both emotional intimacy and sex. Nonmonogamous relationships are still frowned upon, particularly if they involve infidelity to one's primary partner (see McAnulty & McAnulty, chapter 7, this volume). Young adults' romantic relationships usually involve sex, and it occurs fairly early, usually within a few weeks. Although young adults postpone the age at which they marry, they do not wait very long before initiating sex in their dating relationships. In the Add Health survey (K. M. Harris et al., 2009), 61 percent of young women and 70 percent of young men reported having initiated sex within six months of a relationship, often within the first month (for nearly 49% of men and 33% of women). This is not surprising since most young adults view sex as a demonstration of affection for one's romantic partner (Kaestle & Halpern, 2007).

Most adults in the United States experience sexual intercourse prior to marriage, which reflects the widespread acceptability of premarital sex in the culture. Since the sexual revolution, attitudes toward premarital sex have become increasingly tolerant, especially among young adults (Harding & Jencks, 2003). The vast majority of Americans initiate sexual intercourse prior to marriage. Between 90 and 95 percent of adults have experienced sexual intercourse, virtually always before age 30 (Finer, 2007). Consequently, "premarital sex is highly normative behavior" for young adults (Finer, 2007, p. 77). As Regnerus and Uecker (2011) observed, most romantic relationships among young adults involve sexual intimacy, and college students are no exception.

A recent representative sex survey of 13,495 men and women aged 25–44 confirms that monogamy represents the most common pattern in the United States (Chandra, Mosher, Copen, & Sionean, 2011). Nearly 82 percent of women in the survey reported having only one sexual partner in the preceding year, and 8.2 percent of respondents were sexually inactive. Women with less than a high school degree were twice as likely (13%) to have had two or more partners in the preceding year than college-educated women. Similar trends were reported for men: 75 percent of respondents reported having one partner in the preceding year, and 8.6 percent were reportedly sexually inactive. The same trend for education was noted, with college-educated men reporting a lower likelihood of having two or more partners in the past year than their less educated counterparts. Overall, the median number of sexual partners in their lifetime for women was 3.2; the same number for college-educated women was 2.9 partners. For men in the survey, the median number of partners in their lifetime was 5.1; for those with college degrees, the number was 4.8 partners.

In fact, a significant number of college-aged adults postpone sexual initiation and remain virgins. In the Add Health survey, 24 percent of college students were virgins. A more recent survey (Chandra et al., 2011) revealed that nearly 30 percent of women 18–19 years old and 12.3 percent of 20- to 24-year-old women had never had any sexual contact with a man. Over 24 percent of men aged 18–19 years and over 14 percent of 20- to 24-year-old men had no previous sexual contact with a woman.

Other research supports the finding that, contrary to popular stereotypes, college students are typically less sexually active than their less educated counterparts. Regnerus and Uecker (2011) concluded that "the most active sexual behavior—in terms of more numerous partners, frequency of sex, etc.—is found, on average, outside of college" (p. 102). The misperception of college students' sexual behavior is obviously pervasive. College students themselves overestimate their classmates' level of sexual activity (Page, Hammermeister, & Scanlan, 2000; Scholly, Katz, Gascoigne, & Holck, 2005; Stephenson & Sullivan, 2009).

The "hookup" phenomenon clearly seems overstated, in terms of both the typical script and its frequency. Surveys suggest that it occurs rather infrequently (once per year on average across students) and involves sexual intercourse less than half of the time (England, Shafer, & Fogarty, 2010; Fielder & Carey, 2010). When young adults do hook up, it usually occurs with someone they know, often a former dating partner or a close friend (Eisenberg, Ackard, Resnick, & Neumark-Sztainer, 2009; Fielder & Carey, 2010; Grello, Welsh, & Harper, 2006). A significant number of young adults later regret hooking up, women in particular (Eshbaugh & Gute, 2008; Paul & Hayes, 2002), and many have mixed feelings about the experience (Owen, Rhoades, Stanley, & Finchman, 2010). There are, of course, exceptions: some young adults, including college students, are quite sexually active and have regular hookups. In Add Health (K. M. Harris et al., 2009), for example, nearly

15 percent of unmarried men and over 10 percent of unmarried women aged 18–23 years old reported having had over 10 sexual partners in their lifetime. The National Survey of Family Growth (Chandra et al., 2011) yielded comparable estimates: among women aged 20–24 years, 4.6 percent reported having had four or more opposite-sex sexual partners in the preceding 12 months as did 9.5 percent of men in the same age group. Again, the research suggests that college students generally have fewer sexual partners than their less educated counterparts (Chandra et al., 2011; Regnerus & Uecker, 2011).

These trends are largely applicable to most college students: the traditional unmarried heterosexual young women and men attending colleges or universities in North America. Comparable dating trends among other groups, including gay, lesbian, bisexual, and transgendered youths, remain largely understudied (see Kauth and Bradford, chapter 8, this volume). These trends also have a distinctively Western flavor. Comparable trends in other cultures can provide some perspective, so we now turn to another culture for comparison.

A CROSS-CULTURAL COMPARISON: JAPAN

Mating and sexual behaviors are universal activities, present in some form in all cultures. The specific rituals and traditions that exist around mating and sex, however, vary widely cross-culturally. Anthropologists have identified wide variations in sexual behaviors and expectations across cultural groups in nonindustrialized societies (Frayser, 1985; Gregersen, 1986). At the extremes are cultures that encourage adolescents to experiment with and engage in sexual play, such as the Kikuyu of Kenya (Kenyatta, 1953), and groups who see any display of public affection as grounds for public censure, such as the Fulbe of Cameroon (Middleton, 2002). Although the variations are not as extreme, there are clear differences across cultures within more industrialized societies (see Hamon & Ingoldsby, 2003; Hatfield & Rapson, 2005). While there undoubtedly will be some commonalities, especially as people from different cultures more regularly interact and cultural guidelines blend, it is still important to appreciate the cultural and historical context within which the ritual of finding a partner and engaging in sex exists. Culture clashes, as a result of the immigration of people and their cultures, are going to become more common with increased mobility. Germany, for example, has recently considered criminalizing forced marriages (Associated Press, 2010), a practice not present in the traditional German culture, but one that has been imported to Germany by immigrants. To help avoid such culture clashes, we must all become more aware of the differences that exist and the origins of these differences.

What do we know about commonalities and differences across world regions? A number of years ago an international research group (International

Mate Selection Project) looked at predictions about mating preferences based on evolutionary psychology across 37 regions assumed to represent a wide variety of possible cultures (Buss, 1989a). Their focus was on testing five predictions about gender differences that were suggested by evolutionary pressures related to successful mating. Predictions dealt with the importance of age differences, physical appearance, chastity, earning capacity, and ambition. Evolutionary psychology assumes that men prefer potential mates who are most likely to be fertile, and thus able to provide offspring. Younger women and women who appear healthy based on externally available qualities like attractiveness are therefore seen as most desirable. Men also are more likely to have doubts about paternity, so they see chastity as a reassurance of likely paternity (according to the theory, men are disinclined to provide their time and resources in rearing children who were fathered by another man). Women, on the other hand, have no doubts about maternity, so their concerns are expected to focus on the potential mate's ability to provide the resources necessary to support her and her offspring. She, therefore, wants an older man, with ambition to ensure current resources and future earning potential. Overall, across the 37 regions, the basic predictions were supported, with the predicted gender differences in all five areas showing up in virtually all "cultures."

However, in a reanalysis of the same data (Wallen, 1989), the cultures were classified based on the economic status of women in each culture. From a sociocultural perspective, when women have low economic status, they need men to provide them with the resources to support their families. But when women have higher economic status, they have access to the necessary resources without depending on males, so they no longer must choose a mate based on his age and ambition. When gender and culture were both considered as explanatory factors, culture, defined by differences in women's economic status, was a more important factor than gender for three of the five preferences expressed (chastity, ambition, age differences). Apparently, when women have economic status within a culture that allows them to support themselves, their preferences for mates change—and now they are also interested in chastity, but not in older men or men with ambition. So, even as some universals associated with sex and reproduction are evident, culture continues to play an important role in how these universals are expressed. Although social scientists continue to debate the relative contributions of biology and gender to behaviors associated with mate preferences and sexual strategies (see for example Eagly, Eastwick, & Johannesen-Schmidt, 2009), the data clearly indicate a role for both factors. So, how does culture come to shape the way we negotiate our dating and sexual relationships, and the behaviors that characterize these rituals?

One broad conceptualization of culture, distinguishing between individualistic and collectivist societies, focuses on the degree to which cultures emphasize individuality or conformity to the wider group (Markus & Kitayama, 1991; Triandis, 1995, 2001). Triandis argues that the distinctions between these two cultural models are apparent in four primary categories:

1. Self-definitions vary in the degree to which personal or collective aspects of self are emphasized. Do people seek to develop an identity that distinguishes them from others, or do they seek to have a sense of self that is based on connections with others?
2. Goals and aspirations vary to the extent that individual goals take priority over group goals. Do people seek to accomplish what is best for them, or do they consider more carefully the implications of their goals for the wider social group?
3. Relationships vary in the extent to which relatedness is valued over separateness. In seeking a relationship, are you going to submerge yourself in the relationship and focus on what your partner needs, or will your personal freedom and need to have a separate identity be maintained even within your relationships?
4. And, finally, social control varies between individualistic and collectivist societies based on the relative importance of norms versus individual attitudes. Should you feel free to express your individual views, even if they differ from others' views, or should you be bound by the accepted norms, and avoid challenging traditions?

As a result of these distinctions, people who are shaped by the alternative cultural models will be expected to show predictable behavioral differences and selection preferences as they enter into serious relationships.

People within individualistic cultures value the separateness and uniqueness of each individual. As a result, they feel more comfortable expressing themselves, highlighting their differences, and standing out from the crowd. A focus on individual thoughts and personal goals leads to a desire to avoid appearing to simply conform. Instead, people develop their self-identity through their personal initiative and individual accomplishments. The resultant sense of individuality most likely leads to a heightened sense of each person's rights or entitlements, rather than to a sense of duty to others. In evaluating potential dates and mates, individualists may be more likely to expect their partner to meet their needs and also allow them to retain a sense of identity separate from the relationship. When personal needs are not met in a relationship, they may feel more entitled to leave and seek a better match.

The collectivist cultures, on the other hand, promote the needs of the larger group over those of the individual. Typically, in a collectivist culture people define themselves through their connections with others. You are expected to value and respect the relationships that link you across generations and within your family. Conformity is valued and expected because it promotes harmony, a sense of shared meaning, and a strong sense of order. While individual accomplishments are not discouraged, people are expected to demonstrate modesty, rather than engage in self-promotion. Your individual desires or needs often are subordinated to ensure that the broader needs of the group are satisfied, and that your duties are fulfilled rather than your personal desires met. When relationships are entered into, there is a stronger sense of commitment and permanence. Partners should be more sensitive to how their behaviors might impact the other person and strive to avoid disruption. Anything less would be considered selfish.

Earlier, we identified the multiple functions that dating is assumed to serve for most young people, at least for those in the cultures, mostly individualistic, within which of the majority of research on dating has occurred. When cultural expectations are overlaid onto the dating experience, some of these functions may take on less meaning, and other functions may need to be recognized. For example, dating as a means to gain peer group status may be less important when the cultural norms discourage a focus on standing out from the crowd. Additionally, dating as a way to find a long-term partner may be less relevant when family members see their role as finding the "appropriate" mate for you. Arranged marriages, a custom much more common in collectivist cultures, make many of the functions served by dating essentially irrelevant. Even as arranged marriages become uncommon, the cultural values that were embedded in these practices may still persist and influence the dating and mating experience.

To provide a window into the role that culture can play in shaping the dating experience, and influencing early sexual behaviors, we will examine some of the differences found in countries with a strong collectivist cultural history to see if there are important differences in young people from these cultures compared to the abundant findings based on young people in the United States, a highly individualistic society. Obviously, in our highly interconnected world, where television and movies expose people all over the world to the American way of life, people are well aware of cultural differences, and this may be leading to a homogenization of cultures, so-called globalization. Still, the effects of a culture probably leave traces, even as more extreme cultural differences are shrinking.

Many Asian countries are seen as meeting the basic requirements for being viewed as collectivist cultures (Markus & Kitayama, 1991), and information is more available about early romantic and sexual relationships from data collected in China and Japan. Japan and China also represent appropriate comparison countries because they are more comparable to the United States based on their level of industrialization. One noteworthy difference for the United States is that both China and Japan have historical traditions that have supported arranged marriages (Caron, 1998; Hendry, 1995; Xu & Whyte, 1990), marriages that do not depend on individual preferences. In China, for example, marriage has traditionally been viewed as a decision that impacted the larger group, rather than a private choice by two individuals (Ingoldsby & Smith, 1995). These traditions of arranged marriage are no longer common, but it remains true that families have continued to play a much more important and controlling role in partner choices in these cultures compared to in the United States (Murray & Kimura, 2003; Xia & Zhou, 2003). Given this tendency to allow others to influence choices of long-term mates, it would be expected that personal attitudes or desires carry less weight. As evidence of this, when young people in Japan and China are asked if they would marry a person they did not love, they were much more likely to agree than were American youth (Pan, 1993; R. Levine, Sato, Hashimoto, & Verma, 1994). Compared to their American counterparts, in fact, young Chinese do not view passionate love, a highly individualized response to a partner, as a clearly positive experience, believing instead that it has a darker side implying unrequited love or infatuation (Shaver, Wu, & Schwartz, 1991). Chinese youth have views of love that are far more pragmatic (Gao, 2001), with less focus on a special connection between two people.

In a similar vein, given the heavy reliance on family for social support, young people did not have the same expectations about what their potential partner should bring to the relationship. According to Hsu (1985), Chinese youth expect less from marriage because they expect their intimacy needs to be met through their continued connections to family. Japanese youth also appear to have different expectations about what a potential partner must provide, at least when compared to young adults in the United States. When Hatfield and Sprecher (1995) asked college students to rate a series of qualities, indicating how essential it would be that their romantic partner possess these qualities, students from the United States and Japan saw the same qualities as important. Partners who were kind, had a good sense of humor, were expressive, and were intelligent were seen as highly desirable. However, Japanese students tended to rate all of these qualities as less necessary, suggesting that other factors may be more critical. One suggestion is that they are more concerned that a partner has strong ties to their perceived group, facilitating the merging of a potential mate into the existing social network that will continue to be a part of each person's life. Thus a marriage involving members of connected groups, a *shiriai*, is seen as more likely to be successful because it will benefit from the additional existing social ties (Yamagishi & Yamagishi, 1994). In China, marriage has been an important goal to reach, and there has been encouragement to marry young (Hatfield & Rapson, 2006). Even today, pressure exists to find a partner, and to be pragmatic in choosing among prospects. As one young Chinese woman described the pressure to marry, she indicated that "you don't follow the dream . . . find a guy you love, and he loves you, and live happily ever after, it's a bubble—not everyone can get it. That's what my parents taught me" (Gifford, 2010, p. 2). Instead, the parental advice she received was to be sensible: "If a vaguely presentable guy with a good salary and nice habits shows up, you can't be too picky" (Gifford, 2010, p. 2). In other words, find someone who has generally positive qualities, assume that you can build the relationship, and do not expect him or her to meet all your preferences. Contrast that with the focus in the United States of meeting that "perfect person" or soul mate who will have all the qualities you desire, so that a perfect relationship will exist from the very beginning of the match.

A CLOSER LOOK AT CLOSE RELATIONSHIPS IN JAPAN AND THE UNITED STATES

How does culture shape young people to understand what close relationships should provide, and how they should treat their romantic partners? A recent literature review summarizing many findings comparing Japanese and U.S. cultures as they impact the individual beginning soon after birth and continuing through adolescence (Rothbaum, Pott, Azuma, Miyake, and Weisz, 2000) provides a broad model for understanding how Japanese and American relationships differ as a result of cultural influences. Reviewing studies that examine close relationships from infancy through adulthood, the authors find dominant themes that differentiate the experiences of individuals in the two cultures, which ultimately shape what they seek and value in their intimate relationships. In considering the various cultural dimensions that distinguish Japanese and U.S. cultures, Rothbaum et al. (2000) see the individuation-versus-accommodation distinction as critical to understanding close relationships. Individuation is characterized by autonomy, expressiveness, and exploration-separation. Thus, in a culture like the United States where individuation is encouraged, there is a "generative tension" about relationships: a constant tug between seeking closeness and security with others, and desiring freedom to explore, separate, and distinguish oneself from others. Accommodation, the focus in Japanese relationships, emphasizes empathy, compliance, and propriety. Relationships are based on a symbiotic harmony, which requires a continual effort to adapt oneself to meet or fit the needs of others. You are seeking to become connected and a part of the larger whole, and efforts are made to avoid any disruption of existing connections.

How are these views communicated to people in each culture? The process begins early, and continues for years. In infancy, Japanese mothers use vocalizations that draw the infant's attention to her, while mothers in the United States often direct the attention of the child to objects outside the relationship. Japanese mothers' vocalizations are more emotion oriented, designed to lull the child and simulate a conversation, thus keeping the infant's attention on the mother. Japanese mothers also tend to maintain greater physical contact with their children. One indicator of this tendency is that infant carriers, "snugglies," which essentially attach the child to the mother, are more popular in Japan than in the United States, while walkers and swings, which allow the infant to be separate and explore, are more popular in the United States. The result for the Japanese infant is a more symbiotic connection, a mutual focus on each other between the mother and child. In the United States, there is a greater tendency to encourage exploration and separation, while also trying to provide a secure base—creating a generative tension around relationships (Rothbaum et al., 2000).

During later childhood, Japanese parents encourage empathy and emphasize obligations to others, so that Japanese children are discouraged from overtly expressing their own wishes. They are taught that they should rely on others to *sense* their needs. Children in the United States, however, are encouraged to openly express their needs and preferences, and to feel comfortable when their preferences conflict with those of others. While Japanese children are encouraged to avoid creating potential conflicts that might result from asserting their personal needs or desires, U.S. children are allowed to assert their individuality by expressing personal goals and asserting themselves. Even when disciplining children, Japanese parents commonly link inappropriate behavior to the possible consequences for others who may be hurt, or to the possible reactions of others who might judge the child. Consequences of misbehavior are implied to be shared by others within the group, so appropriate behaviors are seen as supporting the group. Individual consequences, like "time outs" or physical consequences, are more commonly used in the United States than in Japan (Rothbaum et al., 2000) to exert control over undesirable behaviors.

Thus, by the time Japanese children reach adolescence and begin to seek relationships with possible mates, they have a very different model for how this new person will fit into their lives, and how they should act within the relationship than do adolescents in the United States. In the United States, this is a time when children move away from their parents, as they seek to become more connected to their peers and establish their individuality. American youth also place an emphasis on exploring sexuality and finding a potential partner for whom there is sexual attraction. For Japanese youth, the strong relationship with family is maintained even as the importance of the peer group grows. While reliance on family for meeting intimacy needs might be seen as a sign of immaturity for an adolescent in the United States, no such stigma is found in Japan (Rothbaum et al., 2000). Given the reduced emphasis on sexual activity as an essential early aspect of romantic relationships, it is not surprising that Japanese youths tend to have their first sexual intercourse at a later age than U.S. youth (Hatano, 1991; Huang & Uba, 1992), although this gap may be decreasing as Japanese youth have been afforded more freedom to socialize (Japanese Association for Sex Education, 2006).

So, when young adults in Japan and the United States begin the serious task of seeking a potential mate, what are their expectations? Rothbaum et al. (2000) characterize Japanese romantic relationships as based on what they call "assurance," which emerges from the expected unconditional loyalty and commitment of a partner. Assurance is embedded in the social network that has been shaped at each stage of development for Japanese youth and that is seen as essential for successful relationships, rather than in an individual relationship between two people. Alternatively, youth in the United States are groomed to see their romantic relationships as trust based (Rothbaum et al., 2000). Trust implies an individual faith that a partner will remain committed, but also an awareness that partners have the freedom to end relationships. The relationship is more narrowly defined, since only the two individuals are seen as relevant, not the larger social network. In Japan, to be loyal is to love (Benedict, 1946), while in the United States, love is more closely associated with passion and the "magic" associated with that special connection between two people. Romantic relationships in Japan have a much stronger sense of companionate love—intimacy, in the form of felt closeness, and commitment are seen as essential, but love is not as reliant on emotion or passion (Rothbaum et al., 2000). According to Toyama (2002), Japanese college students gain both self-esteem and a sense of efficacy when their intimate romantic relationships allow them to express both loyalty and harmony, since these are qualities they believe to be associated with ultimate success in relationships.

Within a Japanese romantic relationship there remains the sense shaped in childhood that directly expressing personal needs is undesirable. Each person expects the other to be able to recognize the partner's needs, and expressing those needs in words would imply that the relationship was not sufficiently close. In other words, if our relationship is truly strong, you will know how I feel and what I need without my having to tell you. This contrasts with relationships in the United States where there is at least some expectation that feelings will be shared and discussed, and that unmet needs should be made clear (Rothbaum et al., 2000). Open communication between romantic partners is viewed as critical to relationship success in the United States.

Kito (2005) found evidence to support the different levels of self-disclosure that would therefore be expected to typify Japanese and U.S. intimate relationships. In samples of college students from the United States and Japan, participants reported on their likely self-disclosure across four relationship types: passionate love, companionate love, cross-sex friendship, and same-sex friendship. Across all four relationships, Japanese students reported levels of self-disclosure that were significantly lower than those claimed by students from the United States.

The Japanese reliance on assurance also might explain the tendency to delay marriage. To develop a relationship based on loyalty and commitment should take more time than one based on passionate love or sexual attraction. In 2006, the average age for marriage in Japan was 30 years for men and 28.2 years for women (Ministry of Health, Labor, and Welfare, 2006), compared to 27.5 and 25.6 years for men and women in the United States (U.S. Census, 2010).

The development of romantic relationships also follows a very structured pattern for most Japanese couples (Farrer, Tsuchiya, & Bagrowicz, 2008). Dating is likely to last a number of years and move through at least one formal transition. For Japanese couples a dating relationship typically becomes a "*tsukiau*" relationship prior to marriage (Farrer et al., 2008). Tsukiau is similar to the outdated tradition of "going steady" that was once common in the United States, in that it implies a publicly recognized exclusive romantic relationship. As of 2005, Japanese couples tended to be in a *tsukiau* relationship for about four years before moving to the next relationship stage—marriage (National Institute of Population and Social Security Research, 2005).

To better appreciate how Japanese romantic relationships evolve, Farrer et al. (2008) collected data from a mostly college student sample and asked them to describe, in narrative form, how their relationship had transitioned from simple dating relationships into *tsukiau*, and what changed in the relationship as a result of the transition. The *tsukiau* relationship begins when one partner makes a formal "confession of feeling" and expresses a desire for commitment. Almost 90 percent of the participants reported that they had experienced this discrete event in their relationship, and it was almost always the male who initiated the request. For many couples, the date of the "confession of feeling" becomes an important anniversary or milestone. A clear expectation after the relationship moves into the *tsukiau* stage is an increased commitment to spend time together and begin to plan a future together. For almost all the couples, formally entering into a *tsukiau* relationship also signaled that a sexual relationship was expected and acceptable. Although many couples in the United States probably go through similar stages, the Japanese experience is much more formalized as part of the dating script, and sexual initiation occurs later in the process than in the United States. For many respondents, the *tsukiau* also appears to signal a change from a more formal connection to one involving greater intimacy, like the connections they have within their families. Rothbaum et al. (2000) have described how for most Japanese there are two sets of rules about revealing anything about oneself to others. Within the family, openness is accepted and expected, but outside the family a more formal and reserved style of interacting is expected where openness is inappropriate. Once couples entered into a *tsukiau* relationship, they reported that they felt free to be more open and to "reveal their true self" to their romantic partners.

Overall, what we see in comparing the mating and dating experiences of Japanese youth and youth from the United States is a very different script. The stages of the processes surrounding dating may be similar, but the beliefs about what to expect from a partnership, and the qualities that define an ideal partner are clearly different. In both cultures, sex is viewed as belonging in the context of a committed relationship. In Japan, premarital sex is tolerated as long as it is discreet and does not interfere with social duties, such as education and family responsibilities (M. I. White, 1993). The two cultures provide alternative frameworks within which decisions about dating and mating will be made.

CONCLUSIONS

This overview of dating trends in young adults illustrates the changes that have occurred in the United States over the past century. Undoubtedly, dating relationships have become less formal, more spontaneous, and often briefer than during the era of courtship. Emerging adults tend to view monogamous relationships as less committed and shorter in duration than their parents and grandparents did. This shift is especially true of young women (Kamen, 2000). However, finding a romantic partner that is suitable and compatible remains an important goal for most young adults, regardless of sexual orientation (Regnerus & Uecker, 2011).

Most dating relationships in the United States today involve sex, and it tends to occur earlier in the relationship than in the past. The double standard, although reduced, is still operational (England et al., 2010). Young women are still expected to be the gatekeepers of sex, and they are judged more harshly than men for departing from the cultural script.

The nostalgia over the older systems of courtship and dating does indeed seem misplaced (B. L. Bailey, 1988). Both systems involved explicit rules and consequences for breaking them, such as a shady reputation. However, the culture seems to exaggerate the sexual exploits of emerging adults, college students in particular. This is not surprising in view of sensational media reports and social critiques. In fact, college students themselves overestimate the extent of sexual activity among their peers.

Cross-cultural perspectives reveal differences in romantic pursuits and ideals. In collectivist cultures, such as Japan and China, dating choices must be compatible with one's loyalty to one's family and not detract from important role obligations, such as being a successful student and being career minded. In contrast, romantic relationships of emerging adults in the United States are built on passionate love, open self-disclosure, and trust, with much less concern for their respective families and for traditions.

Chapter Two

CONDUCTING RESEARCH ON COLLEGE STUDENT SEXUALITY

Michael W. Wiederman

How do we know what college students do sexually? What are their attitudes, feelings, and beliefs about sex? What factors influence these aspects of college students' sexuality? Although far from perfect, our best approach for obtaining answers to these questions is to conduct empirical research. By systematically gathering data, analyzing those data, and making sense out of what those data tell us about the experiences of college students, the goal is to inch closer to answers. It sounds straightforward, but there are usually numerous potential problems to consider and options to weigh (also see Wiederman & Whitley, 2002). In this chapter the primary issues involved in conducting empirical research on college student sexuality will be considered, with an eye toward determining the best options for particular circumstances.

WHAT TYPE OF RESEARCH IS THE BEST CHOICE?

Of course the answer to the question in the section heading depends on the type of research question being asked. Do we want to know what college students do, think, or feel? Those types of questions may call for descriptive studies. Do we want to know how behaviors, thoughts, and feelings are related to each other or to other behaviors, thoughts, and feelings? Those types of questions probably involve correlational research. Or do we want to know what variables influence college students' sexual behaviors, thoughts, and feelings? Questions involving how one variable affects or influences another usually require an experimental approach. How do these types of research differ?

Descriptive Research

Descriptive studies include attempts to determine the prevalence of some attitude, belief, or experience. For example, what percentage of college students have been coerced into a sexual experience with another person? What proportion of college students view sex outside of a committed relationship as morally wrong? Descriptive research also includes attempts to better understand people's experiences by investigating them in greater depth than with simply yes/no questions. So, for example, college students may be asked to describe their experiences of having been coerced into sexual behavior. Who were the perpetrators? What were the circumstances? What forms of sexual behavior were coerced? How did the college students react?

Descriptive research may be considered quantitative or qualitative in its approach. Quantitative studies are focused on numerical data, such as rates and ratings, whereas qualitative studies are focused more on allowing respondents to generate their own descriptions of their experiences, attitudes, beliefs, and so forth. Descriptive studies that are quantitative tend to be focused on establishing estimates of the frequency or prevalence of something, whereas qualitative descriptive approaches tend to be focused on understanding the nature or details of respondents' experiences. In either case, descriptive studies are frequently the first step in research on a particular topic because such research establishes that such a phenomenon exists, and thus warrants further examination. Prior to this kind of exploratory descriptive research, a particular experience, behavior, or belief may have been reported only anecdotally, perhaps in a clinical case report, or news story, or even a work of fiction.

Correlational Research

Once it has been established that particular sexual behaviors, experiences, beliefs, or attitudes exist among college students, often the next step is asking what factors are related to those phenomena. For example, are particular sexual experiences related to specific other sexual experiences? What about possibly being related to specific attitudes, family backgrounds, and so forth? The possible questions about relationships among variables are seemingly endless. Beyond sheer curiosity, however, why would researchers pose such questions, and why would they choose to examine relationships among some variables and not others? Frequently, the choices revolve around attempts to better understand what causes, or at least influences, the phenomenon the researcher is studying. If one variable causes or influences another, the two variables will be statistically related, so examining such correlations is a first step toward researching causes and influences affecting college students' sexuality.

Notice that correlational research is quantitative by necessity. The variables the researcher is examining have to be measured in a quantitative way so that numerical values associated with each variable can be correlated. Coming up with measures of sexuality poses particular potential problems, and some of those issues will be considered below. Here, however, we need to emphasize the relationships between variables. When one variable influences another, the two variables will be statistically correlated, but just because two variables are statistically correlated does *not* mean that one influences the other. Instead of being so wordy, researchers summarize this point with a traditional maxim: "Correlation does not equal causation."

Correlation between two variables is a necessary but not sufficient condition for establishing that one variable influences or affects the other. The problem is that two variables may be statistically related (correlated) due to both being caused by some third variable (or set of variables) rather than one causing the other. For example, suppose that researchers find that college students who report masturbating more frequently also report more frequently engaging in sexual activity with a partner. In other words, there is a positive correlation between frequency of masturbation and frequency of sexual activity with partners. It is tempting to try to explain why masturbation causes more frequent sexual activity with partners (or vice versa). However, it is possible that these two variables are statistically correlated because both are caused by some third variable. In this example, perhaps sex drive, or interest in sexual stimulation, is the causal factor behind both frequency of masturbation and frequency of sexual activity with partners.

Notice that it can be difficult to determine where the causal chain ends, as well as how many variables cause or influence the variables the researcher is attempting to understand. In the example with the correlation between masturbation and sexual activity with a partner, further research might establish that both are caused by sex drive or interest in sexual stimulation. However, this begs the question: What causes differences in sex drive across individual college students? Perhaps there is another "third variable" that explains the correlation between sex drive and frequency of sexual behavior (masturbation and activity with partners). Also, perhaps sex drive is just one of a set of factors that cause or influence college students' frequency of masturbation and sexual activity with partners.

To add yet another layer of complexity, what about the possibility that two variables mutually cause or influence each other? For example, consider the common finding of correlations between sexual attitudes and sexual behavior. When college students who report particular sexual attitudes are also most likely to engage in particular sexual behavior, it is easy to jump to the conclusion that the attitudes cause (or allow) the behavior. Because a correlation does not indicate the direction of causation, it is possible that engaging in the particular sexual behavior affects the college students' attitudes. However, it is also possible that the attitudes lead to the behavior, engaging in the behavior then affects the attitudes, and so on, in an ever-repeating cycle.

These kinds of questions and possibilities are why, typically, multiple studies are required to start to untangle the web of connections among sexuality variables. This distinction between correlation and causation is a hugely important point in understanding research on college students' sexuality, and we will consider it again below when discussing interpretation of research findings.

Experimental Research

If correlation between two variables indicates the *possibility* that one may be influencing the other, how do researchers determine whether one variable actually does influence the other? Traditionally, the gold standard for determining whether one variable affected another was to perform a well-designed experiment. The word "experiment" is frequently used among nonresearchers as a generic term for empirical research, but instead it refers to a specific form of research. At a minimum, a true experiment must include: (1) a manipulation of the variable that is being considered as the possible influence on another variable, and (2) random assignment of research participants to the different conditions or levels of manipulation. Here the word "manipulation" does not mean that the research participants are being manipulated, but rather that the researcher is taking control over the variable being studied, and systematically manipulating that variable so that the researcher can determine whether it affects research participants. This is what is meant by the term "experimental conditions": two or more groups of research participants are created, each being exposed to a different manipulation of the research variable being studied. Frequently, one of the experimental conditions is considered a *control* condition in which the experimental variable is not manipulated at all. That way there is a comparison group that represents what would occur "naturally" (without manipulation by the researcher).

The manipulation of the variable being studied is the first of the two criteria for a true experiment. The second criterion is that research participants are randomly assigned to the experimental conditions (groups). The issue of random assignment is important because the goal is to create comparison groups of research participants who differ in only one way: with regard to the manipulation of the variable being studied. If that goal is met, then any differences in the groups at the end of the experiment presumably must be due to differences in the manipulation, so the researcher can determine what effect (if any) the manipulation had on the research participants. Why is random assignment to the experimental conditions so important? As an example, consider research focused on whether exposure to pornography affects college students' sexual attitudes.

Suppose previous research revealed correlations between the amount of exposure college students had to pornography and the sexual attitudes of those college students. Because correlation does not equal causation, a researcher decides to conduct an experiment on the effects of exposure to pornography on sexual attitudes. Suppose there are two levels of experimental manipulation: one condition consists of one 30-minute session whereas the more intensive condition consists of three 30-minute sessions. For additional comparison, the researcher includes two control groups who spend just as much time viewing wildlife documentaries as the experimental conditions do viewing pornography. However, for whatever reason, suppose that the researcher is unable to randomly assign participants to each of the four conditions (groups). Instead, each college student gets to choose which condition he or she will participate in. Without random assignment, this study no longer meets the criteria for an experiment, but why is that a major problem?

We can imagine ways in which the students who decide to choose each condition probably differ from each other. It is likely, for example, that the students who choose the exposure to the pornography have more liberal attitudes toward pornography, and probably have more experience with pornography, compared to those students who choose to view the wildlife documentaries. So, if measures of sexual attitudes administered after participating in the study reveal differences between the groups, how does the researcher know whether those differences are the result of the experimental manipulation (viewing pornography rather than wildlife films) or were there from the start? It may be tempting to answer that the researcher could simply measure those same attitudes prior to exposures to the experimental conditions. Indeed, this approach would reveal how much change there had been in each group. However, if the goal is to try to determine the effects of exposure to pornography on attitudes among college students in general, this approach would reveal only how 30 minutes or 90 minutes of exposure affects college students who started out with liberal attitudes and possibly extensive experience with pornography prior to the study. If the researcher finds little or no change in this select group, would it be accurate to conclude that exposure to these doses of pornography has no effect on the sexual attitudes of college students generally?

With random assignment to experimental conditions comes the assumption that each experimental group is equal or the same in all ways except what each group experiences during participation in the experiment. Of course this assumption may be wrong. One experimental condition (group) may end up with more or fewer of a particular type of person, just as a fluke of chance. If so, the experimental groups may display differences at the end of the experiment not because of what was manipulated, but because they started out as different. This is less likely to be the case if each group contains a large number of participants, or if the experiment is conducted multiple times. So, in those cases, we can have greater confidence that the results of the experiment were due to the experimental manipulation, and not due to chance fluctuations from one experimental group to the next.

Although we usually think of conducting an experiment as the way to determine what influences a variable, there are numerous sexuality variables for which this would be impossible. As one example, what about researching the influences on the number of different sex partners one has? Or what influences college students to engage in sexual infidelity? Even the previous example of the experiment designed to examine the effects of pornography on sexual attitudes was very limited in the amount of exposure to pornography that could be included in the experiment. Plus, the pornography exposure in the experiment was not the same experience as exposure to pornography of one's own choosing in the privacy of one's own residence. In these cases (and many others), are researchers left without the ability to study influences or effects on college students' sexual attitudes and experiences? Fortunately, the answer is a qualified "no."

When it is impossible to perform an experiment on the relationship between two variables, researchers may choose to try to rule out as many "third variables" as possible as alternative explanations for the link between the two variables of interest. These forms of correlational studies rely on *multivariate* statistical tests; in essence, more than one correlation between the variable of interest and other variables is considered at the same time. Sometimes researchers use such terms as "statistically controlling for" a particular set of variables, or "partialing out" the effects of a particular set of variables. In these analyses, the correlation between variable X and variable Y is determined while statistically "taking out" of the correlation the degree to which these X and Y are correlated with variables A, B, and C. If X and Y are still correlated after statistically controlling for their relationships to A, B, and C, researchers conclude that A, B, and C are not the entire reasons for the relationship between X and Y.

The details of multivariate statistical tests are well beyond the scope of this chapter, but it is important to recognize that, even when performing an experiment is impossible, researchers can try to determine whether particular "third variables" are the causes for the apparent correlation between two variables. One of the primary problems with multivariate approaches, however, is anticipating and accurately measuring all of the relevant variables that may be the actual causes for the correlation between two particular variables. Selecting particular variables to include in the analyses depends on assumptions about what are the most likely explanations for the correlation between two variables in which the researchers are interested.

Because no one study can include all of the possible variables that need to be considered to answer a research question absolutely, once and for all, it is important that researchers perform multiple studies on a particular topic. After several related studies have been conducted, it can be very informative to examine patterns across those studies. Are there solid conclusions that can be drawn based on consistencies in findings, even as each researcher approached the topic differently? Sometimes simply reading these various studies is enough to be able to draw some conclusions. However, there is a more formal method for statistically analyzing other researchers' studies: *meta-analysis*.

In performing a meta-analysis, the researcher gathers all of the studies available on the variables or topic chosen. The results for each of those studies can be translated into a standardized format so that the results across studies can be combined. The results of the meta-analysis may reveal how strongly variables are related to each other, or under what conditions particular variables are and are not related. Also, the results from each study are weighted so that studies that are based on more participants are weighed more heavily than studies that are based on smaller numbers of participants. Whether it is a single study or a meta-analysis of 128 studies, it is important to consider who these students are who participate in the research we depend on to better understand college student sexuality.

WHO ARE THESE STUDENTS, ANYWAY?

Research on college students' sexuality relies on students agreeing to participate, which typically involves sharing sensitive information about themselves, their experiences, attitudes, and reactions, all with total strangers (the researchers). Such participation, even if completely anonymous, still requires time and energy. Who are these students willing to give their time and energy to reveal potentially sensitive information about themselves? What is their motivation for doing so? The reason these are important questions has to do with *generalizability* of the research findings (also see Dunn, 2002, for discussion of sampling issues in sexuality research).

Researchers start with a *population* of interest. Because it is typically impossible, or at least not feasible, to study every member of the population of interest, researchers must rely on studying a selected group, or *sample*, of those individuals. Results are generalizable to the extent that the findings of the study (which are based on the sample) mirror what one would find in the larger population of interest. Ideally, a research sample would be perfectly *representative* of the population of interest (that is, all members of the population would have an equal chance of being included in the research). In reality, this is impossible to achieve as there are always some potential participants who could not be contacted or who refuse an invitation to take part in the research.

The larger concern is the extent to which a particular sample differs from the population of interest. If the people in the sample differ in important ways from the larger population from which they were drawn, we should question the extent to which the findings apply to the people in the population who were not part of the research sample. In such a case, we might refer to the sample as *biased* in the sense that it is not truly representative. Notice that we are not saying that the individuals in the sample are biased toward the topic that is being studied, but rather that the sample as a whole is biased to including more of a particular type of person than exists in the population. One important form of potential sample bias comes from the principle that it is unethical to force people to participate in research. So, by necessity, all such research is based on volunteers. If those who volunteer to participate in research differ overall from those who had the opportunity to participate but chose not to, we have a case of *volunteer bias*.

How does all of this apply to college students who participate in sexuality research? Traditionally, college students have been recruited for sexuality research through the courses taught by either the researchers or their colleagues. So, one form of prevalent sample bias results from the fact that only college students who are enrolled in particular types of courses are liable to be sampled for sexuality research. Traditionally, potential college student participants in sexuality research have been recruited through two primary means: research participant pools and classroom enticement. As we will see, each comes with its own set of issues to consider as to how the resulting samples may be biased.

Particularly at large universities, departments of psychology frequently maintain a college student *subject pool*. The word "subject" here derives from the traditional use of the term in psychology to refer to a participant in a particular study. Typically, the students who comprise the subject pool are those enrolled in an introductory psychology course and who are provided with strong incentives to participate in a predetermined amount of time in research. The incentives may include that research participation is factored into the final course grade or that such participation is a prerequisite for earning credit for the course. Because it is unethical to absolutely require research participation, students are typically provided with an alternative to such participation, which may involve writing a paper or performing community service. However, most students would probably consider the research participation their least troublesome option. The rationale for requiring research participation is that participation in actual psychological research is a valuable educational experience (with the goal of better understanding the process of conducting research in psychology).

There may be hundreds of students who comprise a subject pool during any given academic term at a particular university, and there may be dozens of studies from which each student can choose. Notice that most students who participate in research through a subject pool do not participate in research on sexuality. Typically, students read brief descriptions of each study and select those in which they wish to participate. Even if the description is brief, it would probably be clear which studies involved sexuality and which did not. The potential problem is whether students who choose to participate in the sexuality studies differ from those who choose the nonsexuality studies.

Comparing volunteers and nonvolunteers with regard to their sexual attitudes and experiences is difficult, because doing so would involve asking the nonvolunteers to provide sexual information that they did not volunteer to provide. However, a few studies have involved using different sign-up sheets, although all participants completed the same measures, or asking research participants whether they would be willing to participate in various types of sexuality-related research (see Wiederman, 1999, and the studies reviewed there). In general, college student volunteers for sexuality research are more likely to be male, more sexually experienced, more comfortable with sexual topics, and more liberal in their sexual attitudes compared to nonvolunteers. So, when researchers investigate college student's sexual attitudes and experiences, they may be examining students who differ from in important ways from college students generally.

In addition to some general differences between college student volunteers and nonvolunteers for sexuality research, the more sensitive or revealing the information requested, or the more sexually explicit the requirements of participation, the more likely the sample will deviate from the population (Wiederman, 1999). Typically, if asked to complete a brief, anonymous survey on their sexual attitudes, only a small proportion of college students will refuse. However, if the same sample is asked to complete a face-to-face interview regarding their sexual experiences, a larger proportion will refuse. If the same group is asked to view sexually explicit videos while their genital responses are recorded using specialized instruments, an even greater proportion of students will refuse. The more sensitive or involved the research, the more concerned we should be about the generalizability of the results.

The issues with volunteer bias apply to instances in which the researcher recruits participants from the college courses he or she teaches (or are taught by colleagues). An additional issue arises, however, when potential participants are asked to complete surveys or enroll on a sign-up sheet immediately after being asked for the first time. The researcher may make it clear that participation is voluntary (and perhaps anonymous), but the college students may experience a subtle feeling of pressure by being asked directly (as opposed to impersonal sign-up procedures online).

One last sampling issue to consider is generalizability beyond the college students attending the school from which the sample was drawn. When researchers employ a sample of college students from a particular school in the United States and write, "Based on the findings, it appears that men are more likely than women to stimulate their own genitals for pleasure," the implication is that something was discovered that applies to human males and human females generally. However, research has demonstrated that the college years are a unique developmental period during which individuals' personalities frequently undergo important changes (Caspi, Roberts, & Shiner, 2005), at least some of which may be the result of experiences within intimate relationships (Sturaro, Denissen, Van Aken, & Asendorpf, 2008). So the college years may be a time during which sexual experiences and attitudes undergo more change compared to other periods in life, which may explain why male-female differences in sexual experiences and attitudes are greater in college student samples than in samples of older adults (Oliver & Hyde, 1993; J. L. Petersen & Hyde, 2010). The point is to remember that research results based on college students in one culture may not generalize to adults in general, or even to college students in other cultures.

Does the generalizability of the sample really make that much difference? Like so many questions in life, the answer is "it depends." For descriptive research, where the goal is to assess what proportion of college students have had some particular experience, or how frequently college students engage in some particular behavior or hold a particular belief or attitude, generalizability is extremely important. For correlational research, the importance of generalizability is less clear. If two particular variables are related among college students in general, perhaps it does not matter that the researcher is testing the hypothesis with a biased sample because the relationship should still exist. Of course it is possible, however, that the relationships exist for some groups of people and not others, or that the strength of the relationship between the variables varies across groups.

Only replicating a particular study across various samples reveals whether the results of that particular line of research generalize well. If several researchers, each using somewhat different methods and samples, find generally the same thing, we can have greater confidence that the results of any one of those studies generalizes to the larger population of interest. Of course studies vary not only in the samples they are based on but also in how the variables of interest are measured. Issues of measurement are just as important to consider as are samples.

HOW DO SEXUALITY RESEARCHERS COLLECT DATA?

Variables such as sexual arousal, gender, and attitudes toward rape are each *concepts*. Concepts are useful because the words we use to represent a concept allow us communicate more efficiently than if we had to always describe each the phenomena that a concept captures. Suppose we had no concept labeled "sexual arousal," but in communicating we needed to make reference to that set of experiences. We might have to say something like "You know. That experience when one feels most interested in sexual activity, and blood flow increases to one's genitals, and males get an erection and females get increased vaginal lubrication." It is so much easier to have a shared concept labeled "sexual arousal."

Concepts are extremely useful, but there are downsides. Concepts are constructed by humans, so they do not exist in an absolute sense. Concepts have to be inferred from other indicators. For the example of the concept labeled "sexual arousal," we may use genital blood flow as an indication that sexual arousal is present. However, what if an individual feels sexually aroused but there is no increase in genital blood flow? What about if there is increased blood flow to the genitals but the individual does not "feel" sexually aroused? For many concepts there are various ways to define them, and hence numerous indicators of those concepts. Researchers are usually interested in studying concepts, but to do so, they must decide how those concepts will be translated into concrete measures and sets of circumstances. That is, each of the variables needs to be *operationally defined*.

For example, earlier we discussed a case in which researchers were interested in the effects of exposure to pornography on men's attitudes toward women. In that example exposure to pornography was operationally defined as watching certain sexually explicit video clips in the laboratory. Attitudes toward women would probably be operationally defined as answers to a questionnaire regarding attitudes about women. Or, perhaps the researchers would arrange for the research participant to interact with a female shortly after having viewed the video clips. Notice that researchers are interested in how concepts such as pornography and attitudes are related, yet they are faced with translating those concepts into manipulations and measures that are feasible given their resources. The specific ways they do that are what we mean by the operational definitions of the variables.

In most cases, researchers measure or operationally define their variables in ways that rely on self-reports from research participants. In some cases, researchers are able to measure more directly people's sexual responses.

However, as we will see, both types of measures have their advantages and disadvantages.

Direct Measurement of Sexual Response

Researchers can measure directly the physiological arousal or response associated with sexual stimuli (Janssen, 2002). These methods of gathering data typically are carried out in a laboratory because specialized equipment is needed. Specifically, data on male sexual response are typically gathered using some form of strain gauge consisting of a loop placed around the base of the penis to form a snug fit. Then, as the penis becomes increasingly erect, the expansion in the circumference of the base of the penis stretches the loop. The degree to which the loop is stretched is recorded by a computer connected to the strain gauge via wires. Note that because penises vary in size, the strain gauge has to be calibrated to each research participant. Baseline measurements are obtained for the participant's penis in a nonaroused state as well as at the point of full erection. Then, during the experiment, the researchers are able to determine how relatively aroused the research participant is at any one time.

To measure female sexual arousal and response, researchers typically use a vaginal photoplethysmograph, which consists of a clear acrylic device about the same size and shape as a menstrual tampon. Inside the photoplethysmograph is a light source and a photocell to record the amount of light present. The photoplethysmograph is inserted inside the research participant's vagina and, just as with the penile strain gauge, the photoplethysmograph has wires running from it to a computer. The photoplethysmograph continuously sends data to the computer regarding how much of the projected light is being reflected off of the walls of the vagina. As the research participant becomes increasingly sexually aroused, the walls of her vagina become engorged with blood, and less light is reflected back to the photoplethysmograph. Note that, just like the penile strain gauge, the photoplethysmograph provides data on how relatively aroused the research participant is compared to that individual's baseline measures, but it does not give an absolute measure of sexual arousal that can be compared to other research participants.

Research based on physiological measures of sexual response makes up only a very small proportion of research on college student sexuality, probably for several reasons. For one, physiological measures of sexual response are relevant only to certain research questions (e.g., factors related to sexual dysfunction or sexual response to deviant images). Also, this method of collecting data requires specialized equipment and expertise, as well as research participants who are willing to engage in the highly unusual behavior of having their sexual response monitored by strangers. An alternative method for collecting data is observations made by researchers.

Observations of Behavior

Direct observation of sexual behavior is problematic for several reasons. Doing so without people's knowledge and consent is illegal, and those people who allow researchers to observe them are likely to be unrepresentative of the general population. Even volunteers would probably act differently while being observed than they would in private. There are instances in which direct observation of behavior is possible and useful, but when?

Some behaviors related to sexuality are public, such as flirting with new acquaintances in a bar or displaying affection for a mate. Indeed, researchers have studied these and other topics through direct observation. In such instances, researchers are said to conduct *field research* in that the researchers go out to where people live rather than requiring research participants to come to the researchers. The primary advantage is that researchers are able to observe how people actually behave in real-life situations, especially if the researchers are observing in such a way that the research participants do not know that their behavior is being observed. The primary disadvantage is that there are only a limited number of topics that can be studied through direct observation, especially if the process of observation is to remain hidden from the people being observed. Also, observational researchers are left with only what they can see and hear—the perspective of the research participant is missing. Surveys are a popular alternative method for collecting data on sexuality.

Survey Research

The most common way to gather data on college student sexual behavior and attitudes is through surveys or questionnaires. Surveys are based on asking people questions about their behavior and attitudes, and tallying the responses, typically from large groups of respondents. Still, surveys vary in the extent to which respondents interact with researchers and are anonymous. Whether administered on paper or over the Internet, if the questionnaire does not ask the respondents to identify themselves, and the completed questionnaire is returned in such a way that the researcher cannot identify whose questionnaire is whose, the questionnaire is said to be completely anonymous.

People are most likely to respond accurately and honestly under completely anonymous conditions. However, there are disadvantages to the anonymous questionnaire. Because the respondent does not interact with the researcher, there is no opportunity for either the researcher or the respondent to ask for clarification. If a research participant does not understand a question or a word, he or she is left to guess. If a researcher is faced with a respondent's answer that does not seem to make sense, or conflicts with other answers the respondent provided, there is no way to clarify. Also, people may be less motivated to participate in research when it is easy to opt out of doing so without anyone knowing about it.

To handle these disadvantages, some survey researchers employ trained interviewers to ask questions of research participants. These interviews may be conducted over the telephone or in person (face-to-face). Interviews allow the researcher to have more control, but there are disadvantages. Even if the identity of research participants is not recorded, respondents may not feel anonymous because they are revealing sensitive information directly to a stranger (who does know who the respondent is, at least at the time of the interview). In an attempt to handle this loss of anonymity, some sexuality researchers have aimed for a middle ground by using computer programs to conduct interviews. The computer program presents the questions on the screen, a voice reads each question for the respondent, and there are help windows if the respondent should need clarification.

In summary, there are different methods for collecting data regarding college student sexuality. Each has distinct advantages and disadvantages. Because most sexuality research is based on surveys, and surveys are based on self-reports, it is important to evaluate the factors that may influence self-reports. Collecting accurate self-report data from college students is easier said than done.

MEASURING COLLEGE STUDENTS' SEXUALITY: EASIER SAID THAN DONE?

When researchers ask college students about their sexuality, through either interviews or questionnaires, there are several factors that can influence responses. Unfortunately, researchers have documented that such responses are affected by several other factors, besides the respondents' attitudes or experiences, and these other factors have been lumped together under the terms "response bias" or "reporting bias" (Wiederman, 2002).

Although the forms of response bias are numerous, we will consider the few most troublesome and the ones we should consider when examining any example of research on college student sexuality. First, we will address the primary reasons college student research participants may not provide perfectly accurate answers to researchers' questions, even when they try.

Memory and Recall

Suppose researchers presented the following question to respondents: "With how many different partners have you had vaginal intercourse during your lifetime?" Who would most likely be able to provide an accurate response? Probably those respondents who have never had vaginal intercourse, or who have had one, two, or three partners, would easily be able to recall the exact number of partners.

Consider a second type of example: "How many times during the past 12 months have you used your mouth to stimulate a partner's genitals?" We can imagine that someone who had not performed oral sex during the past year or so would easily produce an accurate response (0 or "none"). However, what about respondents who have had several recent partners or who have had only one partner with whom they have had on ongoing sexual relationship over the previous year? Certainly it is unrealistic to expect that these respondents could remember each instance of oral sex, even if highly motivated and given enough time to try.

How do respondents produce answers to these types of questions about their behavior when it is impossible to recall and count every actual instance of the behavior? In the end, most respondents estimate their experience, and respondents do so in different ways depending on the frequency and regularity of the behavior about which they are being asked. For example, in response to the number of sex partners question, respondents with several partners are liable to give a round, "ballpark" estimate (N. R. Brown & Sinclair, 1999; Wiederman, 1997b). Respondents with more than about 10 partners typically provide numbers that end in 0 or 5 (e.g., 10, 15, 25, 30, 50, 75, 100). Researchers who compute the average number of reported partners and compare groups, say males versus females for example, will end up with averages that look precise (e.g., 4.13 versus 2.27) yet are based on a substantial proportion of respondents who provided global estimates.

Considering responses to frequency questions, such as the oral sex question posed above, it appears that people who have had numerous such experiences go through a reasoning process to arrive at an estimate. The thinking of one hypothetical respondent might go something like this: "Well, my partner and I typically have sex about twice a week or so, and I perform oral sex about half of those times. There are 52 weeks in a year, so I guess I performed oral sex about 50 times during the previous 12 months." The entire line of thinking may take only a second or two. Notice that the respondent does not even attempt to remember each instance because doing so is impossible. How accurate the resulting estimate is depends on how regularly the respondent engages in the behavior as well as the accuracy of his or her recall (or estimation) of that typical frequency. Minor exceptions (e.g., that week the respondent was out of town or was ill or was fighting with the partner) are typically not factored in when arriving at global estimates.

Degree of Insight

Now that we have examined the inherent recall problems in asking people to report accurately on their own behavior, consider how people might attempt to answer the following sexuality questions, and how accurate their responses might be:

1. During what proportion of sexual contacts was a condom used?
2. How did you feel during your first experience of sexual intercourse?
3. How comfortable are you communicating your desires to a sexual partner?
4. At what age did you first stimulate your own genitals for pleasure?

Each of the questions in this list is heavily dependent on the respondent's memory, yet the questions also vary with regard to the degree of insight the respondent needs to have into his or her own mental processes. For example, the second and third questions require insight into one's emotions whereas the first and last questions do not. Conceivably, people who are generally less introspective (less aware of their own feelings and thoughts) will probably have greater difficulty answering the second and third questions, and they may be more prone to providing inaccurate answers as a result.

Now consider questions that require an even greater degree of introspection: "Why did you decide to have sexual intercourse with your current partner that first time that you did? Why did you fall in love with your most recent partner? Why did you break up with your most recent partner?" These questions demand not only recall (memory) but also a great degree of insight into one's own motives and the factors that led to particular emotions and decisions. Humans may not have good insight into these mental processes. This is liable to be true especially with complex feelings and decisions like the ones asked about here.

When asked questions about their motives or decisions, people do readily provide responses. "I felt pressured." "He was the kindest person I had ever met." "We were no longer communicating and just grew apart." These are typical answers people might give to the three questions posed at the start of the previous paragraph, yet how well do they capture all of the complexity that went into decisions to engage in sexual activity with someone for the first time, or the experience of falling in love, or the difficult decision to end a meaningful relationship? It may be that people provide such answers based on stereotypes or beliefs they hold regarding the causes of relationship events. These stereotypes or beliefs may or may not accurately reflect what occurred within the respondent's individual life.

Sometimes researchers ask college students to report what the students would feel or do in a hypothetical situation, such as finding out that their respective romantic partner had cheated on them. Besides needing to clarify what "cheating" would entail, the respondents are being asked to anticipate a situation that would likely elicit very strong feelings in an actual occurrence, yet the hypothetical situation is lacking the rich context in which actual cheating would occur. In other words, when someone discovers that one's partner has "cheated," the discovery occurs in a larger context, including how the cheating was discovered, what the circumstances were, how the person who discovered the cheating feels about that cheating partner generally, and so forth. Asking people to anticipate how they would react in a given scenario will produce a response, but the extent to which that anticipated reaction is in any way similar to how people would actually respond is an entirely different question.

Motivation and Social Desirability

Up to this point we have been talking about problems in accuracy of recall and degree of insight that occur because of the limitations of the human brain, even when motivation and honesty are high. There are also forms of response bias that arise from low motivation to produce accurate responses, or motivation to present oneself in a certain light (regardless of the accuracy of that portrayal).

First, considering lack of motivation, how motivated are respondents when they are participating because of the requirements of one of their college courses? What if they have no such requirement, but are simply asked to participate by an instructor of one of their courses? In contrast, might motivation be higher if participants are paid a substantial amount of money for participating? Or might they be less motivated because they are more likely to be doing it for the money?

There are no definite answers to these questions, but it is important to consider the extent to which participant motivation might affect responses. Also, respondent motivation is liable to vary across participants within any given study. There also may be differences between those who do not answer some questions in a sexuality survey and those who answer all questions.

In addition, some respondents in sexuality studies may distort their responses, consciously or unconsciously, to present themselves in a positive light. For example, if a respondent who has had several sexual partners believes that greater sexual experience is something of which to be proud, she or he may tend to overestimate the lifetime number of sex partners. In contrast, if a respondent feels ashamed of something sexual from his or her past, the respondent may not remember or admit this experience in an interview or on a questionnaire. Researchers refer to these types of distortion as *social desirability response bias*, and such bias may even differ as a function of whether the interviewer is the same or other gender as the respondent. The degree to which respondents believe their answers are anonymous can also alter the degree to which responses are tainted by social desirability response bias.

Besides conscious distortion or deceit in people's sexual self-reports, there are unconscious forms of response bias. In a fascinating example, college women were randomly assigned to two conditions, each involving visualization of the faces of two people known to the participant (Baldwin & Holmes, 1987). In one condition the women were asked to picture the faces of two acquaintances on campus whereas in the other condition participants were asked to visualize the faces of two older members of their own family. All of the women were subsequently presented with the same sexual story and asked to rate their response to it. Interestingly, those college women who had been asked to visualize family members rated the sexual stories less positively than did the women in the other condition. Why? Although we cannot be sure, it is likely that the internal "presence" of the family members led the women to respond more in line with what would be expected by the family members. In a sense, the women's responses were distorted (perhaps unconsciously) by what they had focused on prior to providing their ratings.

We have seen that there are several reasons that the responses research participants give to questions about their sexuality may be inaccurate. These include constraints on memory, inaccessibility to one's own motives or other mental processes, degree of motivation, and tendencies to distort (intentionally or unintentionally) one's responses to be consistent with an image of the self that one wishes to portray. So, research in which respondents have an incentive to participate, are asked direct questions about their behavior over short periods of time, and are assured of anonymity should produce more credible results than research in which participants have little incentive, are asked questions about their behavior over long periods of time or their feelings or motivations, and are unsure of their anonymity. Thus far, the forms of response bias we have focused on involve factors related to the respondent. There are, however, aspects of the research itself that may result in response bias.

Question Wording and Terminology

To elicit self-reports, researchers must rely on words, either spoken or printed, to form the questions and to represent the concepts being studied. The problem is that any time we use words there is the possibility for misunderstanding. Can the researcher be sure that the words used in an interview or in a questionnaire have the same meaning to all respondents as they do to the researcher? Researchers often take great care in choosing the wording for questions, sometimes trying them out on a small sample to work out any problems before actually conducting the study (often referred to as "piloting the questions" or conducting a "pilot study"). For example, would respondents know the meaning of formal sexual terminology such as "fellatio" (performing oral sex on a male) and "cunnilingus" (performing oral sex on a female)? Despite care in question wording, it is easy for different meanings to arise. Consider the following questions:

1. How many sex partners have you had during your lifetime?
2. How often have your and your partner engaged in sex during the past month?
3. Have you ever forced someone to have sex against their will? (Or, have you ever been forced to have sex against your will?)
4. How often do you experience sexual desire?
5. How frequently do you masturbate?

If confronted with these questions in a survey, you might generate answers quite readily, especially if a scale was provided for you to indicate frequency. However, other respondents may interpret the meaning of certain words differently than you do. In the first three questions, what does the term "sex" mean? If you are heterosexual, you are liable to interpret "sex" to mean vaginal intercourse. For many heterosexual individuals, if there was not a penis moving around inside a vagina, there was no "sex." However, others will interpret "sex" to include oral or manual stimulation of the genitals (Sanders & Reinisch, 1999). How does anal intercourse figure into the equation?

What about lesbian college students? Heterosexual definitions of sex rely on the involvement of a penis, and episodes of sex typically are marked by ejaculation from that penis. So, if heterosexual couples are asked the second question ("How often have your and your partner engaged in sex during the past month?"), responses will likely be based on the number of times the man in each couple ejaculated after having been inside his partner's vagina, regardless of the number of orgasms each woman did or did not have. How might lesbian respondents arrive at an answer to the same question? Would the question even have meaning for such respondents?

In the above list of questions, how might the terms "partners," "forced," "sexual desire," and "masturbate" be interpreted by different respondents with different histories, different upbringing, different religious values, and so forth? Does the term "partners" include every individual with whom one has had any sexual contact, or only those individuals with whom one also shared an emotional relationship? How strong does the experience of sexual desire have to be to count? What about a fleeting sexual thought or fantasy? What qualifies as force in a sexual situation?

The last question in the list above had to do with masturbation. This term was chosen intentionally to demonstrate that some sexual words may elicit a stronger emotional reaction than others. Imagine being confronted with the question "How frequently do you masturbate?" versus "How frequently do you stimulate your own genitals for sexual pleasure or release?" Is the second question less threatening and easier to answer? What if the question had been preceded with a statement about masturbation being a common experience? Referring to a particular behavior (e.g., masturbation) as relatively common may lead respondents to be more likely to admit having performed the behavior themselves. When examining the results of a sexuality study, we need to be sensitive to the questions and terminology that were presented to respondents because these are liable to have a substantial effect on the answers the researchers received.

Context Effects

When people respond to questions in a questionnaire or interview, they do not respond to each question in a vacuum. That is, respondents consider the questions that came before and after a particular question when trying to determine what the researchers mean by the question (N. Schwartz, 1999). The impact of certain questions on other questions in the same study is referred to as *context effects*. Because respondents may provide the first appropriate answer that comes to mind, previous questionnaire or interview items may influence responses to a current question because those previous items called to mind particular experiences, attitudes, or feelings. For example, suppose that researchers ask respondents to rate their overall satisfaction with their current dating partners. If this item is preceded by several items having to do with the quality of the sexual aspects of the respondent's relationships, how the respondent feels about his or her sex life is liable to color how he or she rates the overall satisfaction with his or her dating partner.

Conditions and Procedures

Apart from the questions asked and the context in which those items are embedded, researchers may affect respondents' answers by the conditions under which they ask participants to respond. Imagine for a moment answering questions about your first sexual experiences. Under what circumstances would you feel most comfortable and free to do so? Chances are you imagined writing about such experiences, not expecting anyone else to see your answers. Indeed, as a general rule, people are more comfortable and more willing to admit personal, potentially embarrassing information about their sexuality when they are completing an anonymous questionnaire compared to when they believe others have access to their answers. So, all else being equal, we might expect people to be more likely to admit masturbation or extramarital sex when completing an anonymous questionnaire compared to answering the same questions posed in a one-to-one interview. Even within interviews, respondents are liable to be more comfortable with certain types of interviewers compared to other types.

In one study with college students, the researchers manipulated the conditions under which subsamples of the students answered questions about their own extent of experience with masturbation and sexual activity with partners (Alexander & Fisher, 2003). One condition consisted of the standard anonymous surveys that are most commonly used. In a second condition, students were led to believe that, when they were finished completing the surveys, each would be handed to a research assistant, who happened to be a fellow college student of the other gender. In the final condition students were led to believe that, after completing the survey, their answers would be compared to what they reported while connected to a lie detector machine.

The researchers assumed that handing the completed survey to an opposite-sex peer would possibly produce the greatest amount of distortion in responses because the participants did not want to appear to have had too much or too little sexual experience should the research assistant look at their answers. The prospect of being interviewed while connected to a lie detector is assumed to increase motivation to provide accurate and honest answers, so as not to be embarrassed by appearing to lie according to the readout from the machine. Interestingly, in the anonymous-survey condition, the researchers found the typical male-female discrepancy in reported sexual experience, with males reporting more than females. However, in the "hand in the survey to the research assistant" condition, the male-female discrepancy was even larger. Finally, in the lie detector condition there was very little difference between the reported levels of sexual experience between college men and women. Did one gender alter their responses more across the conditions? Yes, and it was clearly the women. This particular study is valuable for reminding us that the conditions under which college students report their sexual experiences and attitudes does matter.

WHAT CAN WE REALLY KNOW ABOUT COLLEGE STUDENT'S SEXUALITY?

Up to this point we have considered aspects of the research that may influence the results. For example, how might the methods of participant recruitment and questioning have affected the answers (data) the research generated? Now we need to examine the issue of what the results or findings actually mean.

Statistical Significance

Researchers generally consider their findings noteworthy only if they are *statistically significant*, and it is only the statistically significant findings that are reported in mass media. To nonresearchers the term "statistically significant" might imply that the results are sizeable or substantial. After all, in common language the word "significant" is synonymous with "important." However, the term as used in science is purely a statistical one that may have little to do with the size or importance of the relationships found among variables. For this reason it is important to understand what sexuality researchers mean when they report that they found a statistically significant difference between groups or a statistically significant relationship between variables.

At the heart of understanding statistical significance is the notion of samples. Recall that, out of necessity, researchers nearly always study samples rather than entire populations. For this reason, there is always the possibility that the particular sample drawn for a given study is unusual simply through random chance. What do sexuality researchers do when faced with this uncertainty that comes along with studying samples rather than populations? They calculate the likelihood that they could have found the results they did in their sample if there is absolutely no difference between the groups, or relationship between the two variables, in the population from which the sample was drawn. If that likelihood is relatively low (usually 5% or less), then the researchers trust (at least for now) that the difference they found reflects the fact that there is an actual difference in the population.

Note that even when a finding is statistically significant, there is still the possibility (up to a 5% chance) that the finding was simply due to chance. So, when researchers set the statistical significance level at 5 percent, then, on average, for every 20 studies (or 20 statistical tests within a particular study) at least one relationship or difference will be statistically significant, yet still simply due to chance. Unfortunately, there is no way to tell which relationships or differences are due to chance without drawing other independent samples to check the consistency of the relationships or differences.

Performing the same research with different samples is referred to as *replication*. If the same findings are replicated across several studies, we can have increased confidence that the findings reflect reality rather than simply a chance finding. Unfortunately, it is the findings that are novel (have not been found before) that are often considered the most interesting, and hence the ones that grab the headlines. So, the findings that are typically reported may be those about which we should be most cautious because they have yet to be replicated.

Practical Significance

Regardless of whether the relationship between two variables, or the difference between two groups, is statistically significant, there is the issue of the absolute size of that relationship or difference. For people in the general public, the primary issue is whether the research findings are large enough to be of practical importance. What we are concerned with is the degree to which particular research findings help us better understand college student sexuality. For example, two or more groups may show statistically significant differences on some variable, yet those differences might be very small in absolute terms such that they have little practical meaning for actual college students. Remember, statistical significance means that the differences are unlikely to be due simply to chance, but these differences can be quite small if the samples they are based on are large samples. Many male-female differences in college student sexuality fit this description (Oliver & Hyde, 1993; J. L. Petersen & Hyde, 2010).

When research results are presented in a way that entails describing one group as having more sexual experience than a second group, it is easy to infer that the members of the first group typically or invariably differ from members of the second group. This may indeed have been the case. However, a statistically significant difference between the groups may have resulted from a small subset of people in the first group who reported extreme amounts of sexual experience. In this case, the typical member of each group may have given very similar responses to the questions researchers posed, yet the groups differ in the average response because of those few respondents who gave atypical reports (and hence inflated their group's average). Describing the members of one group as being different from members of the other group would be misleading.

A similar issue arises when we read or hear some statistic about "the average college student." An example might be, "The average college student has sex with a partner 1.8 times per week." This statement implies that the typical college student, or the majority of college students, has sex with a partner nearly twice per week. However, because statements such as these are based on taking the average across the sample, no one actually reported having sex with a partner 1.8 times per week. Perhaps most college students reported having no sexual activity with partners, and most of the remaining students reported having sex with a partner 4 times per week. The average across the students in this sample might have been 1.8 times per week, but that is not the same as saying that "the average college student" has sex with a partner at that frequency.

In the previous example we used the term "frequency," which refers to how often something occurs in a specific period of time. Sometimes people confuse frequency with "incidence," which refers to the proportion of people who have done something or experienced something in a specified period of time. So, if the yearly incidence of masturbation among college students is 82 percent, that means 82 percent of the college students surveyed reported having masturbated at least once during a given year. The incidence does not reveal anything about the frequency of the behavior. Perhaps it is growing increasingly easy to see how results of sexuality research can be confusing and potentially misleading. Particularly, ways of presenting findings make the situation worse.

Misleading Statistics and Characterizations

It is possible that, regardless of the size of the difference or relationship found, the way researchers describe or visually present their findings implies greater relationships or differences than were actually found. This is not to say that researchers intentionally try to deceive, but there are times when the ways research results are reported can easily lead to misrepresentation of the findings. Suppose you read that researchers found that male college students were more likely than female college students to agree with the statement, "If a woman gets raped, she gets what she deserves." This description portrays men as relatively callous at best and perhaps dangerous at worst.

Now, suppose that the respondents rated their degree of agreement with the statement using a seven-point scale where 1 corresponded to "strongly disagree," 4 corresponded to "neither agree nor disagree," and 7 corresponded to "strongly agree." This is a common method for measuring attitudes in sexuality research. Suppose that the researcher found that the average of the women's ratings was 1.78 and the average rating for men was 2.56. This may have been a statistically significant difference (particularly if it was based on a large sample), yet to say that men were in greater agreement with the statement is misleading because it is clear that both men and women generally indicated disagreement with the statement. Although it may be more accurate to say that men were less likely to disagree with the statement, the findings may not be presented this way. Also, perhaps most of the males disagreed with the statement as much or more than the women in the sample, but a very small group of male respondents agreed with the statement. These few atypical individuals may be responsible for the difference in the averages of the ratings, yet to characterize the men overall as different from the women inaccurately and unfairly characterizes the majority of the male respondents.

Descriptions of research findings can be misleading when they refer to the difference between two groups in relative rather than absolute terms. For example, suppose researchers examined the incidence of masturbation in samples of male and female college students each year for several years. Based on their data, such researchers might conclude something like "The incidence of masturbation has increased more in women than men in recent years." If all you read was the conclusion, you might be led to believe that masturbation is now more prevalent in women than in men, or quickly becoming so. However, suppose that the conclusion is based on finding that the yearly incidence of masturbation among the male college students was rather steady across samples at around 85 percent. Suppose, however, that the yearly incidence among the female college students had been rising in a steady fashion, from initially around 10 percent to about 30 percent in the most recent sample. The researchers might legitimately describe their findings as showing that "the incidence of masturbation among males has not changed, whereas among females it has tripled." Without referring to the actual percentages, the conclusions may prompt an inaccurate image in the minds of readers.

Do the Conclusions Match the Research Design?

Last, are the conclusions sexuality researchers draw from their findings, or the ways in which they characterize their findings, legitimate given the nature of the research? In asking this question, we have come full circle from considering the research design and the inherent limitations involved with each type of research. Now we are considering whether, given those limitations, the conclusions seem warranted.

As an example, suppose sexuality researchers claim that their findings show that college students who live together before marriage have an increased likelihood of divorce. Typically, researchers base such conclusions on the finding that a greater proportion of students who lived together prior to marriage divorced within say five years when compared to students who had not lived together. Although the researchers found such a correlation, the conclusion implies that there is something about premarital cohabitation that causes an increased risk for divorce.

Recall, however, that correlational research does not allow us to draw conclusions about causality. In this case, there may be some other variable or set of variables that is related to both cohabitation and divorce that better explains their apparent relationship. For example, students who live together before marriage may be less religious and hold more liberal attitudes regarding relationships, sexuality, and family compared to those couples who do not live together. People who are less religious and hold liberal attitudes about relationships may also be more open to the possibility of divorce when things are not going well in the marriage. These group differences in religiosity and attitudes (which existed before cohabitation) may best explain why those who chose premarital cohabitation were also more likely to divorce.

Rosenthal (1994) referred to researchers' tendencies to imply causal relationships between their variables as "causism." He noted that writers may not come out and say that their correlational results indicate a causal relationship, yet they may describe their findings using such words as "effect," "impact," "consequence," or "the result of." In using such words when describing relationships between two variables, the implication is that one variable caused the other or at least influenced it. Such words distract the reader from the important point that the results are simply correlational, and that all we can say for sure is that the two variables demonstrate a statistical relationship (and perhaps a weak, yet statistically significant, one).

If researchers do not consider possible third variables that might explain the correlation between any two variables, there is the possibility that the findings will be misleading. For example, in one study the researchers found that religiosity and engaging in risky sexual encounters were negatively correlated among college women (Poulson, Eppler, Satterwhite, Wuensch, & Bass, 1998). That is, those college women in the sample who were most religious were least likely to report having engaged in risky sex. However, they also found that religiosity and risky sex were related to an important third variable: alcohol consumption. It appears that religiosity and risky sex were related to each other because each of these variables was related to likelihood of drinking alcohol prior to engaging in sexual activity.

There are numerous ways in which the limitations or flaws in a research study might be glossed over when it comes to drawing conclusions about the findings. These include making generalizations that are not warranted based on the sample, such as surveying college students about attitudes toward condoms and concluding from those results that people in general hold certain attitudes. It is also common to not recognize the limitations of the measures or questions that were presented to respondents.

For example, researchers may ask college students about their sexual experiences and draw conclusions based on the answers that imply that the respondents did indeed have such experience. To do so does not explicitly recognize the possibility that the answers respondents provided were inaccurate due to problems with memory, difficulty understanding the intended meaning of the questions, and concerns over presenting themselves in a socially desirable (positive) light. To return to the religiosity and risky sex study described above (Poulson et al., 1998), perhaps religiosity was not related to actual consumption of alcohol or engaging in risky sex among the college women in the sample, but rather the most religious students in the sample were most likely to distort their self-reported alcohol consumption and experience with risky sex.

CONCLUSION

In the end, empirical research is the best tool we have for expanding our knowledge about college student sexuality. At the same time, research and researchers are imperfect. There are always limitations to any particular sexuality study. A worthy goal for nonresearchers is to become more savvy evaluators of knowledge claims based on sexuality research. Doing so is a process involving practice, and the first step is learning more about the research process and the choices that are made at various points along the way.

Chapter Three

THEORIES OF SEXOLOGY: WHAT HAVE WE LEARNED FROM COLLEGE STUDENTS?

Sarah E. Ainsworth and Roy F. Baumeister

Few topics can motivate behavior, capture attention, and ignite conversations as readily as sex. Sex is an undeniably important aspect of human behavior, and social scientists have justifiably spent decades collecting data to shed light on the intricacies of sex. In the past half century, the data arsenals of sexuality researchers have expanded rapidly, offering great insight into behavior that most often occurs behind closed doors. This research relies heavily on data collected at university campuses. In spite of the volume of data, the meaning of it all and the larger implications are difficult to interpret given that the field of sexuality research lacks theoretical consensus and integration. This chapter will present an overview of the two leading theories of sex and will review several other theories of sexual behavior.

Prominent sex researchers noted the undesirable state of sexuality theorizing in a special issue of the *Journal of Sex Research* in 1998 (Weis, 1998; also DeLamater & Hyde, 1998). While theory plays a leading role in guiding scientific research in most disciplines, content analyses of two of the top journals in sexuality research revealed a startlingly different trend. Research published in the *Journal of Sex Research* and the *Archives of Sexual Behavior* relegated theory to mere cameo roles. Over a third of the publications in the *Journal of Sex Research* and over half of the publications in the *Archives of Sexual*

Behavior from 1971 to 1990 reported data with no reference to theory (Ruppel, 1994).

The disproportionate number of studies reporting data with no theoretical underpinning reflects in part data collection traditions originating in the Kinsey era. Kinsey encouraged researchers to collect data without the undue influence of major theoretical perspectives. The priority of data over theory evident in the sexology literature also hints at an underlying issue in the field. The explosive growth of the university system has made it easy to collect data, but sex researchers may intentionally shy away from theory to avoid an inhospitable theoretical landscape.

Sexuality researchers who wish to propose new theory or amend theory must be willing to tread on an academic minefield that is dominated by two major theoretical perspectives. The great theoretical divide among sexuality researchers has created an adversarial debate about the nature of sex in which adherents to both groups militantly support their chosen theory. Social constructionists argue that the basis of sexuality is culture and social influence, and the essentialists argue that biology and other innate influences drive sexuality. Researchers on both sides of the divide firmly believe in the superiority of their theory, and challenges to their theory are often met with derision and scorn. To navigate the theoretical minefield of sexuality research, prospective theorists reportedly feel some pressure to align themselves with either major theoretical perspective. Researchers who challenge the status quo by conducting research not in accordance with either major theoretical perspective are punished with hostile reviews and the rejection of their ideas. The partisan nature of sexuality research has forestalled progress in theory development. While the two major perspectives continue to wage theoretical warfare, researchers who propose potentially useful low-level or mid-level theories are ignored or rejected.

The history of contentious debate among sexuality researchers and the reluctance of other researchers to develop theory paint a bleak portrait of the state of sexuality research. In spite of the issues and shortcomings, sexuality research and theory is broadly interesting across a wide variety of disciplines and traditions and will not go out of vogue. In the years to come, researchers can exploit the full potential of sexuality theorizing only by surrendering their agenda and politics. This critical step will allow more thoughtful consideration to ideas that do not align perfectly to either dominant theoretical perspective. Sexuality theory will experience advances in future decades to the extent that researchers are open to new ideas and theories regardless of whether they support or contradict the two traditional theoretical frameworks.

THEORETICAL PERSPECTIVES

Social Constructionist Theory

Social constructionist theories are built around the idea that reality is socially constructed. This means individuals cannot objectively grasp reality. Instead, individuals interpret reality by filtering their perceptions of the world through their preconceptions and biases. The subjective nature of reality is the basis for the social constructionist idea that truth is relative. By arguing that there is no objective reality, social constructionist theories offer a departure from the traditional scientific models of positivism. While the positivism approach to science stresses the use of the scientific method to pursue objective knowledge and reality, social constructionist theories argue that there is no objective reality. Reality will depend on the individual biases, preconceptions, and social context and influence. This reality will vary across individuals and across historical time period and cultural context.

Social constructionist theories of sexuality gained momentum after the publication of highly influential book *The Social Construction of Reality* (Berger & Luckmann, 1966), which outlined the central tenets of the social constructionist theory. The theory emphasizes that language is essential in the social construction of reality because it enables individuals to interpret their world and to share this interpretation with other people. Shared interpretations of reality then become institutionalized through cultural norms and expectations.

Social constructionist theories of sexuality predict that sexual behavior will vary across historical period and time because sexual behavior is based on the social construction of subjective reality, which is variable over time and place. This indicates that sexuality would also vary substantially across the life span. The social influences experienced by a college student are likely to be highly different from those experienced by a retiree. Constructionist theories also emphasize that there are no universal determinants of sexual behavior. Biology may provide the raw ingredients for sex, but sex is not ultimately determined by laws of biology. Instead, sexual behavior reflects the influence of a kaleidoscope of social influences, including religion, education, the media, parenting, and socialization.

Even sexual behaviors that show signs of universality do not escape the influence of culture. The constructionist leader Margaret Mead (1928, 1961) provided an illustration of this constructionist principle in her argument that sexual possessiveness and jealousy are not universal. According to Mead, sexual jealousy and possessiveness result from the tradition in Western culture to frame sex in an emotional context. Cultures that do not view sex as an emotionally laden event, such as Samoa, do not show evidence of sexual possessiveness and jealousy. This research must be considered in concert with the conclusions of other researchers who squarely reject Mead's conclusion that sexual jealousy is not universal (e.g., Reiss, 1986).

Social constructionists' rejection of the universality of sexual behavior is at odds with the essentialist view that sexual behavior is highly influenced by biological principles that know no cultural or social boundaries. Constructionist theorists do not deny that hormones, genes, and biology play a role in sexual behavior, but they question the degree to which these factors ultimately influence sexual behavior. They triumph culture as the ultimate causal force underlying sexual behavior. Subjective experience, social context, and cultural influences outweigh biological factors in determining sexual behavior.

The inherent weakness of constructionist theory is that the focus on the variability and subjectivity of sexual behavior undermines the predictive power of the theory. Social constructionist theorists must have an intimate knowledge of the culture and time period to make broad predictions about sexual behaviors, and these predictions would need to adjust for changes in cultural norms and expectations. Constructionist theories of sex are necessarily cultural specific and historically constrained.

Feminist Theory

The constructionist principle of the variability in subjective reality is reflected in the multitude of the sexuality theories that belong to the perspective. In spite of the diversity of social constructionist theories, feminist theories dominate the social constructionism landscape. The birth of social constructionism coincided with the rise of the feminist movement in the 1970s, which led to the integration of feminist ideals into the framework of constructionist theory. Although there are feminists who are not social constructionists and social constructionists who are not feminists, a large percentage of social constructionists are feminist theorists.

In the 1970s the feminist movement ignited across multiple domains, including sexuality. The sexual revolution was viewed by feminists as a triumph responsible for liberating women's sexual behavior. To be sure, the sexual revolution led to unprecedented changes in women's sexual behavior that extended far beyond the changes observed in men (Ehrenreich, Hess, & Jacobs, 1986; Arafat & Yorburg, 1973; Birenbaum, 1970). Studies of college students indicated that permissiveness toward sex increased during the sexual revolution more for women than for men (K. E. Bauman & Wilson, 1974; Sherwin & Corbett, 1985). Indeed, recognition of this discrepancy was one impetus for Baumeister's research on erotic plasticity, which concluded that female sexuality is generally more malleable and responsive than male sexuality to social and cultural factors (Baumeister, 2000).

The sexual revolution provided constructionist theorists with support for the central notion that sexuality is heavily contingent on cultural influences. Before the sexual revolution fewer than 3 percent of women (38% of men) had sex with five or more partners by age 30, but after the sexual revolution these figures rose to 22 percent of women (49% of men; Laumann, Gagnon, Michael, & Michaels, 1994). The dramatic changes in attitude and praxis bolstered the position of social constructionists. The sexual revolution confirmed to social constructionists that anything is possible in the realm of sex.

The feminist perspective on sexuality and classic feminist works written in the 1970s (e.g., Brownmiller, 1975) continue to influence sexuality research today. In spite of the proliferation of feminist work in sexuality research, it is hard to summarize the movement because what it means to be a feminist differs radically depending on who is asked. As chronicled in the book *Who Stole Feminism?* (Sommers, 1994), feminism cannot be characterized as a uniform movement.

The individuals who started the feminist movement were equity feminists who believed that the men and women are equal (though not necessarily the same). Equity feminists are concerned with promoting fairness and equality between men and women. This is in contrast to radical feminists, who built their movement as an outgrowth of equity feminism. Instead of viewing the each gender as equal and striving to promote knowledge, radical feminists believe that women are superior to men and strive to promote women at all costs. This radical version of feminism borrowed the legitimacy of the equity feminist movement to build an agenda that portrayed men as the unassailable oppressors of women. The following overview of the feminist contribution to sexuality research covers a diversity of viewpoints ranging from equity to radical feminist thought.

The feminist view stresses that sexuality is highly influenced by gender roles assigned to males and females. The social construction of gender roles can be negotiated, and by extension, sex is also negotiable (Tiefer, 1995). This allows the negotiation of gender roles to serve as a mechanism to regulate sex whereby modified gender roles can effectively sexualize or desexualize the act of sex (Weeks, 1991). Several feminist theorists have proposed that sexual authorities regulate sex only when this benefits individuals in power.

Power is a critical feature of many feminist analyses of sexuality (e.g., Riger, 1992; Yoder & Kahn, 1992). Feminist theory endorses the view that men have intentionally oppressed women in the service of maintaining the advantages of patriarchy (the political domination of men over women). In the sexual arena, feminists have theorized that men have intentionally suppressed female sexuality. An early account of the female sex drive characterized it as insatiable and compared human females to female primates who during estrus have sex up to 50 times a day and with every available partner (Sherfey, 1966). Another analysis suggested that the powerful sex drive of women threatened to wreak havoc on prehistoric society (and to make men feel insecure). To prevent these outcomes, men used their greater physical and institutional power to restrict female sexuality and thereby bring it into alignment with male sexuality (Hyde & DeLamater, 1997).

Feminists have also characterized gender differences in sexuality in terms of power. In the 1970s, feminists viewed the existence of gender differences as evidence of double standards created by a male conspiracy to prevent women from experiencing the same sexual pleasures as men. In response to these analyses, feminists tried to minimize or deny gender differences. Nonetheless, a large meta-analysis of 170 studies examining gender differences later provided evidence that males and females differ significantly in incidence of masturbation and in attitudes about casual sex (Oliver & Hyde, 1993). Feminist thinking predicts that these gender differences would dissipate if the institutional power differential between men and women were eliminated. Furthermore, and quite contrary to the feminist analysis of the double standard as a male tool for oppressing women, Oliver and Hyde recorded that women had generally embraced the double standard more than men—indeed every study that found support for the double standard found it to be stronger among women.

The idea that the incidence of masturbation and attitudes toward casual sex could change as a function of the power balance within society stands in sharp contrast to evolutionary theory (see Buss & Schmitt, 1993). Evolutionary theorists propose that innate biological differences between males and females give rise to different reproductive strategies in each gender (e.g., interest in casual sex). These biologically and evolutionarily determined strategies should remain largely consistent despite fluctuations in the societal power balance, although certainly most evolutionary theorists would grant some influence to culture and circumstance. Evolutionary theory offers an alternate view of sexuality that has been elaborated as an alternative to feminist theory and social constructionism.

Evolutionary Theory

Some of the earliest thinkers in psychology mentioned the need to incorporate the evolutionary approach in order to achieve a complete understanding of human social behavior (e.g., James, 1890/1950), but evolutionary theory was not routinely applied to psychological phenomena until the late 1960s. The pioneering evolutionary psychologists centered their research on sex and generated detailed hypotheses incompatible with much of social constructionist sexuality theory. The central emphasis on sex reflected its importance in evolutionary theory: natural selection proceeds based on reproduction, and among mammals sex is a vital part of reproduction. Evolutionary theories and other essentialist theories argue that many sexual phenomena are universal and biologically determined.

The view that human sexual behavior is primarily determined by genes, hormones, and other biological factors was not always well received. Evolutionary theories of sexuality and researchers who endorsed the perspective were for a time regarded with suspicion. Researchers were accused of having an obsession with sex, and people were uncomfortable with the idea that sex reflects forces of nature rather their own personal desires. Many individuals found the idea that sex is largely driven by factors outside of personal control unsettling. Evolutionary theory was sometime criticized for offering a cynical view of sexual behavior that implies that harmful sexual behaviors are biologically determined and cannot be changed or avoided. In this respect, objections to evolutionary theory can be understood as reflecting similar skeptical resistance accorded to other pioneers of research and theory on sex, including Sigmund Freud and Alfred Kinsey.

The building blocks of evolutionary theory are the principles of biological adaptation and evolution by natural selection. Darwin (1859/1964, 1871) proposed that individuals with adaptive physical and psychological features will reproduce at a greater rate than individuals without these features, which are called "adaptations." Adaptations can become characteristic of the entire population over many generations. The preference for sweet-tasting foods represents an adaptation that is now characteristic of the humans. Sweet foods provide nutritional advantages because they are typically rich in calories and provide energy that the body can expend immediately. Human who preferred to consume sweet foods likely ingested a greater number of calories than their counterparts who did not share this preference. This caloric advantage could have helped humans in numerous ways, including by improving physiological functioning and aiding reproduction. The modern availability of sweet foods (e.g., corn syrup) has largely perverted the benefits of the human preference for sweets, but the adaptation historically afforded human ancestors greater reproductive success.

Evolutionary theory predicts that modern sexual behavior and desires evolved from behaviors that helped human ancestors to produce the maximum number of high-quality offspring. Evolutionary adaptations that have bolstered the reproductive success of human ancestors are evident in all aspects of human mating behavior ranging from romantic attraction to the maintenance of long-term relationships (Cosmides & Tooby, 1992; Maner et al., 2003). Gender differences are an inherent aspect of evolutionary accounts of sexuality and reflect the different reproductive constraints faced by men and women throughout the evolutionary past. The classic sexual strategies theory maintains that men and women have adapted different reproductive strategies to overcome the specific reproductive limitations relevant to their gender (Buss & Schmitt, 1993). The foundation of these differentiated sexual strategies is tied to basic differences in biology between males and females.

By virtue of the biology of reproduction, females typically invest more in offspring than males (i.e., a minimum investment of gestation and lactation compared to insemination). This discrepancy in minimal level of parental investment between the males and females, as first noted by Darwin, necessitates that they employ different mating strategies. The gender that invests more in parenting is more discriminating in choosing mates, and the gender that invests less in parenting is less discriminating and must compete more for mates (Trivers, 1972). Choosiness reflects the importance of having only the best sex partners. If a man makes a pregnancy with a suboptimal mate and then a better one comes along, he can reproduce with her within the hour. In contrast, if a woman makes a comparable mistake, her reproductive system is tied up for nine months, and it may be almost a year before she is ready to reproduce again with the better partner. Hence it is more important for her than for him to choose the right mate the first time.

In humans, females invest more on average in parenting than males and are also more discriminating when choosing a partner. Due to their finite lifetime reproductive capacity, women benefit by selecting high-quality partners to maximize the likelihood that each pregnancy results in viable offspring with an adequate chance for survival. The evolutionary perspective predicts that females should seek partners who can provide resources, protection, and commitment to offspring. Research conducted with college students indicates that women typically place particular value on attributes that signal a potential mate's ability to accrue resources, such as social status and dominance (Li, Bailey, Kenrick, & Linsenmeier, 2002; Sadalla, Kenrick, & Vershure, 1987).

The selectivity of females gives rise to the major reproductive constraint experienced by men—access to mates. Men face greater competition for mates compared to women (Trivers, 1972), and to maximize reproductive success in spite of this increased competition, men should pursue females with the greatest reproductive fitness. Accordingly, men tend to highly value traits associated with reproductive capacity, including youth, health, physical appearance, and attractiveness (Li et al., 2002).

In spite of the male preference for beautiful women, there is a chronic shortage of young and beautiful women compared to the numbers of average and below average men who would like to have sex with them. Reproductive odds have not historically favored men. Modern humans are descended from about twice as many women as men (Wilder, Mobasher, & Hammer, 2004), which indicates that most men who ever lived failed to pass on their genes. To secure fertile romantic partners, men employ a greater range of strategies than women to compete with other suitors and are often willing to assume high-risk/high-payoff strategies to acquire mating opportunities (M. Wilson & Daly, 1985).

Evolutionary theory also predicts that men are more likely to favor casual sex than women, and this difference in attitude is well documented (e.g., Oliver & Hyde, 1993). An evolutionary analysis of this data proposes that men have more to gain from casual sex than women. Women have a lifetime reproductive capacity of about 10 offspring (Gould & Gould, 1997; Ridley, 1993) and having casual sex more than about one time per year cannot increase this figure. If anything, casual sex coupled with the attendant lack of commitment from the male partner would translate to worse survival rates for offspring. In contrast to women, men have an almost unlimited reproductive capacity and fertility rates among men vary wildly (e.g., from the unfortunate millions who never reproduced to Ghengis Khan, who allegedly had hundreds of offspring). For men, casual sex can have a startling impact on fertility rates.

The sexual strategies that drive human mating patterns and behaviors are not necessarily conscious processes. In a classic study on casual sex, attractive male and female confederates approached opposite-sex individuals on college campuses and asked whether the individuals would either: (1) go on a date with the confederate, (2) go home with the confederate, or (c) have sex with the confederate (R. D. Clark & Hatfield, 1985). In response to the question about sex, college males almost universally accepted the offer, whereas no college females were willing to have sex with the confederate. The college-age men who were willing to go to bed immediately with the attractive confederate were not likely motivated by the prospect of increasing their reproductive output. Instead, the willingness of the study participants to accept an offer of casual sex reflects adaptive strategies that generations of males have use to gain reproductive advantages.

The sexual strategies put forth by evolutionary psychologists do not always align with societal ideals or morals, and some theorists have accused the evolutionary perspective as endorsing a form of genetic determinism (e.g., Lickliter & Honeycutt, 2003). Evolutionary theorists, however, disagree with this criticism. They propose that culture and learning interact with genes and other biological factors to produce sexual behavior (e.g., Gangestad & Simpson, 2000; Kenrick et al., 2002; D. L. Krebs, 2003).

Social Exchange Theory

Social exchange theories offer an alternate and possibly compatible framework to the social constructionist and evolutionary perspectives for understanding sexuality. Theories of social exchange analyze human social behavior according to economic principles (Blau, 1964; Homans, 1950, 1961; Thibaut & Kelley, 1959). Markets operate based on the interconnected behavior of buyers and sellers who are each motivated to minimize their costs and maximize the profit of their transactions. Social exchange theory, which is actually more of a style of analysis than an outright theory, proposes that human behavior can also be analyzed in terms of costs and benefits. The most common social behaviors will be those that offer more benefits and fewer costs.

The social exchange analysis of human behavior requires an expansive definition of the term "costs and benefits." In contrast to economic theories, the costs and benefits of human social behaviors are not limited to monetary exchange and the exchange of tangible products. Abstract and nontangible social rewards and costs are included in social exchange analyses of behavior. The costs of social behavior can range from heartbreak and disease to a marred reputation and disrespect, and the benefits encompass all varieties of psychological currency, including approval, esteem, prestige, respect, and of course love (see Sprecher, 1988, 1992). Sex also contributes to the social exchange, but it can be classified as either a cost or benefit depending on the specific circumstances associated with the exchange.

Social exchange theories of sexuality are not new arrivals on the sexology scene, but previous attempts to apply social exchange analyses to sex have overlooked the idea that sex itself operates as a female resource (Baumeister & Vohs, 2004). In market terms, women are the sellers of sex, and men are the buyers of sex. This does not imply that all women literally sell sex to men. Instead, women hold a privileged position in the negotiation of sex due to the principle of least interest. Whoever wants something less is in the best bargaining position and has more power (Waller & Hill, 1938/1951). The individual who wants sex less in any relationship has the power to determine when sex will happen and under which circumstances. When it comes to sex, recent reviews of literature have confirmed overwhelmingly that women want it less than men (Baumeister, Catanese, & Vohs, 2001). Because women desire sex less than men, men generally understand that they must offer women some additional benefits (beyond the sex act itself) to make sex appealing. These other benefits can include love, commitment, security, attention, and material resources. These constitute a sort of price of sex, and the price can vary with conditions in the sexual marketplace.

Generally, the price of sex is regulated by principles of supply and demand, and men and women have competing interests. Men benefit sexually if the price of sex is low, and women benefit economically and emotionally if the price of sex is high. Women can maintain a high price for sex by employing the economic principle of scarcity. The value of social rewards diminishes when the rewards are handed out too freely (Blau, 1964), but strictly controlling the supply of sex and other rewards increases their value. Individual women could demand higher prices for their sex by refusing to have sex early in a relationship or without serious signs of commitment, but women who raise the price of their sex above the market average could find it difficult to attract potential buyers because men can find other options that are less expensive. This illustrates that the price for sex is determined by the overall behavior of buyers and sellers, which is contingent on social norms.

The most obvious fluctuations in the balance between supply and demand involve the sex ratio. Few college campuses have exactly as many female as male students. As documented in a classic study of the sex ratio by Guttentag and Secord (1983), sexual norms change as a function of which gender is in the majority—and it is rarely the case that the majority rules! Rather, the norms favor the minority, as is the case in most marketplaces. In sex, women constitute the supply and men the demand. When there are more men than women, demand exceeds supply, and in such cases the price is typically high. That means that sex outside of committed relationships is relatively rare, and a man must usually offer a woman quite a bit in order to have sex. In contrast, when women outnumber men (as is increasingly the case on campuses across the country), then supply exceeds demand, which in sex as with other goods and services leads to a lower price. A surplus of women relative to men tends to produce local norms that favor easy, casual sex without much in the way of commitment. In such a situation, a woman who wants sex only with a committed relationship partner may find it difficult to get such a commitment, because men can obtain sex from other women relatively easily, and each women feels pressure to offer sex rather early and frequently in order to keep the man's interest.

Women could increase the market price of sex by working together to restrict supply. Considerable evidence suggests that this does sometimes happen. Although feminist analyses of sexuality are often based on the underlying assumption that males intentionally suppress female sexuality, recent analyses from a social exchange perspective offer the opposite conclusion. Women are motivated to suppress the sexuality of other women (Baumeister & Twenge, 2002), which could be interpreted as a rational strategy to maintain an appropriately high value of sex. Indeed, this can explain the seeming paradox noted above, which is that support for the double standard of sexual morality has generally been stronger among women than among men. It is in women's collective self-interest to hold up high standards of sexual morality for each other, so that men's sexual opportunities remain scarce and the price of sex stays high.

The restriction of female sexuality by women represents a form of collusion among sellers, and a study of Canadian college students preparing for spring break vividly illustrates how both buyers and sellers collude when navigating the sexual marketplace. Whereas the men in this study agreed before their trip to help each other have as much sexual activity as possible during spring break, the women made pacts to restrict their sexual activities, such as promising to keep others from having sex after drinking (Maticka-Tyndale, Herold, & Mewhinney, 1998).

Individuals who undercut the collective bargaining position of women by "cheap" sexual behavior should be met by the female community with disapproval, ostracism, and other disincentives. Accordingly, women are more likely than men to judge promiscuous women harshly (Millhausen & Herold, 1999). Women also tend to disfavor any practices that lower the price of sex. Compared to men, women hold more negative attitudes about a variety of sexual behaviors, including premarital sex, extramarital sex, and casual sex (Laumann et al., 1994; Oliver & Hyde, 1993; W. C. Wilson, 1975). Pornography and prostitution are no exceptions. These sexual outlets serve as cheap alternatives to sex with women who require commitment and investment, and not surprisingly, college-age women hold more negative attitudes than college-age men toward pornography (Lottes, Weinberg, & Weller, 1993) and prostitution (Klassen, Williams, & Levitt, 1989).

The social exchange theory of sex applied to the sexual revolution offers a radical reinterpretation of the cultural meaning of increased sexual permissiveness. Although feminists touted the sexual revolution as a victory for women, later research indicated that women assessed the rise in sexual permissiveness attached to the sexual revolution more negatively than men (T. W. Smith, 1994). From a social exchange perspective, increased norms of sexual permissiveness effectively lowered the price of sex. Social exchange theorists would agree with feminist author Germaine Greer, who wrote in 1999 that men won the sexual revolution because "the sexuality that has been freed is male sexuality" (Greer, 1999, p. 10). The sexual revolution made sex available at a discounted rate, which translated to more sex for men in a context of less commitment to and investment in their female partners.

Social exchange theories of sexuality also endorse the principle that competition among sellers increases when supply exceeds demand. When there are fewer buyers than sellers, the buyers have greater influence on the rules of the exchange. Sex ratios of males and females within societies reflect the ratio of buyers to sellers. When men are in the minority, the social exchange of sex aligns with the interest of men, and there is more sex (Guttentag & Secord, 1983). During World War II, American college campuses were left with about eight times as many women as men. This hugely disproportionate sex ratio dramatically altered the social exchange rules of sex. Skirt lengths became shorter (Barber, 1999), and social norms were inverted as women were forced to compete for dates. One researcher noted that the shortage of men led women to advertise for prom dates with the added incentive that the woman would cover the expenses and provide the car (J. R. Petersen, 1999). When men are in the minority, they experience sexual advantages that they would not have otherwise.

Social exchange analyses of sexuality propose that economic principles dictate the rules of human courtship and sexual behavior. Sex begins as a female resource based on the fact that women desire sex less than men. Although evolutionary theory can provide a basis for understanding why women desire sex less than men, the social exchange theory is more cultural because it predicts how couples negotiate sex within an organized and meaningful social system.

SEXUAL PHENOMENA

This section will detail how several specific sexual phenomena relate to the overarching theoretical perspectives presented in the previous sections and will mention other directions in theorizing. The social constructionist and evolutionary perspectives currently dominate sexuality theorizing, but theoretical development in the field stands to benefit from focusing more attention to narrow theories that cannot necessarily be classified into either theoretical camp.

Sexual Desire

Social constructionist theories send mixed messages as to whether males or females have higher sex drives. Some feminist theorizing asserts that sexual intercourse is inherently coercive, and men satisfy their higher sex drive by coercing women to have sex with them. Other feminist theories rest on the assumption that the female sex drive is comparable to or even greater than the males' sex drive (e.g., Sherfey, 1966; see also Hyde & DeLamater, 1997).

Evolutionary theory rebukes the claim that the sex drives of each gender are equal and instead proposes that the male sex drive is stronger than the female sex drive (for a review, see Buss & Schmitt, 1993; Oliver & Hyde, 1993). The strong male sex drive is explained as an evolutionary adaptation that helped men reach their reproductive potential. The desire for sex does not always lead to more sex, but it motivates individuals to actively search for sex partners and to take risks for sexual payoffs. Increased mating effort could lead to higher (virtually unlimited) number of offspring in men, but not women because women have a limited reproductive capacity of about one child per year. Evolutionary theory explains that women did not evolve the high sex drive of men because women cannot reproductively benefit from additional sex.

A comprehensive survey of the research literature by Baumeister, Catanese, and Vohs (2001) addressed the question of whether there is a gender difference in sex drive. The answer was a resounding yes, with males showing higher desire for sex on just about every measure. Men rate their desires for sex as more frequent and more intense than women rate theirs. Men think about sex more often, want it more frequently at all stages in a relationship, desire more partners, desire and enjoy more different sex acts, and have more frequent and elaborate sexual fantasies. Men take more risks than women to get sex. They find chastity more difficult to achieve, even when backed by strong personal religious commitments. They initiate sex more often and refuse it less often. They masturbate more, are more willing to pay for sexual stimulation, and are less willing to do without.

The social exchange theory views sex as a female resource precisely because men have a stronger desire for sex than women (Baumeister & Vohs, 2004). The potent desire men have for sex explains why they are willing to offer women other rewards, such as love, commitment, and support, in exchange for sex. If women and men had equal levels of sexual desire, sex could simply be traded directly for sex instead of exchanged for other rewards. If the sex drive of women outpaced that of men, social exchange theory would predict that women would offer men other rewards to have sex with them. In this scenario, it would be common for a woman to buy gifts for a man with the goal of enticing him to come to bed with her. Perhaps she would even tell him she loved him in order to convince him to undress for her. All available empirical evidence strongly supports the view that the male sex drive is greater the female sex drive regardless of how sex drive is measured.

The undeniable gender differences in sexual desire have ramifications for sexual decision making. Error management theory, which is marginally linked to the evolutionary perspective, predicts that individuals want to minimize the most costly errors they experience in relation to reproduction (Haselton & Buss, 2000; see also Maner et al., 2005). The relatively strong sex drive of men compared to women puts men at a disadvantage in the competition for sex partners. If all women had all the sex they wanted, some men would still be left without a partner. Most men will never completely fulfill their sexual desires, and this endemic state of male sexual hunger makes missing the opportunity to have sex the most costly sexual error for men. To avoid this error, men are prone to overinterpret ambiguous signs of sexual interest, such as smiling. Compared to men, women have relatively weaker desire for sex. This puts women in a better position to discriminate among potential partners, but women must still avoid the costly error of having sex with an inadequate or genetically inferior partner. To prevent this error, women are often reluctant to consent to sexual activities and exact high standards when selecting sexual partners.

The gap between male and female sexual desire also has implications for theories about prostitution and pornography. Social exchange theorists suggest that prostitution and pornography are relatively low-cost substitutes that enable men to have sex. Men can turn to prostitution and pornography when the price of courtship is too expensive or when they are unwilling to give certain rewards in exchange for sex. Feminist theorists view male use of prostitutes and pornography as an exploitation of women. These theorists do not link the use of prostitutes and pornography to the strong sexual desire of men because they argue that the male and female sex drives are comparable. Instead, pornography and prostitution represent tools of degradation and exploitation leveraged by a patriarchal society to oppress women. Prostitution and pornography are highly contentious issues that have sparked heated debated among scholars and laypersons alike.

Rape

The scientific discourse on rape is even more divisive than the disagreements concerning the societal implication of prostitution and pornography. Academic conversations about rape often degenerate into intense ideological debates. These nonproductive exchanges have contributed to the inadequacy of the current state of theorizing about rape within the major perspectives in sexuality research.

The majority of theorizing about rape centers on why men rape women. Feminist theories of rape portray rape as a weapon used by men to dominate and exploit women. An influential feminist characterization of rape described it as "nothing more or less than a conscious process of intimidation by which all men keep all women in a state of fear" (Brownmiller, 1975, p. 15). By this account, power rather than sex is the driving force behind rape. The idea that power is the dark force lurking behind the phenomenon of rape has been largely discredited by empirical evidence (for reviews, see Felson, 2002; Palmer, 1988; Tedeschi & Felson, 1994). In spite of the evidence, this conceptualization of rape is still popular among feminists. Men do not rape women to achieve power, but it is possible that women interpret the experience of rape as one in which men have power over them. This would fit with the social constructionist principle that reality is subjective.

Evolutionary theorists have put forth the hypothesis that rape could serve as a biological strategy that some men employ to boost their reproductive odds (Thornhill & Palmer, 2000). Rape as a reproductive strategy could particularly appeal to low-status men. Throughout evolutionary history, women often discarded or rejected low-status men during the mate selection process in favor of high-status men, who could provide more resources for offspring. If women do not willingly mate with low-status men, sexual aggression is a strategy that could enable low-status men to reproduce in spite of female reluctance. Low-status men who raped women would be more likely to pass on their genes than low-status men who refrained from sexual coercion. The authors of this theory admit that the theory suffers from a lack of empirical support. More data are needed to lend support to this theory and to answer the remaining questions.

Several other theories of rape that cannot be classified as belonging to the social constructionist or evolutionary theoretical perspectives have also received attention. An early theory of rape explained the phenomenon as related to a lack of social skills on the part of the rapist. This theory proposed that men who could not charm women into bed sometimes resorted to sexual coercion. Empirical data do not support this theory. Rapists attain more consensual sex than other men (e.g., Kanin, 1985), and social skills are related to the incidence of consensual sex but are unrelated to sexual coercion (Muehlenhard & Falcon, 1990). Another more recent theory of rape states that a constellation of personality factors predisposes men toward rape (Malamuth, 1996). Masculine men who hold negative attitudes toward women, feel victimized by women, and categorize heterosexual relationships as antagonistic or exploitative are more likely to engage in sexual coercion than men who do not share these characteristics. This cautious approach to theorizing about rape is admirable in the sense that it is limited in scope and is based on systematic observations.

The narcissistic reactance theory of rape is another recent, empirically based theory of rape (Baumeister, Catanese, & Wallace, 2002). This theory analyzes rape through the lens of reactance theory (Brehm, 1966). According to reactance theory, options that are taken away are perceived as more attractive, and individuals react to lost options by trying to partake in the off-limits behavior. This reactance can involve aggressive behavior toward the individual who took away the option. When the sexual advances of men are met with refusals for sex, some men will react with sexual aggression toward the woman. The narcissism component of narcissistic reactance theory explains why only some but not all men who have experienced sexual rejection turn to rape.

Most men respond to refusals to have sex with no further advances or attempts (Byers & Lewis, 1988), and only a small minority of men rape women. Narcissistic reactance theory predicts that narcissism increases the chance that reactance to refusals for sex will lead to rape. A hallmark characteristic of a narcissist is an inflated sense of entitlement. Individuals high in entitlement are more likely to become upset when their freedom is curtailed or when an option is taken away from them (Rhodewalt & Davison, 1983). Narcissistic men become convinced through their overblown sense of entitlement that they deserve to have sex with the women who reject them. Narcissistic reactance theory views the obtainment of sex after refusal for sex as the central motivation to rape women and predicts that men will use aggression only to the extent necessary to obtain sex. Sexually coercive narcissists would likely prefer to believe that the sex was consensual because this would provide the greatest ego boost.

Homosexuality

Homosexuality is an area of sexuality research rife for midlevel theorizing because the major theoretical perspectives do not offer adequate explanations. Social constructionist theories could explain homosexuality as a result of upbringing, the media, and other socializing factors. This explanation is suspect considering that Western cultures have traditionally expressed negative opinions of homosexuality and have even endorsed legal, social, and religious sanctions aimed at preventing homosexuality. If homosexuality were the result of social experiences, the threat of violence and discrimination directed toward homosexuals should decrease or eliminate the incidence of homosexuality.

Some feminist theorists have claimed that heterosexuality is not a natural state. These theorists argue that heterosexuality is the result of men wielding their institutional power to pervert sexuality to conform to their version of an ideal social structure. Other feminists argue that culture is sometimes enough to motivate individuals to choose homosexuality. Some women became lesbians during the zenith of the feminist movement to support political rhetoric that likened sleeping with men to sleeping with an enemy (Blumstein & Schwartz, 1997). In the wake of this political movement, sleeping with women represented the most politically correct form of sexuality.

Evolutionary theories have difficulty in explaining homosexuality because it does not fit with the theme that modern human sexuality reflects adaptations that allowed human ancestors to maximize their reproductive output. Homosexuals can increase their reproductive footprint only by sleeping with members of a sex they do not desire. Considering that desire is often a requirement for sex, it is not unreasonable to predict that evolution should have completely eliminated homosexuality. Some evolutionary theorists speculate that homosexuality evolved due to kin selection (Bobrow & Bailey, 2001). Homosexual individuals may not have their own children, but they could indirectly propagate their genes by supporting the children of their close relatives.

Another theory of homosexuality, proposed by Bem (1996), explains that a specific interaction of nature and nurture can lead to homosexuality. Nature endows children with particular temperaments, and these temperaments will lead each child to prefer playing predominantly with males or with females. When children reach adolescence they become attracted to the sex opposite of their childhood playmates because "exotic becomes erotic." This theory explains that the attraction bisexuals have to both genders could result from having played with both boys and girls as children. Similar to other theories of homosexuality, this theory awaits the empirical evidence that could be used to argue for or against it. The unsatisfying state of homosexuality theory makes homosexuality a topic that will lend itself well to future midlevel theorizing.

HOW HAVE COLLEGE STUDENTS INFLUENCED SEXUALITY THEORIZING?

Sexuality researchers have relied extensively on college students. Would the theories presented above change if the majority of sexuality research relied on less restricted samples? Although many sexuality researchers have made painstaking efforts to recruit samples representative of diverse age and demographic characteristics, these samples provide the exception rather than the rule.

College students differ from other segments of the population in important ways. In the realm of sexuality, their preferences and behavioral patterns could be less well established compared to older individuals. Social constructionist theories of sexuality might include age as a crucial moderator. The development of sexual preferences during this period could make college students more susceptible to the influences of norms, the media, and their peer group. These influences are less likely to be significant for older adults, who have well-established sexual routines and preferences. Social constructionist theories could also take into account that college is in itself a distinct culture. Although the specific reasons are not well understood, a nationally representative survey found that education increases sexual permissiveness (Laumann et al., 1994).

The relatively high sexual permissiveness associated with increasing education hints that issues of jealousy and romantic rivalry could apply more to college students than to older adults. Evolutionary theorists posit that the purpose of jealousy is to guard partners against intersexual rivals in order to prevent cuckoldry or the loss of precious resources. Perhaps jealousy is less prevalent in relationships in which women are past the child-bearing age and in relationships in which adult children can support themselves. Older people might also experience less intense romantic rivalry than college students due to decreases in sexual desire associated with aging. Decreased sexual desire should decrease the effort that romantic rivals expend on courting romantic partners. Older people are also more likely to be involved in committed romantic relationships than college students, who often flit from relationship to relationship. If at least some proportion of all people in committed relationships are satisfied in their relationship and not pursuing other partners, the number of potential romantic rivals should be lower among populations with a greater proportion of committed or married couples.

Regardless of overarching theoretical perspective, sexuality theorists have studied gender differences extensively. We speculate that gender differences in sexuality may be smaller in college students than in other populations. In the university system in the United States, the enrollment of women now exceeds that of men. Social exchange theorists predict that when men are in the minority, the sexuality of women will align more with the sexuality of men. Gender differences among college students may also be low because male and female college students likely share similar goals. The college years are often viewed as a time of sexual exploration, and many younger college students, both male and female, are not yet actively looking for long-term, committed relationships.

It is difficult to predict how sexual theorizing could be different if sexuality researchers were consistently able to obtain diverse samples. One method typically employed in sexuality research asks participants to write narratives that recall and reflect on their past sexual experiences. Younger college students do not (presumably) have as many experiences to draw on compared to older adults, so it is theoretically plausible that data collected from older adults more closely approximate that truth. In our view, the availability and willingness of college students to participate in sexuality research compensates for any shortcomings. Data collected from college students have allowed the refinement and expansion of theories of sexuality that otherwise would have been impossible.

CONCLUSION

A comprehensive summary of sexuality theory would be difficult to provide in a single volume and is not possible in a single chapter. The purpose of this chapter was to highlight the overarching theoretical perspectives and to detail several specific midlevel theories of sexuality. The expansion of the university system and the availability of college-age research participants give sexuality researchers unprecedented opportunity to collect the data needed to test new theories, but progress in the field of sexology will ultimately depend on the abilities of sexuality researchers to refine their theorizing.

The advances in sexual theorizing in the past half century have been slowed by the academic and political warfare waged by proponents of the two major theoretical perspectives. Social constructionist and evolutionary approaches to sexuality are indispensable, but the field of sexuality must also look beyond these perspectives in order to make room for midlevel theories. Sexuality researchers must strive to set an agenda of developing and testing new midlevel theories. The ideas that prove meritorious will have the potential to revolutionize the way scientists understand specific sexual phenomena and to redefine problem areas within each of the major theoretical perspectives.

Chapter Four

THE DEVELOPMENTAL CONTEXT OF EMERGING ADULTS' SEXUALITY AND INTIMATE RELATIONSHIPS: A CRITICAL PERSPECTIVE

Mason G. Haber and Charles A. Burgess

The concept of emerging adulthood was introduced in a seminal article by Jeffrey Arnett approximately 10 years ago (Arnett, 2000a). According to Arnett, this period, stretching from the age of majority to the middle 20s, during which most youth are engaged in postsecondary education, is "a time of unparalleled possibilities," during which young adults engage in explorations of worldviews, types of work, intimate relationships, and sexuality, experiences that are thought to provide the foundation for adult identity (Arnett, 2000a, 2004). Since its introduction, behavioral scientists as well as the general public have seized upon emerging adulthood as a clear and intuitively appealing framework for organizing thinking about this period of the life span, resulting in publication of books and edited works (e.g., Arnett, 2004; Arnett & Tanner, 2006), and prominent references in the popular press (e.g., Grossman, 2005; Henig, 2010). Works focusing specifically on emerging adults' sex and intimate-relationship experiences have also been released (Crouter & Booth, 2006; Fincham & Cui, 2011). In prior scholarship, the years of emerging adulthood tended not to be considered discretely, but rather, were thought of as a part of adolescence (e.g., Hall, 1904; Erikson, 1968) or the beginning of adulthood (e.g., Levinson, 1978). In contrast, emerging adulthood has been viewed as potentially constituting its own *life stage*—a distinct, normative period, associated with characteristic and unique developmental tasks, identifiable across a variety of social and cultural contexts (Reifman, 2011).

Emerging adulthood provides an important foundation for understanding sexuality and intimate relationships of college students, by specifying the developmental context in which students' sexuality and love relationships occur. Prior research on college students' sexuality has been criticized as decontextualizing sexuality, by viewing it as a type of "problem behavior" (e.g., Jessor, Donovan, & Costa, 1991). While this perspective may assist in development of preventative interventions (e.g., by identifying factors associated with sexual risk taking), it fails to encompass normative sexuality and intimacy (Lefkowitz, Gillen, & Vasilenko, 2011). Because Arnett's framework seeks to describe normal, healthy behavior during emerging adulthood, it provides a potential means for understanding characteristic qualities of normative sexuality and love experiences among emerging adults. In this view, for example, patterns of more frequent, unstable, and varied sexual activities and intimate relationships among emerging adults may serve a healthy developmental function, by facilitating the discovery of preferred sexual and intimate-relationship choices, thereby furthering the development of identity in this domain of functioning.

Despite the appeal of the concept of emerging adulthood as a means of describing the developmental context of college-age youth, critics have raised issues concerning the both the concept itself and its application to understanding sexuality and intimacy during the period (Amato, 2011; Collins & Van Dulmen, 2006; Côté, 2000, 2006). These criticisms largely center on the use of the framework as a life stage, including questions regarding its *distinctiveness* from other developmental periods, its *universality* across social and cultural contexts, and, correspondingly, the distinctiveness and universality of qualities ascribed to emerging adults' sexual behavior and intimate relationships. Further, questions have been raised concerning whether emerging adulthood is as rosy a phenomenon as Arnett and his proponents would seem to suggest. In an alternative view of the period, advanced by James Côté (2000, 2006), rather than a time of lesser constraint and greater opportunity, emerging adulthood is viewed as an overly prolonged version of Erikson's (1968) "institutionalized moratorium"—a socially structured, sanctioned deferment of developmental tasks—that constrains as often as it provides life choices, and may interfere with the development of mature adult identity. In this view, the distinctiveness of emerging adults' sexual and romantic relationships stems from fewer rather than increased choices, and represents exclusion from rather than exploration of adult sexual and intimate-relationship roles.

In this chapter, we aim to provide a foundation for understanding the developmental context of sexual and intimacy issues discussed in the remainder of the book, through a dialectical consideration of the merits of emerging adulthood as a framework for understanding sexuality and intimacy among college-age youth. A basic description of Arnett's views regarding the period will first be presented, and ways in which this perspective can be used to examine sexuality and intimacy among college-age youth will be described. Following this, a critique will be provided of emerging adulthood as a developmental framework for understanding sexual and intimate-relationship experiences of youth, including a description of weaknesses in the conceptualization of emerging adulthood as a life stage, involving distinctive and widely shared patterns of sexual and intimate-relationship behavior. Côté's views concerning ways in which defining characteristics of emerging adulthood may defer rather than further development will then be presented. The chapter will conclude by describing implications of a dialectical perspective incorporating both the emerging-adult framework and criticisms of it, including specific recommendations for how this dialectical perspective could be used to inform intervention and promotion to improve emerging adults' sexual and relationship health.

A NOTE ON TERMINOLOGY

Regardless of the possible weaknesses of emerging adulthood as a theoretical framework for understanding development in the late teens and early 20s, the term provides a convenient way of referring to college-age youth, differentiating the group developmentally from adolescents and adults. Arnett (2000a, 2004) makes persuasive arguments regarding problems with other terms sometimes used to refer to the period (e.g., "youth," "late adolescence," "young adulthood"). Alternatively, although the term "college age" could be used, it is our position that the increasing complexity of postsecondary educational experiences makes the use of the college environment as a means of distinction more confusing and less meaningful. For example, in recent years, while the modal age of college attendance continues to fall within emerging adulthood, college students have been increasingly likely to be older, to have already made commitments to family, and to be working part- or full-time (Schuetze & Slowey, 2002). Similarly, while most emerging adult youth participate in postsecondary educational settings at some point, only a minority are enrolled at any given time (Amato, 2011; Manning, Giordano, Longmore, & Hocevar, 2011); thus conflation of college and emerging-adult experiences may perpetuate stereotypes that describe both college students and emerging adults poorly. Therefore use of the term "emerging adult" in this chapter should not be understood as an endorsement of the various ways in which Arnett and others have described emerging adults; rather, it simply provides a convenient way refer to individuals in the age group for which the term is used.

DEFINING EMERGING ADULTHOOD

Emerging Adulthood: Defining Features

Arnett has identified five defining features of emerging adulthood based on demographic data describing the objective life experiences of emerging adults (Arnett, 1998; Bumpass & Liu, 2000; Goldscheider & Goldscheider, 1999), and qualitative and structured survey research examining emerging adults' self-reported experiences (Arnett, 1997, 2001, 2004; Larson, 1990; Schulenberg, O'Malley, Bachman, & Johnston, 2005). Examination of the factorial validity of a scale designed to assess experiences of emerging adulthood has provided support for Arnett's five dimensions (Reifman, Arnett, & Colwell, 2006). They have also been examined across diverse groups of emerging adults in the United States (Arnett, 2000b, 2003; Gore, Aseltine, Colton, & Lin, 1997) as well as cross-nationally (Arias & Hernandez, 2007; Facio & Miccoci, 2003; Mayseless & Scharf, 2003). The five characteristics are:

1. *Identity exploration*—exploration of life possibilities in areas of worldviews (e.g., on politics and religious matters), work roles, and love relationships
2. *Instability*—frequent changes in life circumstances, corresponding to residential changes motivated by desire for educational or work opportunities or to live with love and marital partners
3. *Self-focus*—relative freedom from social role commitments (e.g., to a stable job or family) and associated obligations, leading to increased autonomy and focus on one's own needs
4. *Ambiguity and "in between" feelings*—descriptions of self as not completely a child but also not completely an adult, associated with the incremental attainment of psychological markers of adulthood such as accepting responsibility for oneself, making independent decisions, and becoming financially independent
5. A sense of *possibilities*—optimism and high hopes for the future, associated with unique opportunities of the developmental period to improve long-term health and well-being, severing of connections to problematic earlier environments (e.g., a dysfunctional family environment,) and commitments to new social roles and environments, including stable, rewarding love and work relationship roles

Overall, the five defining features of emerging adulthood suggest that certain qualities of sexuality and intimacy among emerging adults need to be explored. First, due to their defining tendencies for identity exploration, emerging adults may be motivated to explore their sexual and relationship identities by pursuing varied sexual and relationship experiences. Second, due to this drive to explore or perhaps other factors (e.g., other types of instability in circumstances) relationships will be more varied and unstable, as reflected by more frequent relationship partners or sexual behavior outside of the context of committed relationships. Third, relationships of emerging adults will be characterized by a focus on self and relative lack of commitment to partners in comparison with other periods. Fourth, emerging adults will experience their own sexual intimate-relationship identities as "in between" (e.g., will see themselves as more capable of commitment than adolescents, but not fully "adult" in their capacities to commit to relationships). Fifth, emerging adults will evidence high levels of optimism regarding future achievement of sexual and relationship goals.

In addition to the five defining features, descriptions of emerging adulthood by Arnett and others (e.g., Tanner, 2006; Côté, 2006) also emphasize its heterogeneity, including heterogeneity in the experiences of each individual (i.e., over the course of emerging adulthood), and of experiences across individuals at a point in time or over time (i.e., levels or patterns across time of relevant experiences). Indeed, longitudinal data show that emerging adults' patterns of attainment of increased independence from parents and commitment to new adult social roles vary strikingly in these ways (P. Cohen, Kasen, Chen, Hartmark, & Gordon, 2003; Côté, 2006). Although describing emerging adulthood as heterogeneous may seem to conflict with attempts to generalize "defining features" emerging adults, Arnett reconciles this apparent contradiction by observing that the shared features of the period promote heterogeneity on other dimensions (Arnett, 2004). In particular, emerging adults' drives to explore and the instability in their living circumstances are seen as contributing to their diverse pathways in establishing their identities and making commitments to adult roles.

Emerging Adulthood: Developmental Tasks

Arnett's conceptualization of emerging adulthood is grounded in part in Erikson's theory of life cycle stages and, more specifically, his ideas regarding the stages of adolescence and young adulthood. According to Erikson, each stage of the life cycle involves a set of developmental tasks, and success in the tasks of each phase provides necessary grounding for tasks in the following phases (Erikson, 1968). Erikson describes the developmental tasks of the adolescent period as contributing to identity development (i.e., "identity vs. confusion") in three domains: love, work, and worldview. In optimal development during the adolescent stage, identity is formed and refined through a process of exploration in each of these areas, resulting in "narrowing selections of personal, occupational, sexual, and ideological commitments" (Erikson, 1968, p. 245). In the following, "young adult" phase, these commitments become the basis for healthy, complementary affiliations with others in the love, work, and worldview domains. By contrast, in cases in which identity is not adequately consolidated, Erikson held that in these affiliative efforts, "which call for significant sacrifices and compromises" (Erikson, 1982, p. 70), youth would be less successful, and could even compromise the as yet incomplete gains in the development identity. Thus he believed that in order to establish productive relationships with others, one must first develop a strong sense of self.

Although Erikson asserted that identity development tasks occurred during adolescence, he did not see the adolescent stage (or any of his other stages) as necessarily corresponding to a particular age range. In addition, he observed that in industrialized societies, adolescence could be prolonged considerably into "young adult" years through a "psychosocial moratorium"—i.e., a deferment of tasks of the following developmental stage (Erikson, 1968, p. 156). However, he believed that regardless of their particular timing, the *order* of stages should be relatively universal. Thus Erikson's view was that developmental tasks of the next period (young adulthood), which he characterized as centering around the challenge of "intimacy versus isolation" (i.e., affiliation with others), would be emphasized in the period following adolescence, whether this occurred in the teens, early 20s, or later. Erikson's belief that formation of the self developmentally precedes formation of mature affiliations with others has been extremely influential, perhaps in part due to its consonance with the relatively individualistic value system of the developed Western context in which his theory was proposed (Gilligan, 1979). However, this ordering of developmental tasks is somewhat controversial, and may in fact vary across individuals, or be more characteristic of women than men (Orlofsky, 1993). An interesting counterpoint to Erikson's view is provided by the views of Sullivan on the development and self and intimacy, formulated at approximately the same time (H. S. Sullivan, 1953). Sullivan also believed that late adolescence and young adulthood were primarily concerned with identity development; however, in direct contrast to Eriksonian theory, Sullivan's approach supposed that identity development primarily followed rather than preceded the emergence of mature patterns of affiliation.

Arnett organizes his own discussion of identity development into the love, work, and worldview categories proposed by Erikson (although he stresses that explorations can occur in other areas as well), placing the greatest degree of emphasis on the domains of love and work. Building on Erikson's recognition that adolescence could be prolonged, Arnett asserts that technological developments in postindustrial societies and increased possibilities for deferment of childbearing have resulted in a pronounced shift in the timing of Erikson's identity-versus-confusion stage, such that identity development tasks now occur primarily *after* the adolescent period, i.e., during the emerging-adult years (Arnett, 2000a, 2004). In accordance with the Eriksonian view that identity development provides the foundation for mature relatedness, Arnett regards the additional opportunities for individual identity exploration provided by the emerging-adult years as providing a more secure foundation for subsequent affiliative commitments, adhering to Erikson's rather than Sullivan's model. By contrast, critics such as Côté (2000, 2006) have adhered more closely to the Sullivan view that affiliation precedes identity development.

EMERGING ADULTHOOD AS AN EXPLANATORY FRAMEWORK: EVIDENCE FOR AND AGAINST

Relatively few studies have attempted to apply Arnett's general ideas regarding emerging adulthood to understanding the patterns sexual behavior and intimate-relationship patterns of emerging adults. Evidence provided by these studies often fails to support the patterns that would be expected based on Arnett's framework. Relevant findings and interpretations are presented below.

Emerging-Adult Relationship Distinctiveness (the "Distinctiveness Hypothesis")

Much of the discussion of the distinctiveness of emerging-adult intimacy and sexuality, or "distinctiveness hypothesis" (Collins & van Dulmen, 2006) focuses on how the primary developmental task ascribed to the period—the development of adult identity through exploration—might impact observed patterns of intimacy and sexuality, as well as the views of sexuality and intimacy among emerging adults. Researchers have also considered whether benefits to health and well-being result from patterns thought to be associated with greater exploration. Others have considered whether other defining characteristics of emerging adulthood, including the self-focus, optimism, and ambiguity described of the period, might be manifested in emerging adults' intimate relationships and sexual experiences, and differentiate these from these experiences in other developmental periods. These issues—whether emerging adults show distinctive patterns in intimate relationships and sexual activities reflecting exploration, whether they see these activities as serving the purpose of identity exploration, and the extent to which they may be distinctively self-focused, optimistic, and ambiguous among emerging adults—are explored in turn.

Distinctiveness of Emerging Adults' Intimate Relationships

In a recent chapter, Collins and Van Dulmen (2006) summarized evidence for and against the distinctiveness hypothesis. Citing multiple reviews (Collins, 2003; Hartrup & Stevens, 1999; Surra, 1990), they asserted that although important shifts in dating behavior appeared to occur just *prior to* the emerging adult years, in late adolescence (i.e., ages 15–17), few features of intimate-relationship expectancies or behaviors differentiate late adolescents and emerging adults. Differences that have been found, they suggested, indicate continuous refinement of relationship functioning from late adolescence through emerging adulthood rather than any disjunction or qualitative change. For example, in a qualitative longitudinal study, narratives regarding close relationships showed increasing structure and complexity at age 25 relative to ages 14 to 17, but focused on similar themes (Waldinger et al., 2002).

Using data from a multiwave longitudinal study following youth from childhood through emerging adulthood (i.e., the Minnesota Longitudinal Study of Parents and Children; Sroufe, Egeland, Carlson, & Collins, 2005), Collins and Van Dulmen (2006) also specifically considered two of Arnett's defining features—identity exploration and instability—and whether these seemed to be evident in the relationship patterns of emerging adults. Greater identity exploration and instability in intimate relationships, they reasoned, would be reflected by a greater number of sexual and relationship partners reported by youth during emerging adulthood than during adolescence. To examine this prediction, they compared the number of dating partners reported in the last two years by youth questioned at ages 19 and 23, and sexual partners reported in the last two years by youth at ages 16, 19, and 23. No differences were shown in number of dating partners reported at age 19 versus age 23. By contrast, increases in sexual partners were reported from age 16 to age 19 and from age 19 to age 23, converging with findings regarding increases in number of sexual partners during this period from other studies (Michael, Gagnon, Laumann, & Kolata, 1994). As Collins and Van Dulmen point out, however, if the explanation for increases in sexual partners was desire for identity exploration (rather than, for example, greater social acceptance of sexual behavior with increasing age), an increase in dating relationships from age 19 to age 23 would also be expected.

Data from other sources also call into question whether emerging adults' relationship patterns show relatively high levels of instability. For example, many emerging adults—particularly those outside of traditional postsecondary settings—marry during the emerging adult years (Uecker & Stokes, 2008). Even college students, although less likely to marry, are most typically in a committed exclusive romantic relationship, usually of some duration. For example, Fincham, Stanley, and Rhoades (2011) found that 57 percent of students in their college sample reported being in a committed relationship, and that these relationships tended be relatively lengthy, with a median duration of over a year.

Collins and Van Dulmen (2006) acknowledge some research that could be seen as supportive of a distinct emerging-adult period. For example, studies have shown changes in everyday social interaction patterns and behaviors over the course of emerging adulthood, including increased opposite sex and decreased same-sex, mixed-sex, and group interactions and greater intimacy in interactions (Reis, Lin, Bennet, & Nezlak, 1993), and decreased conflict (Reis, Collins, & Berscheid, 2000). However, these studies do not pertain to the distinctiveness hypothesis per se, and are in fact consistent with the counterhypothesis that relationship processes (including maturation-related change) during this period are continuous with rather than qualitatively different from those during adolescence.

Distinctiveness of Emerging Adults' Sexual Exploration

Existing evidence suggests that although emerging adults' committed relationships show similarities to those of adolescents, sexual activity patterns differ. First, as indicated above, data from Collins and Van Dulmen's studies as well as other sources suggest that although emerging adults do not have greater numbers of dating relationships than individuals in other periods, they nevertheless have relatively higher numbers of sexual partners. These more frequent or varied sexual partnerships do not seem to contribute to adult identity development, however. Kimmel (2008) provided a vivid critique of the notion that emerging-adult sexual relationships represent a conscious exploration of identity in his work *Guyland*, which focuses on the conspicuous lack of interest shown by many emerging-adult men in the meaningfulness of sex as a way of furthering one's own identity ("it's hard to square such serious self-reflection with the bacchanalian atmosphere of a college weekend"; Kimmel, 2008, p. 39). Others have noted the increasing popularity of labels in the emerging-adult world for sexual activities that are entirely decontextualized from intimacy and seem to stress the inconsequentiality of sex, such as "hooking up"—sexual activities outside the confines of a relationship—or "friends with benefits" (friendships that include sexual involvement without implication of associated emotional intimacy; Desiderato & Crawford, 1995; Puentes, Knox, & Zusman, 2008).

Emerging Adults' Subjective Experience

Arnett's foundational work provides the primary evidence regarding emerging adults' own perceptions of sex and love relationships. He suggests that although emerging adults are interested in committed relationships—and the vast majority, marriage (Arnett, 2004)—many prefer to defer marriage for some time in order to explore a variety of potential partners. Carroll et al. (2007) found that emerging adults tended to define their own subjective ideal age for marriage as 25, regardless of their specific age cohort, suggesting that the subjective time horizon to marriage decreases over the course of the emerging-adult period. In contrast with Arnett's view, which emphasizes exploration, they suggested that the shortening horizon, combined with (or reflecting) a social context of peers' marriages, creates a "culture of marriage" among emerging adults that strengthens as the emerging-adult period proceeds. Supporting this position, research examining motives for sex among emerging adults has found that "intimacy motives" designed to deepen a relationship (e.g., "feeling closer to one's partner") are among the most important motives for this age group, particularly among individuals in exclusive relationships (M. L. Cooper, Shapiro, & Powers, 1998).

An informative case in point illustrating the influence of exploration motives is provided by the common emerging-adult practice of nonmartial cohabitation. If, as Arnett asserts, relationships during emerging adulthood help emerging adults ascertain who to spend their life with, it would appear that moving in with a partner to "test" the relationship would be a typical and particularly useful choice for emerging adults, and in fact, many emerging adults endorse this idea (Thornton & Young-DeMarco, 2001). However, in their research review, Fincham et al. (2011) concluded that emerging adults typically do *not* initiate cohabitation for purposes of testing their relationships. Rather, most emerging adults move in together simply to spend more time with one another or for convenience, and without much deliberation. Fincham et al. (2011) refer to this pattern as "sliding rather than deciding." The motive of testing was cited relatively infrequently in their national study, and was associated with level of relationship dysfunction rather than positive outcomes (e.g., poorer communication, relationship violence, lack of commitment, and lower satisfaction). Conversely, in cases in which cohabitation occurred in the context of a committed relationship—specifically, following engagement—emerging-adult couples were far less likely to show these problems.

Health Benefits of Exploration

Although, generally speaking, romantic relationship involvement in emerging adulthood is associated with at least some improved outcomes (primarily, fewer externalizing problems; Farrington, 1995; Farrington & West, 1995; Van Dulmen, Goncy, Haydon, & Collins, 2008), these benefits appear to result from being in certain types of relationships, including relationships that are committed and secure (Braithwaite, Delevi, & Fincham, 2010; Van Dulmen et al., 2008) of high quality (e.g., equal, supportive, not stressful; Daley & Hammen, 2002; Galliher, Rostosky, Welsh, & Kawaguchi, 1999; LaGreca & Harrison, 2005; Roisman, Aguilar, & Egeland, 2004), and in which relationship partners are supportive of one another's work and education goals (Manning et al., 2011). When frequency of dating relationships or sexual partners—which would seem to better represent a process of exploration than committed involvement—has been examined as a predictor, either no relationship or a detrimental relationship with outcomes has been found (Sroufe et al., 2005). Finally, sexual exploration outside of intimate relationships such as "hookups" has generally been shown to be associated with mental and physical health risks (e.g., Grello et al., 2006).

Self-Focus

M. S. Clark and Beck (2011) recently argued that in the context of intimate relationships, the "self-focus" Arnett ascribed as reflecting identity exploration may actually result from the effortfulness of self-presentation and self-protection tasks at the outset of intimate relationships. Evaluation of a partner and their "fit," by contrast, is often subordinated in self-presentation and self-protection aspects of the relationship initiation process, particularly for individuals who are generally anxious, rejection sensitive, or insecurely attached (Bartz & Lydon, 2006; Beck & Clark, 2009). Thus, although emerging adults may appear to be, and perhaps perceive themselves as being self-focused in an exploratory sense, their self-focus may be due to self-presentation and self-protection concerns.

Optimism of Emerging Adults' Relationships

Arnett describes emerging adulthood as an optimistic time, during which levels of well-being with current circumstances are comparatively high, and emerging adults perceive opportunities to pursue and reach goals to a greater extent than at other phases of the life cycle. To a point, data would appear to support the proposition that emerging adults are similarly rosy in their perceptions of their current and future intimate relationships. High levels of satisfaction with intimate relationships have been reported (Auslander et al., 2007). Further, large majorities of emerging adults indicating a high level of confidence about achieving their future goals (Hornblower, 1997), including a finding a "soul mate" for a stable, happy marriage (Popenoe & Whitehead, 2001). This optimism appears to be brittle, however, and the extent to which it is in evidence may depend on the manner in which questions about the future are framed. For example, contradicting the findings of Popenoe and Whitehead (2001), A. Levine and Cureton (1998) found in a sample of college students that respondents were often unsure of their abilities to establish happy marriage.

Ambiguity

Emerging adulthood has been referred to by Arnett and other commentators as an "age of ambiguity." In Arnett's formulation, this ambiguity provides fertile ground for testing propositions about the self. Critics such as Côté (2000, 2006) have suggested, however, that this ambiguity stems from an active avoidance or deferment of commitment, not in the service of exploring identity but rather to avoid the real-world limitations to identity that a genuine process of exploration—involving meaningful commitment—would provide. Fincham et al. (2011) discuss the lack of commitment and ambiguity in emerging adults' sexual and romantic relationships as a function of social trends that have made the development of relationships both less structured and less secure. These include the disappearance of social customs marking relationship and level of commitment (e.g., "going steady," sharing of class rings), higher divorce rates in recent age cohorts, and the growing number of youth in the United States who experience not one but multiple relationship dissolutions involving one or both parents. Thus, as they begin to contemplate possibilities for their own committed relationships, they argue, emerging adults lack guidance for how to time and express commitment, and have been presented in some cases with many examples of possible harms commitment can bring. The result, they suggest, may be insecure adult attachment patterns, which motivate ambiguity for self-protective rather than self-enhancing purposes.

Implications of Evidence on the Distinctiveness Hypothesis

Even critics of the distinctiveness hypothesis assume that considerable exploration of identity in sex and love relationships occurs during emerging adulthood and that this exploration is beneficial (e.g., Collins & Van Dulmen, 2006; Fincham et al., 2011). The exploration that occurs, however, appears to be qualitatively similar to exploration in adolescence. Perhaps due to fewer constraints on their behavior, the frequency of emerging adults' sexual activity increases, but length and commitment of relationships are similar to those in adolescence, at least up until the point of engagement or marriage. Further, there appears to be little or no evidence that explorations of sexual and relationship behavior are more conscious or influence identity more greatly in emerging adulthood than in adolescence. In fact, where relationships between patterns thought to represent exploration and outcomes have been established, these have tended to show that exploration is detrimental to health. Other emerging-adult defining characteristics, including the optimism, self-focus, and ambiguity, may poorly apply or have more complex meaning when applied to understanding their sexuality and intimate relationships.

Universality of Relationship and Sexual Behavior Patterns of Emerging Adults

Arnett holds that emerging adulthood is a time of "unparalleled opportunity" during which a relative freedom from social constraints allows for wide explorations of worldview, love, and work. However, as summarized below, emerging adults lacking adequate facilitative resources, including economic, social, human, and "identity" capital (Côté, 1997), may not be able to engage in these activities to the same extent or as meaningfully, or may even be harmed by the relative lack of normative structure.

The "Forgotten Half" and the "Traditional" College Student

As reviewed to this point, increasing needs for postsecondary education in postindustrial economies are seen as shaping experiences of emerging adults. In order to complete their educations, many emerging adults defer assumption of adult roles, including demanding full-time work or committed intimate relationships. By doing so, they are thought to be able to focus their resources on the development of their own identities, through exploration of various career and relationship possibilities, protected by the "psychosocial moratorium" that college context represents. This experience is typified by the full-time college student seeking an undergraduate university degree, which requires a relatively lengthy period of education covering much of the emerging adult period (four years but often longer), a type of student that is the focus of much of the research discussed in this book. Further (and increasingly), some emerging adults will extend education even further, making commitments to graduate education, and in some cases, continuing to defer commitments to family and full-time work.

As Arnett himself points out, however (e.g., Arnett, 2000a), experiences of four-year college students do not easily generalize to emerging adults, which, in a classic white paper, were referred to as the "forgotten half"—those who fail to enter postsecondary education and move immediately into the world of work, or in some cases, become disengaged from productive activities or ensnared in the criminal justice system (William T. Grant Foundation Commission on Work, Family, and Citizenship, 1988). Even among students in postsecondary settings, the "typical" experience of full-time, continuous education and deferred adult commitments has become far less so. Arnett warns that lacking exposure to the psychosocial moratorium provided by postsecondary education on a college campus, emerging adults are vulnerable to "identity foreclosure"—i.e., commitment in the absence of exploration—which in the identity development literature is seen as a less optimal identity status for emerging adults than identity exploration, leading to poorer actualization of the self (e.g., Marcia, 1994). However, if a continuous, four-year educational experience is currently accessible to only a minority of youth, it may be that less focus should be placed on facilitating access to this setting and more on promoting other avenues for identity development.

Recent data show that despite increases in the rate of college matriculation since the original publication of the "Forgotten Half" white paper—current data suggest that approximately two-thirds of emerging adults will receive at least some exposure to postsecondary education—the traditional pattern of postsecondary education at a four-year institution may indeed characterize only a minority of emerging adults as a group. For example, census data suggest that among high school graduates through the age of 24, only a third are enrolled in a four-year institution at any given time, reflecting common patterns of discontinuing education or withdrawing for periods of time among matriculated students (Davis & Bauman, 2008; U.S. Census, 2006, cited in Manning et al., 2011). Similarly, analyses of data on emerging-adult women enrolled in the National Longitudinal Study of Adolescent Health ("Add Health") indicated that only 29 percent conformed to a pattern of continuous postsecondary education and deferred family formation (Amato et al., 2008). Thus overall it appears that only about a third of youth fit the profile typically associated with emerging-adult experience of deferring adult role commitments in love and work to pursue education completion.

Among groups with fewer resources, even smaller percentages of emerging adults consistently attending college during the period would be expected. For example, non-Latino Caucasians are substantially overrepresented and African Americans and Latinos underrepresented in four-year college settings (Hudson, Aqillino, & Kienzi, 2005). In an extension of analyses of the Add Health data cited above, Amato et al. (2008) examined a wide range of predictors of membership in the category of women conforming to the continuous postsecondary education and deferred family formation pattern. Analyses of a wide range of predictors of health and positive development in emerging adulthood from developmental and sociological literatures, Amato first reduced these influences to three factors: (1) noneconomic social and psychological resources, including many identified from the life span development literature; (2) family socioeconomic status and youth academic achievement; and (3) conventional values and behavior. These factors (particularly the first two) sharply differentiated privileged (i.e., continuous college attendees) from other groups.

Impact of Exclusion on Emerging Adults

Whether their exclusion influences outcomes economically or through impact on identity development, it is clear that some youth have poorer access to the sorts of opportunities Arnett posits are important for well-being in emerging adulthood. Considering data summarized above, a picture begins to emerge of a society in which emerging adults are sharply bifurcated by intertwined factors of social class and social and psychological resources. Privileged emerging adults are provided with far greater resources and opportunities to pursue identity development. In turn, those excluded from these opportunities are more likely to experience poor developmental, social, and health outcomes. The specific mechanisms through which social disadvantage impacts circumstances and experiences of emerging adults, including those identified by Arnett, deserve far more attention than they have received to the present. In some cases, these outwardly conform to emerging-adult patterns described by Arnett, but can have very different significance. For example, "instability" in living circumstances, driven by changes in cohabitation, is understood by Arnett to reflect a healthy process of exploration. We have already discussed weaknesses in this understanding of instability for *any* emerging adult; however, the significance of instability for poorer emerging adults appears to be more overtly negative. For example, Meier and Allen (2008) have reviewed data on how residential instability may have differing significance for emerging adults based on social class, finding that among poorer emerging adults, instability is far more likely to stem from negative circumstances such as unemployment or incarceration, or events that can adversely impact developmental trajectories such as unplanned childbirth.

EMERGING ADULTHOOD AS INSTITUTIONALIZED MORATORIUM: THE SOCIAL CRITICISM OF CÔTÉ

The previous section examined the capacity of the framework of emerging adulthood to predict and explicate patterns of sexuality and intimacy among emerging adults. Problems in applying this framework to understanding emerging-adult sexuality and intimate relationships were noted. Emerging adults' sexual behavior and intimate-relationship patterns do not seem to reflect defining characteristics of the period in some ways, and even where patterns unfold as predicted, they do not seem to have the desirable effects anticipated. Specifically, the more that emerging adults' intimacy and sexuality appear to reflect motives of exploration, particularly when at the expense of commitment, the less these seem to actually contribute toward maturation or health. Moreover, to the extent these patterns may exist for their ascribed purpose, psychologically or socially disadvantaged emerging adults (or alternatively, those lacking exceptional advantages) do not seem equally capable of benefiting from them.

Côté (2000, 2006), in his critique of the concept of emerging adulthood, addresses this apparent paradox, by suggesting that what currently passes for active exploration of identity, or *developmental individualization* among emerging adults, is actually a deferment of identity development, which in some cases represents an alternative to genuine identity development or *default individualization*. He also argues that the resources required to pursue the more difficult developmental individualization path are both increasingly demanded by and increasingly inaccessible to emerging adults. This situation is attributed to several forces operating in postindustrial societies, including social myths that obscure the identity-related difficulties experienced by emerging adults.

Emerging Adulthood as Deferment

Reviewing the existing literature on identity development during the period, Côte (2006) shows that identity development during adolescence and emerging adulthood typically does not resemble the exploratory process envisioned by Erikson (1968), Arnett (2000a, 2004), and others. First, he observes that there is little evidence for an impact of the college experience on identity development, despite its apparent influence on other variables such as indices of overall psychological well-being (e.g., Pascarella & Terenzini, 1991, cited in Côté, 2006). In addition, summarizing across multiple reviews of the identity development literature (e.g., Van Hoof, 1999; Meeus, Iedema, Helson, & Vollebergh, 1999, cited in Côté, 2006), he argues that exploration-based identity development is relatively uncommon among emerging adults, and is not consistent across time or across different domains of identity (e.g., work, relationships). Rather, identity exploration, where it occurs, tends to happen sporadically, involve patterns of regression as well as progression, and be domain-specific.

Côté also shows that emerging adulthood appears to be a relatively unproductive period for identity development when the outcomes of this process are examined across age groups. To assess identity development outcomes, Côté developed the Identity Stage Resolution Index Scale (ISRI; Côté, 1997), measuring two outcomes of identity development among emerging adults, based on Eriksonian theory, including: (1) *adult identity resolution*—the sense of being a self-sufficient, independent adult in one's own and others' eyes; and (2) *social identity resolution*—finding a social niche, including lifestyle, roles, and identification with a community. Côté (2006) assessed adult and social identity resolution in a sample of college enrolled youth at the outset of, toward the end of, and following emerging adulthood (i.e., in their late teens, early 20s, and late 20s). Analyses showed that although some change in the level of identity development over the course of the first, emerging adulthood period, the incremental increase was much greater during the second time period, from the end of emerging adult to the following, young-adult period. Furthermore, change in the initial, emerging-adult time frame was almost entirely limited to the adult identity subscale, with social identity resolution not showing change until the final point of the study. Even more important to Côté's argument was *who* changed on these indices in his sample. At the final time point, emerging adults enrolled full-time in school showed markedly lower scores on the ISRI; conversely, those working full-time had higher scores. Thus providing a context that would seem to facilitate exploration of possibilities for work and career seemed to result in *less* progress in the outcome identity development, than actually committing to a full-time job. Similarly, comparing single and married youth at T3, Côté found that those in married relationships showed higher scores on the ISRI, whereas single individuals had lower scores.

Although work is needed to further elucidate Côté's findings, they appear to converge with data reviewed earlier regarding commitment in sex and love relationships and its associations with emerging adult health and well-being—namely, greater commitment to adult roles correlates with better outcomes among emerging adults. Côté argues that commitment is more productive for development of identity because it leads to "reality based" resolutions of identity—discovering oneself through adult social role experiences (which involve commitment), rather than simply imagining what one might be through activities that, although ostensibly furthering explorations in love and work, bear little resemblance to those constituting meaningful adult roles (e.g., "hookups").

Identity Confusion and Default Individualization

Côté accepts that there are individuals who do choose to engage in identity explorations during the psychosocial moratorium and show benefits (i.e., developmental individualization); however, as reviewed above, most seem to defer identity exploration. Côté argues that this deferment of identity resolution can be aversive, particularly for the most vulnerable youth. Borrowing from Erikson, Côté refers to this aversive state as *identity confusion*. To reduce identity confusion, Côté asserts that some individuals opt for a sort of pantomiming of identity development through mimicking of popular trends, which he refers to as *default individualization* (Côté, 2006; Côté & Levine, 2002).

Identity Confusion

Data from Côté's survey research (2006) indicate that certain individuals are less likely to make progress in identity resolution, and that early weaknesses in this area are likely to persist over time. In the aforementioned sample of college students at the beginning, end of, and following emerging adulthood, Côté found that lower identity resolution scores tended to persist across time points. Côté also examined the prevalence of high scores on a measure of "identity confusion" (M. Steinberg & Schnall, 2000) designed to assess poor outcomes of the adolescent identity crisis as described by Erikson (1968), corresponding with an aversive psychological state (e.g., agreement with the statement "I feel confused about who I really am"). In Côté's college sample, the prevalence of elevated scores at the third, post–emerging adulthood time point was 38.5 percent, with approximately half of these individuals scoring at a level thought to correlate with significant psychopathology (Côté, 2006). Individuals with these highly elevated scores also tended to score lower than other respondents on the ISRI concurrently and at the prior two time points. Côté interpreted this as signifying that approximately a fifth of his college student sample suffered from identity confusion at the outset of emerging adulthood that persisted throughout the phase. Côté also noted that this prevalence of aversive identity statuses was found despite the fact that sample was composed entirely of college-enrolled students, and therefore would be expected to have relatively greater advantages for pursuing identity exploration than would be found in a more diverse group of emerging-adult youth.

Default Individualization

Because it is highly effortful, involving sacrifice and assumption of social obligations, few individuals will pursue developmental individualization as a strategy for negotiating the Eriksonian identity crisis. Many youth, Côté argues, will opt instead for ways of seeming to establish identity that do not involve effort and sacrifice, or default individualization. These "paths of least resistance and effort" are focused on self-presentation (Côté, 2000, p. 34), and involve mimicking of popular culture such as trends in fashion and music, require little thought or commitment, and thus demand little from youth with limited resources for identity development (Côté, 2006, p. 92). Youth are encouraged to choose this path by cultural forces, as discussed below.

Social Forces and Myths

The social critical perspective has been defined as an approach to inquiry that seeks to offer "explanations of destructive social arrangements and myths, as well as the self-defeating beliefs of people subjected to these arrangements" (Forte, 2007, p. 497). Although Côté suggests that psychological factors can interfere with identity development of emerging adults, he also describes social forces adversely impacting emerging adults' identity development, including: (1) decreasing access to well-paid work opportunities, and increasing requirements for higher education to gain this limited access; and (2) cultural factors promoting the default individualization strategy, including the celebration in popular media of default individualization lifestyles, and the ideology of free choice. These cultural factors also reduce recognition by the general public of identity development problems of youth, by obscuring appreciation of the sacrifice and obligations entailed in genuine developmental individualization. All of these forces are seen as being driven by the demands of a postindustrial market economy.

Limited Access to Work Opportunities and Higher Education Demands

Even if the contribution of college experiences themselves to identity development are limited, credentials resulting from postsecondary educational credentials are important resources for identity development due to their influence on gaining access to work (Côté, 1997). Difficulties in entering the labor market due to increased needs for educational credentials are reflected by lower workforce participation, higher unemployment, and longer school-to-work transitions over time (Bowlby & Jennings, 1999, cited in Côté, 2006), and increased poor outcomes such as incarceration of large numbers of youth (Halperin, 1998). These difficulties effectively exclude youth from the settings in which identity capital could be accrued and issues of identity be resolved, either directly (due to "reality-based testing" of work-related identity) and indirectly, since the income that is generated facilitates starting a family and establishing a stable residence in a community. Youth lacking psychological and social resources, and thus most in need of these opportunities, are also those most likely to struggle to earn higher education credentials.

Popular Culture and the Ideology of Free Choice

Côté points out that default individualization and avoidance of social commitments is celebrated in popular culture, conveyed by mass media. As discussed above, popular culture and mass marketing provide many examples for and opportunities to adopt "badges of individuality" (Côté, 2000, p. 34), ways of distinguishing oneself that require only purchasing products or imitating media examples. Adoption of these symbols is emphasized at the expense of more meaningful, committed activities. Default individualization is also promoted by the "ideology of free choice" (Furlong & Cartmel, 1997, cited in Côté, 2006). This ideology undermines the value of social commitments and social norms, as these inevitably detract from free choice of the individual. In the extreme, free-choice ideology may create a "tyranny of free choice" in which any social commitment is seen as detracting from choices of the individual, and the basis of identity is paradoxically undermined (B. Schwartz, 2000).

Postmodern Market Economy

Côté believes that the factors above, including lack of access and the encouragement of default individualization by popular culture and free-choice ideology, are ultimately driven by the needs of a postindustrial market economy. Efficiency increases lead to a tightening labor market, in which youth are increasing unwelcome newcomers. As fewer youth are able to access work opportunities, education becomes increasingly prolonged, due to both efforts by youth to better compete in a tightening labor market, and their poor options for assuming work roles more rapidly. Youth lacking in resources for identity development suffer disproportionately as a result, since their access to these prolonged educational opportunities is limited and they are less prepared for these environments even where they are accessible. Coté holds that cultural messages promoting default individualization are useful in this context because they reduce motivation of youth to strive to enter the economy in meaningful roles, and focus on consumption of marketed symbols of default individualization instead, driving up demand (Côté, 2000, 2006).

Implications of Côté's Critical Perspective

Côté's arguments regarding how particular social forces have encouraged the deferment of adulthood are inferential and therefore somewhat speculative. As noted above, however, they do provide an explanation of why the more positive conceptualization of emerging adulthood advocated by Arnett has had such wide appeal, despite the increasing social challenges faced by this population discussed in this chapter and elsewhere (e.g., Osgood, Foster, Flanagan, & Ruth, 2005). They also provide an explanation of individual differences in development during the emerging-adult years that result in a minority of youth being able to explore identity in the context of a supportive, institutionalized moratorium, but many (perhaps most) lack these opportunities.

In addition to providing a complementary and critical perspective on the phenomenon of emerging adulthood more generally, Côté's work provides a means for understanding contemporary trends among emerging adults for sexual behavior decoupled from the context of committed relationships such as "hookups" and "friends with benefits." If emerging adults are deferring resolution of their identities, including their identities in the area of sexual and love relationships, increased drive toward forms of sexual expression outside the context of commitment is understandable. Conversely, the continuing tendencies of emerging adults to prefer committed relationships can be understood as representing resilience in this population in the face of social forces that would discourage such commitments.

Côté's perspective may also contribute to understanding emerging adults' sexual behavior and intimate relationships in a more subtle way, by promoting a more nuanced appreciation of the nature of identity development, and highlighting the ways in which social myths may promote a distorted view of the identity development process in the context of emerging-adult sexuality and intimate relationships. In a culture that celebrates free choice—due to dynamics of the market economy, or other reasons—it is important to appreciate how any "exploration" may have little meaningfulness if decontextualized completely from committed social roles.

SUMMARY AND IMPLICATIONS FOR SEXUALITY AND ROMANTIC RELATIONSHIPS

This chapter sought to examine the developmental context of sexuality and intimacy among emerging adults, using the framework of emerging adulthood as described by Arnett (2000a, 2004) as a starting point, but also considering a critical, alternative view, advanced by Côté (2000, 2006), in order to address possible weaknesses of Arnett's framework in explaining emerging adults' sexuality and intimate-relationship behavior. Through combining these two perspectives, a more dialectical understanding of the distinctive form and significance of emerging adults' sexual and intimate-relationship patterns was sought, in order to explain apparent contradictions in existing research evidence, as well as provide a more flexible framework for understanding a more diverse range of emerging-adult sexual and intimate-relationship behavior.

Arnett's approach posits that the years coinciding with a traditional postsecondary educational experience, spanning from the late teens to the early 20s, represent a distinct developmental phase in which emerging adults (1) explore and test their identities in areas of worldview, love, and work; (2) focus primarily on self-development; (3) experience themselves ambiguously, as partially adults and partially not (i.e., "in between"); (4) experience great instability in life circumstances; and (5) are highly optimistic about themselves and their futures. Several corollaries to Arnett's ideas for college students' sex and love relationships were examined in light of existing evidence, including propositions that emerging adults' sex and love relationship behavior and experiences qualitatively differ from those experienced in other developmental periods along the defining dimensions used to describe the period, that this distinct form reflects a healthy striving toward individuation and identity achievement that is essential to normal development, and that this distinct form is shared across socioeconomic and cultural groups. Although limited support for these ideas was identified in some instances, overall, research evidence for these applications for Arnett's ideas was limited and inconsistent. To address this problem, an alternative, critical framework proposed by Côté for understanding the developmental context of college students' sex and love relationships was presented. This framework describes emerging adults as deferring developmental tasks Arnett ascribes to the period, due to either an imposed or actively sought "institutionalized moratorium," and suggests that this moratorium is excessively prolonged and harmful to many young adults.

Using existing data and informed by the Arnett's and Côté's criticisms, some proposals to improve emerging-adult sexual and love relationship functioning and address problems can reasonably be advanced. If, as proposed by Côté, emerging adulthood is extremely heterogeneous with respect to the factors described by Arnett, any approach informed solely by this model will be a poor fit for some young adults and may even be harmful. If, further, many young adults would benefit from earlier foreclosure of exploration and commitment to adult roles, then the task of health professionals could be seen as working to encourage such commitments, by helping emerging adults to

(1) continue but perhaps better structure or limit exploration (and avoid those types of exploration most likely to be destructive); and (2) select and maintain committed healthy relationships that address their needs and allow for growth. Fortuitously, these two strategies appear to correspond to two existing types of approaches to improving emerging adults' sexual and relationship health, namely, a "problem behavior" approach that seeks to reduce risky sexual behaviors, and a "relationship education" approach designed to help in the selection and maintenance of positive intimate relationships. In addition to these approaches, Côté's arguments that emerging adults' difficulties may be due to weakening of support for and de-structuring of the transition to adulthood in contemporary society suggest the possibility of intervening to improve health at higher levels of social analysis, through creating more supportive contexts for emerging adults or even through larger, macrosocial changes. Some preliminary ideas for such efforts are presented in the final section of the chapter.

Problem and Health Behavior Approaches

The problem behavior perspective on emerging adults' sexual health stipulates that risky sexual behavior is one among multiple forms of risk taking (Jessor et al., 1991), which tend to occur at relatively high levels or peak during emerging adulthood (Centers for Disease Control and Prevention, 2002; Johnston, O'Malley, Bachman, & Schulenberg, 2004). This perspective appears to be influential among existing interventions to improve sexual health of adolescents and emerging adults, many of which focus on reducing risky sexual behavior (Robin et al., 2004). Critics of this perspective have pointed out that emerging-adult sexual activity is normative and mostly healthy and therefore that sexual health promotion should not be "deficit-based" in the manner implied by a problem behavior perspective (Lefkowitz, Gillen, and Vasilenko, 2011). Nonetheless, certain types of high-risk behavior such as "hooking up" or unprotected sex might be profitably addressed using a problem behavior model. This is particularly the case given that contemporary approaches (e.g., motivational interviewing, harm reduction) incorporate concern for benefits as well as costs of behavior, incorporate healthy behavioral alternatives, and consider broader social and contextual factors (G. Harper, 2007).

Conclusions of this review would suggest that problem or health behavior approaches could be enriched by attending to how making commitments to adult roles and community may increase the likelihood of better sexual behavior choices. For example, findings of lower rates of risky sexual behavior among religious youth (e.g., Lefkowitz, Gillen, Shearer, & Boone, 2004) suggest that commitments to a religious community or other similar social institution encouraging positive behavioral norms could be protective. Similarly, as work commitments have been found to lead to desistance from other types of problem behaviors (e.g., Roisman et al., 2004), these commitments could reduce problematic sexual behavior among emerging adults as well. Recently, G. Harper (2007) has also suggested that content focusing on ethnic or sexual identity enculturation—helping youth discover or better connect with personal ethnic, sexual, or other cultural identities—could enhance interventions to reduce problematic sexual behavior. Clearly, intimate-relationship commitments are relevant to efforts to reduce risky sexual behavior, as individuals in committed relationships are less likely to engage in risky sex (e.g., unprotected sex with multiple partners; Braithwaite et al., 2010). Commitments to intimate partners have been shown to reduce the incidence of multiple types of problem behavior among high-risk youth, if relationships are with prosocial partners and are healthy (Davila, 2011; Quinton, Pickles, Maughan, & Rutter, 1993). Thus relationship education approaches such as those discussed below might also be a valuable complement to strategies focused on reduction of risky sexual behavior.

Relationship Education Approaches

Relationship education focuses on providing information to facilitate successful relationships, such as information about communication and conflict management, and develop appropriate attitudes and expectations (Fincham et al., 2011). It has been tried and shown to be efficacious in a variety of populations and contexts, including couples at risk for marital failure or relationship violence and couples in transition (e.g., newly married, expecting children) (Jakubowski, Milne, Brunner, & Miller, 2004; D. K. O'Leary, Wooden, & Fritz, 2006). It is a relatively new approach among dating college students but has shown effectiveness in influencing proximal outcomes such as conflict behavior and extradyadic involvement in "real world" college settings (Braithwaite, Lambert, Fincham, & Pasley, 2010; Fincham et al., 2011). Objectives developed for relationship education with college students have included strengthening of healthy relationships, helping to end destructive (e.g., violent) relationships, and assisting students with selecting partners wisely (Pearson, Stanley, & Rhoades, 2008). A particularly appealing feature of this type of intervention is its responsiveness to the lack of deliberation characteristic of many emerging-adult relationship decisions, referred to earlier in this review as "sliding versus deciding." For example, emerging adults are asked to reflect on their relationship beliefs and personality features that may be relevant to their relationships and actively consider specific relationship goals (Fincham et al., 2011).

Relationship education is consonant with both the Arnett and Côté frameworks, as it both encourages healthy exploration and fosters commitment to existing relationships. Consideration of sociocultural barriers to commitment articulated by Côté, including de-structuring of the transition to adulthood and economic exclusion, suggests certain ways in which these interventions could be further enhanced to meet developmental needs of emerging-adult youth. For example, rather than reflecting primarily on how personality impacts relationships (and intraindividual problem framing), emerging adults might be encouraged to actively consider norms in their own sociocultural communities regarding relationships, and how these might inform their efforts to improve their own sexual and relationship health. Given the intertwined nature of family and work goals (Manning et al., 2011), explicit consideration of career plans and how these are impacted by intimate relationship partners (and vice versa) could be helpful. By reflecting on these interrelationships, emerging adults might be able to plan ways of balancing commitments to work and love in an unforgiving economic climate, by selecting partners who have similar career goals or who are otherwise supportive of these goals, or, in established relationships, discussing and negotiating work-family balance issues.

Macrosocial and Critical Approaches

Hallmarks of the critical approach to social problems include analysis at the systemic level, a concern for differences in power, and a focus on types of intervention suited to systemic change and oppression (Forte, 2007; G. Nelson & Prilleltensky, 2010). Côté's critical approach to understanding emerging adulthood as a manifestation of social exclusion—or, more forcefully put, a "frame," which, if accepted uncritically, furthers oppression of youth (Gruendel & Aber, 2007)—suggests radically different strategies for enhancing sexual and romantic relationship health of emerging adults. As a starting point, further critical examination such as pursued in this chapter could enrich discussion of sexual and relationship health, by suggesting ways in which social forces impacting emerging adults may limit the their capacity to fulfill their sexual and intimate-relationship development needs. Much of the existing literature examining emerging adults' functioning in this domain attempts to explain relative health or problems by appealing to their prior functioning in adolescence (e.g., Masten et al., 1999; Tanner, 2006). Although clearly prior functioning impacts well-being and resilience in emerging adulthood in a variety of ways, a focus on individual differences and developmental causes diverts attention from causes at the macrosocial level that impact emerging adults in their current contexts. If emerging adults avoid relationship commitments due to social forces that push against their assumption of adult roles, then strategies that focus on individual-level risk—including preventative as well as treatment strategies—will have limited effectiveness.

In order to address problems of emerging adults on the macrosocial level, social reforms enacted on a broad scale may be needed. These could include government policies that provide greater economic support for young families on a universal rather than selective or "means tested" basis (Kamerman, 1996), educational reforms that "restructure" transition through more diverse, inclusive, and supportive postsecondary school environments, more career-relevant instruction, better structured and more adequately supported pathways from school to rewarding employment, (Bloom, Thompson, Unterman, Herlihy, & Payne, 2010; William T. Grant Foundation Commission on Work, Family, and Citizenship, 1988), community development policies emphasizing needs of young families (Perkins, Crim, Silberman, & Brown, 2004), and programs to provide additional support to marginalized emerging adults such as youth in the juvenile justice or child welfare systems, youth with mental health or other disabilities, socioeconomically disadvantaged youth, or "disconnected" youth (Besharov, 1999; Osgood et al., 2005). Critical resources necessary for navigating transition that are either lacking or poorly distributed, including access to educational and work opportunities, could be identified and prioritized to inform these policy changes. Leadership within marginalized communities is an essential aspect of social transformation (Friere, 1970); thus any of these strategies would need to incorporate concern for youth leadership, as both an outcome of intervention, and a means of guiding social interventions so that they serve the interests of emerging adults, according to their own, critical understandings of their needs (Delgado, 2007).

CONCLUSION

The notion of emerging adulthood as a distinct phase of development has helped to catalyze research on the period and provided an easily understood framework for informing health practices with emerging adults, including practices to improve their sexual and intimate-relationship health and well-being. In adopting emerging adulthood as an organizing framework, however, there is a danger that behavioral scientists and practitioners will reify phenomena that are culturally bound and that, in some respects, may be detrimental to the health and well-being of youth. Incorporating critical perspectives on emerging adulthood, represented in this chapter by the commentary and research of Côté (2000, 2006), can provide a means to profitably use this framework without perpetuating its weaknesses. A dialectical understanding of this sort provides a means for describing general features of sexual and intimate-relationship development during emerging adulthood, while still recognizing (and hopefully, addressing) the social disadvantages among emerging adults overall or in specific vulnerable groups that can contribute to developmental problems.

Chapter Five

SEX, INTIMACY, AND DATING IN COLLEGE

Daniel Perlman and Susan Sprecher

> If we can't say no to sex, what is our yes even worth? Only with self-control can I make a gift of myself. That's the biggest thing with chastity. It frees college students to love. They aren't in it just for taking, they are in it for giving.
>
> Jason Evert ("Why Chastity," YouTube video, January 4, 2008)

> Masturbation can help college students to relieve stress, to fall asleep, or to feel sexually satisfied whether or not they have a partner.
>
> Debby Herbenick (sexual health educator at the Kinsey Institute, from L. Zerbe, "Sex in College: What Every Student—and Parent—Should Know," http://www.rodale.com/college-sex-tips

> A survey of 223 college students shows that vaginal intercourse, receiving oral sex, and being masturbated by a partner received the highest pleasure ratings.
>
> Pinkerton, Cecil, Bogart, and Abramson (2003)

As the above statements indicate, sexuality among college students can be expressed in various personal and interpersonal contexts. These can range from with no one at all (complete abstinence or chastity), to by oneself, to with a single partner, to with multiple partners. The partners can be of the same sex, the opposite sex, or both sexes. They can be casual acquaintances. Most often, however, college students' interpersonal sexual activity is with someone for whom they feel some affection and with whom they have a relationship that includes nonsexual interaction as well. Such relationships have traditionally been referred to as "dating relationships." When the dating relationships are developed and enduring, they are often referred to as intimate relationships.

What exactly is sex? People, even students, do not always agree. For example, in various studies, between 20 and 58 percent of college students in the United States and elsewhere have defined oral genital behaviors as having sex (Byers, Henderson, & Hobson, 2009). McKinney and Sprecher (1991, p. 2) provided a broad definition of sexuality as referring to "sexual behaviors, arousal, and responses, as well as to sexual attitudes, desires, and communication." In this view, the one we will adopt, sex includes a range of sexual behaviors plus the physiological concomitants, the attitudes, the desires, and the communication associated with them.

Another point worth considering before turning to the main sections of this chapter is the extent to which sex is a solitary activity involving just one person versus an interpersonal activity involving a partner or partners. This is a challenging question to answer definitively because to do so requires having information on a full set of solitary and interpersonal activities, each with frequency and duration data. Nonetheless, two studies help address this question: the first involved students taking a human sexuality course (Pinkerton et al., 2002), and the second is a recent nationally representative survey with 471 participants ages 18–24 (Herbenick et al., 2010). Table 5.1 presents selected findings from these studies. Three aspects of these data are noteworthy. First, solitary masturbation is common. Second, there is a gender difference such that males masturbate more than they have vaginal intercourse but females have vaginal intercourse more than they masturbate. Third, although

Table 5.1
Solitary versus Partnered Sexual Activity

	Males	Females
Frequency of masturbation (alone)/month	12.0	4.7
Frequency of intercourse/month	5.8	6.3
Masturbation (alone)	82%	63%
Vaginal intercourse	60%	75%
Received oral sex	60%	67%
Masturbation with partner	43%	36%
Gave/received anal sex	10%	22%

Note: Frequency data are from Pinkerton et al. (2002); percentages of participants are from Herbenick et al. (2010) and refer to the proportion of 18- to 24-year-olds reporting selected activities during the past year.

masturbation is widely prevalent among college-age young adults, when all forms of interpersonal activity are combined it is likely that the frequency of partnered sex is higher than the frequency of solitary sex.

This chapter examines the role of sex in dating and intimacy, focusing on research conducted with college students. We begin by providing an overview to an area of study referred to as *premarital sexuality*. Research in this tradition has focused on assessing young adults' attitudes about sexual behavior in different types of dating (premarital) relationships. This overview also includes a discussion of how premarital sexual behaviors in a dating context have changed over several decades on college campuses. Second, we discuss the influence of the partners' sexual attitudes and prior sexual behaviors on the attraction process between them at the *initiation* stage of a dating relationship. In our third section, we turn to a focus on the role of sex in the *development* of a dating relationship. We consider both the traditional sexual pathway of dating for a period of time preceding sex, and a more recent pathway in which sex occurs first, after which a dating relationship may develop but more often does not. Next, in the fourth section, we consider the interplay of sexuality with other important components of intimacy in the maintenance and continuation of those college romantic relationships that make it beyond the initiation stage. In this section, we also consider the degree to which the quality and quantity of sex in the dating relationship affect whether the relationship is satisfying and long-lasting. Finally, in our last section, we consider three types of factors that influence college students' sexuality, arguing for why considering interpersonal factors is important.

AN OVERVIEW TO SEXUAL ATTITUDES AND BEHAVIORS IN THE CONTEXT OF DATING

It was only a few decades ago that most Americans did not find sex to be appropriate for dating relationships and believed that sex should be reserved for marriage. This section describes how sexual standards and behaviors have changed over time among college students and how the degree of approval of sex in dating depends on the dating relationship's emotional and commitment level.

Attitudes about Premarital Sexuality

Early research on sex among college students focused on their sexual attitudes. College students were asked to respond to measures that assessed their attitudes (or standards) about sex prior to marriage. Ira Reiss (1960, 1967), a pioneer in the study of young-adult *premarital sexuality*, created a sexual permissiveness scale that was administered to several samples of college students, beginning in the 1950s and 1960s. The scale asked students to indicate the acceptability of sexual behavior (for men and women) at four levels of emotional involvement: without much affection, moderate affection, strong affection, and love relationship. This scale and related scales (e.g., Sprecher, McKinney, Walsh, & Anderson, 1988) assess dating or premarital sexual standards with greater validity and discriminability than the single items often used in national studies. For example, the General Social Survey (T. W. Smith, 1994) has included only one question that asks about premarital sexual standards: "If a man and a woman have sexual relationships before marriage, do you think it is always wrong, almost always wrong, wrong only sometimes, or not wrong at all?"

Based on his early research on sex among college students and adolescents, Reiss (1960, 1967) distinguished among four types of premarital standards: (1) *abstinence*: sexual activity is considered wrong prior to marriage; (2) *permissiveness with affection*: sexual activity is permissible if it occurs in the context of affection, love, and commitment; (3) *permissiveness without affection*: sexual activity is permissible as long as both want it; emotional commitment is not necessary; and (4) *the double standard*: sexual activity is considered more acceptable for men than for women.

When Reiss and others (e.g., Erhmann, 1959) first began surveying college students about sexual standards in the 1950s and 1960s, the predominant standards were the abstinence standard and the double standard. This was before the sexual revolution that occurred on college campuses in the early 1960s (T. W. Smith, 1990, 1994). Beginning in the 1970s, however, widespread acceptance was found among college students for sex in the context of love and commitment. Students were endorsing the "permissiveness with affection" standard, and to a lesser degree, the "permissiveness without affection" standard (e.g., Sprecher, 1989; Sprecher & Hatfield, 1996; Sprecher et al., 1988). These standards have also been referred to as a *relational orientation* and a *recreational orientation*, respectively (DeLamater, 1989; Michael et al., 1994). The most dramatic changes over time in sexual attitudes have been found for women (e.g., Wells & Twenge, 2005).

In addition, the double standard has diminished over time (Crawford & Popp, 2003). Whereas college students in early decades responded to the Reiss Premarital Sexual Permissive scale and similar sexual attitude measures with more acceptance of premarital sex for men than for women, this difference diminished over time. One exception is that young adults (especially men) have continued to find it more acceptable for men than for women to have sex in casual relationships or at a very early stage of the relationship such as on the first date (e.g., Sprecher & Hatfield, 1996; Sprecher, 1989).

Although premarital sexual standards continue to be investigated today (e.g., Espinosa-Hernandez & Lefkowitz, 2009), other sexual attitudes are also assessed with college student samples. These include attitudes about "hooking up" (T. A. Lambert, Kahn, & Apple, 2003; Owen et al., 2010) and other forms of casual sex (Buss & Schmitt, 1993), same-gender sexual activity (Herek, 1988), condom use (e.g., Beckman, Harvey, & Tiersky, 1996), masturbation (Weis, Rabinowitz, & Ruckstuhl, 1992), and infidelity versus faithfulness (e.g., Sheppard, Nelson, & Andreoli-Mathie, 1995). In general, today's college students have permissive attitudes about homosexuality, condom use, and masturbation; have mixed attitudes about casual sex; and have generally negative attitudes about infidelity (e.g., Weis et al., 1992; Wells & Twenge, 2005).

The early focus on college students' premarital sexual standards (e.g., Reiss, 1960) was influenced by a sociological perspective, with an emphasis on how sexual standards are associated with social and cultural factors (N. D. Glenn & Weaver, 1979). Studies conducted over several decades have found that college student males have more liberal sexual standards than college student females, particularly in regard to attitudes about sex in the beginning stage of relationships or in casual dating (for meta-analysis reviews, see Oliver & Hyde, 1993; Peterson & Hyde, 2010). In addition, more permissive sexual standards are associated with lower religiosity, being black or Latino (in comparison to being white), having friends who are sexually permissive, and coming from a divorced family (T. W. Smith, 1994; Wells & Twenge, 2005).

Sexual Behaviors

College students' sexual behaviors have also been studied. The most common sexual behaviors assessed with student samples have been incidence of vaginal intercourse (i.e., sometimes referred to as virginity status), age at first sexual intercourse, and number of lifetime sexual partners. Other behaviors have also been assessed among college students including incidence of other specific sexual behaviors (in addition to penis-vaginal intercourse)—i.e., oral sex, anal sex, and foreplay; casual sex with a stranger or acquaintance; incidence of sex with a friend; same-gender behavior; extradyadic sex; viewing of pornography; frequency of sexual behavior; and cybersex (e.g., Peterson & Hyde, 2010). In addition, college students have been asked about their behavioral intentions or willingness to engage in particular behaviors, which are also important to assess because actual behavior can be constrained by lack of opportunities. For example, a majority of college virgins state that they would be willing to have sex if they had the right opportunity, which includes finding the appropriate partner (Sprecher & Regan, 1996).

Various theories would predict a correspondence between sexual behaviors and sexual standards. A sociological analysis would argue that attitudes regulate actual sexual behaviors (DeLamater & MacCorquodale, 1979;

T. W. Smith, 1994). That is, it is assumed that attitudes predict behaviors because attitudes offer guiding principles about what to do in particular situations. Attitude-behavior consistency may also occur because behaviors influence attitudes through self-perception processes (Bem, 1972; Kleinke, 1978). Young adults may find themselves engaging in a behavior of which they had disapproved and then change their attitudes about the behavior as a result of their actions (T. W. Smith, 1994). As a reflection of the attitude-behavior correspondence, college students' incidence of sexual activity and number of partners increased and age at first intercourse decreased on college campuses in the 1960s and in the decades after, at the same time that sexual attitudes were becoming more permissive, as indicated by a meta-analysis of 530 studies conducted between 1943 and 1999 (Wells & Twenge, 2005).

In provocative work, social psychologist Roy Baumeister (2000) has argued and found evidence that attitudes are less congruent with behaviors for women than for men and theorized that it is because women's behavior is affected to a greater degree by situational pressures, relational factors, and social/cultural influences than is men's behavior (i.e., women would be more likely than men to engage in behaviors contrary to their attitudes). Baumeister (2000) refers to the process by which cultural, contextual, and social factors shape a person's sex drive as "erotic plasticity" and concluded, based on a review of the sexuality literature, that women have greater erotic plasticity.

In sum, college students hold normative beliefs (i.e., standards) about what is appropriate sexual behavior in dating contexts for themselves and for others, and these standards have been reliably measured over the past several decades and have become more permissive over time. In addition, a corresponding increase in sexual behaviors has been found on college campuses. Although some research suggests that there has not been a further trend toward permissiveness since the 1980s, and perhaps even a slight decrease in permissiveness due to AIDS and enhanced sex education (e.g., Planned Parenthood Federation of America, 2001; Risman & Schwartz, 2002), most of today's college students are accepting of sex during dating and are sexually active. Nonetheless, college students are diverse, and range from those who choose to abstain from sex, to those who seek frequent sexual partners for short-term, casual relationships. In the next section, we discuss the implications of this variation in sexual attitudes and behaviors for the attraction process at the initial stage of dating relationships.

PARTNERS' SEXUAL ATTITUDES AND PRIOR SEXUAL EXPERIENCE AS AN INFLUENCE ON INITIAL ATTRACTION

When two individuals enter a romantic relationship, or consider the possibility of doing so, their sexual attitudes and prior sexual behaviors can influence the likelihood that they are attracted to each other. In this section, we discuss three interrelated questions:

1. To what degree is sexual permissiveness (versus sexual restrictiveness) desired in or a possible influence on attraction for a partner?
2. Do individuals' own sexual permissiveness affect what they find attractive in a partner?
3. Do those who select each other as romantic partners have greater than chance similarity in sexual attitudes and behaviors?

What Level of Sexual Experience Is Preferred in a Partner?

Studies on mate or partner preferences were first conducted by family sociologists in the 1930s and 1940s (e.g., Hill, 1945), but proliferated beginning in the 1980s due to extensions of evolutionary psychology to predictions about men's and women's differential preferences for qualities in dating and mating partners (e.g., Buss, 1989b). Evolutionary theory argues that men should prefer (more than women) traits in a partner that suggest youth and the ability to reproduce as well as traits that can give them confidence of paternity. The theory further argues that women should prefer (more than men) traits that show that the partner will have the resources to support offspring.

In research using the mate selection list format, the participants—who are most often single college students—are presented with a list of characteristics (e.g., honesty, physical attractiveness, good earning potential) and are asked how much they would desire each in a partner. In some such studies, an item has been included that refers to a potential partner's level of prior sexual activity. For example, in what was perhaps the first mate selection list distributed to college students (Hill, 1945), chastity was included as one of the items. Although college students rated chastity to be somewhat important in a partner in the 1940s (rated to be more important than such traits as intelligence, sociability, and good looks), its importance decreased over time, and recently has been rated as the least important characteristic for a partner to have (e.g., Buss, 1989b; Hoyt & Hudson, 1981; Sprecher, Regan, McKinney, Maxwell, & Wazienski, 1997). Men and women agree about its relative (un)importance, although Buss (1989b) found in his U.S. subsample and some of his other subsamples in a cross-cultural study that men rated it slightly more favorably than did women.

If chastity is no longer an important characteristic in a partner, is sexual experience now desired in a dating partner? The answer is also no. Sprecher and Regan (2002) asked college students how important several characteristics would be in a partner, and found that an item that referred to "sexual experience" was rated as least important (in a list of 14 characteristics). Furthermore, in an earlier study Sprecher et al. (1997) varied how a sexuality item was presented in a mate selection list and found that when the item referred to "considerable sexual experience (had several sexual partners)," it received a lower importance rating than when it referred to "chastity" or "some sexual experience."

A bogus stranger paradigm approach, initially popularized by social psychologist Donn Byrne (1971) to examine the effects of similarity on attraction, has been used to determine how a number of factors might affect attraction to others. In some such studies, sexual information is presented about a hypothetical person, and participants are asked to indicate how attractive the target would be as a relational partner. Across various experiments, information has been manipulated about a target's level of sexual attitudes, lifetime sexual experience, and relational context for his or her past sexual activity. Overall, this research indicates that a target person who is described with a sexually permissive background is perceived to be less desirable as a date or mate than someone who is described with a less permissive background (Bettor, Hendrick, & Hendrick, 1995; Oliver & Sedikides, 1992; O'Sullivan, 1995; Sprecher, McKinney, & Orbuch, 1991).

The degree to which sexual experience, or lack of sexual experience, is desired in a partner or leads to attraction, however, has been found to depend on the type of relationship being considered. Sexual experience is rated as more desirable in a partner and more likely to lead to attraction when the target person is being considered for a short-term, sexual relationship than for a long-term relationship such as marriage (Kenrick, Sundie, Nicastle, & Stone, 2001; Oliver & Sedikides, 1992; Sprecher et al., 1991; Sprecher & Regan, 2002). This greater acceptance (or desire) for sexual activity for a short-term partner than for a long-term partner has been found especially for men. Buss (1998) provided an evolutionary perspective for this sex difference:

> Whereas in the long-term mating context men place a premium on sexual fidelity and abhor promiscuity in a woman (solutions to the problem of uncertainty about paternity), the reverse is true in a short-term mating context, in which men are indifferent to the sexual fidelity of a partner and even slightly desire a partner who is promiscuous (possibly a cue to sexual accessibility). (Buss, 1998, p. 26)

As suggested in the quote above, one explanation for people's desire for a dating partner with less rather than more past sexual experience, particularly for a long-term relationship, is that lack of sexual experience suggests future fidelity; and conversely extensive sexual experience suggests future infidelity. There can be worry that if a partner has had several prior sexual partners, he or she may commit a future infidelity. In addition, people may worry about contracting a sexually transmitted infection from a new partner who had sex with many others.

Although researchers can make a hypothetical person's sexuality salient through mate selection lists and bogus stranger paradigms, in real-life interactions, how do people become aware of a new partner's sexual attitudes and prior sexual history? In developing relationships, the partners' prior sexual relationships can be a "taboo topic," uncomfortable for discussion (Baxter & Wilmot, 1985). Nonetheless, people *say* that they want to ask questions of new partners about their previous sexual partners before having sex (Edgar, Freimuth, Hammond, McDonald, & Fink, 1992). In addition, research on self-disclosure among dating couples indicates that dating partners report that they self-disclose about the sexual experience they had prior to the current relationship (e.g., Rubin, Hill, Peplau, & Dunkel-Schetter, 1980). People may also seek, indirectly, information about a potential partner's past sexual behavior through their social network (Afifi & Lucas, 2008). They can also infer (correctly or incorrectly) information about the other's sexuality based on visible characteristics, including photos on Facebook, clothes, and choice of friends.

Partner Preferences as a Function of Own Sexual Experience

Although most people may find a person who has a history of being sexually permissive less desirable for a romantic relationship than a person who has less sexual activity, the selectors' own past sexual experience can affect the level of sexual experience they desire in a partner. Istvan and Griffitt (1980), in an experimental study, found that sexually inexperienced men and women had a stronger preference than more experienced men and women for an inexperienced partner (see also Sprecher et al., 1997; Wiederman & Dubois, 1998). This can be explained by a similarity-attraction hypothesis, whereby people are more attracted to similar others than dissimilar others. These differences, however, can also be interpreted within an evolutionary perspective. According to Simpson and Gangestad (1992; see also, Simpson, Wilson, & Winterheld, 2004), sociosexual orientation, or how permissive or restrictive an individual is about sex in uncommitted relationships, may play a role in moderating participants' preferences. People who have extensive sexual experience place greater emphasis on selecting mates who are physically attractive and sexually experienced (Simpson et al., 2004).

Matching on Prior Sexual Activity

There is also some evidence that partners in actual couples are similar in sexual attitudes and behaviors, and more similar than would be expected by chance. With a sample of 126 heterosexual couples (most of whom were college dating couples), Cupach and Metts (1995) found a positive correlation between the partners' scores on several subscales of the S. S. Hendrick and Hendrick (1987) Sexual Attitudes scale. These dimensions were general permissiveness, attitudes about sexual responsibility, sexual communication, sexual instrumentality, sexual conventionality, and sex avoidance. The researchers also found that the couples had greater similarity than did a sample of randomly generated pairs from the same sample. More recently, Garcia and Markey (2007) obtained data on the number of prior sexual relationships from both partners of dating, cohabiting, and married couples. They found that the partners' number of prior sexual relationships was positively correlated; i.e., there was matching on prior sexual experience. Separate analyses for different types of couples indicated that the number of prior partners was correlated between the partners among the dating and married couples, but not among the cohabiting couples. In addition, both studies (Cupach & Metts, 1995; Garcia & Markey, 2007) found some support for the hypothesis that similarity between partners was associated with relationship quality.

In sum, attraction, the engine that leads people to enter a new relationship, can be affected by knowledge and assumptions about the characteristics of the other, including their sexual attitudes and prior sexual experiences. Next, we discuss sex and the development of dating relationships.

CASUAL SEX AND THE DEVELOPMENT OF DATING RELATIONSHIPS

Earlier in this chapter we noted that in the 1970s, "permissiveness with affection" became a dominant American standard for sexual behavior. In other words, emotional intimacy and sex were linked. This standard implied a proper sequence of events: first came affection, and then came sex. Various types of sexual activity were coordinated with various degrees of relationship development. Textbook authors still consider the permissiveness with affection standard the most prevalent one in the United States (see Lamanna & Reidman, 2008, p. 131). Not everyone, however, sees sex and affection as linked in an orderly sequence as part of achieving a committed relationship. Akin to what Reiss called the "sex without affection standard," observers also believe a "hook-up" culture operates on college campuses today (Bogle, 2008). Some college students engage in physically intimate behaviors first and then become emotionally involved later, maybe.

> Journalist Tom Wolfe depicts the contrast between generations as follows Only yesterday boys and girls spoke of embracing and kissing (necking) as getting to first base. Second base was deep kissing, plus groping and fondling this and that. Third base was oral sex. Home plate was going all the way. That was yesterday. . . .[Today]

> we can forget about necking. Today's girls and boys have never heard of anything that dainty. Today's first base is deep kissing, now known as tonsil hockey, plus groping and fondling this and that. Second base is oral sex. Third base is going all the way. Home plate is learning each other's names. (description of hooking up, http://books.simonandschuster.com/ Hooking-Up/Tom-Wolfe/9780743519199)

In this section, we discuss the process by which sex can occur prior to the development of the relationship, but that sometimes results in a relationship developing. Hook-ups, booty calls, and friends with benefits (FWB) are each terms that have come into popular and scholarly usage related to sexual activities that can occur outside of loving, committed relationships. Both students and scholars vary somewhat in exactly how they use these terms and the extent to which they see them as separate versus intertwined. We will use common scholarly depictions of each of these terms. We begin by discussing hookups.

Hookups

Hooking up generally refers to a sexually based encounter between two strangers or brief acquaintances in which the partners are not anticipating having a continuing relationship. Paul, Wenzel, and Harvey (2008) defined them as "noncommitted and emotionally inconsequential sexual interactions" (p. 320). Hookups often originate at parties or other situations where drinking is involved; students frequently enter these situations without knowing which particular person they will approach (Paul, McManus, & Hayes, 2000). Hookups often leave the participants, especially females, with mixed feelings such as being desirable yet awkward and confused (N. Glenn & Marquardt, 2001).

Hooking up has become widespread among American college students: it has been reported by 40 percent of participants in a nationally representative phone survey of female students (N. Glenn & Marquardt, 2001), 78 percent of students attending a northeastern state college (Paul et al., 2000), and 51 percent of undergraduates attending a public southeastern university (Penhollow et al., 2007). The variability in reports may be due to such factors as the point in history when the surveys were conducted, the students sampled in terms of gender and geographical region, the exact wording of the questions posed, and other factors.

N. Glenn and Marquardt (2001) identified a number of demographic, social, and contextual factors that give rise to hooking up and other current mating practices of college students. Today's students grew up in an era when many parents divorced, which enhanced the importance of women having a career. The age at which people marry has risen so that most people do not marry until several years after graduating. Sexual relations have become more socially acceptable. In contrast to earlier eras, colleges no longer have responsibilities for supervising dating activities. Instead they are more likely to have coed residence halls. Females often outnumber males on campus five to four, contributing to female competition for male partners. The result of these forces is that current students often begin their sexual activity prior to starting college, are focused on career preparation during college, and delay contemplating marriage until a later time. Hooking up becomes a common, age-specific activity especially among males and children of divorce. It is, however, a practice that fades when students graduate and enter into the next stage of their lives (Bogle, 2008).

Most studies of prevalence of hookups on college campuses ignore the total number of interpersonal sexual experiences that students have. Determining what proportion of sexual encounters occurs in the context of hookups is difficult. The studies of hookups do provide insights into the number of encounters students have with their hookup partners, however. In their national survey, N. Glenn and Marquardt (2001) found that 75 percent of those women who had hooked up had done so less than six times. In Paul et al.'s (2000) study, the students who had hookups reported an average of 10.8 such experiences. Penhollow et al. (2007) reported that the median number of hookups among those who did engage in hookups was two to three times per year. Examined from a slightly different angle, a study of college freshman showed that those in a relationship had penetrative (vaginal or anal) sex more than three and a half times as often as those not in a relationship (Patrick & Maggs, 2009). Our conclusions are that (1) a significant proportion of students engage in hookups but the frequency of hooking up is relatively modest and (2) people's odds of frequently having sex are higher if they are in a dating or committed relationship.

Other Types of Casual Sex

Another route to casual sex among college students is a "booty call." A booty call is contacting a friend or previous hookup partner, often via a late night phone call, with the stated or implied intent of getting together with that person to engage in sexual activities (Bogle, 2008; Jonason, Li, & Cason, 2009). Booty calls and hookups both have an underlying sexual impetus. In contrast to hookups, however, booty calls are often made when the caller is alone rather than in a party situation and are more likely to be directed to a person with whom the caller is already acquainted.

Friendships with benefits, another form of casual sex, involve some degree of sexual intimacy in relationships between friends who define their relationship as platonic rather than romantic (see Hughes, Morrison, & Asada, 2005; Mongeau, Ramirez, & Vorell, 2003). Bogle (2008) describes friendships with benefits as something more than hookups in the sense that friends with benefits care about each other in a way that is not typical of partners who hook up. Estimates of the number of students who have engaged in friendships with benefits have ranged from 49 to 62 percent (Bisson & Levine, 2009). In friendships with benefits, the circumstances leading to sexual activities are varied: partying and alcohol are not such prominent features. Sex is only one of multiple, ongoing activities in which the friends engage. Sexual relations with friends are not necessarily a onetime event; sexual activities may continue for a few months (Bisson & Levine, 2009). When friends engage in sex, it likely involves more affectionate (hugging, kissing, etc.) and genital sexual behaviors than the sexual encounters in hookups (Grello et al., 2006).

Three lines of evidence indicate that friendships with benefits are relationships in which the friendship rather than love predominates. First, consistent with Sternberg's (1987) model of the characteristics of love and friendship, friendships with benefits have the attributes of friendships not those of love: they are moderately high in intimacy but relatively low in commitment and passion (Bisson & Levine, 2009). Second, two-thirds of individuals who have had sex with friends have reported that it improved their friendship (Afifi & Faulkner, 2000), but it typically does not change friendships into romantic relationships (see below). Third, although the motive to have sex in these relationships is strong, students report being significantly more committed to the friendship itself rather than to the sex (Lehmiller et al., 2011).

Relational Aspects of Casual Sex

Hookups, and other forms of casual sex, can be described as a recreational activity that typically involves one or at most a few contacts between partners. From an interpersonal perspective, hookups often look like an interaction rather than an ongoing relationship. So, what aspects of hookups are truly what we would consider relational? Casual sexual activities such as hookups intertwine with relationships in several ways.

First, these activities occur within the context of relationship networks. Students perceive that their peers are involved in hooking up and that their peers are comfortable with it (T. A. Lambert et al., 2003). Students talk with their friends about their experiences in hooking up, perhaps in a way that emphasizes the positive aspects and minimizes the negative (Paul & Hayes, 2002). These perceptions and socializing experiences may make hookups more acceptable to college students.

Second, individuals' ways of relating, including their attachment style (Hazan & Shaver, 1987) and love styles (C. Hendrick & Hendrick, 1986), also influence their engagement in hookups. Students who have a secure attachment style (e.g., they feel comfortable getting close to others) are less likely to engage in casual sex; students who are avoidant (e.g., do not feel comfortable getting close to others) are more likely to engage in casual sex (Stinson, 2010). Students who are anxious-ambivalent (e.g., who worry that others do not want to be as close to them as they would like) are more likely to engage in consensual yet unwanted sexual activity. Apropos of love styles, students who approach love as a game or conquest (ludus style) are more likely to engage in hookups (Paul et al., 2000). For those who have sex with friends, a game-playing approach is associated with the friends with benefits relationship persisting (Hughes et al., 2005).

Third, students' relational status matters. Romantically involved students are less likely to hook up than nonromantically involved students (Paul et al., 2000). Those involved in a romantic relationship at the time of engaging in casual sex are more likely to regret having casual sex (Grello et al., 2006).

Casual Sex as a Pathway to Relationship Development

Casual sex can be part of relationship development (and even decline in cases where ex-partners sustain a friend with benefits relationship). The odds of casual sex leading to a romantic relationship, however, are fairly low, perhaps 10 to 12 percent (Bisson & Levine, 2009; Paul et al. 2000). Nonetheless, there is a chance, and this possibility is a consideration in the decision to have casual sex, especially for women. In an Internet survey restricted to individuals who had engaged in friendships with benefits but not restricted to students, 25 percent of men and 37 percent of women cited a desire to feel closer as a motivation for entering into a sexual relationship with a friend (Lehmiller et al., 2011). Many respondents in this survey also hoped their friendships with benefits would evolve into romantic relationships (24% of men, 43% of women). Nearly a fifth of female students (vs. 3% of males) who participated in hookups believed their most recent hookup experience was the beginning of a romance (Grello et al., 2006). Relevant to those with hope, Paul et al. (2008) articulated conditions they believed enhance the likelihood that hookups will become longer-term relationships (e.g., conscious and consensually chosen entrance into the hookup, small talk and some discussion of future interaction during the hookup, the hookup being a positive emotional experience, absence of regret, and social network support).

In summary, a large percentage of today's college population has engaged in hookups and friendships with benefits. Several demographic trends likely have contributed to sex without affection becoming more socially acceptable. Even though hookups may be only onetime encounters, they are influenced by other relationships in which students are involved as well as by the students' approach to romantic relationships. Hookups are also associated with relationship development, albeit in a somewhat paradoxical manner. Many partners are motivated to engage in sex as a way of increasing closeness with their partners but only a small percentage of hookups lead to long-term relationships. (Of course, advocates of hookups might argue that only a small percentage of any way of trying to establish intimate relationships achieves it goals). The importance of hookups appears to recede in the period after college when graduates become oriented to finding more permanent partners.

SEX IN THE DEVELOPMENT OF ROMANTIC RELATIONSHIPS

Despite the recent focus on hookups and sex without affection, traditionally and often still today sex occurs within the context of intimate relationships. Concerning this, three questions arise: When do couples in more enduring relationships initiate various sexual behaviors (especially sexual intercourse) in their relationships? How is the initiation of sex related to other aspects of their relationships? What strategies do they use to initiate sex?

The Timing of Sexual Intimacy within Developing Relationships

In their classic investigation of sexual intimacy in romantic couples, Peplau, Rubin, and Hill (1977) conducted a two-year longitudinal study of 231 dating couples attending Boston area colleges in the early 1970s. Among these couples, roughly 40 percent had sexual intercourse within one month of when they began dating; approximately the same percentage engaged in sexual intercourse but did so later in their relationship. Just under 20 percent of couples did not engage in sexual intercourse. Peplau et al. classified these couples, respectively, as liberals, moderates, and traditionals. The timing of first intercourse was related to several individual difference factors among the women in these couples (e.g., women in the moderate group tended to be more conservative in terms of religion and attitudes toward women working than those in the liberal group). Peplau et al. described the three types of couples as having different orientations. Traditionals have a moral orientation, believing that premarital sex is wrong. Moderates have a romantic view, seeing sex as an expression of love and caring. Liberals have an erotic view, believing sex can be enjoyed in its own right and that it may be a route to developing emotional closeness.

Approximately a decade after the Boston study, Christopher and Cate (1985) asked dating couples at what point in their relationship they engaged in various sexual behaviors. They used four dating stages: first date, casual dating, considering becoming a couple, and being a couple. They used a 21-item scale that has been shown to represent a reasonably standard progression of sexual behaviors. These start with lip kissing, and then successively move to manipulation of the female breast (over clothes, under clothes, and kissing), manual manipulation of the genitals, oral-genital contact, face-to-face sexual intercourse, and various "advanced" sexual activities (e.g., mutual oral-genital stimulation, ventral-dorsal sexual intercourse). They identified four groups.

- *Rapid-involvement couples* (7%), who typically engaged in intercourse on their first date
- *Gradual-involvement couples* (31%), who reported a gradual increase in sexual activity, beginning orgasmic sex during the period—starting after nine weeks—they were considering becoming a couple
- *Delayed-involvement couples* (44%), who refrained from direct genital touching and sexual intercourse until the period—starting after 22 weeks—they became a couple
- *Low-involvement couples* (17%), who had lower than average levels of sexual intimacy at the various dating levels, engaging in genital touching but refraining from intercourse even after becoming a couple

Stepping back from these two ways of dividing couples, we conclude that there seem to be three main categories: couples who engage in sexual intercourse fairly soon in their relationship, before they have strong emotional bonds and are still considering their future level of involvement (liberals, rapid-involvement and gradual-involvement couples); couples who wait until they are more emotionally bonded and consider themselves as a couple (moderates and delayed-involvement couples); and couples who refrain from sexual intercourse (traditionals and low-involvement couples).

Timing of Sexual Activities and Relationship Properties

There is some evidence that among the couples in the Christopher and Cate (1985) study who had sex (all but the low-involvement couples), the dating stage when the couple initiated extensive sexual involvement was associated with the couple experiencing heightened conflict. In interpreting this, the researchers suggested the possibility that "couples may be bargaining over issues of commitment versus sexual involvement: women may want more commitment, while men may want more sex" (p. 284). Consistent with this, L. L. Cohen and Shotland (1996) found that men expect to engage in sex sooner than do women. For example, in relationships where they are physically attracted and emotionally close, men expect sex after 4 weeks, women after 13. Interestingly, the timing of when sexual intercourse occurred in Cohen and Shotland's study was more strongly associated with women's expectations than with men's. Both L. L. Cohen and Shotland (1996) and Peplau et al. (1977) entertain the notion that women are the main "gatekeepers" of sexual initiation in developing relationships.

Metts (2004) had midwestern university students recall the extent, in their most recent relationship, to which they and their partners had expressed love and commitment prior to the couple's first "significant" sexual involvement. She found that the more students had expressed love and commitment before the couple's first sexual significant involvement, the more they reported that their degree of understanding and satisfaction was enhanced in the period immediately afterward. Regrets immediately afterward, on the other hand, were reduced to the extent that students had expressed love and commitment before the couple's first significant sexual involvement. Furthermore, presex expressions of love and commitment predicted the stability of relationships over time: those participants whose relationships were still ongoing at the time of the survey reported higher levels of presex love and commitment than those whose relationships had ended.

As a framework for understanding these patterns, Metts (2004) referred to script theory (e.g., Metts & Cupach, 1989), the idea that much of sexual behavior seems to follow a social script that instructs members of a society as to sequences of events as well as appropriate behavior and the meanings to attach to those behaviors. Metts observed that "sequences that reflect cultural expectations about sexual episodes in romantic relationships might function as a more positive force in relationship development than those that do not" (p. 138).

Peplau et al. (1977) compared moderate versus liberals on a number of dimensions. In the area of emotional intimacy, moderates were generally more intimate at the beginning of the study: they felt they understood their partners better, felt closer to their partners, had higher scores on a measure of love, and gave higher estimates of the probability that they would get married. In the area of physical intimacy at the beginning of the study, liberals were generally more intimate: liberals had intercourse more frequently than moderates (four to five times per week vs. two to three) and, among women, liberals reported a higher degree of sexual satisfaction than did moderates. In terms of outcome measures taken two years after the study had begun, there were no differences between groups: at that point in time, the timing of first intercourse was not associated with how satisfied the couples were with their relationships nor with the status of couples (separated, still dating, or married).

The studies by Metts (2004) and Peplau et al. (1977) provide somewhat different views of how the sequencing of love and sex affects the stability of relationships. Metts found that expressing love first increased the odds that couples would still be together whereas Peplau et al. failed to find an impact of having sex early in the relationship on whether couples stayed together. The studies were done in different eras and used different ways of assessing the sequencing of love and sex. Perhaps even more important is the design of their studies. Metts asked students individually about their most recent relationship and included all students regardless of how long that relationship lasted. Peplau et al. recruited students who were "going together." To be in the study, both partners had to participate. Nearly a quarter of the couples had been together for more than nine months at the beginning of the study. Peplau et al.'s recruitment procedures may have eliminated early-sex couples who did not continue their relationships very long, and their absence from the Boston study may have minimized the observed effect of early casual sex on relational persistence.

Influence Strategies in Sexual Encounters

Progressing to more advanced levels of sexual intimacy in relationships involves interacting in specific situations: requesting new sexual activities and responding to those requests. How do college students go about that?

In an early study of this issue, McCormick (1979) asked 229 students at UCLA to describe the tactics they would use to avoid or achieve having sexual intercourse with a partner. Students had to imagine being alone with an attractive opposite-sex partner whom they had known for under three weeks and with whom they had "necked" but had not yet had sexual intercourse. McCormick classified the students' descriptions of what they would do into 10 different categories. Students most frequently reported indirect strategies such as seduction and body language for having sex. They mentioned more direct, forceful strategies such as coercion and moralizing to avoid sex. Somewhat to McCormick's surprise, men and women generally used the same ways of achieving each goal. However, given that people of both sexes relied heavily on indirect strategies for having intercourse, men relied more heavily on seduction while women relied more heavily on body language. Table 5.2 gives examples from the students' essays of the four predominant strategies described for achieving sex and the four predominant strategies mentioned for avoiding sex.

In a second study, which used a hypothetical approach, students were asked to imagine that they were members of a couple who had been dating for either three weeks or two years (Humphreys & Newby, 2007). They were then asked to assess the likelihood of their using various tactics to introduce a new sexual behavior into the relationship. In imagining themselves in a relationship of two years, they believed they would be more likely to use verbal strategies to introduce a new sexual behavior than they would in a relationship of only three weeks. Humphreys and Newby see this trend as consistent with other evidence that the longer couples date, the more they self-disclose sexually.

Subsequent studies have asked students about actual behaviors. A study of Canadian students in various stages of dating relationships who kept a daily record of their dating and sexual experiences for a week showed that men were

Table 5.2
Examples from Student Essays of Strategies for Having or Avoiding Sex

Strategy	Example
Major Strategies Used for Having Sex	
1. Seduction	First of all, I would put on some soft music and offer her some wine, then I would start kissing her gently and caressing her body . . .
2. Body Language	I would test the limits by holding hands, sitting closer . . .
3. Information	I would casually ask if [my partner] wanted to have sex.
4. Relationship Conceptualizing	I would tell my date that we have a very strong, close relationship and that it is time to express it through sexual intercourse.
Major Strategies Used for Avoiding Sex	
1. Coercion	If he still insisted on making love, I'd remind him that it's my apartment and he can just leave.
2. Logic	I would give reasons why I didn't want to make love . . . like fear of pregnancy.
3. Moralizing	I would state directly that type of relationship is reserved for marriage.
4. Relationship Conceptualizing	I would tell her the relationship had only just begun. I don't feel we are ready for sex at this stage.

Note: Based on McCormick (1979).

more likely than women to initiate sexual activity but women were as likely as men to respond positively to engaging in the desired behavior (O'Sullivan & Byers, 1992). Eighty percent of requests for sexual activity were accepted. Again in this study, men and women used similar strategies to initiate sexual activity. These students also used indirect and nonverbal means of initiating sex more than they did direct verbal requests. The more students went on dates and the more advanced the stage of their dating relationship, the more likely it was for sexual activity to be initiated.

In a questionnaire study done at a university in the southwestern United States several years ago, students reported on their most recent date. Emotional and physical closeness strategies enhanced the probability of actually having sex, while use of logic and reason decreased the probabilities of having sex (Christopher & Frandsen, 1990). Emotional and physical closeness included items such as: "Told my partner how much I liked him or her," "Did something special for my partner," and "Flattered my partner." Logic and reason included items such as: "Used logic," "Suggested limiting our sexual interaction," and "Claimed to be knowledgeable about how sexual we should be."

To sum up regarding the initiation of sexual intimacy in developing relationships, some couples have sexual intercourse early in their relationship before romantic bonds have been clearly established, others delay having intercourse until emotional bonds have emerged, and still others do not have intercourse even after love flourishes. Couples may experience conflict around the time they initiate having intercourse. In the period shortly after introducing significant sexual activity, couples who had stronger presex emotional attachments report a greater boost in their relationship than couples who had weaker presex emotional attachments. Similarly, during the first few months of their relationships, moderate couples who waited at least a month before having intercourse enjoyed emotionally closer relationships than liberal couples who initiated intercourse in advance of forming clear emotional bonds. Indirect and nonverbal strategies (e.g., seduction strategies such as soft music and body language) are often used to initiate new sexual activities in the early stages of relationship development. More verbal strategies may emerge later. Men and women use many of the same tactics to initiate sexual activity although men are more often the initiator than women. More direct, verbal strategies (e.g., logic and moral reasoning) are used to refuse sexual overtures. Within dating couples, however, most sexual overtures are accepted.

In our next section, we discuss how the sex in the relationship is related to other aspects of the intimate relationship.

SEX IN COMMITTED DATING RELATIONSHIPS

The sexual aspect of the relationship is only one dimension of dating relationships. In this section, we first discuss how sex is an element of important qualities or dimensions of close, dating relationships. Second, we review research showing how sex is associated with the quality of the dating relationships (e.g., satisfaction).

Sex as One Element of Other Important Relationship Dimensions

Scholars of close relationships have identified several important qualities of relationships, including intimacy, sharing of information, interdependence, and love (e.g., R. S. Miller & Perlman, 2009). As noted many years ago by Sprecher and McKinney (1993), sex is one component (among multiple components) of several higher-order constructs that refer to defining characteristics of close relationships.

First, sexual expressions can be considered to be *self-disclosure*. As noted by Reiss (1989), sexual partners "reveal their emotions and responses in their sexual interaction and thereby learn more about each other" (p. 10). Sex is also an act of *intimacy*. For example, a popular assessment of relationship intimacy is M. T. Schaefer and Olson's (1981) multidimensional intimacy scale, which includes sexual intimacy among five types of intimacy. Sex can also be considered an expression of *love*. When people are asked why they have sex with their partner, the most frequently mentioned reason is love and affection (e.g., Christopher & Cate, 1984; M. L. Cooper et al., 1998). Therefore sex can be used as a way for intimate partners to express love, sometimes referred to as a "love act" (Buss, 1989a). Another important dimension of relationships is *interdependence*, and one way that partners can be interdependent is by spending time with each other having sex. Sex can also be considered to be an act of *maintenance*. Couples use various maintenance strategies to maintain their relationships, and one maintenance strategy is physical affection and sexual activity (e.g., Dainton, 1991). A final example of "sex as a component of higher-order constructs" is sex as an act of *exchange*. Dating partners exchange many resources in their relationship, including sex, love, money, and information (e.g., Cate, Lloyd, Henton, & Larson, 1982). As a result, complex trade-offs can occur by which sex is exchanged for other resources in the relationship (Sprecher, 1998).

Associations between Sex and Relationship Outcomes

Perhaps the most frequently studied issue about intimate relationships is what factors lead them to be satisfying and long-lasting. A strong positive association has been found between sexual satisfaction and general relationship quality. Although much of the research on this topic has focused on married couples, the positive association between sexual satisfaction and relationship quality has also been found in dating relationships among college students (see Byers, Demmons, & Lawrance, 1998; S. Davies, Katz, & Jackson, 1999; Sprecher, 2002). Sexual satisfaction is also found to be positively associated with other indicators of relationship quality, including love (Sprecher & Regan, 1998), commitment, and the likelihood that the relationship will last (Sprecher, 2002).

Because not all dating couples have sex, and among those who do there is considerable variation in the frequency, it is also important to examine how the incidence and quantity of sex are related to relationship outcomes, such as satisfaction and whether the relationship stays together or breaks up. Earlier we reported that Peplau et al. (1977), in their study of dating couples, found no association between level of sexual activity at Time 1 of their study with satisfaction and stability assessed two years later. However, Simpson (1987), in a three-month longitudinal study of students involved in dating relationships, found that couples who were sexually active at Time 1 were more likely to still be together at Time 2, even controlling for other variables such as length of relationship, satisfaction, and closeness. In another longitudinal study of university dating partners, Felmlee, Sprecher, and Bassin (1990) also found that level of sexual intimacy was a positive predictor of relationship stability, although in their study, the index of sexual intimacy did not remain a significant predictor once other variables were included in a multivariate analysis. Most of the research examining the association between sexual frequency and relationship outcomes has focused on married couples, and found a positive association (for a review, see Christopher & Sprecher, 2000). No research, to our knowledge, has examined how frequency of sex in college students is associated with overall relationship quality.

The causal order between sex (quality and quantity) and relationship outcomes can be in either direction. Having (frequent) sex and being satisfied with the sex can lead partners to become happy with their overall relationship (conversely, problems with sex can lead to a decrease in overall relationship quality). In addition, the overall quality of the relationship can affect the couple's desire to have sex and the likelihood that they are happy with the sex.

Whichever the direction of causality, sex is linked with how our relationships turn out. This brings to a close our examination of sex in the development of relationships. Let us recap some main points and then address one last issue: Why is considering the interpersonal context of sex very important?

SUMMARY

So far, this chapter has consisted of five main sections. In a first main section, we traced the history of premarital sexual standards in the United States. Since the 1950s what Americans have considered acceptable sexual behavior has shifted from two earlier standards (abstinence and a double standard sanctioning sex for men but not for women) to two contemporary standards (sex in the context of affectionate relationships and sex without affection, e.g., hookups). Along with this, the prevalence of sexual behavior increased at least until the 1980s. Today, most students are sexually active.

In a second section, we examined how partners' sexual attitudes and prior sexual experience influenced how attracted potential partners are to one another. When asked about the importance of various characteristics in a potential dating partner, neither chastity nor extensive sexual experience is considered very important, according to recent research. Nonetheless, in experimental studies of attraction, potential partners with less sexual experience were somewhat preferred. This is especially true when seeking a partner for a long-term relationship. There is also evidence that individuals seek partners with sexual histories similar to their own.

In a third section, we looked at casual sex and the development of relationships. Hookups, friendships with benefits, and booty calls all have become part of today's college life. Although hookups may be only brief interactions, they occur in the context of participants' network of relationships and are influenced by relational factors. People, especially women, entering hookups often are seeking to forge a romantic relationship although this outcome is rare.

In a fourth section, we discussed the timing of introducing sex in developing relationships and the strategies partners use. Some couples engage in sexual intercourse in the early stages of their relationship before establishing strong emotional bonds; others become sexually involved after romantic bonds have been established; and still others refrain from coitus even after romantic ties exist. Couples who delay intense sexual involvement until they achieved a degree of emotional intimacy generally have better outcomes. Students often use nonverbal and indirect strategies to initiate sex but use more direct, verbal strategies to refuse it. Partners generally respond positively to their partner's efforts to initiate sexual behaviors.

In a fifth section, we looked at how sex and other aspects of relationships are related. We argued that sex involves self-disclosure, intimacy, love, interdependence, relational maintenance, and exchange. Thus sex is a facet of several of the defining characteristics of close relationships. We also noted that sexual satisfaction is strongly related to general relationship quality.

LEVELS OF EXPLANATION

In each section of this chapter, we have focused on the interpersonal aspects of college students' sexual attitudes and behaviors. College students' sexuality can, however, be explained at various levels: the individual, the factors beyond the couple themselves (e.g., environmental forces, macrolevel influences at the institutional or national/societal level), or in between at the interpersonal level (involving the actor and the actor's partner or other key people). As is true with virtually all social behavior, no one factor is likely to perfectly predict sexual attitudes and activities. Instead, multiple factors from all three domains are likely to combine together in either an additive or more complex fashion to determine what people do.

The Individual Level

Individual approaches for explaining people's premarital sexual standards look at how properties of the individual influence that person's sexuality. They focus on personality traits as well as characteristics of the individual including their physical attributes, their moral values, and the like. The famous British psychologist Hans Eysenck (1976) was a leading earlier exponent of this viewpoint. One of Eysenck's cogent arguments for using an individual-difference approach to predict sexual behavior is rather simple. Eysenck pointed out that many sex researchers such as Kinsey have tried to provide descriptive statistics for entire groups. For instance, Kinsey reported the average number of times per week that Americans have sexual intercourse (1.67 and 1.7 times per week among males and females age 18–24 according to Laumann et al.'s [1994] more recent data). However, Eysenck maintains that such statistical averages are virtually meaningless. The variability hidden by these means is so great that averages tell little, if anything. One person may have intercourse only two or three times a year, while another person may have intercourse two or three times a day. Eysenck concluded that sex researchers should examine these individual differences in behavior. He also contended that one of the best ways to account for the variability in people's sexual behavior is via personality traits. To verify his viewpoint, Eysenck surveyed German students. He found that *extroversion was associated with greater and more varied premarital sexual activity* (i.e., being nonvirginal, having premarital sex more frequently, etc.).

In this same individual-difference tradition, Snyder, Simpson and Gangestad (1986) have looked at how self-monitoring intertwines with premarital sexuality. Self-monitoring has been defined as the self-observation and self-control of expressive behavior and self-presentation guided by situational cues to social appropriateness. Individuals high in self-monitoring scan their environment; they alter their behavior and self-presentation to fit the situation. Individuals low in self-monitoring attune to their own affective states and values; they tend to present themselves and behave consistently across situations. High self-monitors have a less committed orientation in their dating relationships: they have shorter relationships, have dated more partners over their lifetimes, and have more desire to form relationships other than their current partner. Given these differences in their approaches to intimate relationships, Snyder et al. argued that high versus low self-monitoring college students would manifest differences in their sexuality. As expected, students high in self-monitoring had a less restrictive view of sex than students low in self-monitoring. In particular, students high in self-monitoring

- Had more accepting attitudes toward casual sex
- Had more frequent fantasies of sex with other partners
- Had a larger pool of current admissible partners
- Envisioned having a larger number of partners in the future
- Reported a larger number of "one-night stands"
- Reported a larger number of partners in the past year
- Reported a larger number of lifetime partners.

In short, individual differences in self-monitoring were systematically related to students' sexuality.

The Societal Level

Other scholars emphasize how macro factors such as the culture in which we live influence sexuality. Reiss and Miller's (1979) autonomy theory of premarital sexual permissiveness was an early version of this viewpoint. Seeing tension between a courtship subculture that emphasizes the *rewards* of sexuality and a family subculture that stresses the *risks*, they argued

> To the extent young people are free from the constraints of the family and other adult-type institutions, they will be able to develop their own emphasis on sexuality. The physical and psychic pleasures connected to human sexuality are rewards basically to the participants and not to their parents. . . . Thus, the autonomy of young people is the key variable in determining how sexually permissive one will be. (p. 83)

Reiss and Miller believed this courtship autonomy was largely culturally determined.

The impact of culture can be seen in cross-national studies (Widmer, Treas, & Newcomb, 1998). Sexual attitudes vary dramatically depending on one's culture: for example in Widmer et al.'s survey, 11 percent of Swedes and 59 percent of Americans versus 89 percent of people in the Philippines believed having premarital sex is wrong.

The Importance of the Interpersonal Level

Although we consider factors at the individual and societal levels to be useful in explaining students' sexuality, why do we give special attention to the interpersonal level? A basic reason is that much of students' sexual activity occurs with a partner. As we have already seen, in our society the interpersonal relationship between those partners is considered by many to be crucial in determining what sexual behaviors are acceptable. Romantic partners often try to actively influence one another, and every dyad, as a dyad, has properties of its own, develops a unique pattern of behavior, and has a history.

In essence, a dyad is different from the sum of its parts. For one thing, there are phenomena and processes such as interpersonal power and influence that occur only at the interpersonal level. Even if partners' behaviors are simply the average of the way the two individuals behave, each person may act differently in a relationship than they would by themselves. And, the behavior of a couple may not always be the average of what the partners bring to the relationship.

To illustrate these ideas, consider a virginal male named John who can form an emotionally intimate, new relationship with sexually inexperienced Mary, with sexually experienced Sally, or with Jake. If dyadic considerations made no difference, John would not be likely to engage in sexual intercourse with his new partner regardless of the new partner's previous sexual experiences. Furthermore, if averaging is all that mattered, the couples consisting of one virgin and one experienced partner should each have the same likelihood (50%) of engaging in intercourse regardless of which partner was sexually experienced. However, as available evidence clearly demonstrates, neither individual determination nor averaging necessarily operates in this circumstance. In Peplau et al.'s (1977) classic study of seriously dating couples, what they found was as follows. Every virginal male in the study began engaging in coitus if he dated a sexually experienced female for some period of time. None persisted in their previous behavior of being abstinent. The same was not true for every virginal female who partnered with a sexually experienced male. Only two-thirds of virginal females began engaging in coitus. The other third did persist in being abstinent. So whether it was the male or the female who was experienced mattered in predicting the probability of the couple's sexual activities; a simple averaging did not occur. Peplau et al. interpreted their findings from a role perspective, claiming that men initiate sex and women limit it. Their overall pattern of results suggests that in this domain, women's preferences matter more—women are the party with the greatest power. In any case, these and other similar results testify to the importance of how the interplay of the two partners in a relationship shapes what the couple does.

From a scholarly perspective, the dyadic perspective is important because it opens up new questions about sexuality that can be researched (see Perlman & Campbell, 2004). For example in this chapter we have discussed research on how past sexual histories influence to whom we are attracted and how partners go about requesting and refusing sex.

A final reason that the dyadic level of analysis is important is because sex is literally a life-and-death matter. Sex is essential for the perpetuation of the species, and as Reiss and Miller (1979) imply, it can be one of life's great pleasures (cf. Pinkerton et al., 2003). Unfortunately, however, there is also a dark side to sexuality: sexual dysfunction and discomfort, jealousy, sexual coercion and abuse (Spitzberg, 1998), sexually transmitted diseases (e.g., chlamydia, genital warts, genital herpes; see Weinstock, Berman, & Cates, 2004), unplanned pregnancies, etc. These life-and-death aspects of sexuality involve the interaction of two people.

Other levels contribute to the positive and negative aspects of sex, too. Nonetheless, the dyadic level adds a piece that others do not. Let us briefly consider just one example, use of contraceptives. Contraceptives can serve two important functions: to avoid unplanned pregnancies and to prevent the spread of sexually transmitted diseases. Two examples will suffice as a demonstration of how relationships intertwine with contraceptive practices. First, in a study of adolescents engaging in sexual intercourse for the first time in their lives, 52 percent of those who "just met" their partner used *no method* of birth control compared to 24 percent of those "going steady" (Manning, Longmore, & Giordano, 2000). Second, in a sample of young adults aged 17–22, Ku, Sonenstein, and Pleck (1994) advanced and found support for the "sawtooth hypothesis." According to that hypothesis, within each relationship condom use tends to be frequent at the beginning and then decline but increases again when a new relationship is begun (albeit condom use at first intercourse with a new partner declined some with age). As relationships progress, the use of other forms of birth control increased. When asked their reason for using condoms, the participants in this study voiced concern about pregnancy much more frequently than they mentioned protection against disease.

In sum, we have noted that individual and societal factors, as well as interpersonal ones, influence college students' sexual behavior. We appreciate that it is worthwhile to consider the complex intersection of casual factors in multiple sources, as explanations of diverse aspects of sexuality. Nonetheless, in this chapter we have featured the ways college students' sexuality is influenced by the students' personal relationships, especially their relationships with their sexual partners. We have offered various reasons why this level of analysis is especially important:

- Much of students' sexual activity occurs with a partner.
- Partners influence one another.
- A dyad is different from the sum of its parts so considering interpersonal factors opens additional questions for sex researchers.
- Aspects of our interpersonal relationships have an impact not made by other factors on the important positive and negative life outcomes associated with our sexuality.

As with many sexual behaviors, books are ultimately an interpersonal endeavor between author and reader. In our relationship with you, we hope you are better informed and that in some small way this chapter helps you to have more fulfilling and satisfying sexual relationships. All best wishes.

Chapter Six

LOVE, COLLEGE STYLE

Pamela C. Regan

By the time most men and women finish their first year of college, they have fallen in love at least once and have experienced their first "serious" romantic relationship (Regan, Durvasula, Howell, Ureño, & Rea, 2004). Indeed, most college-age adults believe that forming a successful love-based relationship is essential for their personal happiness, view love as an essential ingredient in marriage, and will not consider forming a long-term relationship with someone they do not love. For example, over 40 years ago, Kephart (1967) asked more than a thousand U.S. college students the following question: "If a boy (girl) had all the other qualities you desired, would you marry this person if you were not in love with him (her)?" More than one-third (35%) of the men and three-fourths (76%) of the women responded affirmatively and said they were willing to marry without love. However, by the mid-1980s there was evidence of a dramatic shift in attitude—one that continues to characterize college students today. When Simpson, Campbell, and Berscheid (1986) asked a group of university students the very same question, only 14 percent of the men and 20 percent of the women indicated that they would marry someone they did not love if he or she were "perfect" in every other respect. Similar results have been reported in more recent investigations, with researchers finding even lower percentages of young adults in college samples willing to consider marriage without love (e.g., Allgeier & Wiederman, 1991;

R. Levine et al., 1995). For example, only about 10 percent of the 1,043 college students in Sprecher et al.'s (1994) survey responded affirmatively to Kephart's (1967) question; that is, 90 percent steadfastly refused to consider marrying someone with whom they were not in love. Love—and the relationships it produces and fosters—clearly plays a significant role in the lives of college students.

This chapter explores the love experiences of college-age men and women. We begin by exploring college students' attitudes and beliefs about love and romance. Next, we discuss the attributes that college students seek in their potential love partners (along with the partner characteristics they hope to avoid). We then consider the different types of love that young adults can experience. Finally, we examine the dark side of college love, with a focus on unrequited love and obsession.

WHAT DO COLLEGE STUDENTS BELIEVE ABOUT LOVE?

A number of specific love-related beliefs have been examined by relationship researchers over the past several decades. Some researchers have focused on beliefs about the association between love and sexual activity. Others have examined the ideology of romance, which includes such idealistic beliefs as love at first sight and the notion of a "soul mate" or "one true love." Still other scholars have attempted to delineate young adults' mental models of love. In this part of the chapter, we consider these three areas of research.

College Students' Beliefs about Love and Sex

> Well, I can't speak for anyone else, but for me, the only way I'd have sex with someone was if we were deeply in love. If two people are in love, then sex seems like a natural way to express those feelings. (19-year-old female university student interviewed by the author)
>
> The decision to have sex is a personal choice that everyone should be free to make. Some people have sex just because they enjoy it, or because they have the chance to do it. That's fine; it's a personal decision. Other people, and I'm one of them, think that sex is best when it's done out of love, with someone you're involved with. (20-year-old male university student interviewed by the author)

As the quotations above illustrate, many college students view love and sex as intimately connected. In fact, attitude surveys conducted around the United States reveal that the majority of young adults feel that sexual activity is most appropriate when it occurs between two people who are involved in a loving, committed relationship. In one of the first empirical investigations of sexual standards, Reiss (1964) reported that students from five high schools and colleges (and adults from a national probability sample of the U.S. population) were increasingly more accepting of premarital sexual intercourse between two people as their relationship became characterized by correspondingly greater amounts of affection and commitment. For example, as the relationship progressed from relatively little affection to strong affection, and then to love and engagement, people believed that intercourse was more acceptable. Similarly, the majority (80%) of the college students in Peplau et al.'s classic (1977) study indicated that it was "completely acceptable" for couples who love each other to engage in sexual intercourse, whereas only 20 percent found sexual intercourse with a casual acquaintance to be completely acceptable. More recently, Roche and Ramsbey (1993) asked a large sample of undergraduates to indicate how appropriate they thought sexual intercourse would be between partners at five different stages of dating. The results of their survey revealed that sexual intercourse was viewed as increasingly acceptable as the partners moved from dating with no particular affection (Stage 1, endorsed as acceptable by fewer than 1% of college students), to dating with affection but not love (Stage 2, endorsed by only 5%), to dating and being in love (Stage 3, considered acceptable by 22%), to dating each other only and being in love (Stage 4, endorsed by 56%), and finally to engagement (Stage 5, viewed as acceptable by 69% of students).

Cross-sectional research reveals that U.S. college students are becoming more sexually permissive (for a review, see Willetts, Sprecher, & Beck, 2004). In particular, although young men and women continue to view sex as most appropriate when it occurs between committed relational partners, there is a trend toward greater acceptance of sexual activity in casual dating relationships. Sherwin and Corbett (1985), for example, examined normative expectations about sexual activity in various types of dating relationships on a college campus. Three groups of students—the first surveyed in 1963, the second in 1971, and the third in 1978—were asked to indicate the extent to which various sexual activities generally were expected to play a part in the relationship between casually dating, steadily dating, and engaged couples. The results provided evidence for increasingly liberal campus sexual norms among both men and women over the 15-year period. For example, none of the men and women in the 1963 sample expected sexual intercourse to occur in a casual dating relationship; by 1978, however, 17 percent of the men and 9 percent of the women viewed intercourse as a normal part of casual dating.

A more recent investigation by Wells and Twenge (2005) confirmed these results. These researchers first identified 45 individual research studies conducted in the United States between the years 1955 and 1989 that had examined attitudes toward premarital sex. Next, for each study they gathered information on the year of data collection and the participants' average attitude score. Finally, in order to determine whether attitudes toward premarital sex had changed over time in U.S. society, Wells and Twenge calculated the correlation between average attitude scores and years of data collection. The results clearly revealed that attitudes toward premarital sex had become considerably more permissive over time. Specifically, only 12 percent of young women surveyed during the mid-to-late 1950s (1955–59) approved of premarital sex. By the mid-1980s, however, 73 percent of women approved of premarital sexual intercourse. Young men displayed a similar shift in attitude over time; 40 percent of men surveyed in the 1950s approved of premarital sex compared to 79 percent of men surveyed in the 1980s.

In sum, although there is evidence that intercourse is becoming an increasingly accepted part of casual dating relationships, young adults today continue to associate love with sexuality and to view sexual activity as most appropriate when it occurs in the context of a committed, love-based relationship.

The Romantic Ideology of College Students

By the time they reach college, men and women have developed a vast array of (not necessarily accurate) beliefs, expectations, values, attitudes, and assumptions about love and romance from their own previous relationship experiences as well as from observing the relationships of their peers, family members, and others in society. One of these assumptions concerns the association between love and marriage. As we discussed earlier in the chapter, most college students strongly subscribe to the notion that love is an essential prerequisite for marriage. Other romantic beliefs include the idea that love strikes without warning and often at first sight, the belief that there exists only one true love for each person (a "soul mate"), the idea that true love endures forever, and the notion that love can conquer all obstacles. The most thorough measure of *romanticism* was created by Sprecher and Metts (1989), who drew on previous measurement instruments and theoretical statements about romantic ideology in crafting the Romantic Beliefs Scale. The Romantic Beliefs Scale contains items that reflect the essential tenets of romantic ideology:

- *Love Finds a Way*: "If a relationship I have was meant to be, any obstacle can be overcome." "I believe if another person and I love each other we can overcome any differences or problems that may arise."
- *Love at First Sight*: "I am likely to fall in love almost immediately if I meet the right person." "When I find my 'true love' I will probably know it soon after we meet."
- *One and Only ("Soul Mate")*: "There will be only one real love for me." "Once I experience 'true love,' I could never experience it again, to the same degree, with another person."

- *Idealization*: "The relationship I will have with my 'true love' will be nearly perfect." "The person I love will make a perfect romantic partner; for example, he/she will be completely accepting, loving, and understanding."

At least two variables—sex and age—are associated with romantic beliefs. For example, college-age men generally score higher on the Romantic Beliefs Scale than do their female counterparts (e.g., Sprecher & Metts, 1989, 1999; Weaver & Ganong, 2004). There also appear to be age differences in romantic beliefs, with younger students more likely to subscribe to an idealized vision of love and romance than older students. For example, Knox, Schacht, and Zusman (1999) surveyed a large sample of university undergraduates about several specific romantic beliefs. Their results revealed that younger students (19 years of age or younger) were more likely than were older students (20 years of age or older) to believe that "you can fall in love the first time you see someone" (54% vs. 36%) and to agree that "all problems can be solved if there is enough love" (61% vs. 43%). A similar age difference was reported more recently by another group of researchers (Medora, Larson, Hortaçsu, & Dave, 2002).

Idealized romantic beliefs are associated with several aspects of relationship quality, including (not surprisingly) feelings of love for the partner. Men and women students who strongly endorse the romantic ideal generally report higher levels of passionate love and liking for their partners than do their less romantic counterparts, and they tend to fall in love with their partners at an earlier stage in their relationships (Sprecher & Metts, 1989). Moreover, highly romantic students think about the relationship more during a partner's absence (Cate, Koval, Lloyd, & Wilson, 1995) and express higher amounts of satisfaction with and commitment to the partner and the relationship (Sprecher & Metts, 1999; Weaver & Ganong, 2004; but see Metts, 2004). Young adults who subscribe to a generalized romantic ideal may be more likely to feel passion, more eager to commit, and more inclined to view their partners and their relationships in a positive light than are less overtly romantic men and women.

College Students' Mental Models of Love

In addition to exploring specific beliefs about love and romance—such as whether love and sex (or love and marriage) "go together," whether love can truly "conquer all," and so forth—relationship researchers have also investigated young adults' mental representations or mental models of the concept of love. This research typically utilizes a *prototype approach*, which is specifically designed to capture what people think of when they are asked about love, how they differentiate love from related concepts (e.g., liking), how they form their conceptualizations of love, and how these conceptualizations or mental representations influence their behavior with relational partners.

The Hierarchy of Love

According to Rosch (e.g., 1973, 1975, 1978), an early pioneer in the use of prototype analysis, natural language concepts (e.g., love, dog, apple) can be viewed as having both a vertical and a horizontal dimension. The former concerns the hierarchical organization of concepts or relations among different levels of concepts. Concepts at one level may be included within or subsumed by those at a higher level. For example, the set of concepts fruit, apple, and Red Delicious illustrate an abstract-to-concrete hierarchy with superordinate, basic, and subordinate levels.

Using the methods originally developed by Rosch, some researchers have investigated the hierarchical structure of the natural language concept of love. Shaver and colleagues (Shaver, Schwartz, Kirson, & O'Connor, 1987), for instance, found evidence that *love* is a basic level concept contained within the superordinate category of *emotion* and subsuming a variety of subordinate concepts that reflect types or varieties of love (e.g., *passion*, *infatuation*, *liking*) (see Figure 6.1). That is, most college students consider passion, infatuation, and liking to be types of love, which in turn is viewed as a type of positive emotion.

The Prototype of Love

Concepts like love also may be examined along a horizontal dimension. This dimension concerns the differentiation of concepts at the same level of inclusiveness (e.g., the dimension on which such subordinate level concepts as Red Delicious, Fuji, and Granny Smith apples vary). According to Rosch, many natural language concepts have an internal structure whereby individual members of that category are ordered in terms of the degree to which they resemble the prototypic member of the category. A *prototype* is the best and clearest example of the concept (the most apple-like apple [e.g., Red Delicious]). Individuals use prototypes to help them decide whether a new item or experience belongs or "fits" within a particular concept. For example, in trying to decide whether or not he is in love with his girlfriend, a college student might compare the *feelings* ("I'm happy when she's here and I'm sad when she's not"), *thoughts* ("I think about her all the time"; "I wonder what it would be like to be married to her"), and *behaviors* ("I arranged my class schedule so that we can spend time together") he has experienced during their relationship with his prototype—his mental model—of "being in love" ("People who are in love miss each other when they're apart, think about each other constantly, imagine a future life together, and spend a lot of time with each other"). If what the student is experiencing "matches" his prototype, he is likely to conclude that he is, in fact, in love with his girlfriend.

The prototype approach has been used to explore the horizontal structure of a variety of relational concepts, including love. Fehr and Russell (1991), for example, asked a sample of university students to generate as many types of love as they could in a specified time and then asked another group of students to rate these love varieties in terms of prototypicality or "goodness-of-

Figure 6.1. The Hierarchy of Love and Other Emotions. Research conducted by Shaver, Fehr, and their colleagues (Fehr & Russell, 1991; Fischer, Shaver, & Carnochan, 1990; Shaver, Schwartz, Kirson, & O'Connor, 1987) suggests that young adults conceptualize love as a basic level concept contained within the superordinate category of emotion. In addition, young adults view love as containing a variety of subordinate concepts that reflect types or varieties of love; of these, maternal love is viewed as the most prototypical variety.

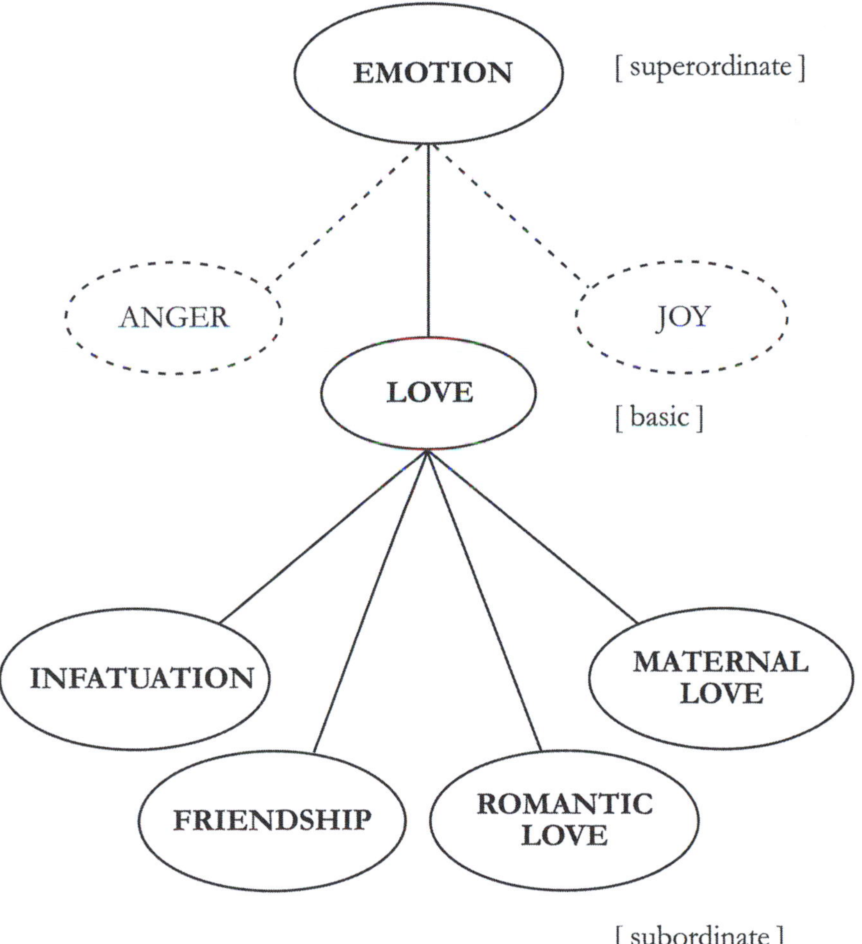

example." Of the 93 subtypes generated, students rated *maternal love* as the best or most prototypical example of love, followed by *parental love*, *friendship*, *sisterly love*, *romantic love*, *brotherly love*, and *familial love*. Students considered *infatuation*, along with *puppy love*, *patriotic love*, and *love of work*, to be the least prototypical examples of love. Similar results were reported by Fehr (1994) in a more recent investigation.

Researchers also have identified college students' beliefs about the prototypic features (as opposed to types) of love. For example, in an earlier demonstration, Fehr (1988) asked one group of undergraduates to list the characteristics of the concept of *love* and a second group to rate how central each feature was to the concept of love. Features that her participants believed were central or prototypical to love included *trust*, *caring*, *honesty*, *friendship*, *respect*, *concern for the other's well-being*, *loyalty*, and *commitment*. Features that were considered peripheral or unimportant to the concept of love included *see only the other's good qualities*, *butterflies in stomach*, *uncertainty*, *dependency*, and *scary*.

In sum, research on beliefs about love and romance indicates that most college students continue to view love and sexuality as intimately connected, consider love to be a necessary prerequisite for marriage, are at least moderately "romantic" (though become less so over time), and conceptualize love as a positive emotion that is distinct from other emotions, that can take on many forms, and that possesses several essential features.

WHAT ATTRIBUTES DO COLLEGE STUDENTS SEEK IN A LOVE PARTNER?

The literature on *mate preferences*—the characteristics that men and women consider important and desirable in their potential romantic partners—is enormous and encompasses a large number of empirical studies. These studies generally indicate that young adults overwhelmingly prefer romantic partners who possess intelligence, emotional stability, warmth and expressiveness, an honest and trustworthy disposition, an exciting overall personality, and a physically attractive appearance. In two of the first documented examinations of mate preference, both conducted during the late 1930s and early 1940s, Christensen (1947) and Hill (1945) asked students at their respective universities to rank order a list of characteristics in terms of their importance in a romantic partner. The two most important attributes, according to both samples of students, were "dependable character" and "emotional stability." Men and women also emphasized a "pleasing disposition" and "mutual attraction or love." Other researchers have since replicated these results using the same or very similar lists of features (e.g., Hudson & Henze, 1969; McGinnis, 1958; Regan & Berscheid, 1997). Table 6.1 illustrates these findings.

Table 6.1
The Stability of College Students' Mate Preferences over Time

	Rank Order					
	Men			Women		
Characteristic	**1945**	**1958**	**1969**	**1945**	**1958**	**1969**
Dependable character	1	1	1	2	1	2
Emotional stability	2	2	3	1	2	1
Pleasing disposition	3	4	4	4	5	4
Mutual attraction	4	3	2	5	6	3
Good health	5	6	9	6	9	10
Desire for home/children	6	5	5	7	3	5
Refinement/neatness	7	8	7	8	7	8
Good cook/housekeeper	8	7	6	16	16	16
Ambition/industriousness	9	9	8	3	4	6
Chastity	10	13	15	10	15	15
Education/intelligence	11	11	10	9	14	7
Sociability	12	12	12	11	11	13
Similar religious background	13	10	14	14	10	11
Good looks	14	15	11	17	18	17
Similar educational background	15	14	13	12	8	9
Favorable social status	16	16	16	15	13	14
Good financial prospect	17	17	18	13	12	12
Similar political background	18	18	17	18	17	18

Note: Mate preferences among U.S. college students have remained fairly constant over time. Most young men and women emphasize positive personality attributes and mutual attraction when considering someone for a long-term romantic or marital relationship. Data from R. Hill (1945) and Hudson and Henze (1969).

More recently, Regan and colleagues (Regan, Levin, Sprecher, Christopher, & Cate, 2000) asked a large sample of college students (close to 600) to indicate their preferences for a wide variety of characteristics. Both sexes reported desiring a long-term romantic partner who possessed a great deal of the following attributes, in order of importance:

1. *Prosocial personality attributes.* First and foremost, participants desired a mate who possessed prosocial personality attributes related to interpersonal responsiveness. Men and women emphasized the importance of a good sense of humor and an exciting personality, and they sought someone who was expressive and open, and who had a friendly and sociable disposition.
2. *Characteristics related to intellect and mental drive.* Only slightly less important were characteristics related to intellect and mental drive. Both men and women sought a partner who was intellectually gifted and driven—who possessed intelligence, who was educated, and who was ambitious.

3. *Physically appealing attributes.* Although considered less important than the first two attribute categories, participants also desired a mate who was physically appealing. Both men and women emphasized a physically attractive, athletic, sexy, and healthy appearance when indicating what they hoped to find in a long-term romantic partner.
4. *Similarity.* In addition, similarity—on demographic characteristics, values and attitudes, and interests and hobbies—was considered relatively important by the participants.
5. *Characteristics related to social status.* The least important (but still moderately desired) partner attributes were those related to social status and economic, financial, or material resources. Specifically, participants preferred a partner who was above average with respect to earning potential, who possessed at least moderate social status, and who had access to material possessions.

Men and women not only tend to prefer the same set of features when considering a potential mate, but they appear to possess similar aversions. Research on undesirable partner attributes conducted by Cunningham et al. (1996; also see Ault & Philhower, 2001; Cunningham, Druen, & Barbee, 1997; Cunningham, Shamblen, Barbee, & Ault, 2005) reveals that college-age men and women are equally repulsed by dates who consistently violate social norms and rules of conduct, including drinking to excess, cheating at games, gossiping about others, arriving late all the time, and lying. In addition, they seek to avoid selecting a partner who is oversexed —who brags about sexual conquests or skills, constantly talks about or mentions previous relationship partners, or gazes longingly at other men or women. They also seek to avoid dating individuals who display bad habits or uncouth behavior such as poor hygiene, inappropriate table manners, a loud speaking voice, or a shrill laugh. A more complete list of these undesirable partner attributes, called *social allergens* by the researchers, is provided in Table 6.2.

Table 6.2
Social Allergens: What College Students Seek to Avoid in a Romantic Partner

Dimension 1: Someone who uses his or her appearance to get attention
For example:
– dresses in a provocative, seductive manner
– uses a lot of cologne or perfume
– takes a long time to get ready to go out
– is overly concerned with the way he or she looks
– always wears “designer” clothing
– dyes his or her hair
– has had cosmetic surgery to change the way he or she looks (a nose job, breast implants, liposuction)

Table 6.2 (Continued)

Dimension 2: Someone who is intrusive
For example:
– is competitive with you (at work, in leisure activities, etc.)
– demands that you serve him or her in front of others ("Get me some water")
– comments about your driving
– is a know-it-all
– has to pay your way all the time
– insists on helping you when you have not asked for assistance
– likes to speak in baby-talk to you
– tries to control how you act in public

Dimension 3: Someone who is insensitive
For example:
– puts his or her feet on the furniture
– asks embarrassing personal questions
– leaves his or her things everywhere
– asks for your advice but doesn't follow it
– complains constantly about personal problems
– honks the horn instead of coming to the door
– frequently asks for help or emotional support
– tries to get out of paying his or her own way

Dimension 4: Someone who has bad habits
– has poor table manners
– has a shrill laugh or talks in a loud voice
– has bad breath
– gets really upset over minor problems
– stands too close or stares inappropriately
– is careless with your things
– constantly plays on the computer

Dimension 5: Someone who is profane or "punk-like"
For example:
– uses a lot of profanity
– has a lot of body piercings (studs in eyebrows, nose, tongue, nipples, etc.)
– has two or more tattoos

Dimension 6: Someone who is oversexed
For example:
– looks longingly at other men or women while out with you
– brags about his or her sexual conquests or skills
– constantly talks about past relationship partners
– has had a lot of previous relationships
– acts "hard to get"

Dimension 7: Someone who violates social norms (rules of conduct)
For example:
– drinks too much alcohol
– gambles frequently

(Continued)

Table 6.2 (Continued)

– is a risky or unsafe driver
– cheats at games
– arrives late all the time
– is often angry
– smokes
– gossips about other people
– never helps out around the house
– lies to people

Note: Cunningham and his colleagues (e.g., 1996) have identified a number of attributes that college students find particularly repellant in a potential date, organized in the table from least (uses appearance) to most (violates social norms) repellant. Data from Cunningham, Barbee, and Druen (1996) and Rowatt et al. (1997).

In sum, the existing research indicates that most college students are attracted to a potential partner who not only fulfills their desires but who also manages to avoid doing the things that repulse or annoy them.

WHAT TYPES OF LOVE DO COLLEGE STUDENTS EXPERIENCE?

Many relationship scholars have attempted to understand the various forms that love relationships can take and the different varieties of love that people can experience. Two of the more common classification systems were developed by Sternberg (e.g., 1986, 1998) and Lee (e.g., 1973, 1988). Each of these systems can be used to understand the love relationships that young men and women establish during their college years.

The Triangular Theory of Love

Sternberg (e.g., 1986, 1998, 2006) conceptualized love in terms of three basic components that form the vertices of a triangle: intimacy, passion, and decision/commitment. In addition, he developed a 45-item scale to assess these three basic elements (1997, 1998).

The Basic Components of Love

The *intimacy* component is primarily emotional or affective in nature and involves feelings of warmth, closeness, connection, and bondedness in the love relationship. Examples of items that assess this component of love include "I feel close to _____," "I feel that I can really trust _____," "I feel that I really understand _____," "I have a warm relationship with _____," and "I share deeply personal information about myself with _____." The *passion* component of love is motivational and consists of the drives that are involved in romantic and physical attraction, sexual consummation, and related phenomena. Items that capture these more intense, physical, and exciting elements of romantic relationships include "Just seeing _____ excites me," "I especially like physical contact with _____," "I find _____ to be very personally attractive," "I adore _____," and "I would rather be with _____ than with anyone else." The *decision/commitment* component is largely cognitive and represents both the short-term decision that one individual loves another and the longer-term commitment to maintain that love. Items that assess these feelings of stability, commitment, and permanence include "I view my commitment to _____ as a solid one," "I have confidence in the stability of my relationship with _____," "I plan to continue in my relationship with _____," "I am certain of my love for _____," and "I will always feel a strong responsibility for _____."

Types of Love Relationships

According to Sternberg's model, these three basic components of love combine to produce eight different love types, summarized in Table 6.3. *Nonlove* (no intimacy, passion, or decision/commitment) describes casual interactions that are characterized by the absence of all three love components. The majority of the personal relationships formed by college students can be defined as nonlove—casual associations with classmates, coworkers, or acquaintances that lack a great deal of depth or emotional connection. *Liking* (intimacy alone) relationships are also relatively common and essentially reflect friendship. These associations contain warmth, intimacy, closeness, and other positive emotional experiences but lack both passion and decision/commitment. *Infatuation* (passion alone) is an intense, "love at first sight" experience that is characterized by extreme attraction and arousal in the absence of any real emotional intimacy and decision/commitment. In *empty love* (decision/commitment alone) relationships, the partners are committed to each other and the relationship but lack an intimate emotional connection and passionate attraction. This type of love is often seen at the end of long-term relationships; for example, two best friends from high school who head off to different universities might wish to maintain their bond but find it difficult to do so as their lives move in separate directions and they form new relationships. *Romantic love* (intimacy + passion) consists of feelings of closeness and connection coupled with strong physical attraction. *Companionate love* (intimacy + decision/commitment) is essentially a long-term, stable, and committed friendship that is characterized by high amounts of emotional intimacy, the decision to love the partner, and the commitment to remain in the relationship. This type of love is often seen in "best friendships" that are nonsexual or in long-term romantic relationships in which sexual attraction has faded. Couples who experience *fatuous love* (passion + decision/commitment) base their commitment to each other on passion rather than deep emotional

Table 6.3
Sternberg's Typology of Love Relationships

	Love Component		
Kind of Love Relationship	**Intimacy**	**Passion**	**Decision/ Commitment**
Nonlove	Low	Low	Low
Liking	High	Low	Low
Infatuation	Low	High	Low
Empty Love	Low	Low	High
Romantic Love	High	High	Low
Companionate Love	High	Low	High
Fatuous Love	Low	High	High
Consummate Love	High	High	High

Note: According to Sternberg (e.g., 1986), the three basic components of love—intimacy, passion, and decision/commitment—combine to produce eight different types of love relationship. For example, infatuation-based relationships are characterized by relatively high levels of passion but relatively low levels of intimacy and commitment, whereas companionate love relationships demonstrate the opposite pattern (i.e., high levels of intimacy and commitment coupled with low levels of passion).

intimacy. These "whirlwind" relationships are typically unstable and at risk for termination, but might be quite common among students in their early college years. Finally, *consummate love* (intimacy + passion + decision/commitment) results from the combination of all three components. According to Sternberg, this is the type of "complete" love many men and women strive to attain, particularly in their romantic relationships.

Because the three basic components of love occur in varying degrees within a relationship, the love relationships of most college students will not fit cleanly into one particular category but will reflect some combination of categories.

The Styles (Colors) of Love

Another contemporary theory of love that can be applied to the experiences of college students is the typology developed by Lee (e.g., 1977, 1988). In this novel approach, each variety of love is likened to a primary or secondary color (hence the title of Lee's [1973] book, *Colours of Love*). Lee's theory has produced a widely used measurement instrument, called the Love Attitudes Scale (C. Hendrick & Hendrick, 1990), which has been administered to numerous student samples over the years. This instrument has provided a great deal of information about the love experiences of young adults.

Primary and Secondary Love Styles

According to Lee's theory, there are three primary colors or styles of loving that college students can feel. The first, *eros*, is an intensely emotional experience that is similar to passionate love. In fact, the most typical symptom of eros is an immediate and powerful attraction to the beloved individual. A college student who loves erotically is "turned on" by a particular physical type, is prone to fall instantly and completely in love with a stranger (that is, experiences "love at first sight"), rapidly becomes preoccupied with pleasant thoughts about that individual, feels an intense need for daily contact with the beloved, and wishes the relationship to remain exclusive. Erotic love also has a strong sexual component; according to Lee, the typical erotic lover is "eager to get to know the beloved quickly, intensely—and undressed" (1988, p. 50). For example, not only does erotic love begin with a strong physical attraction, but the erotic lover usually seeks some form of sexual involvement fairly early in the relationship and enjoys expressing his or her affection through sexual contact. Items from the Love Attitudes Scale that assess this love style include:

- My partner and I were attracted to each other immediately after we first met.
- My partner and I have the right physical "chemistry" between us.
- I feel that my partner and I were meant for each other.

The second primary color or style of love is *ludus* (or game-playing) love. The ludic lover views love as an entertaining game—one that is to be played with skill and often with several partners simultaneously. The typical ludic lover has no intention of including the current partner (or partners) in any future life plans or events, and dislikes any sign of growing involvement, need, or attachment from the partner. At heart a commitment-phobe, the ludic college student avoids seeing the partner too often, believes that lies and deception are justified, and expects the partner to remain in control of his or her emotions. In addition, ludic lovers tend to prefer a wide variety of physical types and view sexual activity as an opportunity for pleasure rather than for intense emotional bonding. Items that capture this love style include:

- I try to keep my partner a little uncertain about my commitment to him/her.
- I believe that what my partner does not know about me will not hurt him/her.
- When my partner gets too dependent on me, I want to back off a little.

Storge is the third primary love style. Described by Lee (1973) as "love without fever or folly" (p. 77), storge resembles Lewis's concept of affection in that it is stable and based on a solid foundation of trust, respect, and friendship. A young adult adopting this approach views and treats the partner as an "old friend," does not experience the intense emotions or physical attraction to the partner associated with erotic love, prefers to talk about and engage in shared interests with the partner rather than to express direct feelings, is shy about sex, and tends to demonstrate his or her affection in nonsexual ways.

Sample items from the Love Attitudes Scale that reflect this love style include:

- It is hard for me to say exactly when our friendship turned into love.
- I expect to always be friends with my partner.
- Our love is really a deep friendship, not a mysterious mystical emotion.

Like the primary colors, these primary love styles can be combined to form secondary colors or styles of love. The three secondary styles identified by Lee contain features of the primaries but also possess their own unique characteristics. *Pragma*, a combination of storge and ludus, is "the love that goes shopping for a suitable mate" (Lee, 1973, p. 124). The pragmatic college student has a practical outlook to love and seeks a compatible partner. Over time, he or she develops a list of desired features or attributes and then selects a romantic partner based on how well that individual fulfills the requirements (similarly, he or she will drop a partner who fails to "measure up" to expectations). The following items measure this approach to love:

- I considered what my partner was going to become in life before I committed myself to him/her.
- I tried to plan my life carefully before choosing a partner.
- In choosing my partner, I believed it was best to love someone with a similar background.

Mania, the combination of eros and ludus, is another secondary love style that may characterize some college students. Manic lovers lack the self-confidence associated with eros and the emotional self-control associated with ludus. This obsessive, jealous love style is characterized by self-defeating emotions, desperate attempts to force affection from the beloved, and the inability to believe in or trust any affection the loved one actually does display. The manic lover is eager, even desperate, to fall in love and to be loved. He or she begins immediately to imagine a future with the partner, wants to see the partner daily, tries to force the partner to show love and commitment, distrusts the partner's sincerity, and is extremely possessive. According to Lee (1973), people with a manic approach to love are "irrational, extremely jealous, obsessive, and often unhappy" (p. 15), as can be seen in the following Love Attitudes Scale items:

- If my partner and I break up, I would get so depressed that I would even think of suicide.
- When my partner does not pay attention to me, I feel sick all over.
- Since I've been in love with my partner, I have had trouble concentrating on anything else.

The last secondary color of love is *agape*, a combination of eros and storge. Agape represents an all-giving, selfless love style that implies an obligation to love and care for others without any expectation of reciprocity or reward. This love style is universal or inclusive in the sense that the typical agapic lover feels that everyone is worthy of love and that loving others is a duty of the mature person. With respect to their own personal relationships, young adults who love in this manner will unselfishly devote themselves to the partner, even stepping aside in favor of a rival who seems more likely to meet the partner's needs (e.g., "He's really the better man for you, so even though we are happy and you mean everything to me, I love you too much to keep you—you should be with him."). Although Lee believed that many lovers respect and strive to attain the agapic ideal, he also believed that it was difficult to obtain in practice. That is, he felt that the give-and-take that characterizes most romantic relationships precludes the occurrence of purely altruistic love (although near-agapic experiences can and do occur). Items that purport to measure this love style include:

- I would rather suffer myself than let my partner suffer.
- I cannot be happy unless I place my partner's happiness before my own.
- When my partner gets angry with me, I still love him/her fully and unconditionally.

Research on Love Styles

Numerous empirical investigations using the Love Attitudes Scale have been conducted with young adult samples. These studies reveal three general findings. First, in accord with other research demonstrating *homogamy* (i.e., similarity or "like pairing with like") in mate selection, there is a tendency for individuals with similar love styles to end up together. That is, erotic lovers typically fall in love with other erotic lovers, storgic lovers form romantic relationships with other friendship-oriented lovers, agapic people pair with other equally selfless lovers, and so on (e.g., K. E. Davis & Latty-Mann, 1987; Morrow, Clark, & Brock, 1995).

Second, some love styles appear to be more strongly associated with relationship satisfaction than others. In particular, relationship satisfaction appears to be higher when partners possess an erotic, storgic, or agapic orientation to love, and—perhaps not surprisingly—relationship satisfaction seems to be lower when partners adopt a ludic love style (Fricker & Moore, 2002; S. S. Hendrick, Hendrick, & Adler, 1988; Meeks, Hendrick, & Hendrick, 1998).

Third, there appear to be several individual and group differences in love style. For example, although sexual orientation does not appear to be associated with love styles (for a review, see C. Hendrick & Hendrick, 2006), there are fairly robust sex differences. Researchers commonly find that women score higher on the love styles of storge and pragma than do men, whereas men score higher on ludus (e.g., Dion & Dion, 1993; C. Hendrick & Hendrick, 1988; C. Hendrick, Hendrick, Foote, & Slapion-Foote, 1984; C. Hendrick, Hendrick, & Dicke, 1998; S. S. Hendrick & Hendrick, 1987, 1995; Le, 2005; Rotenberg & Korol, 1995; Sprecher & Toro-Morn, 2002). In addition, a number of recent investigations report higher scores among men than among women on the agapic love style (S. S. Hendrick & Hendrick, 2002; Lacey, Reifman, Scott, Harris, & Fitzpatrick, 2004; Sprecher & Toro-Morn, 2002). There also are multicultural differences in love style. Within the United States, for example, Asian American students often score lower on eros and higher on pragma and storge than Caucasian, Latino, and African American students (e.g., Dion & Dion, 1993; C. Hendrick & Hendrick, 1986).

These differences notwithstanding, it is important to keep in mind that not all young adults possess one approach to love, and the emotional tenor of any given relationship does not necessarily remain fixed over time. A student who meets, dates, loves, and leaves several different partners over the course of his or her college years may find that his or her approach to love changes with each new partner. Alternately, a student's orientation to love may change during the course of one particular relationship. For example, the preoccupation and intense need associated with a manic love style may occur more often during the beginning stages of a romantic relationship, when the partners are uncertain as to their feelings and the future of their union. Later, these feelings may be replaced by more storgic or erotic feelings.

THE DARK SIDE OF COLLEGE LOVE

The love relationships that most men and women form during their college years provide them with an opportunity to express and experience happiness, satisfaction, commitment, passion, joy, warmth, and a host of other positive outcomes. But these same relationships can also serve as a potent source of emotional pain and psychological hurt. In this part of the chapter, we consider two distressing (and, unfortunately, increasingly common) love-related experiences: unrequited love and romantic obsession.

Unrequited Love: When a College Student Loves in Vain

The experience of loving another person typically is associated with a wonderful and rewarding mix of positive outcomes, events, and feelings. However, love—particularly when it is *unrequited* or not reciprocated by the beloved—has the potential to be just as strongly associated with negative outcomes. In fact, of all the forms of interpersonal rejection that people can experience, perhaps none is as acutely painful as romantic rejection.

In one of the first empirical investigations exploring the dynamics of unrequited love, Baumeister, Wotman, and Stillwell (1993) asked a sample of college students to provide written accounts of situations in which they had experienced nonmutual romantic attraction. Each participant wrote two autobiographical stories—one from the perspective of the *would-be lover* who was romantically attracted to an uninterested other and one from the perspective of the *rejector* who did not reciprocate another's romantic attraction. Analysis of these written accounts revealed that unrequited lovers experienced a host of both positive and negative emotions. Many (44%) would-be suitors reported that their unreciprocated passion caused them pain, suffering, and disappointment; jealousy and anger (which were usually directed at the loved ones' chosen partners); and a sense of frustration. Similarly, 22 percent experienced worries and fears about rejection. In addition to these unpleasant experiences, however, the lovelorn suitors also reported many pleasant emotional outcomes; in fact, positive feelings far outweighed negative ones in the accounts they gave of their experience. For example, happiness, excitement, the blissful anticipation of seeing the beloved, sheer elation at the state of being in love, and other positive emotions were reported by the majority (98%) of would-be suitors. More than half (53%) also looked back upon their unrequited love experiences with some degree of positive feeling. In explaining this finding, the researchers noted the following:

> Apparently, positive feelings can be remembered in a positive way even if the memory is linked to suffering and disappointment. People remember the warmth of their feelings for another person, and the memory is at least somewhat pleasant. Some of our participants expressed gladness at being able to preserve the friendship that could have been jeopardized if their romantic overtures had become too insistent. Others simply treasured the memory or retained a soft spot in their heart for the one they loved. (Baumeister & Wotman, 1992, p. 60)

When the researchers examined the experiences reported by the rejectors, however, they found little evidence of positive outcomes. Specifically, although roughly one-fourth (24%) of the rejectors reported feeling flattered by the attention of their admirers, the majority also viewed these unwanted advances as annoying (51%), felt uncomfortable about delivering rejection messages (61%), and experienced a host of negative emotions, including anger, frustration, and resentment (70%). In addition, their recollections of the entire experience were far less suffused with warmth, with only 33 percent indicating any positive affect in retrospect. The researchers concluded:

> Unlike the would-be lover, it was hard for the rejector to feel that his or her life had been enriched by this experience. For many, apparently, it was a useless and

> pointless set of aggravations. They were forced to respond to a situation they never wanted, and these responses were difficult for them, bringing uncertainty, guilt, aggravation, all of which went for naught. For some, a valued friendship was destroyed in the bargain. Thus they had plenty to resent and regret. (Baumeister & Wotman, 1992, p. 62)

Other researchers have reported similar findings (e.g., Sinclair & Frieze, 2005). Unrequited love clearly is an emotionally difficult experience for both the rejector and the would-be suitor. Unfortunately, it also is a common event in the lives of college students and—other than waiting patiently for the pain to pass with time—there appears to be no easy way to recover from the distress brought about by romantic rejection.

Romantic Obsession: When a College Student is Stalked

A female university student interviewed by the author of this chapter described the devastating effects of a romantic obsession:

> At first I thought it was sort of cute and romantic that he wanted to be with me all the time. He would ask me to give him a detailed account of my day, all the places I went, the people I talked with, the things I did. . . . I felt flattered that I had a boyfriend who loved me so much. But then it got out of hand. I mean, he wouldn't even let me drive to the store by myself! After we broke up, he began calling me at home, usually several times a night . . . I think what really made me realize that I needed to take some action and tell people what was going on was when he started spying on me. One morning, I was standing by the window looking outside and I noticed his car. He was just sitting there, watching me. I have no idea how long he had been there, but it really scared me. I felt trapped and violated.

A male university student provided a similar description of his experience:

> I met a woman I thought I liked. She was attractive, bright, seemed to have a good sense of humor and to be stable and well-grounded. We went out on a couple of dates and it turned out that we didn't have that much in common, so I didn't pursue the relationship. No big breakup or anything, we just weren't suited to each other. That should have been the end of it, but it wasn't. She lived about 10 miles from me, and she would drive over to my neighborhood, park in front of my house, and then go jogging around the block for what seemed like hours. I would see her as she passed my house again and again, every single day . . . She was everywhere I went and she did her best to invade every single moment of my day. My friends laughed about it and made jokes about what a lucky guy I was to have this woman chasing after me, but believe me it wasn't funny. Fortunately, I relocated due to my job and I haven't seen her since.

By the time they finish college, most young adults have experienced romantic rejection. And although these experiences are not pleasant, the majority of men and women manage to successfully negotiate them. In some cases, however, unreciprocated attraction can lead to obsession and a harmful (and potentially dangerous) behavioral syndrome called *relational stalking*. Relational stalking refers to a situation in which one person (the pursuer or stalker) desires and actively attempts to create or obtain an intimate relationship with another person (the target or victim) who either does not want this particular kind of relationship or who wants no relationship at all (see Emerson, Ferris, & Gardner, 1998; Spitzberg & Cupach, 2003). Relational stalking behavior possesses three characteristic features: (1) intentional and persistent contact (or attempted contact) by the pursuer that is (2) unwanted and (3) psychologically aversive (unpleasant or offensive) to the recipient. In addition, although legal definitions vary across the United States (and other countries), relational stalking typically becomes a crime when it poses a credible threat that places the recipient in reasonable fear for his or her safety (see Cupach & Spitzberg, 2004; Meloy, 2007).

Surveys of college samples reveal that relational stalking is disturbingly common, with rates ranging from 12 percent to 40 percent, and with women at greater risk than men for this type of victimization (e.g., Coleman, 1997; Haugaard & Seri, 2003; Logan, Leukefeld, & Walker, 2000; Spitzberg & Cupach, 2003; Turmanis & Brown, 2006). In addition, sizeable numbers of both male and female students report having been the target of unwanted pursuit or "prestalking" behaviors including receiving undesired or unsolicited letters, notes, phone calls, visits, or gifts, or being followed or watched (Herold, Mantle, & Zemitis, 1979; Jason, Reichler, Easton, Neal, & Wilson, 1984). Most victims are acquainted with their stalkers; in fact, former romantic partners represent the largest category of relational stalkers (Spitzberg & Cupach, 2007).

What factors contribute to relational stalking? Although there is some evidence that personality disorders and social skills deficits increase the likelihood of engaging in unwanted pursuit (see Cupach & Spitzberg, 2008), interpersonal factors appear to play the most important role. For example, relational stalking may emerge from the normal courtship process—in particular, from the indirect manner in which relationship initiation is typically enacted. A student who wishes to convey romantic interest to another will tend to rely on indirect cues to signal his or her attraction (see Regan, 2008). These indirect behaviors—eye contact, smiling, casual conversational gambits—may pass unnoticed by the target (or may be noticed but not interpreted as a serious bid for a relationship); consequently, the target may fail to clearly communicate acceptance or rejection. In the absence of any direct and unequivocal response one way or the other, the pursuing student may conclude that the target student reciprocates his or her feelings and may persist in the pursuit behavior. Indeed, research conducted with college student samples reveals that men and women often engage in persistent pursuit or prestalking behaviors during the early stages of courtship (Sinclair & Frieze, 2002; S. L. Williams & Frieze, 2005) as well as after the unwanted termination of a romantic relationship (Dutton & Winstead, 2006). In addition, they often fail to accurately perceive the negative impact that their behavior has on the objects of their desire (Sinclair & Frieze, 2005; also see K. E. Davis, Ace, & Andra, 2000).

The environmental or sociocultural context also promotes behaviors that are implicated in relational stalking. For example, a commonly held romantic assumption (and one that is frequently portrayed in movies, literature, and other media) is that "persistence pays." Hopeful suitors may continue in their efforts to gain affection from a seemingly uninterested partner because they believe that their persistence will ultimately be rewarded—in the face of their unwavering devotion, the beloved will eventually "come around" and return their affections. By making it difficult for both pursuers and targets to recognize when pursuit behaviors have crossed out of the realm of "normal courtship," these contextual factors—the ambiguity that frequently surrounds relationship initiation and the cultural glorification of persistence in the face of romantic disinterest or rejection—create a situation that is conducive to relational stalking.

Data gathered by Cupach and Spitzberg (1998, 2004, 2008; Spitzberg & Cupach, 1996, 2002) and others (e.g., Brewster, 2003; Turmanis & Brown, 2006) reveal that pursuers use a variety of tactics to promote relationships with their unwilling targets. Some of these strategies are *mildly intrusive*, including unexpectedly "showing up" at places frequented by the target, leaving repeated messages, giving gifts and other tokens of affection, using third parties to obtain information, and making exaggerated expressions of devotion or affection. Many of these milder forms of pursuit involve variations of flirting behavior and most targets consider them to be annoying but not terribly frightening or bothersome. They are also the most frequently experienced. For example, approximately 60 percent to 75 percent of the student participants in Spitzberg and Cupach's studies reported that their pursuer engaged in the following activities:

- Repeatedly called them on the phone
- Sent letters or gifts
- Asked them if they were seeing someone romantically
- Called and hung up without speaking
- Begged them for another chance
- Watched or stared at them from a distance
- Refused to take hints that he/she was not welcome
- Made exaggerated claims about his or her affection
- Gossiped or bragged about the supposed relationship with others

Moderately invasive behaviors range from surveillance of the target (e.g., following, monitoring, or watching the target, driving by the target's home or place of work), trespassing, stealing information or property, intentionally sabotaging the target's reputation, and intruding on the target's friends and family. These forms of harassment are much more aggravating and distressing to the target. *Extremely intrusive or invasive* behaviors are those that are most likely to pose a credible safety threat and induce fear (in which case the behaviors would legally constitute stalking). These tactics include threatening to harm the target or his or her loved ones, physically restraining or assaulting the target, injuring or killing the target's pet(s), coercing or forcing the target to engage in sexual activities, damaging the target's property, and invading the target's home or work.

Given the range of invasive and threatening actions in which pursuers commonly engage, it is hardly surprising that victims of relational stalking often experience a number of negative emotional reactions, including fear, anxiety, paranoia, depression, self-blame, and anger. In addition, they may change their lifestyle and patterns of social activity, develop a heightened distrust of others, and exhibit sleep disturbances, illness, and other physical symptoms (Amar, 2006; Spitzberg & Cupach, 2001).

One fundamental question for researchers in this area concerns coping responses to victimization. What responses, for example, are most effective at minimizing or eliminating stalking or intrusive behavior? What strategies can college students who are being victimized by a stalker use to reduce their risk of negative outcomes in these situations? Unfortunately, there is little systematic empirical work in this area; however, some professionals believe that statements and actions that directly and unequivocally convey rejection are most effective at managing unwanted attention (e.g., De Becker, 1998). For example, a student should refuse gifts and other forms of attention offered by the pursuer, should directly state his or her disinterest, and should cease all further contact and communication with that person. In addition, students should inform others of the situation, should document all stalking-related occurrences, should take steps to improve and/or increase security at their schools, workplaces, and homes, and should devise a plan that allows for immediate escape if they feel threatened (see Leitz-Spitz, 2003).

SUMMARY

Love plays an important—and central—role in the lives of college students. Most college-age men and women believe that finding love and establishing a committed, love-based relationship is essential for their personal happiness, and very few would even consider marrying someone (even a "perfect partner") in the absence of love. Researchers interested in the love experiences of young adults have identified a number of commonly held beliefs, attitudes, and assumptions about love and romance. This research generally reveals that most college students associate love with sexuality. Specifically, although attitudes toward sexual activity in casual dating relationships are becoming more permissive over time, young men and women today still view sexual activity as most appropriate when it occurs between partners who love each other and who are in a committed romantic relationship. In addition, some college students (particularly male and/or younger cohorts) possess a fairly idealized vision of romance, subscribing to such beliefs as the notion that love strikes without warning and often at first sight, the idea that there exists only one true love for each person (a "soul mate"), the belief that true love endures forever, and the notion that love can conquer all obstacles. Although the degree to which young adults subscribe to this constellation of romantic beliefs varies, the majority of men and women possess a similar mental representation of love itself, conceptualizing this concept as a type of positive emotion that can take on multiple forms (e.g., romantic love, maternal love, infatuation). Of these many forms, maternal love seems to be the universally agreed-upon "best example" or prototypic form of love. One of the most frequently studied aspects of college love concerns the mate preferences of young adults. This large body of empirical work indicates that men and women overwhelmingly prefer and seek to establish love relationships with partners who possess intelligence, emotional stability, warmth and expressiveness, an honest and trustworthy disposition, an exciting overall personality, and a physically attractive appearance. And when they do find such a partner, college students adopt a variety of different approaches when entering and maintaining a love relationship—some tend to love in a more erotic and passionate manner; others love in a more companionate and friendship-oriented way; still others love selflessly (or selfishly). Of course, not all love experiences are positive. During the course of their college years, men and women are likely to experience some form of romantic unpleasantness, including rejection by someone they love and/or unwanted pursuit or victimization from someone they may have rejected themselves. For college students—as for all of us—love clearly is a multifaceted and many-splendored experience.

Chapter Seven

INFIDELITY IN COLLEGE DATING RELATIONSHIPS

Richard D. McAnulty and David P. McAnulty

Alfred Kinsey and colleagues elicited a great deal of controversy when they reported that nearly half of married men and over one quarter of married women admitted to having had an affair by age 45 (Kinsey et al., 1948, 1953). These rates of marital infidelity were shocking for at least two reasons. First, at the time there were strong sanctions against extramarital sexual activity. More recent surveys reveal that the vast majority of adults in the United States still disapprove of marital infidelity under any circumstance (J. A. Davis, Smith, & Marsden, 2003; Laumann et al., 1994). Second, the reported rates were higher than anyone expected.

Infidelity remains a topic of widespread interest in popular culture, routinely featured in popular media such as soap operas (B. S. Greenberg & Busselle, 1996; B. S. Greenberg & Woods, 1999) and daytime talk shows (B. S. Greenberg, Sherry, Busselle, Rampoldi-Hnilo, & Smith, 1997). But as T. W. Smith (2006) lamented, "There are probably more scientifically worthless 'facts' on extramarital relations than any other facet of human behavior" (p. 108). Although this is probably an overgeneralization, the literature on infidelity in dating relationships is definitely limited, due in part to the potential difficulties in defining a dating relationship. Because dating relationships often lack the formal commitment to sexual and emotional exclusivity that characterizes marriage, violations of the exclusivity may be more difficult to define. Dating partners may rely on an implicit agreement of what is acceptable without having articulated the precise extradyadic behaviors that are unacceptable. The expectations or "rules" for dating may be especially unclear in contemporary culture (DeGenova & Rice, 2005).

Even though the rules for marital infidelity are clearer, it is apparently more common in younger cohorts, presumably because they have been married for a shorter period of time and are struggling with the transition from having multiple sexual partners prior to marriage to a monogamous sexual partnership (T. W. Smith, 2006). If true, dating patterns may be predictive of marital adjustment. Some authors (e.g., Drigotas, Safstrom, & Gentilia, 1999) have speculated that the causes of dating infidelity carry over into marriage; however, we found no empirical tests of this assumption. Regardless, dating patterns and associated problems are important topics of inquiry of their own right.

In one recent pair of reviews, Blow and Hartnett (2005a, 2005b) addressed infidelity in committed relationships, but they were primarily concerned with marital infidelity. In this review, we are concerned with the literature on infidelity in dating relationships. It does not include studies on infidelity among married or cohabiting couples unless those studies also included unmarried, noncohabitating couples. Some researchers have suggested that dating patterns and expectations for exclusivity are more variable among gay and lesbian couples (e.g., Blumstein & Schwartz, 1983; LaSala, 2004a, 2004b). Because the vast majority of studies in this area have relied on unmarried heterosexual college students, we limit our discussion to this group, although there is clearly a need for research with other samples to assess the generalizability of the major findings. For the sake of simplicity, we use the term "infidelity" to refer to any form of emotional or sexual intimacy with a person other than one's primary partner. Defining infidelity, however, has proven to be a vexing problem for researchers, so our review begins by addressing this topic.

DEFINING INFIDELITY

The literature reveals various operational definitions of infidelity. Indeed, the terms commonly used to refer to infidelity (cheating, having an affair, being unfaithful, stepping out on, extradyadic involvement) betray the ambiguity in meanings. This problem is evident in most of the relevant research, including studies of marital infidelity (see Blow & Hartnett, 2005a, for a review). The earliest studies tended to rely on narrow definitions of infidelity, particularly marital infidelity, in most cases, limited to engaging in sexual intercourse with a person other than the primary partner while being involved in an exclusive and committed relationship (see Lieberman, 1988, for example). This narrow definition is problematic for several reasons. First, it does not capture the full range of behaviors that most students consider forms of infidelity. Second, other types of infidelity are apparently more common and often just as troublesome for the parties affected by the transgressions. Finally, significant variations in operational definitions of infidelity make comparisons across studies and over time difficult. Therefore narrow definitions of infidelity tend to underestimate the extent of the phenomenon.

The relevant literature reveals two general approaches to defining infidelity. One approach is to allow respondents to define the term. For example, some researchers asked participants if they had ever been "unfaithful" (Sheppard, Nelson, & Andreoli-Mathie, 1995) or if either they or a partner had "cheated" on the other (Afifi, Falato, & Weiner, 2001; Feldman & Cauffman, 1999a; Grello et al., 2006). Others have used broad descriptions such as "romantic or sexual behavior with someone other than the primary partner" (Allen & Baucom, 2004). Such approaches are potentially problematic if participants do not share the same definition of cheating or infidelity. In these studies, investigators have revealed that students have divergent views of such seemingly basic terms as having sex and what constitutes a sexual partner. Over one third of college students would not label another person a sexual partner even though they had performed oral sex on that individual (Randall & Byers, 2003). Similar findings have been reported by researchers who have studied students' definitions of virginity and having sex (Bogart, Cecil, Wagstaff, Pinkerton, & Abramson, 2000; L. M. Carpenter, 2001; Sanders & Reinisch, 1999; Trotter & Alderson, 2007). For instance, Trotter and Alderson (2007), although not directly investigating infidelity, found that a group of 155 college students included a broader range of sexual behaviors in their definition of what constitutes a "sexual partner" than what constitutes "having sex." Predictably, most men and women viewed behaviors such as vaginal or anal intercourse as both "having sex" and being "a sexual partner." However, as the authors note, "few participants included deep kissing, oral contact with nipples, or masturbatory behaviors in their definitions of 'having sex.' " Significantly more participants, though, viewed these same behaviors in their definition of a "sexual partner." Such findings suggest that college students display different scripts for sexual behavior in general than for sexual fidelity. The former script would appear to minimize sexual restraint, while the latter would minimize extradyadic sexual activity in dating relationships.

Therefore with regard to approaches that allow the respondents to define infidelity, it seems imprudent to assume that students share the same definitions of cheating or even of sexual activity (see Forste & Tanfer, 1996). Even though in one study Randall and Byers (2003) found a high level of agreement in college students' definitions of infidelity, it seems advisable to ask respondents what they consider infidelity to ensure that their understandings are consistent. The development of the Perceptions of Dating Infidelity Scale (PDIS) represents a recent effort to gain greater clarity regarding what college students, as well as older dating couples, consider infidelity (Mattingly, Wilson, Clark, Bequette, & Weidler, 2010; Wilson, Mattingly, Clark, Weidler, & Bequette, 2011). Relying on a factor analytic method, these researchers identified three dimensions of behaviors that were perceived as cheating, suggesting that a dichotomous approach (cheating vs. not cheating) may be inadequate. The factors were labeled (1) explicit behaviors, which included oral sex, intercourse, heavy petting/fondling, dating, and kissing; (2) deceptive behaviors, including flirting, fantasizing, lying, and withholding information; and, (3) ambiguous behaviors, including dancing, hugging, buying/receiving gifts, talking on phone/Internet, and eating/drinking with another.

The second approach is to provide participants a definition of infidelity. Although this approach promises consistency in criteria for defining infidelity, its usefulness hinges on the accuracy of the criteria. Some early researchers did not include some common sexual practices in their list of potential extradyadic sexual behaviors. Both Hansen (1987) and Feldman and Cauffman (1999b) omitted oral sex in their surveys. Feldman and Cauffman (1999b) queried their 417 college students about experiences with extradyadic "petting" and sexual intercourse to measure betrayal, but did not include any questions about oral or anal sex. Hansen (1987) asked participants if they had experienced "extradyadic relations" in the form of "erotic kissing, petting, or sexual intercourse." In that study, petting was defined as "sexually stimulating behavior more intimate than erotic kissing and simple hugging, but not including full sexual intercourse." It seems questionable to include oral sex as a form of petting. Petting usually refers to fondling or "sexual touching," and surveys that make a distinction between fondling and oral sex produce different frequencies (see Wiederman & Hurd, 1999, for example).

In contrast to the limited definitions of many researchers, college students generally have very broad definitions of infidelity. Moreover, very few gender differences appear in students' definitions. For most students, spending excessive time with another person and virtually any form of extradyadic physical intimacy qualify as infidelity. In their survey of 164 Canadian college students, Randall and Byers (2003) found that all forms of extradyadic physical intimacy qualified as infidelity to the vast majority. Over 90 percent of participants agreed that "deep kissing/tongue kissing," oral contact with nipples, oral sex with or without orgasm, and masturbation to orgasm in the presence of another person, would count as being unfaithful if their partner engaged in any of these acts. Vaginal and anal intercourse yielded near unanimous agreement. Yarab, Sensibaugh, and Allgeier (1998) derived a list of 29 behaviors suggested by students as examples of unfaithful behaviors. This list included many behaviors not typically included as forms of infidelity, including having sexual fantasies about a person other than the primary partner and having even mild romantic feelings for another person. In a subsequent study, Yarab, Allgeier, and Sensibaugh (1999) found that men and women alike rated a variety of extradyadic "romantic attachments" and sexual behaviors as "highly unfaithful in dating relationships" (p. 311), including flirtation. Wiederman and Hurd (1999) asked students if they had ever gone on a date with someone other than their primary partner "while involved in a serious dating relationship." They also queried participants about their experiences with extradyadic romantic kissing, kissing and fondling, receiving and performing oral sex, and sexual intercourse with a person other than their primary dating partner. Differences in the reported frequencies of the various acts suggest that although all qualified as infidelity, respondents do make distinctions between them.

In every study but one, virtually every respondent labeled extradyadic intercourse as a form of infidelity. The results of the study by Roscoe, Cavanaugh, and Kennedy (1988) are anomalous in that only 41 percent of the students identified having sexual intercourse with a person other than one's primary partner as constituting being "unfaithful." More students (57%) identified "dating/spending time with another" as "unfaithfulness." These findings may be due to the open-ended format used in the question: "What behaviors do you think constitute being 'unfaithful' to a dating partner provided the couple is in a serious dating relationship (in other words, they have assumed that they are to date only each other)?" There are several possible explanations for this finding. Many of the participants may not yet have initiated sexual intercourse and, therefore, it might appear irrelevant to their perspective of infidelity. Alternatively, they may have assumed that extradyadic intercourse would invariably be included and needed not be listed. The lack of follow-up questioning makes it impossible to evaluate students' responses, but nearly all students in the other studies consider that extradyadic sexual intercourse qualifies as infidelity.

In their review of infidelity research, Blow and Hartnett (2005a) offered the definition of infidelity as a "sexual and/or emotional act engaged in by one person within a committed relationship where such an act occurs outside of the primary relationship and constitutes a breach of trust and/or violation of agreed upon norms (overt and covert) by one or both individuals in that relationship in relation to romantic/emotional or sexual exclusivity" (pp. 191–192). These researchers have developed a clear definition, but we find no research on the process by which dating couples themselves develop implicit or explicit norms regarding exclusivity. Anecdotal reports suggest that many couples reach a point in the relationship when they agree to exclusivity. How couples reach this point and the manner in which it is negotiated are essential to understanding what would constitute a breach. In the end, they not only expect that their dating relationships should be emotionally and sexually exclusive, some even seem to expect "mental exclusivity" because extradyadic fantasies qualify as infidelity to some individuals (see Yarab et al., 1998).

THE PREVALENCE OF DATING INFIDELITY

Prevalence estimates of dating infidelity are complicated by inconsistencies in operational definitions and other factors, such as social desirability. Broad definitions of infidelity tend to yield higher estimates. As we noted previously, narrow definitions may produce more reliable estimates, although they probably do not capture the full extent of pertinent extradyadic involvements. In their review of infidelity in committed relationships, Blow and Hartnett (2005a) concluded that the most reliable estimates were derived from nationally representative samples of married, heterosexual couples and focused on extramarital sexual intercourse. In their National Health and Social Life Survey (NHSLS), for example, Laumann et al. (1994) revealed that 25 percent of married men and 15 percent of married women admitted to at least one lifetime experience of extramarital sexual intercourse. When measured over the preceding year, the prevalence was less than 4 percent. A consistent finding is that the rates of extramarital intercourse increase over the duration of marriage (Wiederman, 1997a).

Because dating relationships are usually shorter in duration than marriages, one might expect lower prevalence rates of infidelity because the relationship may still be in its "honeymoon" phase, and partners have simply had less time for extradyadic involvements. However, this does not seem to be the case. Dating women are more likely than married women to report having a "secondary sex partner" (18% vs. 4% respectively; Forste & Tanfer, 1996), possibly the result of the lower degree of formal commitment that characterizes dating relationships. Cohabitating women have rates of infidelity similar to those of dating women, which may support the idea that both kinds of relationships are less committed and less exclusive than marriage (Forste & Tanfer, 1996). Another possibility stems from social mores; married persons may be less likely than individuals in dating or cohabitating relationships to admit to infidelity because it is viewed as a more serious transgression (Blumstein & Schwartz, 1983). Alternatively, college students may actually have more social opportunities for infidelity than their married counterparts (e.g., parties attended by numerous available potential partners). Opportunities may interact with degree of relationship commitment to determine a person's likelihood of infidelity: for a person with low relationship commitment, relatively few opportunities might be required in comparison to a person who is highly committed to the relationship, a topic that we will revisit later.

Recent broad-definition surveys of students in dating relationships report relatively high prevalence rates. Allen and Baucom (2006), for example, found that 69 percent of the 504 students they surveyed reported engaging in some form of infidelity in the previous two years. Each respondent's definition of infidelity—romantic or sexual behavior with someone other than one's primary partner—could have included noncontact activity such as flirting with another person. Indeed, a vast majority of students in committed dating relationships report having flirted with someone other than the primary partner while in a dating relationship, although they may not have considered it "cheating" at the time. A true/false single-item definition of infidelity ("I have never been sexually unfaithful to my partner") in a subsequent study yielded a 33 percent rate of infidelity among premarital dating couples (Allen et al., 2008).

More recently, Hall and Fincham (2009) reported that 35 percent of 287 college students in an exclusive dating relationship indicated they had been physically and/or emotionally unfaithful to their current romantic partner. Among those who had cheated, infidelity was further classified as physical (29%), emotional (28%), or both physical and emotional (43%). Finally, these investigators attempted to gain information regarding the duration of infidelity. They found that the majority (50%) reported extradyadic relationships lasting from one to four weeks, while 29 percent described the infidelity as a "one-night stand" (lasting less than 24 hours) and another 21 percent as long-term involvement. These findings suggest there are a number of different types of infidelity in college populations.

The reported rates of extradyadic involvement decline steadily as the contact becomes more physically intimate. Although extradyadic flirtation and kissing are highly prevalent, oral sex and intercourse are less common. The reported prevalence of actual extradyadic sexual contact in dating relationships is generally in the range of 50 percent or lower. Over 65 percent of men and 39 percent of women in Hansen's (1987) study reported extradyadic erotic kissing, but only 35 percent of men and nearly 12 percent of women reported extradyadic intercourse. Yarab et al. (1998) reported that 90 percent of men and 81 percent of women in their survey had engaged in extradyadic casual flirtation, but fewer than 45 percent of men and 38 percent of women reported sexual intercourse with someone other than their primary partner. Wiederman and Hurd (1999) noted that 68 percent of the men and 61 percent of the women engaged in extradyadic romantic kissing. Actual extradyadic oral sex and intercourse were engaged in by approximately half of the men and one-third of the women in the survey. Men were more likely than women to report experience with all forms of extradyadic activity except kissing and receiving oral sex, the rates of which were equal with women's reports.

The perspective of experiencing a partner's infidelity offers additional, although very generalized, data on prevalence. In her study of community samples of heterosexual and homosexual men and women, Harris (2002) found that 70 percent of the participants had experienced partner infidelity, defined has "having a partner cheat on you." No separate data for dating individuals are available from this study. Focusing more specifically on dating college students, Berman and Frazier (2005) found that 61 (15%) of their sample of 394 reported having been the victim of infidelity, while 72 (18%) admitted having been unfaithful, with infidelity defined as "a romantic, sexual, or emotional relationship with someone other than the primary partner that was kept secret from that partner and that would have been unacceptable to the partner had he/she known." Interestingly, 36 percent of the victims reported they had also cheated on their partner. The relatively low levels reported in this study might be related to the young age of the sample (mean age of 21). Alternatively, specific aspects of the definition of infidelity that was given (kept secret, unacceptable) might have allowed respondents to exclude certain extradyadic behaviors. In any event, because infidelity is often secretive and undiscovered, the above figures may represent low-end estimates.

Gender differences in prevalence rates of infidelity have been addressed in several studies. With respect to sexual fantasies, while both men and women commonly report fantasizing about someone other than their partner (98% and 80% respectively), the difference in rates is significant (Hicks & Leitenberg, 2001). Additionally, for men in a relationship, a majority of sexual fantasies involve someone other than their current partner, while for women, a majority of fantasies involve their current partner. In at least one study, gender was a significant predictor of self-reported inclination toward extradyadic sexual activities, although actual behavior was not assessed (McAlister, Pachan, & Jackson, 2005). Finally, in studies of self-reported extradyadic behaviors higher prevalence rates have been reported for men than women, with the possible exception of extradyadic romantic kissing (e.g., Hansen, 1987; Wiederman & Hurd, 1999). This finding is consistent with the literature on married or cohabitating individuals, which suggests men are generally more likely to engage in extradyadic sexual activity relative to women (Atkins, Baucom, & Jacobson, 2001; Træen, Holmen, and Stigum, 2007; Treas & Geisen, 2000). At the same time, the observed gender difference does not consistently hold up for younger individuals (e.g., < 39 years of age), among whom rates of infidelity are comparable for men and women (Atkins et al., 2001; Træen & Martinussen, 2008).

The purported gender difference in infidelity, which has also been reported in surveys of other sexual behaviors, warrants an explanation. Several researchers, for example, have noted that men consistently report a higher number of past sexual partners than women (Allen & Baucom, 2004; Garcia & Markey, 2007; Laumann et al., 1994; Oliver & Hyde, 1993; Wiederman, 1997b), a consistent finding generally attributed to sampling bias or self-presentation bias (Baumeister & Tice, 2001). One possible source of sampling bias could be due to the men having extradyadic sexual encounters with women who were excluded from the sample, such as younger female high school students. Another possibility is that men engaging in infidelity do so mostly with women who are unattached, perhaps by lying about their own relationship status. Alternatively, a smaller number of women may be having extradyadic sexual encounters with a relatively larger number of men. Self-presentation biases could result from gender differences in definitions of cheating and sexual partners, although this explanation seems unlikely, as we have previously noted. Another possible source of presentation bias could involve overreporting by men and underreporting by women (J. A. Davis & Smith, 1991). In their reports of lifetime number of sexual partners, men are more likely than women to use "ballpark" figures or "round up" their estimates (N. R. Brown & Sinclair, 1999; Wiederman, 1997b), causing them to overreport. Given the widespread disapproval of infidelity, however, this effect seems rather unlikely. Underreporting of infidelity by women seems more likely, but this factor has not been systematically evaluated. Arguing against any gender bias in self-presentation, the study by Grello et al. (2006) revealed no actual gender differences in rates of extradyadic casual sexual encounters among students. Nor did Feldman and Cauffman (1999b) find any gender differences in reported rates of extradyadic dating, emotional involvement, kissing, and petting. If the early-married cohort reflects dating behaviors, Wiederman's (1997a) research further supported the idea that no gender differences occur in extradyadic involvement.

The lifetime prevalence of dating infidelity is higher than the reported rates over a one-year or two-year period, perhaps due to greater opportunities combined with fluctuations in degrees of commitment to the relationship. For men, the amount of dating experience is positively correlated with extradyadic involvement (Hansen, 1987). The evidence for women is mixed: Hansen (1987) found that relationship length did not correlate with rates of infidelity in women, but Forste and Tanfer (1996) found a significant relationship between these variables. Another possibility for explaining variation is that infidelity represents a repetitive pattern of behavior for some individuals.

At least one study supports the popular notion that "once a cheater, always a cheater." Wiederman and Hurd (1999) found that individuals who had participated in extradyadic sexual behavior once were highly likely to have experienced it again. The vast majority of men and most women who have experienced extradyadic kissing, fondling, oral sex, or intercourse have done so more than once. In terms of extradyadic sexual intercourse, nearly 86 percent of men and 62percent of women who reported the behavior have repeated it. Unfortunately, we find no other study on patterns of dating infidelity over time. Repeated infidelity may reflect low commitment to a relationship, a threshold effect (once a person has crossed that line, any subsequent transgression seems less serious), or some other individual characteristic (such as sexual permissiveness) that merits empirical study. In view of the shorter duration of dating relations relative to marriage, it may come as somewhat of a surprise that these "serial infidelity" rates are higher than the 35 percent rate reported in married samples (Allen & Rhoades, 2008). Further research is needed to determine the extent to which the high rate of repeated infidelity across dating relationships can be replicated, as well as to elucidate intraindividual and relational factors that are associated with this phenomenon.

ATTITUDES TOWARD DATING INFIDELITY

One consistent finding across studies is that a decided majority of young adults disapproves of any form of infidelity. Almost universally, they disapprove of marital infidelity (Widmer, Treas, & Newcomb, 1998), which they view as immoral, socially reprehensible, and often illegal. Although they connect fewer sanctions with dating infidelity, it too meets with widespread disapproval. Of note, these findings may be limited to heterosexual populations, as recent evidence suggests a more tolerant view of "open relationships" among gay men in committed relationships (LaSala, 2004a, 2004b), although in such cases, due to the absence of dissimulation and the fact that extradyadic sexual behavior is an accepted aspect of the relationship, it may not be accurate to refer to such acts as infidelity.

In the first survey of college students' attitudes toward dating infidelity Lieberman (1988) revealed that two-thirds disapproved, with no gender differences. Sheppard et al. (1995) also found that both male and female students disapprove of infidelity in both married and committed dating relationships, although males rate both forms of infidelity as less unacceptable than do females. Knox, Zusman, Kaluzny, and Sturdivant (2000) reported that two-thirds of the students they surveyed disapproved of dating partner infidelity and would terminate a relationship because of it. Nearly half of the sample reported that they had actually done so.

Although the majority of students disapprove of infidelity, the degree of disapproval is apparently influenced by the context. Infidelity motivated by being in a troubled relationship meets with less disapproval (Feldman & Cauffman, 1999b). Similarly, if the infidelity results from a strong attraction, it is less condemned than if it occurs out of spite, to test the primary relationship, or simply because the culprit simply believed the infidelity would not be discovered. Infidelity that is deliberate rather than opportunistic seems to be more widely condemned (Feldman & Cauffman, 1999b). Still, overall, the perspective on dating infidelity remains rather negative among college students. In fact, one recent investigation found that even individuals who have cheated on a partner consistently describe cheating as reprehensible (Anderson, 2010). Indeed, in a qualitative study of 40 university males who were or had been in a heterosexual dating relationship lasting at least three months, the investigator found that while a full 65 percent of this British sample acknowledged cheating (ranging from kissing to intercourse), all of these men voiced disapproval of their own actions.

Betrayal of sexual exclusivity in marriage is a more serious transgression than dating infidelity to most people, whether community samples (Blumstein & Schwartz, 1983) or college students (Lieberman, 1988; Sheppard et al., 1995). This social sanction may explain why students who acknowledge their extradyadic involvement are less worried about being judged negatively than individuals who have engaged in marital infidelity (Allen & Baucom, 2006). However, students view both as serious breaches. Although the context of the infidelity influences disapproval ratings, to most students infidelity in any committed relationship is never justified.

In addition to attitudinal surveys, further evidence of the general disapproval of dating infidelity comes from the fact that most individuals involved in extradyadic sex keep the activity secret from their primary partner. Allen and Rhoades (2008) reported that 62 percent of their sample of men and women who had cheated reported that their partner did not know about the infidelity. For the community sample (whose extradyadic involvement occurred in the context of a marriage or engagement), 78 percent of partners were unaware of the infidelity, perhaps reflecting the greater unacceptability of marital infidelity. Hall and Fincham (2009) found that 46 percent of partners were reportedly unaware of the extradyadinc involvement. Since all of these estimates are self-reports obtained from the unfaithful partners, the potential exist for inflated rates, perhaps to reduce cognitive dissonance. In actuality, fewer of the deceived partners may have been aware of the infidelity.

REACTIONS TO INFIDELITY

Emotional Impact

Reactions to partner infidelity are generally negative. Hansen (1987) found that 72 percent of women and 77 percent of men reported that their partner's behavior had hurt the relationship to some degree. The impact on the unfaithful partner is likewise generally negative. According to Feldman and Cauffman (1999a), the most common reaction reported by men and women who have been unfaithful to their partner is feeling guilty (63%). Some ambivalence is evident, however, as nearly as many students report positive emotions (such as happiness or excitement) as negative reactions. One-third of the sample experienced confusion, shame, and feeling "immoral." It is not surprising that male and female students in committed relationships who engage in an extradyadic casual sexual encounter report more regret afterward than do unattached students who had "casual sex" (Grello et al., 2006). Hall and Fincham (2009) found that undergraduates who had been unfaithful to their current romantic partner experienced greater depressive symptomatology, more shame, greater guilt, more intrusions, more avoidance, and less self-forgiveness, compared to those participants who had not been unfaithful. Other emotional consequences of infidelity include fear and anxiety, particularly of discovery and an associated relationship breakup (Anderson, 2010). And, in fact, one of the most common end results of infidelity by a partner is termination of the relationship (Harris, 2002).

Relationship Dissolution

Over half of the participants in Roscoe et al.'s (1988) survey would terminate (44%) or consider terminating (16%) the relationship with an unfaithful partner (see also Knox et al., 2000). Over half would discuss the incident with the partner in hope of understanding or explaining it. Although a small number of respondents report that they would forgive the transgression or retaliate, their actual reactions may be different.

Moving beyond hypothetical infidelity and relational impact, Afifi et al. (2001) investigated the differential impact of infidelity based on the manner in which actual dating infidelity came to light. They observed four general discovery methods: (1) unsolicited partner discovery (31.5%), where the infidelity is revealed by the transgressor's unsolicited disclosure; (2) solicited discovery (19%), where the partner discovers the infidelity after confronting the transgressor; (3), "red-handed" discovery (7.5%), where the partner accidentally walks in during an act of infidelity; and (4) unsolicited third-party discovery (42%), where the infidelity is uncovered by an unsolicited third-party disclosure such as being told by others about it, sometimes the "other" person. In their sample of 115 undergraduates who had been in a dating relationship where either they or their partner cheated on the other, the researchers found that discovery method was clearly related to relational dissolution. Termination of the relationship was most likely when the infidelity came to light through solicited discovery (86%) and "red-handed" discovery (83%), followed by third-party discovery (68%), and least likely following unsolicited partner disclosure (44%). Similarly, unsolicited disclosure was most highly associated with forgiveness and had the least negative impact on relationship quality. Conversely, "red-handed" discovery and third-party discovery produced the most relational damage and were least likely to be forgiven. Paradoxically, solicited discovery, although almost always resulting in termination of the relationship, was associated with higher likelihood of forgiveness and lesser relational damage than either "red-handed" or third-party discovery.

Gunderson and Ferrari (2008) conducted a similar investigation using hypothetical vignettes with 196 undergraduate students, 66 percent of whom had never experienced infidelity firsthand. Respondents reported that discovery method would not differentially affect forgiveness following sexual cheating by a partner. However, they believed that both the presence of an apology and the frequency of occurrences would impact the likelihood of forgiveness and of ending the relationship. The discrepancy between these findings regarding discovery method and the earlier finding by Afifi et al. (2001) may result from the hypothetical nature of the study. On the one hand, students who have not experienced infidelity may not be capable of predicting their actual responses accurately. On the other hand, compared to real-life discoveries of infidelity where the experience is quite vivid and details such as the frequency of occurrence are often hard to ascertain, brief vignettes give clear-cut facts with significantly less emotional impact. It is plausible to believe that these differences might distort individuals' predictions of their own reactions.

Jealousy

Another common reaction to infidelity, or threatened infidelity, is jealousy. The literature on jealousy in reaction to hypothetical partner infidelity has been prolific, spurred in large part by evolutionary theorists (see, e.g., Buss, Larsen, Westen, & Semmelroth, 1992). Although a review of that literature is beyond the scope of this chapter, we want to address a few points relevant to our review. Typical studies employ hypothetical scenarios that require participants to imagine a partner's infidelity and anticipate their reactions to it (Mongeau, Hale, & Alles, 1994; Mongeau & Schulz, 1997; Nannini & Myers, 2000; Wiederman & LaMar, 1998). Results have generally supported the prediction that men would be more upset by sexual infidelity (presumably due to the evolutionary need of males for certainty about paternity) while women are more upset by emotional infidelity (presumably due to the evolutionary fear of increased likelihood of desertion by a mate who is emotionally attached to someone else). Moreover, such findings have been replicated cross-culturally (Fernandez, Vera-Villarroel, Sierra, & Zubeidat, 2007; for a comprehensive review, see for example, Sabini & Green, 2004). However, a number of studies have failed to confirm the evolutionary predictions (e.g., Sabini & Silver, 2005).

Although this research design is simple and efficient, several researchers have revealed that individuals' predicted reactions to hypothetical scenarios are sometimes different from their actual reactions. Harris (2002) recruited four community samples: gay men, lesbians, heterosexual women, and heterosexual men. Using a forced-choice format, participants were asked if they would be more upset by imagining their "partner trying new sexual positions" with another person or falling in love with that person (see Buss et al., 1992). Across groups, a large majority of respondents picked emotional infidelity as more upsetting. The heterosexual men were more likely than any other group to report that sexual infidelity was more upsetting, although 74 percent of them chose emotional over sexual infidelity as most upsetting. When participants were asked about their actual reactions to partner infidelity, no group differences emerged, as all were more distressed by emotional infidelity and over half reported that the relationship had ended because of it.

Allen and Baucom (2006) found differences between persons who had actually engaged in infidelity and those asked to imagine their reactions to doing so. Individuals who only imagine being unfaithful to a partner report higher levels of anticipated distress and remorse than do persons who have actually had the experience. The authors concluded that individuals who actually engage in dating infidelity seem either to feel justified or at least to minimize its impact in order to reduce cognitive dissonance (p. 315). Gender differences in response to the hypothetical scenarios are inconsistent; where such differences do occur, they are only modest (see Harris, 2003; Nannini & Myers, 2000; Sheppard et al., 1995; Yarab et al., 1999). Across studies, and considering all participants, infidelity in any form elicits jealousy and constitutes a threat to the relationship.

The aftermath of dating infidelity, however, is not inevitably negative. According to Hansen (1987), approximately one-fourth of students who participate in extradyadic involvement report that it actually improved the primary relationship. This claim seems to be a matter of perspective, because individuals feel much less positive about their partner's infidelity: only 7 percent to 12 percent of students whose partners were unfaithful reported that their relationships benefited from it. Similar reports were obtained in a community sample of 398 married or cohabitating couples in Norway (Træen & Martinussen, 2008). In this study, 46 percent of men and 43 percent of women with extradyadic sexual activity reported having told their partner about the affair. Of these, 47 percent of women said their relationship was unaffected while 29 percent claimed the relationship improved. For men, the corresponding numbers were 31 percent and 35 percent, respectively. Unfortunately, no corroborating data from the victim of extradyadic sexual activity were reported.

MOTIVES FOR INFIDELITY

In their review, Drigotas and colleagues (1999) delineated five categories of motives for infidelity: sexuality, emotional satisfaction, social context, attitudes-norms, and revenge-hostility. Sexuality motives include the desire for variety and dissatisfaction with the primary sexual relationship. Emotional satisfaction might imply relationship dissatisfaction, ego bolstering, and/or emotional attachment to the other person. Social contextual factors refer to opportunity and absence of the primary partner. Attitudes-norms include sexually permissive attitudes and norms. Revenge-hostility applies to infidelity that occurs in retaliation for some perceived wrong by the partner. Barta and Kiene's work (2005) compresses the categories of the earlier study and seems to eliminate the social context factor: they derive four factors from the Motivations for Infidelity Inventory they administered to students: dissatisfaction, neglect, anger, and sex. Obviously, infidelity can result from multiple motives.

Feldman and Cauffman (1999a) found that sexual attraction was the most commonly reported motive: 53 percent of their participants endorsed it. Partner absence was a close second (48%), followed by feeling unable to resist the opportunity. Sexual dissatisfaction and insecurity about one's relationship were reported by one-third of participants who engaged in infidelity. Vindictiveness was not a common motive in their study. No gender differences were found in motives for infidelity. Barta and Kiene (2005) reported that dissatisfaction with the primary relationship and feeling neglected were the two most commonly cited motives in their sample of 120 students. Sexual motivation and anger were listed as motives by only a minority of their respondents, with men more likely than women to identify sex as a motive. These results are consistent with findings from the literature on marital infidelity, which identifies sexual dissatisfaction, preoccupation with sex, and relationship problems such as invalidation and poor communication as significant variables (e.g., Allen et al., 2008; Træen & Martinussen, 2008).

In Grello et al. (2006), a previously unstudied factor emerged: the finding that extradyadic encounters involved less affection than encounters with the primary partner suggests that these different relationships serve different needs. Men and women in committed dating relationships who had a casual sexual encounter reported having engaged in fewer affectionate behaviors (such as holding hands and hugging) with the third party than did unattached persons who also experienced a casual sexual encounter. Affectionate behaviors are perhaps reserved for the primary partner; restricting them may implicitly signal that the casual encounter is only sexual and just a "onetime" thing (Grello et al., 2006).

The implication of sharing affection between partners creates other issues. Several studies have examined the role of relationship factors in infidelity. Allen and Baucom (2006) investigated the contribution of self-esteem needs, love needs, intimacy needs, and autonomy needs among three groups: a group of students who engaged in infidelity, a community sample that reported marital infidelity, and a sample of students instructed to imagine having engaged in infidelity. Compared to the students who had engaged in infidelity, the marital infidelity group was more likely to endorse intimacy reasons (felt neglected and lonely) and self-esteem needs. The marital infidelity group was also more likely than the student groups to report having been in love with the extradyadic partner. The authors concluded that, because marital infidelity is a more serious transgression than dating infidelity, married individuals might require higher levels of multiple motives to betray their spouses.

In subsequent research, Allen and Rhoades (2008) provided further differentiation between types of infidelity. In a sample of 345 undergraduates and 115 community volunteers who had reported extradyadic involvement, these investigators found distinct subtypes of affairs. Relationships where the individual was more emotionally involved with the extradyadic partner were characterized by a gradual onset, by a platonic beginning, and by greater likelihood of self-esteem motivations (e.g., to feel good about themselves). Conversely, less emotionally involved extradyadic relationships were either actively sought out or developed quickly. Similarly, at least for students, the greater the number of extradyadic partners, the less emotionally involved the extradyadic relationship was.

Lewandowski and Ackerman (2006) evaluated the relationship between need fulfillment and self-expansion needs and the susceptibility to infidelity, examining five types of need fulfillment (intimacy, companionship, sex, security, and emotional involvement) and three types of self-expansion (self-expansion, inclusion of the other in self, and potential for self-expansion) as predictors of the self-reported likelihood of engaging in dating infidelity. As hypothesized, all five need fulfillment variables were negatively correlated with susceptibility to infidelity, as were all self-expansion variables. Limited by its reliance on self-reported susceptibility to infidelity, the study would have been strengthened by adding a measure of actual infidelity because self-reported susceptibility may not always predict participation.

In a study employing a prospective design, Drigotas and colleagues (1999) used the investment model to predict actual dating infidelity. Simply, the model states that commitment to a relationship is a function of relationship satisfaction, alternative quality (the extent to which alternatives to the relationship are viewed as attractive), and investments (tangible and intangible) in the relationship. Dissatisfaction with one's current relationship combined with the prospect of a desirable alternative partner could erode commitment to the relationship and increase the likelihood of infidelity. According to the model, lack of commitment to one's relationship is ultimately at the root of infidelity. In study one, degree of commitment to the relationship at the start of a semester was predictive of subsequent emotional and sexual infidelity. The findings revealed that "individuals who were more committed, more satisfied, had fewer alternatives, and were more invested in their relationships were less likely to be unfaithful to their partners" (p. 513). Study 2 essentially replicated these findings showing that the degree of commitment was predictive of infidelity among students on spring break. Commitment was also predictive of the number and intensity of interactions with opposite-sex strangers over the break. Lower commitment was associated with more frequent and more intimate interactions with strangers, thereby creating opportunity for infidelity.

Relationship satisfaction, however, has not uniformly been found to predict dating infidelity. Hall and Fincham (2009) followed 284 undergraduate students in exclusive dating relationships over a four-week period. Relationship satisfaction was associated with infidelity only in the cross-sectional analyses. In contrast, initial relationship satisfaction was not predictive of subsequent infidelity in the longitudinal analyses. The authors concluded that "although individuals who engage in infidelity may be dissatisfied with their primary relationship this dissatisfaction does not appear to drive extradyadic involvement" (p.156).

Possible motives for dating infidelity are numerous and varied—and possibly inaccurate, given the retrospective nature of most studies and the widespread disapproval of infidelity (see Allen & Baucom, 2006; Drigotas et al., 1999). The limited research on motives for infidelity reveals that relationship factors should be carefully considered, particularly the degree of commitment to the relationship. As Drigotas et al. (1999) recommended, "Paying attention to one's partner's commitment would be a very diagnostic tool in the prediction of partner infidelity" (p. 520).

Allen and Baucom (2006) have suggested that motives for dating infidelity might differ from those behind marital infidelity. Therefore we cannot assume that the relevant research on marital infidelity can be generalized to dating relationships (e.g., Glass & Wright, 1985). At the same time, some of the motives related to marital infidelity may serve as a starting point for future investigation with college dating samples. In particular, social exchange theories, including but not limited to the investment model mentioned above (Drigotas et al., 1999), have been evaluated as explanatory models for extramarital sexual behavior. Sprecher (1998) identified the interpersonal model of sexual satisfaction, the outcome-interdependence theory (i.e., relationship rewards and costs), and equity theory as other examples of social exchange theories with relevance to sexual fidelity. For instance, Prins, Buunk, and VanYperen (1993) found that relational inequity was associated with marital infidelity. They concluded that "deprived as well as advantaged women had been involved in more extramarital relationships than women who felt equally well off" (p. 49). Whether the relationship between relational equity and infidelity can be extended to a dating college population awaits empirical confirmation.

PREDICTORS OF INFIDELITY

The search for potential predictors and other correlates of infidelity in committed relationships is in its infancy. The few variables that have been studied include religiosity, personality type, love style, and sexuality-related attitudes and behaviors. Each of these, however, has been investigated in very few studies. Because most samples used in the studies are relatively homogeneous (i.e., unmarried heterosexual college students), restrictions of range in scores could attenuate potential relationships between the variables and infidelity.

Demographic Variables

As mentioned earlier in this chapter, gender differences have appeared both in terms of extradyadic fantasies and extradyadic behavior. Further research is needed to more fully determine the extent and nature of gender differences in extradyadic involvement. Similarly, future investigations with more diverse populations are required to determine whether race is a significant predictor. Preliminary data suggest that infidelity rates are higher among married or cohabitating African American men and women, compared to whites (Treas & Giesen, 2000; Whisman & Snyder, 2007).

Religiosity

While various indices of religiosity have been correlated with greater rates of marital fidelity, particularly religious affiliation (Burdette, Ellison, Sherkat, & Gore, 2007), religious attendance (Atkins & Kessel, 2008; Treas & Giesen, 2000; Whisman & Snyder, 2007), and belief in the Bible as the literal/inspired word of God (Burdette et al., 2007), research findings regarding dating couples are minimal. Certainly, general sexual behavior in college students has been associated with religiousness, including church attendance and denominational affiliation (Burdette, Ellison, Hill & Glenn, 2009). With particular regard to infidelity in dating couples, Hansen (1987) derived a religiosity score that combined self-rated importance of religion and frequency of church attendance. It was negatively correlated with infidelity for women, but not for men. Wiederman and Hurd (1999) used two ratings of the importance of religion in participants' lives, but these did not predict extradyadic activity. More recently, Mattingly et al. (2010) found that individuals who self-identified as religious and who reported that their religious beliefs/values influenced their beliefs regarding appropriate romantic relationship behaviors were more likely to perceive a wider range of behaviors (i.e., Perceptions of Dating Infidelity Scale Ambiguous Behaviors) as cheating. However, this study assessed attitudes rather than acts of infidelity. Finally,

Fincham, Lambert, and Beach (2010) examined the impact of prayer on infidelity in a college population. In a series of studies that followed students in dating relationships for four to six weeks, they found that prayer for one's dating partner was associated with a reduced likelihood of infidelity acts (emotional and physical). The findings held true when the prayer-for-partner group was compared to three control conditions: neutral activity, undirected prayer (i.e., not specifically for one's partner), and positive-thoughts-about-partner.

Altogether, these initial findings suggest that religious behaviors and attitudes may be predictors of dating infidelity. However, the relationship between religiosity and infidelity may be moderated by other factors. For instance, in predicting marital infidelity, religiosity showed little to no effect for individuals who reported "pretty happy" or "not too happy" marriages, compared to individuals in "very happy" marriages for whom the religiosity effect was strong (Atkins et al., 2001).

Attitudes

Sexuality-related attitudes have also been investigated in relation to infidelity. Sexually permissive attitudes were predictors of infidelity in several studies. Attitudes related to sex outside of committed relationships have proven useful, as expected. Sociosexual orientation (self-reported willingness to engage in sexual encounters without emotional attachment) is related to infidelity, with this factor partially mediating the relationship between gender and a sexual motivation for engaging in infidelity (Barta & Kiene, 2005). Seal, Agostinelli, and Hannett (1994) had previously found the sociosexual orientation was related to self-reported willingness to engage in infidelity. They also reported that men were more likely to express an interest in extradyadic relations than women. The second part of the study included a behavioral measure of participants' willingness to engage in extradyadic dating; the gender difference disappeared, but sociosexual orientation remained a significant predictor of willingness to go on a date with someone other than one's primary partner. A ludic love style (a playful and cavalier view of romantic relationships) and sexual sensation seeking were unique predictors of past sexual and dating infidelity in one study (Wiederman & Hurd, 1999). Permissive attitudes toward infidelity are predictors of self-reported infidelity for women and men (Hansen, 1987). Accepting attitudes toward infidelity are also related to overall sexual permissiveness and earlier initiation of sexual intercourse (Barta & Kiene, 2005; Feldman & Cauffman, 1999b).

Closely related to sexual attitudes, sexual behaviors are another predictor of infidelity. Indeed, Whisman and Snyder (2007) have suggested that a broad attitudinal construct of "traditionality," as reflected by religiosity, fewer lifetime sexual partners, and decreased likelihood of cohabitating before marriage, helps account for a lowered disposition to infidelity, among women. Træen et al. (2007) reported that among married or cohabitating couples with extradyadic experience, the mean number of lifetime sex partners was 15.3, compared to 7.9 for those without extradyadic experience.

Attachment

Research on attachment style and infidelity has yielded interesting results. Individuals with a secure attachment style have less accepting attitudes toward infidelity than those with avoidant and preoccupied styles, but there was no difference in terms of actual infidelity in one sample (Feldman & Cauffman, 1999b). Allen and Baucom (2006) found that individuals whose attachment style causes them significant anxiety over possible abandonment (i.e., fearful and preoccupied types) are more likely to complain of neglect in their primary relationships and to identify a need for intimacy as a motive for infidelity, whether actual or imagined, than those with low anxiety (the secure and dismissive attachment styles). Bogaert and Sadava (2002) also reported a relationship between anxious attachment styles and past infidelity in a community sample.

In one of the more detailed studies of attachment and infidelity (Allen & Baucom, 2004), the investigators compared a sample of undergraduates and a community sample, all of whom reported extradyadic involvement in the past 2 years. The distribution of attachment styles for the college sample—secure (26%), fearful (21%), preoccupied (36%), and dismissive (17%)—corresponded to base rates for undergraduate populations. However, within this sample of students who had engaged in extradyadic involvement, there was a strong relationship between attachment style and total number of extradyadic partners in the past two years. Specifically, dismissive males exhibited the highest number of partners of all groups. Among women, those with preoccupied attachment styles had significantly more partners than securely attached females. Additionally, college students exhibiting fearful and preoccupied styles were most likely to describe the extradyadic relationship as "obsessive" in nature.

Personality

Two studies examined the relationship between personality traits, the "Big Five" traits, and infidelity. Orzeck and Lung (2005) administered a questionnaire to measure the Five Factors to a sample of 104 college students who also completed the same instrument to describe their dating partners. Participants who reported infidelity scored higher on Extroversion and Openness, but lower on Conscientiousness than the "noncheaters." Higher levels of Extroversion may reflect a more socially active lifestyle, which presents more opportunities for meeting extradyadic partners. Lower Conscientiousness may be associated with unreliability and erratic behavior. An interesting finding was that the participants who reported infidelity rated their partners lower on all five factors relative to those who reported no past infidelity. These lower ratings may be due to perceived incompatibilities and resulting relationship dissatisfaction, which could be motives for infidelity. Alternatively, these might serve as justifications after the fact. Somewhat different findings were reported by Barta and Kiene (2005) who found that individuals admitting to infidelity scored higher in Neuroticism and lower in Agreeableness than their counterparts. The lower level of Conscientiousness in the infidelity group was replicated (Orzeck & Lung, 2005). Personality factors may influence the types of motives given for engaging in infidelity. Extroversion and female gender predicted reporting relationship dissatisfaction as a motive for infidelity. Neuroticism was related to claiming neglect as a motive. The combination of high Neuroticism and low Agreeableness predicted reporting anger as a motive for infidelity (Barta & Kiene, 2005).

In sum, certain personality factors seem to interact with relationship variables in influencing a person's likelihood of being unfaithful to a dating partner. Tolerant attitudes toward infidelity, insecure attachment styles, and personality traits associated with erratic behavior seem to be related to extradyadic involvement, possibly as a function of opportunity and dissatisfaction with the primary relationship. In fact, McAlister et al. (2005) found that a combination of person factors (e.g., number of prior sexual partners, dysfunctional impulsivity), relationship factors (e.g., relationship satisfaction) and environment factors (e.g., quality of alternatives) predicted propensity toward extradyadic kissing and sexual activity. Unfortunately, the study measured only self-predicted tendencies in response to hypothetical scenarios, rather than actual behavior.

There is clearly a need for more research on possible correlates of dating infidelity. Researchers have only begun to explore the contribution of such factors as attachment style and personality traits on infidelity. It seems likely that a number of individual differences interact with relationship factors, such as level of commitment, and with contextual variables, like opportunity, to ultimately determine a person's likelihood of engaging in infidelity. We agree with Blow and Hartnett (2005b) that there is a need for studies on individuals' vulnerability to infidelity and on the process by which individuals decide to engage in infidelity, particularly the process by which costs and benefits are evaluated. An example of individual vulnerability to infidelity is the association between childhood sexual abuse (i.e., forced sexual intercourse before age 16) and later marital infidelity among women (Whisman & Snyder, 2007). Although yet to be studied, a similar relationship might exist for college dating relationship infidelity.

Internet Infidelity

The Internet has had a profound impact on human social and sexual behavior (M. L. Cooper, McLoughlin, & Campbell, 2000). Accordingly, a growing number of studies have explored online infidelity both in marital and in dating relationships, although data are still limited. To date, most of the research on "cybercheating" among college students has concerned itself with perceptions of infidelity, usually comparing reactions to hypothetical online and offline behaviors that might be construed as unfaithful. Despite the fact that online interactions are not physical and could be considered strictly fantasy, evidence to date reveals that cybercheating is perceived as being as real as face-to-face cheating (Whitty, 2005).

In an investigation of attitudes toward online and offline infidelity comprising 1,117 individuals, Whitty (2003) constructed a questionnaire and asked participants to rate a number of acts of potential infidelity. Attitudes toward both online and offline activities were assessed. Online behaviors included viewing pornography, engaging in hot chat with strangers, hot chat regularly with the same person, engaging in cybersex with strangers or regularly with the same person, sharing deep emotional and or intimate information with a person of the opposite sex, and maintaining a nonsexual relationship with someone of the opposite sex online. Results indicated that younger participants were more likely to view various online sexual activities as infidelity relative to older participants. A factor analysis yielded three moderately correlated factors, which were labeled "sexual infidelity," "emotional infidelity," and "pornography." Perhaps the most significant finding was "that online acts of betrayal do not fall into a discrete category of their own" (p. 376). Instead, each factor included both online and offline behaviors. So, while the results do suggest that a range of what is considered infidelity exists, most likely based on the perceived threat to the relationship, perceptions of online and offline behaviors are not dramatically different.

A more recent factor analytic study (Docan-Morgan & Docan, 2007) examined college students ratings of 44 possible acts of online infidelity, ranging from chatting about a favorite sports team with a person met in a chat room or having intellectual e-mail conversations with a person met online to disclosing love to someone met in a chat room or having cybersex with someone met in a chat room. The authors identified two factors, each characterizing a different type of infidelity: superficial/informal acts and involving/goal-directed behavior. Predictably, the latter category was perceived more negatively (i.e., more likely to be considered infidelity). This study suggests that a number of online acts that are nonsexual in nature are viewed as infidelity. Interestingly, individuals were more likely to see their partner's hypothetical online infidelity as less acceptable than their own hypothetical online infidelity.

Henline, Lamke, and Howard (2007) asked 123 college students who were in exclusive dating relationship to nominate online behaviors they would consider "unfaithful." The four most frequently nominated behaviors were online sex (45%), emotional involvement (39%), online dating including making plans to meet/actually meeting (37%), and sexual interactions/flirting (37%). The authors also investigated online versions of the infidelity scenarios used to assess jealousy with offline behavior (e.g., Buss et al., 1992). Results suggested that a large majority of participants, both men and women, identified emotional online infidelity as more distressing than online sexual infidelity. These findings differ from the commonly observed tendency (at least using the method of hypothetical scenarios) for men to be more distressed by sexual than emotional infidelity, relative to offline behaviors. A plausible explanation for this discrepancy lay in the fact that both men and women believed an emotional attachment to an online contact was more likely to lead to a face-to-face encounter than an online sexual interaction. A more recent study, however, replicating the forced-choice jealousy scenario method with both a student sample and a general-population sample (Groothof, Dijkstra, & Barelds, 2009) found that responses to online infidelity matched those to offline behaviors. Men were more upset by their partner's sexual involvement than emotional bonding with someone else online, by their partner trying different sexual actions via webcam than falling in love with an Internet contact, and by the sexual aspect of Internet infidelity than the emotional aspect of Internet infidelity.

A major shortcoming of the body of research regarding online dating infidelity is the absence of data on actual prevalence rates. Whitty (2003) found that 36 percent of her sample admitted to some experience in hot chatting. However, prevalence for other online behaviors were not reported (e.g., cybersex, pornography). Other studies did not obtain base rates of actual behaviors. A related shortcoming refers to the excessive reliance on hypothetical infidelity scenarios (Docan-Morgan & Docan, 2007; Groothof et al., 2009; Henline et al., 2007; Whitty, 2003, 2005). We found no study that examined response to occurrence of actual Internet infidelity among dating couples. Yet, as with the studies of jealousy and offline infidelity, it is quite probable that reaction to actual infidelity would differ from those to hypothetical scenarios.

RESEARCH LIMITATIONS

The literature on dating infidelity suffers from the same limitations as the research on marital infidelity (Blow & Hartnett, 2005a). With few exceptions, all data are derived from self-report measures. Given the widespread disapproval of infidelity in any context and the apparently high prevalence of extradyadic involvement, it seems likely that results are influenced by social desirability. As Feldman and Cauffman (1999b) concluded, "Acts of betrayal are likely to be underreported, whereas disapproving attitudes toward such behavior are likely to be overstated" (p. 245). By its very nature, infidelity is an illicit and clandestine practice that defies investigation (Charny & Parnass, 1995). One method that may be useful for evaluating the reliability of infidelity data would be to compare the individual's self-report to that provided by the "third party." Although fraught with ethical, methodological, and logistical complications (it would require participants to identify the third parties in order to recruit their participation), this method may yield some answers (see E. P. Ochs & Binik, 1999, for the use of couple data in sex research). Agreement between two individuals, however, does not ensure that the data are valid.

Another limitation is that the few studies on dating infidelity rely almost exclusively on samples of college students. The vast majority of participants in the relevant studies are unmarried Caucasian college students. Although the study of dating practices among college students is a legitimate topic of inquiry, it is important to also evaluate other groups. Research on dating practices and infidelity in high school students, older unmarried adults, and divorced persons would be useful for evaluating the generalizability of the findings. Research on same-sex couples is very limited (Blumstein & Schwartz, 1983; LaSala, 2004a, 2004b).

Longitudinal research to assess patterns of infidelity over time is also needed. If infidelity is a pattern for some persons, what attitudes, experiences, and traits predict susceptibility to the pattern? In the studies reviewed, the few longitudinal investigations ranged from four weeks to four months. Longer follow-up periods would provide important information regarding infidelity over the entire course of typical college relationships. Additionally, longitudinal designs would allow the study of individuals who are serially unfaithful, across dating relationship. Similarly, the extent to which dating infidelity predicts marital infidelity is an important question. Although popular lore suggests that behavior patterns in dating relationship predict marital adjustment, this hypothesis has not been tested. Related to this, the long-term sequelae of infidelity are relevant from the perspective of both the participants and their partners. Finally, the literature on dating infidelity is largely atheoretical. Commenting on a larger problem, Baumeister, Maner, and DeWall (2006) noted that much sex research accumulates in a theoretical vacuum. Outside of the studies of jealousy to hypothetical partner infidelity, few have attempted to explain dating infidelity from a theoretical perspective. Drigotas and Barta (2001) suggested that the study of infidelity would benefit from the combined perspectives of evolutionary theory and the investment model. Whereas both perspectives emphasize the role of exchanges in relationship satisfaction and the inverse relationship between relationship satisfaction and the attractiveness of alternative partners, the evolutionary viewpoint postulates different motives for infidelity in men and women. The investment model, on the other hand, focuses more on factors that are beneficial or detrimental to relationship commitment for both genders, including satisfaction and degree of investment. Other social exchange models, such as the equity model, point to potentially significant factors such as power within the relationship, perceived costs and benefits, and availability of attractive alternatives. We would add that additional perspectives, such as script theory, could shed light on possible gender differences in infidelity, attitudes toward extradyadic involvement, and students' definitions of infidelity. As Randall and Byers (2003) have observed, a broad and inclusive definition of infidelity may serve to reinforce the cultural script that promotes monogamy and fidelity. Conversely, a narrow definition of sex may reinforce the script that emphasizes sexual restraint. Finally, changing scripts for dating and sexual exclusivity could create some ambiguity about when extradyadic sexual activity qualifies as infidelity.

FUTURE DIRECTIONS

Research on dating infidelity could offer important insights into sexuality and intimacy. It could provide valuable information about the nature of commitment in dating relationships, potential gender differences, and the process by which couples negotiate problems in relationships, such as betrayal. Such findings could lead to applications in the field of couples' therapy.

Several interesting questions remain unanswered. Information on the other person involved in infidelity is lacking—what might be called the "third-party problem." Although infidelity was not a primary focus, the study by Grello et al. (2006) of casual sex among college student is an exception (21% of the students who participated in casual sex were involved in a committed dating relationship at the time). In order to better understand the context of infidelity, there is a need to study the perspective of the third party. How often do unfaithful partners misrepresent their relationship status, as in the popular stereotype of the married man who strategically removes his wedding band? What were the motives, justifications, and reactions to the infidelity for the third party? It would also be important to understand individual characteristics, including personality traits and relevant attitudes, from the partner's perspective. Some researchers have suggested that infidelity could result from the third party's intentional pursuit of a person who is in a committed relationship, so-called "mate poaching" (Schmitt & Buss, 2001; Schmitt et al., 2004). Davies, Shackelford, and Hass (2007) reported that 54 percent of the male students and 34 percent of the female students in their survey admitted to having knowingly poached a person in a committed dating relationship for "sexual relations." An even larger number of students (70% of males and 80% of females) reported that they had been the objects of attempted poaching, and 38 percent of both genders claimed to have been "successfully poached" for a sexual encounter. A significant number of men (64%) and of women (74%) claimed that others had attempted to poach their partners, with some success (22% of men and 30% of women reportedly had a partner who gave in to the pursuer). It would be informative to learn of the factors that differentiate those who give in to poaching from those who do not. Although infidelity can result from poaching by a third party, it has not been possible to determine how many cases of infidelity might be explained by this strategy. It seems likely that situational (such as opportunity) and relationship factors (such as low commitment or ongoing conflict) are also important. If poaching is indeed a widespread phenomenon, what makes a person vulnerable to the third party's pursuit? Finally, some, if not many, instances of infidelity probably involve some degree of receptivity and even initiation by the cheating partner, even if only providing subtle cues of ambivalence about one's availability.

Over the past decade, a number of researchers (see Amato et al., 2007) and social critics have lamented the changes in the institution of marriage. The median age at first marriage has steadily risen, divorce rates remain relatively high, and alternatives to marriage have become increasingly popular. We wonder whether the "institution" of dating, as popularized during the 1950s in most Western cultures (Gordon, 1978; Hareven, 1977), is undergoing a similar transformation. For example, the script for dating in contemporary culture appears to be changing (DeGenova & Rice, 2005; Sessions-Stepp, 2007). College dating has reportedly become more informal, which may reflect a revision of such former scripts as "going steady" in favor of "hanging out" and "hooking up" (Bogle, 2007; Grello et al., 2006; Manning, Giordano, & Longmore, 2006; Paul et al., 2000). The study of infidelity could shed light on the changing meanings of commitment and exclusivity in contemporary college dating relationships.

The study of dating infidelity illustrates the inconsistency between stated attitudes and actual behavior. Although the vast majority of college students disapprove of most forms of extradyadic intimacy, a majority of them report having cheated on a dating partner at some time. A variety of motives and predictors of infidelity have been identified, most of which can be conceived of as (1) individual characteristics, such as demographics, attitudes, and traits; (2) relationship variables, such as sexual and general satisfaction, commitment to the relationship, and perceived equity; and (3) environmental variables, such as availability of alternatives. In the final analysis, it is likely that more comprehensive studies will allow clarification of the interaction between these categories of variables in the prediction of dating infidelity.

Chapter Eight

SEXUAL ORIENTATION AND COLLEGE STUDENTS

Michael R. Kauth and Andrea Bradford

By the time American adolescents are old enough for college, most will already be sexually active (W. D. Mosher, Chandra, & Jones, 2005), and some youths will have already identified ("come out") as gay, lesbian, or bisexual (Savin-Williams, 2005), if only to close friends or Internet acquaintances. Recent evidence suggests that lesbian, gay, and bisexual (LGB) youth are "coming out" at a younger age, often by age 15, and are using the Internet to facilitate this process (Elias, 2007; Grov, Bimbi, Nanín, & Parsons, 2006; Savin-Williams, 2005). Whether LGB or curious young people are certain about their sexual identity when they arrive on campus, the college environment's diverse student population, their relative independence from parental oversight, and the presence of alcohol and substances present an opportunity for students to explore their sexuality and self-identity (Wetherill, Neal, & Fromme, 2010).

In this chapter, we will review the general process of sexual-identity development for LGB college students. In the first half of the chapter, we will review what LGB youth often seek to understand about same-sex sexuality. We will briefly discuss the interaction of gender orientation and sexuality, including transgenderism. In the second half, we will discuss the role of the college environment in the formation of sexual identity for LGB students and suggest several helpful campus and online resources for students. Where we are purposefully including transgender individuals in the discussion, we will use the acronym LGBT.

FROM SEXUAL ATTRACTION TO A SEXUAL ORIENTATION

It is likely that most LGB college students have been aware of a pattern of erotic feelings since before puberty, by ages 10 and 11 (McClintock & Herdt, 1996), although a small percentage of youth may never have had erotic feelings. Males tend to experience these feelings as sexual attraction, while females often experience erotic feelings as romantic attraction. Usually, people find their sexual interests directed toward one sex or the other. Sexual and romantic attraction, arousal, and sexual behavior toward adolescents or adults of the same sex, different sex, or both sexes are generally referred to as *sexual orientation* (J. M. Bailey, 2008; Kauth, 2005). *Homosexuals/gays* or *lesbians* are people with same-sex sexual attractions. *Heterosexuals/straights* are people with different-sex sexual attractions, and *bisexuals* are individuals who are sexually attracted to both sexes. Young people often hear the words "gay," "lesbian," "fag," "dyke," and others used as insults, although they may not have understood their meaning. Particularly among young people, "gay" may be used to mean stupid or inferior (e.g., "That's so gay"); while not directly related to sexual orientation, this still carries connotations of queerness or impugned masculinity. When used as a noun, "gay" or "homosexual" refers to a same-sex-attracted person or to a social identity. As an adjective, however, "homosexual partner" may refer to the sex of the partner, the sexual behavior of two individuals, the partner's self-identity, or a kind of person. Sex researchers attempt to avoid this kind of imprecision in language by restricting word use, by identifying what aspect of sexual orientation is of interest, or by generally referring to attraction to males as *androphilia* and attraction to females as *gynephilia*.

Although most youths experience sexual and romantic attraction to different-sex individuals, many may also experience some same-sex attraction (Savin-Williams, 2005). More people experience same-sex attraction than identify as gay or lesbian. Women appear less likely than men to experience exclusive heterosexual attraction, yet men are more likely than women to identify as nonheterosexual (J. M. Bailey, 2008; Savin-Williams & Cohen, 2007). Regardless of sexual orientation, boys typically initiate sexual activity at an earlier age than girls (Cavazos-Rehg et al., 2009; Grov, et al., 2006), and by late adolescence about 75 percent of American 18- to 19-year-olds have engaged in sexual activity with a partner to orgasm (W. D. Mosher et al., 2005).

A small number of people (about 1%) describe themselves as asexual and report no sexual attraction and no desire for sex with a partner, although some masturbate or engage in sex anyway (Bogaert, 2006; Prause & Graham, 2007). Recently, asexual individuals have become more public and have organized supportive real-world and virtual communities (e.g., The Asexual Visibility and Education Network (AVEN), http://www.asexuality.org/). While the causes of asexuality are not well established, it is thought to be a function of low sexual desire caused by one or more biological processes (Prause & Graham, 2007).

CAUSES OF SEXUAL ORIENTATION

Same-sex-attracted youth typically wonder how they got this way and may look for clear answers in religion or science. There are many varied and strong beliefs about the causes of same-sex attraction. The scientific literature is clear, although far from complete. Comprehensive reviews of the literature (e.g., LeVay, 2010; G. Wilson & Rahman, 2005) have concluded that sexual orientation is likely *predisposed* before birth due to several biological processes, such as genes and sex hormone exposure, although these processes differ for males and females. A predisposition for same-sex attraction still depends on postnatal biological processes and environmental interactions, including social experiences, for development. For instance, early behavioral traits associated with same-sex sexual orientations like gender nonconformity (e.g., female tomboyish activities or male avoidance of rough-and-tumble play) may strongly influence the children's experiences in the world (Hammack, 2005). In addition, early same-sex affectional desires and feelings are likely to shape social relations, emotions, and children's view of themselves. Prior to puberty, youths are often already aware of a pattern of same-sex emotional and sexual desires that will later lead to their identification as gay, lesbian, or bisexual (Herdt & McClintock, 2000).

Although early social and sexual experiences may affect one's later sexual feelings and functioning, there is no evidence that early experiences determine adult sexual orientation (LeVay, 2010; G. Wilson & Rahman, 2005). That is, people do not become gay or straight because of certain childhood experiences; and there is also no convincing evidence that adult sexual orientation can be changed through treatment (American Psychological Association, 2009). A controversial study by Spitzer (2003) of 200 religious, married men and women who had completed interventions to become heterosexual found that a few highly motivated people can be taught to minimize same-sex feelings and find pleasure in heterosexual relations, despite continued same-sex attractions. That is, people may choose to act or not act on certain sexual feelings (and may do so for many reasons) without a change in their primary attractions. This may also explain why some people "come out" late in life after years of living a heterosexual life. Further, some women and many bisexuals claim to be more attracted to the person rather than the person's gender, which may look to others like a change in sexual orientation when a partner of a different sex is chosen (Diamond, 2008; Weinberg, Williams, & Pryor, 1994).

Biological research has suggested that male homosexuality is linked to a maternal lineage, and female homosexuality with prenatal androgen exposure (LeVay, 2010; G. Wilson & Rahman, 2005). Possible genetic markers for male homosexuality have also been found (Hamer & Copeland, 1994). The evolutionary origins of these phenomena are unknown, although several hypotheses have been proposed. Kauth (2000) and Muscarella (2000) have argued that rare exclusive same-sex attraction is an effect of population-level, same-sex eroticism that may have benefited our ancestors within sex-segregated societies. In other words, erotic attractions may have facilitated alliances with older or younger same-sex individuals in competition for resources, including mates. Vasey and VanderLaan (2010) have found more prevalent helping behaviors among same-sex attracted males in Independent Samoa (called *fa'afafine*) consistent with the idea that traits beneficial to kin will be favored. A separate line of research suggests that mothers who have a gay son have more children on average (Camperio-Ciani, Corna, & Capiluppi, 2004), which suggests that male-male attraction may be a by-product of a trait for maternal fertility. Although these hypotheses are intriguing, additional evidence is needed to support an evolutionary advantage for homosexuality.

SEXUAL BEHAVIOR, IDENTITY, AND BISEXUALITY

Late adolescence and early adulthood - the college years - are a time for trying out and establishing a personal identity (Erikson, 1994). One aspect of identity is sexuality, or sexual identity. In an anonymous survey of nearly 8,000 U.S. and Canadian college students, over 97 percent of men and women identified as heterosexual (Ellis, Robb, & Burke, 2005). Only about 3 percent of respondents identified as homosexual or bisexual. However, nearly 15 percent of students acknowledged at least some attraction to both sexes; and 9 percent reported both male and female partners. Thus more students experience same-sex attraction than engage in same-sex behavior or identify as LGB. Even so, people may engage in sexual behavior for reasons other than sexual attraction, for instance, because of uncertainty regarding sexual feelings, convenience, or intoxication. Many gay men and lesbians report having different-sex partners before adopting a gay or lesbian identity (Savin-Williams, 2005), and some lesbian-identified women continue to occasionally have sex with men (Diamant, Schuster, McGuigan, & Lever, 1999). For women, sexual attraction may be less specific to sex of partner and more associated with subjective feelings about the person and the setting than for men (Chivers, Rieger, Latty, & Bailey, 2004; Diamond, 2007; Rieger, Chivers, & Bailey, 2005). Yet women are not necessarily more likely than men to identify as bisexual. Some studies find more women than men who identify as bisexual (W. D. Mosher, Chandra, & Jones, 2005), and others do not (Laumann et al., 1994).

On the other hand, Chivers and colleagues (2004; Rieger et al., 2005; J. M. Bailey, 2008) have suggested that male bisexual orientation (as opposed to bisexual behavior) is rare or nonexistent because bisexually identified men tend not to show strong physical arousal patterns (erection) to both male and female sexual stimuli (e.g., photos). Rieger at al. (2005) likewise found that some bisexually identified men responded physically more like gay men (preferring male stimuli) and others like heterosexual men (preferring female stimuli). In general, men tend to show category-specific physical arousal patterns, responding to one sex and not the other. However, Kauth (2006) has argued that male bisexual arousal patterns may indicate qualitatively different attractions to men and women.

SEXUAL IDENTITY FORMATION

Despite the fact that most college students identify as heterosexual, we know very little about the process of heterosexual identity formation. One study asked 26 heterosexual college students to write about their own identity development (Eliason, 1995). Most men described adopting a heterosexual identity by *rejecting* homosexuality, consistent with men's general experience of attraction directed toward one gender. However, most women described entertaining the *possibility* of a lesbian or bisexual identity before adopting a heterosexual identity, consistent with women's more social, flexible experience of sexual attraction. Worthington, Savoy, Dillon, and Vernaglia (2002) proposed a conceptual model of heterosexual identity formation that begins with gender socialization and the association of gender nonconformity with homosexuality. In this model, heterosexual identity is defined more by what one is not (homosexual) rather than by what one is.

By contrast, we have much more information about gay and lesbian identity formation. Numerous models of gay and lesbian identity formation have been described. Most of these are linear stage models that have been criticized for being rigid, failing to account for social and cultural context, and assuming the need to disclose (Eliason & Schope, 2007). None has been strongly supported by data. Common themes among the models include (1) early feelings of differentness, (2) moving toward identity acceptance, (3) disclosure of identity to others, (4) pride and cultural immersion, and (5) identity synthesis/integration. In their review, Eliason and Schope (2007) concluded that gay and lesbian identity formation is a lifelong, highly individual process that may include some or all of these themes. Many individual factors appear to influence the pathway of identity formation, such as perceived support networks, self-confidence, culture and ethnicity, personally held stereotypes, feelings of rejection or isolation, and internalized homophobia (Stevens, 2004). For many, sexual identity is just one of several identities (e.g., race/ethnicity, gender, religious) that must be integrated into a whole self, if possible. One difference in identity development between gay men and lesbians is the role of sex. Gay and bisexual men are more likely to have their first sexual experience with someone they met for the purpose of having sex, while lesbians are more likely to have their first same-sex experience with a close, trusted friend (Dempsey, Hillier, & Harrison, 2001).

Greater public tolerance of homosexuality over the past decade may help to explain why LGB youth are coming out earlier. In 2010, for the first time, more than 50 percent of Americans viewed gay and lesbian relationships as morally acceptable; and disapproval of gay and lesbian relations dropped to its lowest point (43%) in a decade (Saad, 2010). Increased media attention to gay issues like marriage and the rights of gay soldiers to serve openly may be driving public attitudes. "Normal" gay characters and storylines are now common in mainstream television programs and on premium cable series, as opposed to crude stereotypic depictions of gays and lesbians as pathetic, sad victims, or harmless clowns. Positive media images of gays and lesbians have been shown to positively influence attitudes toward homosexuality, especially among social conservatives (Calzo & Ward, 2009). Also, younger people, many of whom interact with LGB peers, have more positive attitudes toward gays and lesbians and are replacing older, negative cohorts (Saad, 2010).

Media such as books, magazines, television, and movies have long provided information about homosexuality to young people seeking to understand their sexual selves. Today the Internet plays a dominant role in identity formation for LGB adolescents by providing access to enormous amounts of information in seconds and linking with LGB people in virtual communities (Bond, Hefner, & Drogos, 2009; C. Ryan & Futterman, 1998). Teens can explore their sexuality, ask questions, and share their experiences in chat rooms, special interest websites, blogs, social networks, instant messages, tweets, and virtual worlds (Hillier & Harrison, 2007). The connectivity to information and to LGB people provided by the Internet may be particularly important for isolated, marginalized, and rural LGB teens (Ross & Kauth, 2002). *Second Life*, a virtual world, offers bars, nightclubs, beaches, and even island resorts for LGB avatars to meet and simulate the experience of real-life encounters. The Internet has also provided a popular means for LGB people to meet sexual partners via personals sites, chat rooms, and social networking (Daneback, Månsson, & Ross, 2007). In fact, LGB people are more likely than heterosexuals to use the Internet to search for sexual partners (Lever, Grov, Royce, & Gillespie, 2008). These services are no longer limited to personal computers. Free mobile smart-device applications like Grindr use global positioning system technology to locate nearby same-sex attracted men. In many ways, the Internet has made finding other LGB people infinitely easier, which may in some ways speed up identity development.

Although LGB college students today may find it relatively easy to gain information and social support and become more quickly comfortable with their sexuality, social stigma regarding homosexuality remains prevalent. Campus environments vary in their support of LGB students and may present conflicting messages about acceptance of LGB people or intolerance of antigay speech and behaviors (Wilkerson, Ross, & Brooks, 2009). Social stigma regarding homosexuality contributes to low self-esteem among LGB individuals, self-hatred, social isolation, health risks, and vulnerability to violence and discrimination (Herek, Chopp, & Strohl, 2007). LGB college students, compared with heterosexual peers, remain at increased risk for heavy drinking, depression, suicidal thoughts, and sexually transmitted infections, including HIV (Kisch, Leino, & Silverman, 2005; Lindley, Nicholson, Kerby, & Lu, 2003). Bisexual men and women are at particular risk and are more likely to report mental health problems than gay/lesbian and heterosexual peers (Dodge & Sandfort, 2007).

GENDER ORIENTATION, ROLES, AND SEXUALITY

Gender underlies most aspects of sexuality. *Gender orientation* refers to the adoption of a self gender identity. Boys and girls are socialized from birth to think of themselves as male or female, respectively. *Gender role* refers to the behaviors (e.g., dress, mannerisms, speech, sexual attitudes) that convey that one is a man or a woman. Men's stereotypic gender role is to be always interested in sex, have multiple partners, maintain an emotional distance from partners, and perform as sexual penetrators (Stokes, Miller, & Mundhenk, 1998). Women, on the other hand, are stereotypically expected to be more cautious about sex, choosy about partners or chaste, emotionally intimate, and sexually submissive to men (Oliver & Hyde, 1993). Heterosexuality is a central way that men and women manifest gender (Hamilton, 2007). For men, heterosexuality is demonstrated by their ability to seduce women, while for women it is their ability to attract men's attention as a desired sexual object. Lesbians are stigmatized for violating the female gender role because they are not interested in men's sexual attention.

In terms of desired features in a sexual partner, gay/lesbian and heterosexual men and women are not so different. Gay and heterosexual men both share similar interests in uncommitted sex, visual sexual stimuli, and physically attractive partners, while lesbians and heterosexual women share similar interests in committed sexual relationships and older partners (J. M. Bailey, Gaulin, Agyei, & Gladue, 1994). However, conflict occurs when gender boundaries are more than temporarily crossed. On average, gay men and lesbians report more gender-atypical behaviors than heterosexuals (J. M. Bailey & Zucker, 1995; Lippa, 2005; Rieger, Linsenmeier, Gygax, & Bailey, 2008) and have different occupational interests than heterosexuals (Lippa, 2005). Although many gay men and lesbians appear and behave in a gender-typical manner, those who transgress traditional gender roles are more visible and are the usual subjects of gendered stereotypes. Typically, gay men are perceived as being effeminate and sexually passive, while lesbians are perceived as being masculine. Perhaps because gay men are thought to commit a double gender violation by "abandoning" masculinity and "adopting" femininity, heterosexual men report more negative attitudes toward homosexuality, especially male homosexuality, than do women (Herek, 2002, 2009). Although definitions of masculinity and femininity vary across cultures, as do attitudes toward homosexuality (Lippa & Tan, 2001), college students may find that the social and cultural context on their campus permits little or no gender role variation.

Gender Variance

Gender also affects sexuality through gender orientation variance. *Transgenderism* is a continuum of perceived inconsistency with one's gender role. *Transgender* individuals view their "real" gender as inconsistent with their biological sex and may live full- or part-time as the other sex (Lawrence, 2007). *Transvestites*, individuals who dress in the clothes of the other sex for sexual arousal, are transgender. Intersex individuals, those born with incompletely differentiated genitalia, fall on the extreme end of the transgender continuum. However, female impersonators, like drag queens, who dress as caricatures of women for entertainment are not transgendered. *Transsexual* is a medico-psychiatric term used to label transgender people who view their "real" sex as different from their biological sex and may seek to alter their physical appearance partially or completely through surgery. Not all transsexuals desire to complete surgical reassignment. There remains some confusion among scholars and the trans community regarding the differences between and preferences for the terms "transgender" and "transsexual." Clearly, gender orientation is independent of sexual orientation (Byne, 2007). Transgender people may be androphilic, gynophilic, attracted to both sexes, or attracted only to transpeople.

Devor (1999) has described a 14-stage, lifelong model of transsexual identity formation, based on interviews with intersex and transgender individuals.

This model is similar to early models of gay/lesbian identity formation with the addition of stages for gender identity confusion, discovery and acceptance of transgenderism, and transitioning. Self-disclosure may lead to rejection by family and friends; and transgender students may be particularly vulnerable to rejection, isolation, and marginalization (Beemyn, Curtis, Davis, & Tubbs, 2005). Supportive campus resources can make self-acceptance easier for transgender students.

CAMPUS LIFE FOR GAY, LESBIAN, BISEXUAL, AND TRANSGENDER (LGBT) STUDENTS

An important determinant of an LGBT student's experience on campus is the general campus climate toward nonheterosexual community members (Stevens, 2004). *Climate* refers to characteristics of institutions that shape their members' behaviors and experiences; these characteristics are related to policies, social norms, and events, but they also emanate from numerous "unspoken rules" that are often diffuse and difficult to pinpoint. Consequently, *climate* is challenging to define precisely. Research on campus climate for LGBT students has defined *climate* primarily in terms of perceived discrimination or hostility toward LGBT persons. However, even when overt homophobia is minimal, the campus's structural features, policies, and climate may be biased to favor heterosexual people and practices. Other important elements of campus climate include the presence of resources for LGBT students; LGBT-inclusive programs and services; and policies or rules to protect LGBT students, faculty, and staff from discrimination (Rankin, Weber, Blumenfeld, & Frazer, 2010; for review, see Rankin, 2003).

Although climate can be thought of as a shared perception of "how things are" in a given environment, minority groups may perceive campus climate differently from those in majority or privileged groups. For instance, a heterosexual student who "knows of" gay and lesbian peers and holds ambivalent attitudes toward same-sex relationships may perceive the campus climate quite differently than a lesbian classmate who struggles to find fellow students or faculty who openly identify as gay or lesbian. Indeed, studies have found that heterosexual students relative to LGBT peers tend to underestimate the degree to which a campus is discriminatory toward nonheterosexuals (R. D. Brown, Clarke, Gortmaker, & Robinson-Keilig, 2004; Waldo, 1998). Bisexual students perceive campus climate even more negatively than gay and lesbian students (Rankin, 2003).

Differences in perceptions of antigay climate are also found among other minority group members. Studies have found that African American students are comparable to Caucasian students in their personal attitudes toward gay men and lesbians (Jenkins, Lambert, & Baker, 2009; Rankin et al., 2010), although at least one study has suggested that African American students *perceive* antigay sentiment on campus slightly more strongly than Caucasian peers (Waldo, 1998). This experience too is a function of the general social environment of the college campus. The socially conservative climate of many religiously affiliated institutions and historically African American colleges and universities, for instance, may contribute to environments that are less accepting of nonconforming gender expression or nonheterosexual identification and behavior (S. R. Harper & Gasman, 2008). Although few studies have examined other factors related to perceived climate, such as experience with sexism or contact with LGBT students, limited evidence suggests that women (relative to men) and upper-division students (i.e., junior year or higher, relative to lower classifications) are more likely to perceive antigay climate on campus (R. D. Brown et al., 2004).

The outcomes of a hostile, invalidating environment for LGBT students are numerous (see Wright's chapter on homophobia in this volume), although the direct effects of antigay campus climate are difficult to quantify because campuses vary in other important ways as well. Regardless of setting, LGBT college students are likely to experience some degree of chronic psychological and physiological stress associated with their status as a sexual minority ("minority stress," Meyer, 1995). Belonging to an LGBT-identified organization or social group appears to act as a buffer to minority stress (Westefeld, Maples, Buford, & Taylor, 2001). On the other hand, for some this buffer may be limited if students are "out" only on campus and not in other significant areas of their lives, such as their hometowns or families of origin (Rankin, 2003).

Below we briefly describe several social and structural features of college campuses that may shape the developmental experiences of LGBT students. Although not exhaustive, the features described cover key facets of the campus climate for LGBT students. These features include attitudes of campus members, visibility and representation of LGBT people, and inclusion of LGBT students.

Attitudes of Students, Faculty, and Staff

Although there may be greater social tolerance of LGBT persons in general, homosexuality remains stigmatized. Negative attitudes can be manifest in a variety of ways, from overt homophobic acts such as antigay jokes, name-calling (e.g., "fag," "lezzy"), threats, physical assault, or property damage to more subtle behaviors such as exclusion from a group or downplaying the importance of LGBT issues. The overt and covert attitudes of peers, faculty, and staff toward LGBT students are central to the campus climate. In a survey of 5,149 college students, staff members, faculty members, and administrators, LGB respondents were significantly less likely to feel comfortable with the general campus climate than their heterosexual counterparts, although overall comfort was high for most groups (Rankin et al., 2010). Transgender respondents were least likely to feel comfortable with the campus climate. LGB respondents (23%) were nearly twice as likely to report experiencing harassment as heterosexuals (12%), and transgender students (35%) were more likely to report harassment than men and women (20% and 19%, respectively). However, 61 percent of LGB campus respondents reported being targets of demeaning remarks compared with heterosexual peers (29%); and gay-identified men (66%) were more often the targets of derogatory remarks. Lesbians (53%) were more likely to be ignored or excluded. Bisexual and transgender students in particular may face alienation from both heterosexuals and nonheterosexuals.

Experiences with antigay attitudes on campus may vary across contexts and within groups. For instance, heterosexual students who privately express favorable or supportive attitudes toward LGBT students in surveys may downplay their support when asked to speak publicly in a peer group setting (Jurgens, Schwitzer, & Middleton, 2004). In an earlier survey of 1,669 college students, staff, faculty, and administrators, 63 percent of LGB students reported being harassed in public space on campus, while 40 percent experienced harassment in their place of residence and 30 percent in the classroom (Rankin, 2003). In response, 40 percent of LGB students reported concealing their sexual orientation in the past year to avoid harassment. However, concealment may not be sufficient or effective to avoid harassment. Often people are targeted for harassment because they are *perceived* to be LGB. What is more, the same advances in technology that permit greater access to information and to virtual communities for LGBT students also provide new ways of bullying ("cyberbullying") by quickly disseminating hurtful information to a wide audience through social media like Twitter (Elias, 2007). Private images (e.g., nude photos of the sender) sent to an intimate partner ("sexting") may be instantly transmitted to everyone in the former partner's cell phone address book. Further, phone cameras and tiny webcams may be used to spy on an individual's private life. Recently, an 18-year old Rutgers University student, Tyler Clementi, jumped to his death from the George Washington Bridge, after his roommate and a fellow student secretly used a webcam to view Clementi's intimate encounter with a man in his dorm room and streamed it to the Internet (J. Schwartz, 2010). The roommate "tweeted" friends to tune in to the webcast. Clementi was not open about his sexual orientation, but his roommate believed that he was gay and had made an earlier attempt to spy on him via webcam.

Double Minorities

LGBT students who are also a member of a minority group—a "dual minority"—may be especially vulnerable to antigay attitudes and harassment on campus. The term "dual minority" refers to membership in at least two distinct minority groups, which may be defined by sexual orientation, race, ethnicity, ability, social class, country of origin, or other sociocultural characteristics. Here, we focus specifically on the experiences of LGBT people of color. LGBT college students of color are more likely than Caucasian LGBT students to experience harassment and conceal their sexual identities and are less likely to feel comfortable in the campus environment (Rankin et al., 2010). Transgender students of color are particularly likely to perceive harassment on campus. LGBT students of color not only face the double threat of race-based and antigay discrimination, but they may also have greater difficulty navigating within their social groups. Asian, Hispanic, and African American communities, for instance, tend to hold more conservative attitudes toward homosexuality than Caucasians (Ahrold & Meston, 2010). Consequently, LGBT ethnic minority students may hide their sexual orientation from their family and community to avoid the perception that they have rejected their community and their family (Savin-Williams & Cohen, 2007). At the same time, LGBT people of color may experience discrimination and alienation from Caucasian LGBT peers (Rankin et al., 2010). Similar identity-management challenges may be experienced by LGBT students with disabilities and LGBT students from poverty- and working-class backgrounds, although these and other varieties of "dual minority" experiences are less addressed in the literature.

Although women now comprise a larger portion of the student body than men on many campuses, sexist attitudes toward women, including conflicting standards of sexual conduct, persist. Correspondingly, some evidence suggests that lesbians more than gay men have difficulty in adjusting to college and feeling a sense of belonging on campus (Longerbeam, Inkelas, Johnson, & Lee, 2007). Several issues complicate the development of a lesbian or bisexual identity for college women. First, women are disproportionately the targets of sexual harassment and assault on campus, primarily by men (Banyard et al., 2007; Cortina, Swan, Fitzgerald, & Waldo, 1998). Second, women who defy a passive gender role and endorse greater assertiveness, ambition, and other so-called masculine personality traits are especially likely to experience sexual harassment (Berdahl, 2007). These conditions contribute to a reduced sense of personal safety on campus for lesbian or bisexual women, as well as pressure to conform to gender expectations and limited safe space for exploration of sexual identity. However, ironically, even as female homosexuality is shunned or ignored, women may find that female-female sexual behavior is encouraged or rewarded in certain heterosexual contexts, provided it is performed for the gratification of men (Hamilton, 2007).

Representation and Inclusion

The degree to which LGBT students, faculty, and staff are "out" and welcomed in public spaces is another important feature of campus climate. In a survey of 14 campuses, 64 percent of LGB college students reported being "out" on campus (Rankin, 2003). The proportion of "out" students was highest for lesbian and gay male students (83% and 80%, respectively) and lowest for bisexuals (48%). Although there are many reasons why students may or may not choose to disclose their sexual orientation, the campus climate, which may vary across campus, is an important determining factor (Rankin, 2003). Various campus "subclimates" may result in greater representation of sexual-minority faculty, staff, and students in some spaces than in others. For example, course offerings that focus on issues of gender and sexuality are more likely to attract LGBT (and questioning) students and are typically concentrated in the humanities and social science fields. Such courses provide exposure to theories of gender and sexuality and to the works of sexual-minority scholars, writers, and artists. Some colleges and universities now offer majors, minors, or concentrations in gender studies, sexuality studies, queer studies, and/or gay and lesbian studies. An unofficial listing of such programs, maintained by John Younger at the University of Kansas, can be found at http://people.ku.edu/~jyounger/lgbtqprogs.html.

Visibility of LGBT students in some spaces does not necessarily indicate that sexual diversity is distributed across multiple spheres of campus life. The inclusion and participation of LGBT students in campus organizations and functions is an essential component of overall LGBT-positive campus climate. Longerbeam and colleagues (2007) reported that, relative to heterosexual peers, LGB students were marginally less likely to participate in certain campus activities such as intramural sports but likely to participate more frequently in political and social activism events and arts and music performances. Similarly, C. S. Carpenter (2009) found that gay and lesbian students were more likely to view political activities and the arts on campus as important, relative to heterosexual peers. Gay men also placed greater importance on involvement in student organizations and volunteer work than did heterosexual men.

Although well represented in campus political activism and the arts, LGBT students have been less welcome in other groups and organizations. Collegiate athletics in particular continue to be a relatively volatile space for LGBT people, even within schools that are otherwise more generally inclusive (Krane & Barber, 2005; Roper & Halloran, 2007). While the National

Collegiate Athletic Association prohibits discrimination on the basis of sexual orientation, homophobia and heterosexism are entrenched in sports culture. For instance, until relatively recently some coaches have attempted to forbid same-sex sexual activity among their players. Particularly in women's sports, a tactic known as "negative recruiting" has been used to deter student-athletes from entering some programs by insinuating that certain coaches or players are gay or lesbian. Proactive educational campaigns, such as the Women's Sports Foundation's *It Takes a Team!* initiative, have aimed to eliminate these practices and promote a more inclusive environment for LGBT student-athletes. A few recent high-profile stories of collegiate and professional athletes who have publicly come out as gay and lesbian suggest that the culture of silence may be changing, if slowly (Wharton, 2007).

Greek organizations, often associated with traditional gender roles (Kaloff & Cargill, 1991), have been another important target of efforts to educate members about LGBT issues, involve LGBT students, and improve the campus climate. Hinrichs and Rosenberg (2002) reported that the presence of Greek organizations on campus predicted a more negative campus climate for LGBT students, although at the level of the individual student Greek affiliation was a weaker predictor of attitudes toward homosexuality. The heterosexist climate of many fraternities and sororities has been the target of several initiatives aimed at improving attitudes toward and inclusion of LGB members. Greek-specific ally programs and other educational outreach efforts such as the Lambda 10 Project (http://www.lambda10.org) have been established to address sexual-orientation concerns in this population. In addition, campus-based Greek organizations such as Delta Lambda Phi and Gamma Rho Lambda have been formed specifically to be inclusive of sexual-minority students.

The inclusiveness of religious activities on campus is another indicator of the overall climate for LGBT students. Despite clear proscriptions against same-sex sexuality by many faith traditions, young LGBT persons may seek spiritual communion in religion (Love, Bock, Jannarone, & Richardson, 2005; Ritter & O'Neill, 1989). Whether LGBT students are religious, they may be affected by religious attitudes toward homosexuality and by institutional policies and programs on campus (Getz & Kirkley, 2006). Religiously affiliated schools, particularly those that espouse conservative beliefs, may create a campus culture that is unsupportive and even hostile to same-sex sexuality. For instance, students who apply to Oral Roberts University in Tulsa, Oklahoma, must sign an Honor Code Pledge that specifically prohibits "any homosexual activity" (ORU Online Campus Degree-Seeking Application, n.d.); and recently Jerry Falwell's Liberty University's School of Law hosted a two-day campus conference on the spiritual consequences of same-sex attraction and the legal implications of gay rights (Liberty Counsel, 2010). Other religiously affiliated institutions have adopted a neutral or even an affirming stance toward LGBT students. Emory University, for example, a Methodist-affiliated institution, boasts an Office of Gay, Lesbian, and Transgender Life (Emory University, n.d.); and the Roman Catholic-affiliated University of San Diego sponsors students, faculty, staff, and alumni as Rainbow Educators to present campus workshops on diversity and sexual orientation (University of San Diego, 2010).

Many college campuses have programs that promote contact with LGB students and faculty. In general, social contact with LGB people predicts positive attitudes toward homosexuality (Liang & Alimo, 2005). Juniors and seniors, for instance, report more positive attitudes toward homosexuality than freshman and sophomores, perhaps because older students have had more opportunity for contact with fellow students who are gay (E. G. Lambert, Ventura, Hall, & Cluse-Tolar, 2006).

SPECIFIC RESOURCES FOR LGBT STUDENTS

Resources for LGBT students, once virtually unheard of on college campuses, have multiplied substantially in the past two decades. While some colleges and universities may largely "support" LGBT programs and services for self-promotion, the increase in campus resources, nevertheless, illustrates a growing awareness of LGBT students' needs. Below we describe some common initiatives and services that have been developed to address the needs of LGBT college students on campus.

Institutional Policies

At the most basic level, institutional policies are influential by prohibiting discrimination based on sexual orientation or gender expression. These policies affect not only hiring and admissions decisions but also the ability for student organizations to discriminate against LGBT students. Although private universities have more latitude in permitting discrimination, many public universities are at a minimum subject to state or local laws regarding discrimination based on sexual orientation. In the absence of such state or local laws, a number of institutions have adopted their own antidiscrimination policies—for example, the University of North Dakota (2010). Even so, the efficacy of these policies depends strongly on enforcement and commitment from senior administrative officials. Recently, the U.S. Supreme Court upheld a California institution's right to deny formal recognition and funding to a Christian student organization that prohibited membership of gay men and lesbians (*Hastings Christian Fellowship v. Martinez et al.*, 2010). Even so, in early 2010 the Virginia attorney general notified the state's public schools and universities that they lacked the authority to ban discrimination based on sexual orientation (Helderman, 2010). The outcome of this decision on Virginia campuses is still uncertain.

LGBT Student Organizations

Many colleges and universities provide some support for "identity-based" campus organizations to promote cohesion and social support for members of underrepresented or nonprivileged populations. Eisenberg and Wechsler (2003) reported that in 2000 most of 119 colleges surveyed had at least one "well-established" student organization for LGBT students. The proportion of schools with such organizations has no doubt grown in the last decade. Larger schools may even have separate groups organized around specific cultural identities, such as Latina/Chicana/Raza lesbians or gay and lesbian Muslims. Although relatively little research has addressed the nature or effect of these groups, LGBT students' needs for social support are well described. For some, an LGBT student organization may be a student's first or only point of contact with LGBT peers, particularly in rural or isolated regions.

"Safe Zones"

The presence of heterosexual allies who are supportive of LGBT students and who openly identify themselves as such can help to contribute to an inclusive climate for LGBT students. "Safe zone" programs generally consist of heterosexual students, faculty, and/or staff who openly support LGBT students and who have received training in and a means of displaying their support publicly—for example, through a placard posted on one's office door. One of the first such programs began at Ball State University in 1992 (University of Illinois at Chicago, n.d.). There is no single model for "safe zone" programs, and thus their form varies from campus to campus. Poynter and Tubbs (2008) recently reviewed the development and characteristics of some successful LGBT ally programs. A list of campuses with LGBT ally training programs is available at http://www.LGBTCampus.org.

Housing

Previous research suggests that antigay sentiment can "cluster" geographically by residence hall (Bowen & Bourgeois, 2001). Institutional bans on antigay discrimination are designed to protect LGBT students in residence halls from harassment by roommates, fellow residents, and residence hall staff. In addition, some colleges and universities have designated LGBT-themed or LGBT-friendly spaces in residence halls. Berkley's Unity House, for instance, is designated for residents who are interested in LGBT and women's studies programs (University of California at Berkeley, n.d.). Other institutions have adopted gender-neutral housing policies, which relax traditional requirements for same-sex housing arrangements. Such policies have been adopted by more than 50 colleges and universities, some of which also extend gender-neutral restrooms and other facilities to other campus locations (The National Student Genderblind Campaign, 2010).

Health Services

Health service providers in college and university health centers are not immune to antigay bias and benefit from specific training to provide comprehensive care of LGBT students. Although study findings vary in the extent to which LGBT and heterosexual students differ in health status, bisexual men and women may be at particular risk for several poor health outcomes (Diamant & Wold, 2003; Dodge & Sandfort, 2007; L. S. Steele, Ross, Dobinson, Veldhuizen, & Tinmouth, 2009). According to a survey conducted by the Association for University and College Counseling Center Directors (Barr, Rando, Krylowicz, & Winfield, 2009), LGBT students make up over 10 percent of the clientele in college counseling centers. Greater mental health service needs, for example, by LGBT students may not reflect a greater incidence of psychopathology so much as a need for coping resources to manage the developmental, environmental, and social challenges faced by most LGBT students. The inability to cope with stressors may lead to health risk behaviors, depression, and even thoughts of suicide. In recent years, many campuses have initiated campaigns to increase awareness of student depression and suicide and have made 24-hour telephone counseling services available.

A small handful of studies have examined the influence of campus health resources on LGBT students' lives. Although the effect of specific resource availability on LGBT students' well-being is unclear, the opportunity for social affiliation that campus resources present appears to be especially important. Surprisingly, Eisenberg and Wechsler (2003) found that greater availability of LGBT resources was associated with a larger proportion of students who had engaged in same-sex sexual behavior, although whether greater resources was a cause or effect is unknown. This study also found that greater LGBT resource availability was associated with lower rates of smoking in bisexual women and lesbians but greater rates of binge drinking in bisexual and gay men, perhaps because of more opportunities for social activities that involve alcohol. Interestingly, the presence of LGBT resources on campuses was also associated with safer sex practices (condom use) by both LGBT and heterosexual students (Eisenberg, 2002).

In addition to institutional resources, an increasing number of unaffiliated resources are available to current and future LGBT college students. A recent

Google search turned up over 16 million links to "gay lesbian college student resources" (September 24, 2010). Websites such as CampusPride.org and books such as *The Advocate College Guide for LGBT Students* and the Princeton Review's *Gay and Lesbian Guide to College Life* attest to the increasingly mainstream visibility of sexual-minority students. Select additional Internet resources are listed below:

LGBT chats
- Gay chat (http://www.chat-avenue.com/gaychat.html)
- *Yahoo!* LGBT chats (http://dir.yahoo.com/society_and_culture/cultures_and_groups/lesbian__gay__bisexual__and_transgendered/chats_and_forums/)
- Teenspot.com (http://www.teenspot.com/chat/)

LGBT Resource Centers
- Gay Student Center (http://gaystudentcenter.student.com/)
- Human Rights Campaign LGBT campus group directory (http://www.hrc.org/issues/youth-campus)

LGBT Scholarship information
- FinAid (http://www.finaid.org/otheraid/gay.phtml)
- CollegeScholarships.org (http://www.collegescholarships.org/scholarships/lgbt-students.htm)

Campus LGBT groups
- University of Missouri, St. Louis gay group PRIZM (http://www.umsl.edu/~prizm/)
- Harvard College Queer Students and Allies (QSA) (http://www.hcs.harvard.edu/~queer/)

LGBT-friendly campuses
- Campus Pride (http://www.campuspride.org/shop.asp)
- Campus Climate Index (http://www.campusclimateindex.org/)
- University of Utah LGBT Resource Center guide to finding a college (http://www.sa.utah.edu/lgbt/resources/college.htm)
- Consortium of Higher Education LGBT Resource Professionals (http://www.lgbtcampus.org/)

LGBT news
- The International Gay, Lesbian, Bisexual, Trans and Intersex Association (http://ilga.org/)
- 365 Gay (http://www.365gay.com/)

Civil rights and freedom of expression
- Lambda Legal Defense (http://www.lambdalegal.org/)
- Soulforce (http://www.soulforce.org/index.php)

LGBT studies
- Wakefield State University Library (http://www.lib.wsc.ma.edu/GLS.htm)
- GLBT Historical Society (http://www.glbthistory.org/)

SUMMARY

LGB youth appear to be "coming out" at a younger age while still in high school, and by the time they are ready for college most adolescents, including LGB youth, are sexually active. Although the college years have traditionally been a time of self-exploration and personal identity formation, this process may start at an earlier age for LGB youth. One factor that may account for this change is a growing social tolerance for homosexuality. LGBT issues are often in the news, and LGBT characters are increasingly portrayed by the media and the entertainment industry as normative. For the first time, more than half of Americans now view same-sex relationships as morally acceptable, and disapproval of same-sex relationships is at its lowest point (43%) in a decade. A second factor that may account for LGB youth coming out earlier is widespread access to and use of the Internet. Mass media has always played a critical role in the coming out process for LGB individuals by providing information about same-sex-attracted people and where they can be found. The Internet has made access to information infinitely easier. For instance, information about the biological causes of same-sex attraction and the coming out process are a "click" away. Chat rooms, personals websites, blogs, e-mail, instant messaging, phone applications, and virtual worlds make it relatively easy for LGB youth to find others like them and find potential sexual partners.

For many same-sex attracted men and women, healthy identity formation is aided by accurate information about sexual orientation and the coming process. Recent comprehensive reviews of the scientific literature conclude that same-sex sexual orientation is likely a biological predisposition that is often but not always associated with other gender-related traits. Development of a same-sex sexual orientation then is a product of the interaction between the individual's own cognitive, social, and behavioral traits and preferences and the social environment, including the family, the ethnic culture, and general social culture. Sex differences also contribute to variation in sexual orientation and sexual behavior. For instance, regardless of sexual orientation, men tend to be more category-specific in their sexual attractions (that is, attracted only to men or only to women), while women tend to be more context focused in their attractions (that is, aroused by the sexual nature of the situation). The process of LGB and T identity formation appears to be a lifelong process with common developmental phases or tasks. At present, current developmental models are more descriptive than evidence based.

Despite somewhat greater social acceptability, antigay attitudes remain prevalent and significantly influence LGBT identity formation. Attitudes toward LGBT people vary across ethnic groups, as well as by educational level, religious faith, political beliefs, and region of the country. Antigay and antitransgender attitudes place LGBT youth at risk for verbal and physical harassment or assault as well as discrimination. Use of the Internet to cyberbully individuals represents a new mode of antigay harassment that can quickly cross boundaries of privacy. A hostile message, compromising photo, or live video can instantly be disseminated to a wide audience. Recent suicides of gay youth have focused attention on antigay bullying in general. As a consequence of antigay attitudes and behaviors, LGBT youth are vulnerable to experiencing low self-esteem, heavy drinking, depression, and suicide.

For many individuals, an LBGT identity is one of several potentially conflicting identities that must be integrated into a personal identity. This process of identity integration can be particularly difficult for LGBT youth of color and for those who come from cultures that emphasize family and reproduction or collective interests over the individual. The college campus represents another social environment that may be supportive or hostile to LGBT students, depending on the campus climate. More welcoming campuses provide relatively safe spaces for LGBT students. For many, the college campus may be the first space in which a young person can express their sexuality and gender openly. Additionally, certain academic fields or spaces may offer more supportive "subclimates." Meanwhile, other campus climates may stigmatize, silence, or ignore LGBT community members. Student, faculty, and staff attitudes toward LGBT campus members are an important contributing factor to the campus climate as are institutional policies, services, and programs. For instance, college nondiscrimination policies that include sexual orientation, the presence of LGBT student organizations on campus, health services for sexual minorities, and specific programs to increase awareness about LGBT issues contribute to an open, supportive climate. The Internet provides a means for LGBT students to research the campus climate and available resources before they arrive. A number of key Internet resources for LGBT students and family members are provided throughout the text and at the end of this chapter.

Chapter Nine

A NEGATIVE CAMPUS CLIMATE: SEXUAL HARASSMENT AND HOMOPHOBIA

Lester W. Wright Jr. and Anthony G. Bonita

INTRODUCTION

Campus climate is a concept that serves as a "temperature gauge" to describe the learning environment of a college or university campus. A campus with a positive climate is welcoming and receptive, while campus with a negative climate would be perceived as nonwelcoming, cold, and alienating (Cress, 2008). The campus climate affects the faculty and staff as well as the students. Sexual harassment and homophobia are just two examples of behavior that can lead to a negative campus climate. These behaviors will be described separately; however, they can occur together, as in the case of a person who is sexually harassed due to a perception that the he or she is homosexual. The information presented is intended to focus on homophobia and sexual harassment as they pertain to college students, the university setting, and the extracurricular activities associated with a university. Comparisons will be made to other settings, such as business, industry, and the military, to demonstrate similarities and differences, as the recourse one has for being victimized depends on the setting in which it occurs. Factors related to the victims and the perpetrators will be described, as well as the effects on the victims. Finally, prevention and intervention methods will be shared and new areas of research will be suggested.

SEXUAL HARASSMENT

Definitions and a Brief History of Sexual Harassment

Sexual harassment has been interpreted by the U.S. Supreme Court to be a form of sex discrimination that is prohibited by Title VII of the Civil Rights Act of 1964. Sexual harassment has a long, well-documented history and extends beyond our borders. For example, accounts of sexual harassment are known to have occurred against African American women during the time of slavery in the United States; however, this behavior predates any legislation that protected individuals from such abuse. The concept of sexual harassment and protection from the behavior did not gain much momentum until activists began fighting for women's rights (Farley, 1978; MacKinnon, 1979). Even after legislation was passed to protect workers from sexual harassment, many of the early sexual harassment cases that were filed were not successful. Title VII does not actually contain any language specifically prohibiting sexual harassment, so many cases had to work their way through the courts in several jurisdictions until the U.S. Supreme Court settled the inconsistencies in the rulings. It was not until the mid-1970s that the courts began to issue verdicts in favor of the plaintiff for sexual harassment.

The Equal Employment Opportunity Commission (EEOC) in 1980 developed guidelines against sexual harassment and provided a definition for the behavior based on Title VII. The courts are not required to follow the EEOC guidelines; however, since the guidelines were written the courts have been more inclined to hear the cases brought before them and to rule in favor of the plaintiff. Sexual harassment is defined by the United States EEOC guidelines as:

> Unwelcome sexual advances, requests for sexual favors, and other verbal or physical conduct of a sexual nature constitute sexual harassment when (1) submission to such conduct is made either explicitly or implicitly a term or condition of an individual's employment, (2) submission to or rejection of such conduct by an individual is used as a basis for employment decisions affecting such individual, or (3) such conduct has the purpose or effect of unreasonably interfering with an individual's work performance or creating an intimidating, hostile, or offensive working environment. (U.S. Equal Employment Opportunity Commission, 1980, pp. 74675–74677)

The EEOC guidelines list two types of sexual harassment that are illegal. *Quid pro quo*, a Latin term that translates to "something for something," is when sexual requests or demands are made for employment or academic benefits. This behavior is seen as a form of bribery and can occur, for example, when a harasser, such as a supervisor, promises a reward, such as being employed or receiving a promotion, in return for sexual requests, or threatens punishment, such as being fired or not receiving a promotion, if the demands are rebuffed. On a college campus, this type of harassment could occur between a professor and a student when it is either implied or stated that a reward, such as a higher grade or extra credit, will be delivered if a sexual request is granted. This form of harassment, often stated as an explicit proposition, is generally the most recognizable type.

The second type of harassment, the hostile workplace environment, occurs when ridicule, insult, or intimidation are severe or pervasive enough to create an abusive atmosphere or to alter the working conditions of the employee. Many different types of behavior and or comments can make an environment uncomfortable or hostile. Examples of a hostile workplace would be when an employee receives sexual comments based one's attire, if pornography or sexual material is visible in the workplace, if repeated requests to go out on dates are made, or when sexually explicit language is commonly used. This form of harassment is more difficult to prove (McCandless & Sullivan, 1991) and is often decided on the "totality of circumstances," which takes into account the context in which the behavior or comments occur. A mere offensive utterance or an isolated joke or comment does not rise to the level of a hostile workplace; the behavior must be widespread and extreme.

Till (1980) elucidated how sexual harassment can occur in various settings, including college campuses, with the following five examples. Gender harassment occurs when suggestive stories are told, offensive jokes are made, seductive or crude sexual remarks are stated verbally, and nonverbal behavior, such as staring, leering, or ogling, is exhibited. Sexual seduction can be considered harassment when it includes unwanted discussion or questions related to personal sexual matters, unwelcome seductive behavior, attempts to establish sexual relationship despite discouragement, and invasion of privacy such as repeated phone calls or repeatedly asking someone out on a date.

The "quid pro quo" examples include sexual bribery, which can be subtly implied or direct blatant bribery for sexual cooperation; being actually rewarded for sexual cooperation; and sexual coercion or threats, which include subtle or direct threats of retaliation for noncooperation, or if someone engages in unwanted sexual behavior because of threats. Physical harassment can occur on its own or in combination with verbal harassment. Sexual imposition describes a range of behaviors from deliberate touching to unwanted attempts to touch or fondle someone to unwanted attempts at intercourse that result in the victim crying, struggling, or pleading (Till, 1980).

The first sexual harassment cases that were successful in the courts were based on employer-employee harassment in business and industry (see *Meritor Savings Bank v. Vinson* and *Harris v. Forklift Systems, Inc.*, for details on these cases). The case of *Oncale v. Sundowner Offshore Services, Inc.*, was the first case in which the courts held that victims of same-sex sexual harassment were also protected under Title VII. The opinion of the judge in this case stated that harassing conduct did not have to be motivated by sexual desire to justify discrimination on the basis of sex. Eventually, lawsuits were filed alleging harassment between teachers and students as well as student-on-student harassment. As with the initial cases of harassment in business and industry the early cases of sexual harassment in academia were not successful. However, by the 1990s several cases were successful in the courts.

Sexual harassment in academia that is between the employer and employee is covered under Title VII. If, however, the harassment is between a teacher and a student, or is student-on-student harassment, the behavior is covered under Title IX of the Education Amendment (1972). Title IX states that:

> No person in the United States shall, on the basis of sex, be excluded from participation in, be denied the benefits of, or be subjected to discrimination under any education program or activity receiving Federal financial assistance. (Cengage, 2003)

The case of *Franklin v. Gwinnett County Schools* in 1992 was decided by the U.S. Supreme Court on the issue of teacher-on-student harassment. Lower courts had heard similar cases and their rulings were inconsistent, so the U.S. Supreme Court took on this case to prevent future inconsistencies. The *Franklin* case involved a high school girl and her coach and included forced intercourse. The girl claimed that the school officials knew the harassment was occurring but did nothing to stop it so she transferred to another school. The Court ruled that the student was entitled to monetary damages under the provisions of Title IX.

The U.S. Supreme Court heard the case of *Davis v. Monroe County Board of Education* in 1999 to decide the issue of student-on-student sexual harassment. This case is important because it addresses the issue of peer sexual harassment among students, showing how sexual harassment can occur beyond a prototypical supervisor-supervisee harassment example. This specific case involved physical contact and sexual slurs from peers that were so severe that the student victim considered taking her own life. The Court ruled that school districts could be held liable if they act with deliberate indifference to known student-on-student sexual harassment that is so severe as to effectively deny the victim access to an educational program or benefit. The Court also ruled that teasing and name-calling based on gender differences are not covered unless the harassment is harsh and pervasive.

Statistics and Scope of Sexual Harassment

Sexual harassment in educational settings, both verbal and physical acts, has been found to begin as early as elementary school and continues throughout the educational process, into one's career. Sadker and Zittleman (2005) found that four out of five girls and almost as many boys experience some type of sexual harassment. The American Association of University Women conducted a national survey of girls and boys in public schools in 2001 and found that approximately 80 percent of students experienced some form of sexual harassment at some time during their school life. The students' most common reactions to harassment included avoiding the person who bothered or harassed them, talking less in class, not wanting to go to school, changing their seat in class, and finding it difficult to pay attention. Gruber and Fineran (2008) found that girls experienced more harm than boys; they reported suffering from lower self-esteem, poorer mental and physical health, and more trauma symptoms.

Sexual harassment on college campuses is a commonly occurring behavior that is often ignored and infrequently reported. Reason and Rankin (2006) found that women reported experiencing harassment more than men. Most instances of sexual harassment are instigated by men against women. Men who are harassed are most often harassed by other men. Woman-to-woman sexual harassment is rarely reported but does exist (Taylor, 1994). Student-to-student or student-peer harassment is the most common form of sexual harassment on college campuses (C. Hill & Silva, 2005), which contradicts the stereotype of harassment occurring only between a professor and student.

Various studies, using different methodologies and different questionnaires, have found different prevalence rates of sexual harassment. Clodfelter, Turner, Hartman, and Kuhns (2010), using an online survey, found that almost a quarter (22.7%) of the college-student participants reported being sexually harassed. When the definition of sexual harassment included sexist remarks and "gender harassment" the incidence rate for undergraduates is close to 70 percent (Paludi, 1996). M. L. Kelley and Parsons (2000) found in their university study that 30 percent of staff, 22 percent of faculty, 43 percent of administrators, 20 percent of undergraduate students, and 19 percent of graduate students reported sexual harassment. Undergraduate students more often reported other students as being responsible for the sexual harassment, but graduate students were more likely to report faculty as perpetrators. Kalof, Eby, Matheson, and Kroska (2001) conducted a study of undergraduate students and found that 40 percent of women and 28.7 percent of men had been sexually harassed by a college professor or instructor. This study shows that both men and women are perceiving sexual harassment, but not in equal numbers. Although men and women on college campuses may experience some type of sexual harassment during their college experience, less than 10 percent report the behavior to faculty or administration (C. Hill & Silva, 2005). Minority women are more likely to be sexually harassed and less likely to report the behavior than White women (Paludi).

Since many instances of sexual harassment are not reported, the actual occurrence of sexual harassment is difficult to know. Published statistics are likely to underestimate occurrences of the actual behavior, especially if they rely on victims reports of harassment. Reasons for discrepancies in prevalence rates, such as why student reports of harassment are lower than university faculty or employees, could be that university employees may be more knowledgeable about what constitutes sexual harassment. Therefore when they are the victim of harassment, they are better able to identify what infraction occurred in order to report it (M. L. Kelley & Parsons, 2000). Methodological issues in research can also create varied reporting rates. Researchers who employ a direct-question approach, such as asking a student "have you been sexually harassed," will be more likely to record lower rates. An alternative approach, such as providing a list of behaviors in the form of a checklist, can be used and is often more accurate since respondents have to report only what behaviors or actions have been directed toward them without having to label it as harassment or not (Chan, Lan, Chow, & Cheung, 2008). It could also be that the victims fear they will not be believed or that they will be retaliated against for making an allegation. Students are often reliant on faculty for grades and letters of recommendations for jobs or internships and may feel pressure because they do not want to jeopardize their futures.

Prevalence rates of sexual harassment on campus are comparable to the rates for the military, which range from 60 percent to 79 percent (Sadler, Booth, Cook, & Doebbeling, 2003). Rates of sexual harassment in business and industry are also comparable to those found on campus.

Victims of Sexual Harassment

Women are more likely to report sexual harassment when it occurs, while men are more likely to accept the behavior and remain silent. Ways that individuals have dealt with the sexual harassment are to deny the harassment, avoid the harasser, or treat the harassment as a joke rather than reporting it. In many instances other individuals in the workplace or educational setting will witness the harassment and will file charges against the harasser on behalf of the actual target or as a result of being offended by the harassing behavior; this type of complaint is called secondhand sexual harassment (Cengage, 2003).

The types of harassment men and women experience on campus differ as do their reactions to the harassment. Female victims are more likely to be the targets of sexual jokes, comments, gestures, or looks. Males are more likely to receive sexual harassment in the form of antigay comments such as being called "gay" or another homophobic slur. Threats of physical violence were more often experienced by male students, while actual physical assaults were most experienced by women (Reason & Rankin, 2006).

Some groups of students are at greater risk for being sexually harassed than others. Students who identify as gay, lesbian, bisexual, and transgendered

(LGBT) are more likely to be harassed than their nonsexual minority counterparts (C. Hill & Silva, 2005). The EEOC has taken the position that sexual harassment that involves same-gender individuals is also illegal.

Barickman, Paludi, and Rabinowitz (1991) identified additional groups of women who are at higher risk for sexual harassment. Those who are at greater risk include: graduate students whose careers are determined by association with their major adviser, students in small colleges or small academic departments, women in male-populated fields, economically disadvantaged students, physically or emotionally disabled students, women students who work as resident assistants in dormitories, women who have been sexually abused, and inexperienced, unassertive, or socially isolated girls and women.

Consequences of Sexual Harassment

The effects of sexual harassment are costly at the personal level as well as to the institution and society. Meta-analysis research confirms that sexual harassment experiences are negatively associated with psychological health, physical health conditions, and job-related outcomes (Chan et al., 2008). Psychological reactions can include body image issues associated with eating disorders in women, depressed mood, anxiety, difficulty concentrating, and lower self-esteem. Reactions to harassment can be similar to those of domestic abuse including feelings of anger and betrayal (Huerta, Cortina, Pang, Torges, & Magley, 2006). Women tend to respond more negatively to sexual harassment than men (C. Hill & Silva, 2005); however, it is likely that men are unaware of and underreport the effects of the harassment. Female students are more likely than male students to feel embarrassed, angry, less confident, and afraid after the harassment has occurred (C. Hill & Silva, 2005). Physical symptoms may also result, in the form of sleeping problems, head and neck pain, fatigue, and gastrointestinal problems (Huerta et al., 2006).

Researchers examining the effects of sexual harassment in the workplace have found decreased job satisfaction, lower organizational commitment, withdrawing from work, physical and mental illness, and symptoms of post-traumatic stress disorder (Willness, Steel, & Lee, 2007). On college campuses, Paludi (1996) reported that 15 percent of female graduate students and 12 percent of undergraduate students changed their major or educational program due to sexual harassment. J. Adams, Kottke, and Padgitt (1983) found that 13 percent of participants avoided working with certain professors due to the risk of sexual harassment. Female victims suffer more significant educational consequences of harassment, in that they are more likely to find it hard to pay attention or concentrate while in class. Also, female students, more than male students, are more than males likely to be disappointed in their college experience (C. Hill & Silva, 2005). Other symptoms include decreased productivity, class attendance, and satisfaction with courses (Fitzgerald, 1993). Researchers found that LGBT students who were sexually harassed were more likely to drop out of their college or university as a way of escaping or preventing sexual harassment.

Perpetrators of Sexual Harassment

Men are more likely than women to sexually harass another person. Ménard, Hall, Phung, Ghebrial, and Martin (2003) found that men were twice as likely to sexually harass and three times more likely to be sexually coercive when compared to women. Both men and women are more likely to be harassed by a man (C. Hill & Silva, 2005). One potential influence on the gender difference in the perpetration of sexual harassment on college campuses is that there are more men in positions of power in academia.

Several individual variables have been identified that may influence one's likelihood to engage in sexual harassment. If a person lacked knowledge of the rules for the organization, that person could violate the rules seemingly unknowingly. An individual who has personal or emotional problems that impact their judgment may sexually harass another (Carr, 1991). Sexual harassment was also predicted among men if the person was a victim of child sexual abuse, demonstrated increased hostility, or possessed adversarial heterosexual beliefs (Ménard et al., 2003). Brunswig and O'Donohue (2008) identified individual variables including problems with self-control, engaging in cognitive distortions, lack of victim empathy, and issues with perspective taking as contributing factors to sexual harassment. Identifying these variables and factors can be instrumental when designing intervention programs aiming to reduce sexual harassment on campus.

Resolving Sexual Harassment

As stated earlier, many instances of harassment are ignored or go unreported. If the victim of harassment chooses, there are several options to resolve an offense. The victim can take personal action and confront the harasser; file a grievance with the employer or the union, if applicable; and or take legal action. The response to an offense might vary depending upon individual differences and the perceived severity of the offense. It is important to document the offense, have witnesses who can corroborate the complaint, file a complaint with the employer or educational institution, and give the officials a chance to respond before filing a formal complaint to the EEOC or instigating a lawsuit. Many institutions have a "zero-tolerance" policy for sexual harassment and will release an employee if he or she engages in harassing behavior. The fines levied against institutions and the monetary awards given in lawsuits make it too risky to retain a faculty member or student employee who has been found to have harassed someone.

Preventing Sexual Harassment

It is important for administrators of institutions to have policies and procedures in place that clearly explain their positions on sexual harassment and the consequences for the behavior. One of the areas in which there is wide disagreement over policy is consensual relationships between faculty and students. Some administrators argue that these relationships are never consensual due to the faculty member's position of authority. Others think that consensual relationships are not part of the institution's business. It is important for students and faculty alike to know and understand the policies of their institution. Many institutions have training sessions for students, staff, and faculty so that each knows what constitutes sexual harassment and how it will be handled. Both the accuser and the accused have rights during the process. It is important to understand how to handle an allegation before it ever occurs since mistakes can be made that make the charges more serious as well as more detrimental to those involved. It is important not to engage in retaliation since the outcome of that behavior can have consequences even if a charge of sexual harassment is not upheld.

Treatment programs are available for those who sexually harass. One of the important treatment objectives is to make sure that perpetrators can identify the harassing behaviors they committed as well as other potentially harassing behaviors, in order to prevent these actions from occurring again in the future. Skills training for the perpetrator is an important aspect of treatment since sexual harassment may occur as a result of a person lacking a proper social repertoire and other social skills. Other important aspects of treatment programs include assessment and change of the perpetrators' "myth acceptance" and of any negative attitudes toward women. Brunswig and O'Donohue (2008) suggest that these goals can be accomplished by providing alternative interpretations to common cognitive distortions and beliefs such as victim blaming, feelings of entitlement, minimizing problems, overgeneralization, and rationalizing behavior.

Awareness training is a key component of prevention and can provide knowledge about sexual harassment, which helps to decrease inappropriate behavior and change perceptions of harassing behavior (Frisbie, 2002). University undergraduate students who were considered likely to sexually harass watched a training video of different examples of sexual harassment and had a discussion of what was viewed. Those who participated had increased knowledge about sexual harassment and decreased inappropriate behavior (Frisbie, 2002).

Future Research

Additional research is needed in the prevention and treatment of sexual harassment. Programs are needed to increase awareness, address factors that are correlated with harassment, as well as change the negative reactions displayed by victims of harassment. Long-term follow-up research is also needed for these treatment programs to see not only if change in behavior occurs but how long is it maintained. Additionally, not as much is known about female perpetrators of harassment and male victims of female perpetrated harassment.

HOMOPHOBIA

Definitions and a Brief History of Homophobia

We as a society differentiate and label people based on their sexual orientation, which is a socially constructed phenomenon that takes into account one's emotional, physical, and sexual attractions. Additionally, we have endowed individuals based on their sexual orientation with characteristics that may or may not be salient to them (Wolf-Wendel, Toma, & Morphew, 2001). Homophobia is a type of discrimination that individuals who are attracted to same-sex individuals may experience as a result of their actual or perceived sexual orientation.

The term "homophobia" was coined in 1972 to describe the dread of being in close quarters with homosexual men and women as well as the irrational fear, hatred, and intolerance by heterosexual individuals of homosexual men and women (Weinberg, 1972). Since the term was introduced, many researchers, authors, and activists have written on the topic and redefined the construct. Debates exist whether homophobia, which literally means "fear" of homosexuality, is a true phobia, in the way arachnophobia is an extreme fear of spiders, or if the construct should be renamed. Others question if the private thoughts of the individual (e.g. attitudes, prejudices, cognitions, etc.) should be part of the construct or if only overt behaviors are important. Herek and Gonzalez-Rivera (2006) describe homophobia as a form of sexual negativity and discrimination. Homophobia, regardless of the specific definition or whether it is a true phobia or not, is a type of prejudice and discrimination that demeans and intrudes upon the rights and behavior of gay and lesbian individuals.

The sources of discrimination faced by sexual minorities on college campuses can range from individuals who work at or attend the institution, to the policies of the institution, as well as to the larger community in which the institution is situated. Given that many high schools currently have LGBT student alliance organizations and that more students are "out" (i.e., are public about their sexual orientation) when they enter college, prospective students are looking for colleges and universities that provide an atmosphere of respect and equality. Many university officials are currently examining their policies and are creating or improving campus organizations that support sexual minorities to make the campus climate as safe and welcoming as possible.

University officials also realize that diversity among its faculty is important in changing the culture on campus, and many are offering benefits to gay and lesbian staff and faculty that are on par with what heterosexual employees receive. Policies of inclusion and fairness, if consistently practiced and enforced from the top administration down through the faculty and staff to the students, help to provide a venue in which all students, sexual minorities included, can thrive. Additionally, communities that have antidiscriminatory policies and states that have hate crimes legislation provide added layers of protection against discrimination and make campuses safer.

In order to understand homophobia on college campuses, it will be useful to have a brief history of how homosexuality was viewed and treated in the past. Homophobia, or negative reactions to sexual minorities, has a long history in the larger society. Laws making homosexual behavior illegal have been around for centuries, and proscriptions for same-sex behavior exist in religious holy books. Until recently, individuals who identified as homosexual were labeled as mentally ill. They could not serve in the U.S. military or obtain security clearances that would allow them to hold certain jobs in the federal government. If a parent came out as gay or lesbian during a divorce, custody of children could be denied on that basis alone.

In the last four decades, many events have taken place that have changed the lives of sexual minorities. The Stonewall riots in New York City in 1969 were seen as a major turning point for the gay rights movement. Since then, some legislation has been passed to protect sexual minorities and some laws restricting the rights of sexual minorities have been repealed. Some states have allowed gay marriage or civil unions to take place, while others have passed constitutional amendments that prohibit such behavior. President Clinton added sexual orientation to the nondiscriminatory policy for federal civilian employees in 1998, and President Obama in 2010 added gender identity to the EEOC policy. There are still approximately 1,000 rights that are not accorded to sexual minorities that heterosexual citizens have. The road for gay rights has not been smooth, nor without controversy. The vestiges of the laws and proscriptions on same-sex behavior and the prejudices of those in charge of the institutions continue to present many obstacles to equality on college campuses. Many challenges, no doubt, lie ahead as attempts are made to take away the recent gains that have been made and as further gains are attempted. Those who oppose equality for same-sex rights often see gay and lesbian individuals as transgressive, as violating rules or laws (LeVay & Valente, 2006), and oppose change based on their interpretation of the law or on religious grounds.

Statistics and Scope of the Problem

It is difficult to provide accurate prevalence rates for homophobia due to many of the definitional issues related to the construct described above. Blumenfeld (1992) viewed homophobia as existing on many levels and proposed that it must be assessed and understood on the personal, interpersonal, institutional, and societal levels. A major issue, however, with obtaining accurate prevalence rates is that regardless of the level on which it exists, many acts of homophobia go unreported to the police or university authorities. Additionally, the prevalence rates obtained through research can be affected by many other variables, e.g., the methodology of the study, the questions asked, the location of the study, the year the study was conducted, etc. Some researchers ask general questions and treat verbal assaults and physical assaults similarly to overt homophobic actions. Others will classify behaviors differently so it is difficult to compare prevalence rates across studies.

Rates of homophobia rise and fall over time as the mood of society changes. Acceptance rates for gay and lesbian individuals had risen quite steadily since the 1970s; however, the trend peaked in the mid-2000s and has declined somewhat since then (G. F. Kelly, 2011; Saad, 2008). The downturn in acceptance rates could be due to the events in the news, such as priests having sexual contact with children (Saad, 2008) or as a result of the politics at that time.

The percentages of gay and lesbian individuals who have been victims of homophobia range from around 75 percent to 94 percent depending on how homophobia was defined and what types of assaults were assessed (D'Augelli & Rose, 1990; Herek, 1989, 2002, 2004). The behaviors that were assessed in the above studies ranged from verbal threats to use of a weapon. Additionally, D'Augelli and Rose found that nearly all of the students who had been victimized expected future harassment. The high rates of abuse in recent studies demonstrate that even though acceptance rates for gay and lesbian individuals have risen over the past decades, the prevalence of homophobic attacks is still alarmingly high.

Heterosexist speech (Burn, 2000) and silence (LeVay & Valente, 2006) are other ways in which homophobia is promulgated. Heterosexist speech such as using the term "gay" to describe something as undesirable or stupid is hurtful and demonstrates the insensitivities of those who use the term in that manner. Words such as "queer," "faggot," and "dyke" are regularly used as a way to insult someone (Burn, 2000; Lovell, 1998). These terms are so common in language today that it is almost impossible to measure how frequently they are used and how much damage they do. Burn, Kadlec, and Rexer (2005), however, pointed out the incongruity behind the intent and reception of such behavior. They found that heterosexual individuals often use these terms without meaning to express sexual prejudice. Burn (2000) found that while antigay prejudice was predictive of antigay behavior, about half of her participants used heterosexist speech without having antigay prejudice. Teachers, coaches, political figures, religious leaders, and so on who remain silent when a homophobic slur or heterosexist speech is used send the message to those in attendance that this behavior is condoned and acceptable. Advertising campaigns and public service announcements on television have been used in an attempt to combat the silence surrounding heterosexist speech and to help raise awareness of the issue; many of these ads target teenagers and young adults.

Homophobia is not only a problem in the United States. Researchers have found antigay sentiment and discrimination to exist in many other countries. Thurlow (2001) found heterosexist language used in a pejorative manner to be very common in Britain. M. Davies (2004) conducted a study in the United Kingdom and found that men more so than women have higher negative affective reactions toward gay men. Homophobic behaviors were found to be higher among male than female college students in Italy, and it was found to be present in the Italian military (Lingiardi, Falanga, & D'Augelli, 2005). Several individuals per week are reportedly killed in Latin America and Mexico as a result of their sexual orientation (J. S. Greenberg, Bruess, & Conklin, 2011). In Brazil, 2,509 gay men were murdered between 1997 and 2007 (Ruscombe-King, 2009).

Bisexual men and women also face discrimination that is similar in form and impact to what gay men and lesbians experience. Biphobia is the term used to describe the negative attitudes about bisexuality and bisexual individuals (Bennett, 1992). Mulick and Wright (2002) confirmed that bisexual people face discrimination from the straight and gay communities, what R. Ochs (1996) described as double discrimination. The general public, as well as the scientific community, has many questions regarding bisexuality. MacDonald (1981) identified four broad beliefs about bisexuality. They are as follows (1) bisexuality can exist and is a valid sexual orientation, (2) bisexuality is a transitory state, (3) bisexuality is a transitional state, and (4) a bisexual individual is denying his or her true homosexual orientation. These differing beliefs and a lack of knowledge are thought to contribute to the prejudice and discrimination that bisexual individuals experience. Not only do bisexuals face overt discrimination for their lifestyles from both the gay and straight communities, their sexual orientation is not even recognized to exist by many.

It seems that until we have a better grasp on the extent of the problems that sexual minorities face and how the prejudice and discrimination can be expressed, we should consider our estimates of the prevalence and who is the likely perpetrator to be preliminary.

Campus Climate and Related Issues

While many university administrators, faculty, staff, and students are trying to make campus life more comfortable for sexual minorities, they encounter a lot of opposition, from both within and outside the institution. Law, policies, governing bodies, administrators, donors, faculty, staff, and students who oppose gay rights present challenges. The campus climate changes every semester as staff and students enter and leave campus, and the direction of that change is not always positive. Every semester colleges and universities are flooded with freshman students, many of whom are 18 years of age and still trying to figure out their identities, sexual and otherwise. D'Augelli and Rose (1990) found that Caucasian heterosexual first-year university students exhibited strongly biased views about lesbians and gay men; over one-half believed male homosexual behavior to be "plain wrong," and they labeled gay men as "disgusting." This finding demonstrates that students are beginning their higher education with preconceived ideas about and opinions of groups of people that are learned before ever stepping onto a college campus.

Researchers have found that homophobia generally decreases with age and as a result of education, so individuals who graduate from college are likely to be less homophobic than when they entered the institution at age 18. However, a lot of homophobic abuse and violence can be expressed in the meantime. Additionally, many college students are on their own for the first time when they go off to college. This is an opportunity for them to come out and engage in behavior that they suppressed while living at home around friends and family. Gay and lesbian individuals in various stages of the coming-out process are more likely to experience acts of homophobia because they are more visible and vocal about their sexual identity.

Homophobia in Collegiate Athletics

College athletics is one area in which the level of homophobia exhibited is above and beyond that found on other parts of the campus (Wolf-Wendel et al., 2001). Athletes are often thought of as the ideal man or woman and are sometimes accorded hero status. These attributes are often at odds with the stereotypes of homosexual individuals.

Student athletes, coaches, and athletic directors are often homophobic and heterosexist, by trying to maintain the heterosexual norms regarding speech and behavior. At best, those in intercollegiate athletics embrace a "don't ask, don't tell" policy, and, at worst, they are unwilling to allow gay and lesbian athletes to participate on their teams. One coach reported adding a swimming program to his university rather than a softball team in response to Title IX requirements because women's softball is associated with lesbian athletes. Some coaches use a practice called "negative recruiting" to attract players to their program by suggesting the predominance of lesbians at other programs, while promoting that their team is heterosexual (Wolf-Wendel et al., 2001).

Athletics, particularly team sports, emphasize cohesion within the team and not the individuality of its members. Expression of one's homosexual orientation is seen as detrimental to issues of trust and team building and therefore is discouraged. Most of the homophobia experienced by college athletes does not involve physical abuse or verbal threats. The majority of the behavior according to Hekma (1998) and Price (2000) involves the normalization of homophobic language and the prohibition of gay and lesbian discourse, identity, and behaviors, which in effect makes gay and lesbian athletes invisible. One can see how closeted college athletes must be in other aspects of their lives in order to not be exposed to their teammates and coaches, particularly if scholarships are involved or if a contract with a professional team is a possibility.

While it appears that homophobia is pervasive in college athletics, there are instances in which a gay athletes received support from their teammates and the campus communities (Hekma, 1998; Wolf-Wendel et al., 2001). Those involved in college athletics seem to be more forgiving of gay and lesbian athletes being out if the heterosexist norms are maintained and if the homosexual athlete is good at the sport and contributes to helping the team win (Anderson, 2002). It is a heavy burden for gay or lesbian athlete to bear when deciding to come out, given that a positive reaction from his or her teammates, coach, and campus community is not guaranteed.

Homophobia in college athletics, while still pervasive, is reportedly decreasing. According to interviews by Wolf-Wendel et al. (2001), the situation today for gay and lesbian athletes is much better than it was decades earlier. If we look back at other forms of discrimination as a road map for what might lie ahead for gay and lesbian athletes, we can examine how racial minorities broke into college athletics. Racial minorities had a very difficult time being accepted in many areas of society, including higher education and athletics, for decades after laws were passed to end segregation, so perhaps the same will be true for sexual minorities if and when laws are passed that forbid discrimination.

Perpetrators and Correlates of Homophobia

There have been many correlates and predictors of homophobia identified over the last several decades. Homophobia has been thought to stem from ignorance about homosexuality, believing in myths regarding homosexual individuals, and as a result of judging homosexual individuals to be immoral. Gender of the perpetrator has been found to play a role in homophobia. Negy and Eisenman (2005) found that heterosexual males express more hostile attitudes toward sexual minorities than heterosexual females. The negative attitudes are more often directed toward gay men than toward lesbians; however, some researchers have found that men are more homophobic toward gay men and women are more homophobic toward lesbians (Herek & Gonzalez-Rivera, 2006; Kite & Whitley, 1996). Wright, Adams, and Bernat (1999) using the Homophobia Scale found that heterosexual women displayed a passive aggressive type of homophobia to gay men. They reported liking gay men and being their friends yet also reported talking about them behind their backs. This could be devastating to gay men if they confide in heterosexual women whom they think are their friends. These men could be exposed for being gay if they are not out, or their private behaviors could be broadcast to others as a result of trusting these female friends. While women might not be outwardly hostile to gay men and commit violent acts against them or their property directly, this type of homophobia can be just as harmful if not more since the gay male is being betrayed by someone who pretended to be his friend.

Other researchers have found that women who were homophobic held authoritarian attitudes, believed in sex role egalitarianism, had less contact with gay men and lesbians, and believed in the importance of feminine attitudes to participants' femininity (Basow & Johnson, 2000). Given that gender is a broad category, researchers have also examined gender role to subclassify individuals within each gender (Goodman & Moradi, 2008). Franklin (2000) found that the primary offenders of homophobic acts are young men who endorse a masculine ideology and whose peers oppose homosexuality. Other attitudinal and behavioral correlates of homophobia that are documented in the literature will be discussed below.

According to LeVay and Valente (2006), homophobia may result from a lack of empathy. For example, a heterosexual man, when he thinks about two men having sex, imagines himself as one of the men involved in the act. Since he is heterosexual he is turned off or disgusted by the notion, and he transfers this aversion to men who have sex with men. What he has failed to do is to think about the behavior from the perspective of the gay man (LeVay & Valente, 2006).

Internalized homophobia is the term used to describe the shame, anger, and self-hatred one experiences due to having same-sex attractions. These thoughts and feelings may develop when a person accepts the negative societal stereotypes about homosexuality. Internalized homophobia is thought to interfere with the development of a positive homosexual identity and can lead to such negative outcomes as depression, anxiety, demoralization, guilt, low affect, low self-esteem, substance abuse, high-risk sexual behavior, or suicide (Gencoz & Yuksel, 2006; Meyer, 1995; Parrott & Zeichner, 2008; Rosser, Bockting, Ross, Miner, & Coleman, 2008). A person with internalized homophobia may also engage in negative behaviors toward other sexual minorities. Homophobic individuals, some of whom are unaware of or are denying their homosexual attractions, may try to avoid LGBT individuals or they may act out aggressively toward these individuals (H. E. Adams, Wright, & Lohr, 1996). A negative campus climate can facilitate internalized homophobia if the person feels unsafe in coming out or being out on campus.

Fear of AIDS is positively correlated to being homophobic (Harrell & Wright, 1998; Long & Millsap, 2008). However, as more is learned about HIV/AIDS and how it is spread, the correlation between fear of AIDS and homophobia has been found to be lower than it was 20 years ago (Cline & Johnson, 1992). Fear of AIDS and homophobia appears to be greater among certain ethnic groups. It is unclear to what extent race is an indicator of a person's antigay prejudice, but the perception is that African Americans are less accepting of homosexuality than Caucasians (Herek & Capitanio, 1995; Lewis, 2003; Waldner, Sikka, & Baig, 1999). There are several hypotheses as to why this perception exists, ranging from the disparity in the ratio between eligible minority men and women to the importance of religion that is frequently associated with the black community (Jenkins et al., 2009). Religiosity, church attendance, and having conservative ideology are correlated with having a more negative attitude toward homosexuality (Herek, 1991; Hinrichs & Rosenberg, 2002). Diversity orientation refers to one's level of interaction with and interest in people from groups other than one's own, e.g., racial, ethnic, religious, or socioeconomic status. Mohr and Sedlacek (2000) found that students who had high diversity orientation were more likely to have a gay or lesbian friend or even want one; they also found that shyness was a barrier to having a gay or lesbian friend due to the potential awkwardness of saying the wrong thing and being offensive during a social interaction.

Right-wing authoritarianism is used to describe people who accept traditional values and authorities and are likely to follow instructions of those in positions of power. Duncan, Peterson, and Winter (1997) and Basow and Johnson (2000) found that those who score high in right-wing authoritarianism are more homophobic; they tend to organize their world in terms of power hierarchies and tend to think of sexual minorities as an out-group since they challenge authority through specific actions or simply by their existence.

Researchers have also looked at attitudes and behaviors that negatively correlate with homophobia, indicating tolerance or acceptance. Attributes predicting acceptance of gay, lesbian, and bisexual persons are female sex, liberal sex-role attitudes, membership in more liberal Protestant denominations, attendance at colleges that do not have Greek letter social organizations, and having positive contacts with gay, lesbian, or bisexual individuals (Hinrichs & Rosenberg, 2002).

Consequences of Homophobia on the Victims

Franklin (2000) reported that being targeted for attack because of one's sexual orientation takes a tremendous toll on victims. Homophobia leads to social inequality on college campuses and contributes to a negative campus climate. The negative campus climate in turn affects a student's ability to successfully complete their schooling and have a positive college experience (Cress, 2008), and will make it less likely that they will come out (Burn et al., 2005; D'Augelli, 1989). Moreover, Rhoads (1994) described cases in which gay men consider suicide, face depression, feel isolated, fear for their own safety, and have increased levels of anxiety as a result of homophobia. Remafedi (1994) reported that gay and lesbian teens attempt suicide at a little over three times the rate for heterosexual youth. He stated, however, that the actual suicide rate is similar across youth and viewed these attempts as cries for help.

Lesbian athletes have been found to experience negative psychological ramification such as low self-esteem, low confidence, high stress, and increased substance abuse, and homophobia can negatively affect athletic performance of both gay men and lesbians (Krane, 1996; Rotella & Murray, 1991). Female athletes reported the need to separate themselves from the stereotype that all female athletes are lesbians by labeling other athletes on other teams or athletes at other universities as being lesbian. Thus they increased their level of homophobic speech in order to draw attention away from themselves.

It takes only a few acts of abuse or violence to suppress or restrict the behavior of those who fear being victimized. This uncertainty about the campus climate and issues regarding safety make it risky for LGBT to come out since once it is known that one is a sexual minority they are at risk for discrimination and or violence. Homophobia and sexual discrimination can lead to abnormally high levels of chronic stress and reduce one's sense of self-esteem (Meyer, 1995). Chronic stress is correlated with depression, higher suicide rates among sexual minorities during young adulthood (D'Augelli, 1992; Rotheram-Borus, Hunter, & Rosario, 1994; Savin-Williams, 1994), risky sexual behaviors (Folkman, Chesney, Pollack, & Phillips, 1992; Rotheram-Borus, Reid, Rosario, & Kasen, 1995), eating disorders (M. B. Feldman & Meyer, 2007), school problems, and substance abuse (McCabe, Boyd, Hughes, & D'Arcy, 2003).

Bullying, Cyberbullying, and the Effects of Technology on Homophobia

Bullying can involve behaviors that are sexually harassing and homophobic in nature. A cluster of suicides of four teens in two years in Ohio reflects the tragic outcome of peer bullying. One teen was bullied for being gay; another boy was bullied because others suspected him of being gay due to the way he dressed and acted in class. Another was ridiculed for her thick accent, and called a "slut," while the fourth was mocked for having a learning disability. Technology such as digital cameras, webcams, and the Internet provide many benefits and make life easier in many ways. However, each of these technologies can be used to invade someone's privacy. The Internet and social networking sites, in particular, have made possible a new type of behavior called cyberbullying that can be used by homophobic persons to hurt others in ways that were not previously possible. Not only can someone post information about you that you might not want known, they can post pictures or video as well. In 2010, Tyler Clementi, an 18-year-old college student at Rutgers University, committed suicide after his roommate and a classmate secretly used a video webcam to broadcast Tyler in a sexual encounter with another man. Tyler was so devastated by this act that he committed suicide by jumping off the George Washington Bridge, after leaving a goodbye message on his Facebook page saying "Jumping off the gw bridge sorry" (Friedman, 2010). Prior to the Internet we knew who the bullies were in school, on the playground, or on the bus. The Internet provides anonymity so that anyone can be a bully, and they have a worldwide audience.

What Can Be Done to Alleviate the Problem on Campus?

Lance (2008) stated that in contemporary American society people remain predominantly heterosexual, believing that heterosexuality is superior morally, socially, emotionally, and behaviorally to homosexuality. It seems as though reducing homophobia is an uphill battle that is being fought on many fronts. It is important that these initiatives begin early and continue throughout one's development. Hennning-Stout, James, and MacIntosh (2000) recommend implementing school-wide programs that emphasize zero tolerance of antigay harassment beginning in elementary school.

University administrators need to do their part by establishing policies of inclusion and setting good examples. Faculty and staff need to be trained on identifying the different forms of homophobia, and they need to learn how to intervene when it occurs. Issues related to homophobia should be included in students' orientation to university life so that they know what will be tolerated and what the penalties will be for violating those policies. R. D. Brown et al. (2004) suggest targeting specific groups, such as freshman students, in general, and male students, in particular, using a variety of intervention strategies. Some of the suggested strategies include enrolling students in freshman seminars, having them participate in other first-year courses, and delivering those interventions in a variety of settings, for instance classrooms and dormitory or living quarters.

Many authors of psychology textbooks on human sexuality are trying to incorporate information about sexual orientation throughout their texts rather than having only one chapter on sexual orientation. In doing so they are attempting to help students realize that sexual orientation is affected by and affects many areas of a person's life. However, there are many disciplines in which authors do not include pertinent information related to sexual orientation in their texts. An examination of textbooks for teacher preparation programs conducted by Macgillivray and Jennings (2008) found that 95 percent of textbooks made no reference at all to same-sex sexuality and those that did often negatively portrayed people who identify as LGBT. Sexuality, when it was mentioned, was defined most often as heterosexuality and few references were made to homosexuality. Some groups have attempted to pass what is called "No Promo Homo" legislation that will make it difficult for educators to bring up LGBT issues for fear of censure (Macgillivray & Jennings, 2008). Cannon and Dirks-Linhorst (2006) found that gay and lesbian issues are largely ignored in criminal justice curricula, despite the fact that biases that affect race and gender are often discussed. They also point out that students educated by these curricula obtain employment in the field but have not been formally trained in the issues that LGBT individuals face in the criminal justice system. A lack of education on LGBT issues can have an impact in policing, the courts, corrections environments, substantive criminal law, and even criminological research (Fradella, Owen, & Burke, 2009).

Authors and educators are encouraged to continue their attempts to include and normalize LGBT issues so that students are appropriately trained and can do the best job possible once they enter their chosen fields. It is no doubt that these omissions and inaccuracies in academic texts as well as the other issues discussed previously contribute to the negative campus climate. Accurate information needs to be added to the curriculum of teachers in training in order improve their knowledge of and preparedness for these issues in a classroom setting.

While the atmosphere in many high schools, which is the predominant source of college freshmen, is changing, it is important to remember that change can occur slowly. Colleges and universities should expect an increase in homophobic behavior as incoming college students are confronted, perhaps for the first time, with sexual minorities. Understanding the homophobic attitudes of college students toward sexual minorities as well as their lifestyles is critical to effecting a more positive environment for gay, lesbian, and bisexual individuals on our campuses (Hinrichs & Rosenberg, 2002; Mueller & Cole, 2009). One's identity, regardless of whether it is a racial identity, a heterosexual identity, or a homosexual identity, is healthier when individuals are in supportive environments.

Researchers need to continue to determine what causes and maintains homophobia so that future discrimination can be prevented. Perhaps college administrators could look to, as was suggested by Wolf-Wendel et al. (2001), what was done to reduce racism on campuses as a way to reduce homophobia. Educational workshops and training sessions could be held to inform those in charge what homophobia is, how it is displayed, how detrimental it is, and how it can be reduced. Campus officials could invite LGBT graduates back to campus to give talks to promote equality; coaches could do the same with LGBT athletes to speak to their teams. Additionally, higher education administrators could lobby for inclusion of sexual orientation to be included in nondiscrimination policies at the state and federal levels.

Educators who can teach specific units on LGBT issues or incorporate the information throughout the course are encouraged to do so. It is unknown exactly how to go about changing the atmosphere on campus, but several researchers and educators have used speaker panel presentations and peer educators to increase exposure to LGBT issues. Results from the research on speaker panels in reducing homophobia is promising; however, some researchers have had mixed or inconclusive results (Hugelshofer, 2006; E.S. Nelson & Krieger, 1997). Questions that need to be answered have to do with determining if attitudes change more than behavior as a result of the panel (Chng & Moore, 1991), or how much can be attributed to the experiential component of the panel, when it was one element in a semester-long human sexuality course (Guth, Lopez, Rojas, Clements, & Tyler, 2004; Pettijohn & Walzer, 2008; Wright & Cullen, 2001). Devine, Evett, and Vasques-Suson (1996) proposed that the lack of congruence between tolerance level for and behavior toward gay and lesbian individuals might be the result of high levels of social anxiety and low levels of interpersonal self-efficacy. Mohr and Sedlacek (2000) indeed found that many incoming college students indicated anticipation of discomfort in starting a friendship with a gay or lesbian person. Having some scheduled structured events in which straight students interact with gay and lesbian students could alleviate this problem early on. It appears that no one type of intervention is adequate due to the differences in reasons for avoidance of such interactions and relationships.

CONCLUSION

Sexual harassment and homophobia are behaviors that not only lead to a negative campus climate but can have devastating effects on the victims.

Institutions of higher learning should set the example for the rest of society that fairness and equality should prevail for all individuals. A college or university setting should be a safe place for individuals to explore behavior and create knowledge; however, prejudice and discrimination can prevent this from happening both on the personal level and at the level of scientific investigation. Progress has been made; however, more needs to be done. Think back to some examples of these behaviors you have observed and determine how you reacted at the time or at a later time. How will you react in the future?

Chapter Ten

SEXUAL RISK TAKING AMONG COLLEGE STUDENTS: CORRELATES AND CONSEQUENCES

Virginia Gil-Rivas

Young adulthood is a period of the life span when individuals are exploring educational, occupational, and romantic possibilities. Normative expectations for sexual activity, the lack of social pressure to get married, and diminished parental and adult supervision that characterize young adulthood may increase the likelihood of sexual activity and sexual risk taking among young adults (Arnett, 2000a). The college environment provides plentiful opportunities for meeting potential partners and sexual exploration and thus may increase the likelihood of risk taking among young adults (Braithwaite et al., 2010). For example, current estimates suggest that between 50 to 75 percent of young adults "hook up," or engage in sexual encounters that occur on one occasion and where partners are not expecting future encounters (Owen et al., 2010). These encounters can include a range of behaviors such as kissing, oral sex, and intercourse. Although sexual and romantic explorations are normative experiences among young adults, sexual risk taking can have serious health consequences for young adults. Sexual risk taking involves engaging in unprotected sexual activity (i.e., vaginal, oral, anal), having multiple sexual partners, having sex with someone one does not know well or trust, using alcohol or drugs before or during sex, engaging in unplanned and impulsive sexual activity, and inability or failure to discuss risky sexual behaviors prior to engaging in sexual activities (M. L. Cooper, 2002; Turchik & Garske, 2009).

HEALTH CONSEQUENCES OF SEXUAL RISK TAKING

Sexually transmitted infections (STIs) are one of the major health concerns in the United States with an estimated annual direct cost of $14.7 billion (Centers for Disease Control and Prevention [CDC], 2007). Recent estimates by the CDC indicate that 19 million Americans become infected every year, and nearly half of those infected (46.7 %) are adolescents and young adults. These estimates also revealed that women, ethnic minority groups, and men who have sex with men (MSM) are particularly vulnerable to STI infections (CDC, 2010b).

Approximately 25 diseases are primarily transmitted through sexual contact. Not including infection with the human immunodeficiency virus (HIV), the most common STIs in the United States are: chlamydia, gonorrhea, syphilis, genital herpes, and human papillomavirus (HPV). Of these diseases, chlamydia, gonorrhea, syphilis, and HIV/AIDS are closely monitored due to their significant impact on the health of the American population (CDC, 2010b).

Chlamydia is the most common STI among adolescents (15–19 years old) and young adults (20–24 years old), and in particular among women (CDC, 2010b). Gonorrhea is the second most common STI among young people. These bacterial infections are frequently asymptomatic and can be detected only through testing. If untreated these infections can result in pelvic inflammatory disease, lead to ectopic pregnancy (pregnancies occurring outside the uterus), undesirable pregnancy outcomes (e.g., eye disease and pneumonia in infants), and permanent infertility for both men and women. Moreover, chlamydia infections place women at a greater risk of contracting HIV if exposed to the virus (CDC, 2010b).

Human papillomavirus (HPV) is a common infection that affects nearly 20 million Americans and at least 50 percent of sexually active men and women become infected at some point in their life. Although most people who are infected with HPV do not develop symptoms or health problems, in some cases HPV can cause genital warts or can contribute to several forms of cancer. Specifically, HPV is related to the development of cervical, vulvar, vaginal, and anal cancer as well as cancer in the head and neck (CDC, 2009).

Syphilis is a curable sexually transmitted bacterial infection that can also be transmitted to the fetus during pregnancy or childbirth. Infection rates are higher among young adults aged 20–29 years (CDC, 2010b), with the highest rates among MSM (CDC, 2010b). In the late stage of the disease, infected individuals develop cardiovascular and neurological diseases (e.g., loss of motor coordination, paralysis) and blindness. Importantly, syphilis can eventually result in death (CDC, 2010b), and individuals with syphilis sores are two to five times more likely to contract HIV compared to those without this condition.

HIV can be transmitted via unprotected sexual activity (i.e., exchange of semen, blood, and vaginal fluid) and blood-to-blood contact (e.g., needle sharing). Although the virus may not produce symptoms years after infection, it can be transmitted to others during this time. Over time, HIV destroys immune cells (CD4 and T cells) and eventually symptoms of infection appear. If untreated or undiagnosed, the immune system is gradually damaged and the individuals' ability to fight infections is seriously compromised leading to the diagnosis of acquired immune deficiency syndrome (AIDS) and eventual death. Approximately 40,000 individuals contract HIV every year in the United States, with rates of new infections remaining stable between 2006 and 2009 (Prejean et al., 2011). Although rates have remained stable in the general population, infection rates among people aged 13–29 years have increased by 21 percent, with the highest rates among MSM, in particular among African American men (Prejean et al., 2011). Although there is no cure for HIV/AIDS, treatment has resulted in a growing number of persons living longer, healthier and more productive lives (CDC, 2003). Unfortunately, approximately 25 to 40 percent of those infected continue to engage in sexual risk taking, increasing the likelihood of HIV transmission or reinfection (Kalichman et al., 2001).

Despite the potential health and social consequences associated with sexual risk taking and public health efforts to increase awareness of these consequences, a large number of young adults continue to engage in these behaviors. For example, despite the fact that condom use reduces the likelihood of unwanted pregnancies and the risk of becoming infected with STIs, only 45 percent of males and 38.7 percent of females aged 18–24 years report condom use (Reece et al., 2010). In fact, although knowledge about potential risks is an important factor in sexual risk taking, it does not appear to be the most important predictor of behavior; rather, a variety of individual, social and cultural factors may help explain why young people continue to engage in risky sexual activities (Kershaw, Ethier, Niccolai, Lewis, & Ickovics, 2003). A brief summary of these factors is provided below.

INDIVIDUAL FACTORS ASSOCIATED WITH SEXUAL RISK BEHAVIORS

Several factors have been hypothesized to play an important role in risk taking among young adults. First, the need for experimentation is an important component of identity development during young adulthood that may contribute to a greater likelihood of risk taking (i.e., substance use, driving while intoxicated), and in particular, to sexual risk taking (Arnett, 2000a; Braithwaite et al., 2010). In addition, individuals in late adolescence and early adulthood may have difficulties regulating their behavior and evaluating potential costs and benefits in situations involving emotional arousal (L. Steinberg, 2004), and this may be especially true if it involves sexual arousal.

Risk-taking behaviors seldom occur in isolation (Jessor, 1991); in fact, sexual risk taking frequently co-occurs with the use of alcohol and drugs (McKirnan, Ostrow, & Hope, 1996; Zweig, Lindberg, & McGinley, 2001). Alcohol use is higher among college students compared to young adults who are not attending college (O'Malley & Johnston, 2002). At a global level, heavy (drinking more five or more drinks in a row) and frequent alcohol use are associated with a greater likelihood of having multiple sex partners and unprotected intercourse (M. L. Cooper, 2002; Randolph, Torres, Gore-Felton, Lloyd, & McGarvey, 2009). Several explanations for the association between alcohol use and sexual risk taking have been offered. Some researchers have suggested that alcohol has the ability to reduce sexual inhibitions through its impairing effects on individuals' ability to think about potential negative consequences. Thus, under the influence of alcohol, individuals mainly focus on their sexual arousal and have a limited ability to focus on the more distant consequences associated with these behaviors (C. M. Steele & Josephs, 1990). Others have suggested that this association is not the result of the pharmacological effects of alcohol, but rather the result of individuals' beliefs (expectancies) about alcohol's ability to increase their sexual arousal and reduce inhibitions. Therefore individuals are likely to drink in anticipation of sexual encounters or in response to specific situations and then behave according to those expectations (George et al., 2000; Lang, 1985). To date, the empirical evidence provides support for both of explanations. Specifically, the effect of alcohol on sexual risk taking appears to vary depending on the strength of coexisting inhibiting (e.g., perceived costs and benefits) and disinhibiting forces (arousal). Simultaneously, individuals' alcohol expectancies play a role in promoting alcohol use in sexual situations or in anticipation of these situations, leading to risk taking (M. L. Cooper, 2002; George, Stoner, Norris, Lopez, & Lehman, 2000). Thus both the impairing effects of alcohol and individuals' expectations of increased arousal and disinhibition in situations that are novel and viewed as desirable appear to play a role in sexual risk taking.

It is important to note that some investigators have not found a significant relationship between alcohol use and expectancies and preventive behaviors such as condom use. A recent study among college students (Randolph et al., 2009) showed that perceived risk for HIV infection was the strongest predictor of condom use. Further, the relationship between alcohol use, alcohol expectancies and sexual risk taking has been found to vary based on the social context. Specifically, alcohol use and alcohol expectancies have a stronger relationship with condom use in sexual encounters with a new partner compared to encounters with a regular partner (Corbin & Fromme, 2002; Vanable et al., 2004).

Marijuana is one of the drugs most frequently used by college students with approximately 20 percent of students reporting use within the last 30 days (O'Malley & Johnston, 2002). As in the case of alcohol, the relationship between drug use and sexual risk taking is complex. At a global level, drug use before or during sex is associated with having multiple sex partners and weak peer norms for condom use. However, it is unclear whether this association is causal or holds with all types of partners (Stall & Purcell, 2000) or situations. In fact, several factors might explain this association. Some drugs can have a significant impact on sexual behavior; for example, amphetamine and crack cocaine users frequently report that these drugs increase their levels of sexual desire, sexual stamina, and reduce sexual inhibitions (Ross & Williams, 2001). In some circumstances, these drugs are used "strategically" to achieve these effects, particularly in situations or settings that promote sexual risk-taking behaviors (e.g., bars, dance clubs, parties) (Green, 2003). In sum, these findings suggest that alcohol and drug use may not play a causal role in sexual risk taking; rather, it appears that other factors (e.g., personality, beliefs) may explain their co-occurrence (Ross & Williams, 2001; Weinhardt & Carey, 2000). In either case, sexual risk taking and substance use, especially alcohol, are related and frequently co-occur among college students.

Sensation seeking (the tendency to seek novelty and excitement and the willingness to take risks in order to have these experiences) and impulsivity (the tendency to act without planning or deliberation; Zuckerman, 1994) have been found to be associated with several risky behaviors (Zuckerman & Kuhlman, 2000) and may contribute to sexual risk taking among college students. For example, a quantitative review by Hoyle, Fejfar, and Miller (2000) of 53 studies of college and high-risk populations (e.g., MSM), concluded that these two personality characteristics predicted a variety of sexual risk behaviors, including frequency of unprotected sexual intercourse, sex with strangers, number of sexual partners, and having sex while intoxicated. Sensation seeking appears to contribute to sexual risk taking in the following ways: (1) by interfering with individuals' ability to engage in safe sex in the "heat of the moment" (Pinkerton & Abramson, 1995; Bancroft et al., 2003), and (2) by the tendency of individuals who are high in sensation seeking to report low levels of perceived risk after engaging in these behaviors (Zuckerman, 1979). The empirical evidence also suggests that personality characteristics interact with other individual and situational factors to predict sexual risk taking (Hoyle et al., 2000). For example, Kalichman, Cain, Zweben, and Geoff (2003) found that sensation seeking was directly associated with higher expectations of increased sexual arousal and disinhibition while under the influence of alcohol. In turn, these expectations were associated with alcohol use in sexual situations and with unprotected intercourse with nonprimary sex partners. Thus it is possible that personality plays a role on sexual risk taking through its impact on individuals' expectations, beliefs, attitudes and norms.

Cognitive Factors

Individuals' intentions to engage in a particular behavior are hypothesized to be strong predictors of future behavior by several health behavior models, such as the theories of reasoned action (Ajzen & Fishbein, 1997) and planned behavior (Ajzen, 1991). These intentions are the result of attitudes (i.e., a positive versus a negative evaluation of a behavior), subjective norms (i.e., individuals' perceptions of what others approve of), and perceived behavioral control (i.e., ease or difficulty associated with engaging in that behavior). A meta-analysis of 42 studies of predictors of condom use provided support for these theories. As expected, individuals' intentions to use condoms were explained by their attitudes about condom use, subjective norms, and perceived behavioral control (Albarracin, Johnson, Fishbein, & Muellerleile, 2001). However, the strength of these associations differed by gender, age, ethnic background, and education. Specifically, behavioral control had a stronger association with actual condom use among younger, less educated, and ethnic minority groups (Albarracin, Kumkale, & Johnson, 2004). Likewise, the association between intentions and perceived behavioral control was stronger among women, younger individuals and ethnic minorities. Subjective norms and intentions had a stronger association with condom use among youths, males, and individuals with higher levels of education.

Risk perceptions are also viewed as key contributors to a variety of health behaviors by several theories of health behavior (i.e., health belief model [Rosentock, Strecher, & Becker, 1994]; protection motivation theory [R. W. Rogers, 1983]). Importantly, individuals in general, and adolescents and young adults in particular, appear to have a tendency to underestimate their health risks despite having the knowledge that some behaviors are "risky." For example, a recent study of college students examined explanations for unprotected sexual intercourse (O'Sullivan, Udell, Montrose, Antoniello, & Hoffman , 2010). Some of the explanations offered by students involved biased evaluations of risky behavior, specifically, feeling that somehow they were invulnerable; ignoring or dismissing risk; and accepting inadequate alternatives. These biased risk perceptions influence young adults decisions regarding unprotected sex and other risky behaviors.

Self-efficacy, defined as beliefs about one's ability to exercise control over one's behavior and the demands associated with particular situations (Bandura, 1994), has been found to be an important predictor of intentions to engage in safe sex practices. In general, higher levels of self-efficacy regarding one's ability to negotiate safe sex with a partner, prevent HIV/AIDS infection, and refusing unprotected sex predict the frequency of condom use (Parson et al., 2000). The strength of this relationship appears to vary by gender, such that the perceived ability to negotiate safer sex is a stronger predictor of protected sexual intercourse among women compared to men (LoConte, O'Leary, & Labouvie, 1997).

The review presented above suggests that although behavioral intentions, expectations, and beliefs are important predictors of sexual risk taking, other factors may influence the magnitude of this association. In fact, many studies examining the association between cognitive factors and sexual risk taking have been criticized on various grounds. First, these studies assume that an individual's decision to engage in sexual risk-taking behaviors is based on informed and rational decision-making processes. However, the evidence suggests that many decisions about sexual risk taking are taken in the "heat of the moment" (R. S. Gold, 2000). Second, the extent to which cognitive factors play a significant role in sexual risk taking might be influenced by social norms regarding sexual risk behaviors and power inequalities in relationships (Amaro, 1995). Some women, for example, may not feel empowered to negotiate safer sex with their partners, especially if they perceive their peers' norms as supportive of sexual risk taking. Finally, the characteristics of a relationship such as level of commitment and love may influence individuals' intentions, expectations, and attitudes about specific sexual practices (L. J. Bauman & Berman, 2005). Below we present a selective overview of social and contextual factors associated with sexual risk taking.

CONTEXTUAL FACTORS ASSOCIATED WITH SEXUAL RISK BEHAVIORS

Aspects of the social context such as the characteristics of dyadic relationships (e.g., closeness, length of the relationship), gender roles, and group and social norms play an important role in predicting sexual risk behaviors among young adults.

Characteristics of the Dyadic Relationship

Sexual risk taking is strongly influenced by individuals' feelings toward a particular partner (J.A. Kelly & Kalichman, 1995). For example, in the context of committed heterosexual (O'Sullivan et al., 2010) or homosexual

(Hays, Kegeles, & Coates, 1997) relationships, individuals are more likely to view condoms as unnecessary. This attitude toward condom use might be explained, at least in part, by difficulties in evaluating risk in the context of close and intimate relationships, gender roles, and the meaning given to unprotected intercourse in this context (Impett & Peplau, 2003). For example a recent daily diary study among college students revealed that perceived closeness and intimacy with one's partner was associated with perceptions of reduced risk associated with unprotected intercourse (O'Sullivan et al., 2010). In addition, for some couples, the exchange of body fluids is viewed as a sign of greater intimacy and commitment (Odets, 1994; Sobo, 1995). Thus a request for condom use might be interpreted as a lack of commitment, mistrust, a sign of infidelity, or a lack of concern for the pleasure of one's partner (A. O'Leary, 2000). Unfortunately, the epidemiological evidence suggests that individuals in long-term committed relationships frequently engage in sexual encounters outside of their primary relationship (Adimora et al., 2002; see also McAnulty & McAnulty, this volume). In addition, one's feelings toward a sexual partner, the extent to which couples are able to discuss STI/HIV concerns, the use of condoms, and their views about sexual risk behaviors play an important role in predicting sexual risk taking (DiClemente & Wingood, 1995). For example, among young MSM, Molitor, Facer, and Ruiz (1999) found that individuals' ability to discuss safe sex with their partners predicted the frequency of unprotected anal intercourse. Finally, differences in age among partners also contribute to sexual risk taking. Females who are involved with older males are more likely to engage in unprotected intercourse, to have sex while under the influence of alcohol or drugs, to experience sexual coercion by their partner, and to have unintended pregnancies (Gowen, Feldman, Diaz, & Yisrael, 2004), compared to those with similar-aged partners.

Gender roles also play an important role in predicting sexual risk behaviors, behavioral choices, and the ability to initiate and maintain behavioral changes. Among women, the tendency to place a greater emphasis on maintaining harmony and connectedness and providing support in their relationships (Simon, 1995) contributes to their tendency to put their partners' needs above their desire to protect themselves from STI/HIV infection (Misovich, Fisher, & Fisher, 1997). In fact, women frequently avoid making requests to use condoms if they expect that such requests will lead to conflict or violence (Wingood & DiClemente, 1998). Cultural beliefs about women's sexual roles and behavior also act as barriers for women's ability to negotiate safe sex practices with their partners (Gomez & Marin, 1996; St. Lawrence et al., 1998). For example, traditional gender roles assign women less decision-making power, interfering with women's ability to make decisions that go against their partners' wishes

(Amaro, 1995). These power inequalities also contribute to women's vulnerability to violence within their intimate relationships (Amaro, 1995). Among college women, over one-third report having been pressured or forced to engage in sexual activities (see Calhoun, Mouilso, & Edwards, this volume). Women with a history of sexual victimization are more likely to experience further victimization, to report a history of STIs (El-Bassel, Gilbert, Rajah, Foleno, & Frye, 2000), and to be at a greater risk for HIV infection (Garcia-Moreno & Watts, 2000) compared to women without such histories. Thus the amount of power women hold in relationships is an important predictor of both the frequency of condom use and exposure to sexual coercion (Pulerwitz, Gortmaker, & DeJong, 2000). These findings suggest that women's intentions to avoid risky behaviors and their knowledge and skills about how to prevent HIV/STI infection might not be the strongest predictors of sexual risk taking. Rather, women's behaviors are greatly determined by their partners' attitudes and behaviors about safe sex practices (Logan, Cole, & Leukefeld, 2002).

Power inequalities and sexual coercion not only occur among women; in fact, a study conducted by Kalichman and Rompa (1995) found that 29 percent of gay and bisexual males had experienced sexual coercion involving attempted or completed unprotected anal intercourse. Men with a history of victimization are also more likely to avoid talking with their partners about the use of condoms for fear of the potential consequences (Kalichman et al., 2001). These findings suggest that aspects of close interpersonal relationships are important contributors to sexual risk taking and STI/HIV infection.

Social Influences

During young adulthood, individuals are more likely to cohabitate with a romantic partner, to explore what type of life partner they would like to have, and to have relationships that are characterized by greater intimacy (Arnett, 2000a). Outside of the dyadic relationship, members of one's social network play an important role in predicting sexual behaviors. For example, individuals' perceptions of their peers' attitudes toward risky behaviors in general (e.g., alcohol and drug use) and norms regarding sexual intercourse and condom use (Kinsman, Romer, Furstenberg, & Schwarz, 1998) are associated with the frequency of condom (K. S. Miller, Forehand, & Kotchick, 2000) and birth control use (Vesely et al., 2004), and the frequency of unprotected sexual intercourse (Hart et al., 2004). For example, among women (Sikkema et al., 2000) and gay men (Kegeles, Hays, & Coates, 1996) individuals' beliefs about the attitudes toward safer sex held by members of their community and social groups are important predictors of the frequency of condom use.

CONCLUSION AND FUTURE DIRECTIONS

As suggested by this review, individual, social, and environmental factors act independently or jointly to influence sexual risk taking among college students. Moreover, the relative importance of these factors may vary by age, gender, cultural background, and relationship characteristics. Although the literature suggests that prevention intervention efforts have been successful at reducing sexual risk taking, these interventions are not equally effective for all populations. Prevention intervention efforts need to be tailored to address the specific needs of each population (DiClemente, Wingood, Vermund, & Steward, 1999) and the meaning given by the individual or the community to these behaviors (Ostrow, 2000). Moreover, changes in treatment, social attitudes, and socioeconomic conditions may impact the extent to which these interventions will be effective in the future. Overall, several key characteristics of successful prevention intervention programs have been identified: the interventions (1) are based on theoretical models and address the interplay between attitudes, beliefs, expectations, behaviors, and environmental influences; (2) are designed with an understanding of the contextual and behavioral factors influencing sexual risk taking and behavior change; (3) focus on specific sexual risk-taking behaviors (e.g., unprotected anal intercourse, condom use); (4) provide education regarding STI/HIV infection and safe sex practices; (5) provide modeling and training in sexual communication, negotiation, and assertiveness skills; and (6) address the role of situation factors and social and peer norms in sexual risk taking (DiClemente et al., 1999; J. A. Kelly & Kalichman, 2002). Please see the following chapter by Harper and colleagues for a more detailed discussion of sexual risk reduction interventions targeting college students.

Chapter Eleven

EMPIRICALLY BASED SEXUAL RISK REDUCTION INTERVENTIONS FOR UNIVERSITY AND COLLEGE STUDENTS

Gary W. Harper, Diana Lemos, Jessica Velcoff, and Joseph G. Benjamin

INTRODUCTION

Adolescents and young adults between the ages of 15 and 24 acquire nearly half of all new sexually transmitted infections (STIs) in the United States, even though they represent only 25 percent of the sexually experienced U.S. population (Centers for Disease Control and Prevention [CDC], 2009). Recent data from the National Longitudinal Study of Adolescent Health revealed that 15 percent of young adults between the ages of 18 and 26 have had an STI within the past year (Wildsmith, Schelar, Peterson, & Manlove, 2010). Unplanned pregnancies are also a growing concern for college-aged young women, with more than one-third (1.1 million) of all unplanned pregnancies occurring among unmarried women in their 20s (National Campaign to Reduce Teen and Unplanned Pregnancy, 2008). Various studies have indicated that college and university students engage in a range of high-risk sexual activity, and results are mixed on the degree to which colleges and universities provide adequate sexual health education and services (Hou, 2009; Rimsza, 2005; P. D. Smith & Roberts, 2009).

In the fall of 2009, the American College Health Association surveyed 34,208 students from 57 colleges and universities across the nation regarding their general health. Sexual health-related results indicated that a little over half of sexually active students used condoms during vaginal intercourse in the past 30 days, and only 30% used condoms during anal sex and 6% during oral sex (American College Health Association, 2010). In addition, just over half used contraceptives (including condoms) during sex, 13 percent had used emergency contraception, and 4 percent experienced unintentional pregnancies. Only 36 percent received information at their college or university on pregnancy prevention, and 51 percent reported that they had not received STI prevention information.

Koumans et al. (2005) surveyed 736 colleges and universities to estimate the number of such institutions providing STI education or services nationally. The authors found that 91 percent of the schools provided some form of STI education, most commonly via flyers or posters. About two-thirds of schools provided individual counseling, lectures, or health fairs. In addition, 60 percent of schools had an on-campus health center. Among the campus health centers, 66 percent provided STI services and 54 percent provided contraceptive services. Only 52 percent of schools provided condoms. The authors also found that larger and private schools were more likely to have health centers, and schools with health centers were more likely to provide a greater array of STI services. Unfortunately, to the authors' knowledge there are no publications that systematically evaluate the effectiveness of university or college-based sexual health interventions across the country. Individual or comparative research on sexual health intervention effectiveness in colleges and universities is also sparse, and to date no comprehensive literature reviews have been published to demonstrate the effectiveness of various interventions specifically designed for college and university students.

The purpose of this chapter is to offer an overview of interventions that have been empirically proven to reduce sexual risk taking and associated negative sexual health outcomes among university and college students in the United States. We conducted a systematic literature review of empirically tested interventions published in peer-reviewed journals and offer details regarding successful interventions. This information will be helpful in planning future sexual risk reduction interventions on college and university campuses that build upon existing empirical literature.

LITERATURE REVIEW METHODS

A rigorous and comprehensive review of interventions that have been empirically proven to reduce sexual risk taking and associated negative health outcomes was conducted by systematically searching electronic literature databases, bibliographies of relevant articles, and book chapters that described STI, HIV, or pregnancy prevention programs for young adults. To be included in the current review the articles had to meet the following criteria:

(1) published in a peer-reviewed journal between January 1980 and September 2010, (2) described the effects of an intervention designed to reduce sexual risk-taking behaviors, (3) described an intervention that was delivered to college or university students in the United States, and (4) utilized an evaluation or research design that involved a minimum of pre- and posttest assessment (regardless of whether or not a comparison condition was used).

Four online databases (i.e., PsychInfo, Google Scholar, ERIC, PubMed) were initially used to search for articles that met the inclusion criteria. The keywords used in these searches included multiple combinations of the following terms: "HIV," "STI," "STD," "unplanned pregnancy," college," "students," "university," "interventions," and "programs." As subsets of intervention programs were distinguished, modified search criteria included the following population-specific terms: "men," "women," "female students," "male students," "gay," "lesbian," and "transgender." Once it was determined that articles met the inclusion criteria, the bibliographic references were reviewed to identify additional relevant articles that had not been identified in the original searches. Book chapters that detailed descriptions of sexual risk reduction interventions for young adults (including those specific to college/university students) were also identified through the online databases, and their reference sections were reviewed for appropriate articles.

A total of 27 articles met the criteria for inclusion in this review. A coding sheet was created to independently code each of these articles. Ten percent of the studies were coded by two of the authors to check for reliability, producing 98 percent agreement. The coding sheet included information regarding the demographic characteristics of the participants and university/college setting (e.g., age, ethnicity, geographic region), characteristics of the intervention (e.g., theory, methods, delivery location, content), characteristics of the evaluation (e.g., design, measures), and characteristics of the outcomes (e.g., behavior, attitude, intentions).

Data from these 27 articles were reviewed in two primary ways. First the characteristics of the articles were examined quantitatively, primarily using the data collected on the coding sheets. After these data were tabulated, more in-depth qualitative reviews of the interventions described in the articles were conducted. For this review, the interventions were divided into three categories—those that addressed sexual risk reduction for general college student populations, those that addressed gender-specific issues and populations, and those that addressed lesbian/gay/bisexual-specific issues and populations.

QUANTITATIVE OVERVIEW OF INTERVENTIONS

The student populations for the interventions in our review ranged in size from 39 to 578 students (mean = 159), and the mean age of participants across studies was 20. Most of the interventions were delivered to both females and males (n = 19), with six programs being female-specific and only two being male-specific. Complete data on race/ethnicity of the participants were offered in only 10 of the articles (with another 10 offering partial data), and based on those data the vast majority of the students served in these interventions were white (46.5% to 97.9% of the student populations across 17 studies). African American (n = 13 studies) and Latino/a (n = 9 studies) students were the second and third most represented ethnic/racial groups, constituting 17 percent of student populations served in their respective studies. With regard to sexual orientation, nine of the studies reported the percentage of students who were heterosexual (range = 92% to 100%) and only one study reported the percentage of students who were lesbian/gay/bisexual (LGB) (2.9%). The vast majority (64%) did not mention the sexual orientation of the student participants.

The characteristics of the colleges and universities where these interventions took place revealed a fair degree of geographic diversity. Of the 20 studies that offered information about their geographic region, the majority of institutions were located in the Midwest (n = 5), followed by the West (n = 4) and the Northeast (n = 4), then the South (n = 3), and finally the Southwest (n = 2) and the Mid-Atlantic (n = 2) regions. Only five studies specified urban or rural settings, with the majority being located in an urban environment (n = 4). Information regarding public versus private institutions was offered for 14 studies, and the vast majority (n = 12) were conducted in public institutions. All of the private institutions were universities. Of the public institutions only one was a community college and the remainder were universities.

Information regarding characteristics of the intervention revealed that although the vast majority of the interventions were delivered to students on campus (with no further information being offered as to the specific location), two took place at a campus health center and one in residence halls. The most common interventionists were campus peer leaders (n = 9) and research staff members or graduate students (n = 8), followed by physicians/nurses (n = 3), health educators (n = 2), and HIV test counselors (n = 2). With regard to intervention implementation, 12 of the interventions were presented to students on an individual basis, with the majority occurring through either small-(n = 10) or large-(n = 4) group delivery. Three interventions used web- or computer-based technology for all or part of the intervention delivery. Although various intervention delivery strategies were utilized in these studies, the most common was the use of lectures (n = 14) followed by media presentations (n = 9) and group discussions (n = 7). Other interactive delivery strategies were also reported, and these included condoms skills practice (n = 7), role plays (n = 5), and condom demonstrations (n = 5). Additional delivery strategies were reported in single studies, and these included skits, condom purchase practice, goal setting, contraceptive skills practice, decisional balance worksheets, and an occasion card to inform sex partners of STI screening and treatment.

The majority of the interventions were based in health behavior change theories or models. The two most frequently used frameworks were social cognitive theory/social learning theory (n = 7) and the information-motivation-behavioral skills (IMB) model (n = 6). Motivational enhancement/motivational interviewing was used as the framework for three of the interventions, and the health belief model and theory of reason action/theory of planned behavior were each used in two interventions. The AIDS risk reduction model and protection motivation theory were each used in one intervention. With regard to the evaluation/research designs used to assess the interventions, the vast majority (n = 17) used an experimental design, with five using a quasi-experimental design and four using a single-group design.

The evaluations of the 27 interventions focused on an array of sexual risk reduction related outcomes. Table 11.1 offers details regarding the targeted outcomes, as well as the number of interventions assessing each outcome and the specific interventions demonstrating a positive effect on each outcome.

Table 11.1
Outcomes Assessed in 27 Sexual Risk Reduction Interventions

Outcome	Significant Effects/ Assessed	Articles Demonstrating Positive Outcomes
Increases in General STI/ HIV Knowledge	11/12	1. Doherty & Low (2008) 2. Evans, Edmundson-Drane, & Harris (2000) 3. J. D. Fisher, Fisher, Misovich, Kimble, & Mallory (1996) 4. Gracia Jones, Patsdaughter, Jorda, Hamilton, & Malow (2008) 5. Kyes (1995) 6. E. C. Lambert (2001) 7. J. A. Miller & Gilman (1996) 8. O'Grady, Wilson, & Harman (2009) 9. Shulkin et al. (1991) 10. Sikkema, Winett, & Lombard (1995) 11. Weiss, Turbiasz, & Whitney (1995)

(Continued)

Table 11.1 (Continued)

Outcome	Significant Effects/ Assessed	Articles Demonstrating Positive Outcomes
Increases in Condom Use Intentions/Sexual Risk Reduction Intentions	8/11	1. Bryan, Aiken, & West (1996) 2. Eitel & Friend (1999) 3. Evans, Edmundson-Drane, & Harris (2000) 4. J. D. Fisher, Fisher, Misovich, Kimble, & Malloy (1996) 5. LaBrie, Pederson, Thompson, & Earleywine (2008) 6. O'Grady, Wilson, & Harman (2009) 7. Shulkin et al. (1991) 8. Weiss, Turbiasz, & Whitney (1995)
Increases in Condom Use	8/14	1. Chernoff & Davison (2005) [men only] 2. Eitel & Friend (1999) 3. J. D. Fisher, Fisher, Misovich, Kimble, & Malloy (1996) 4. Kiene & Barta (2006) 5. LaBrie, Pederson, Thompson, & Earleywine (2008) 6. Sanderson (1999) 7. Sanderson & Jemmott (1996) 8. Weiss, Turbiasz, & Whitney (1995)
Increases in Positive Attitudes toward Condoms	4/8	1. Bryan, Aiken, & West (1996) 2. J. D. Fisher, Fisher, Misovich, Kimble, & Malloy (1996) 3. Sanderson & Jemmott (1996) 4. Shulkin et al. (1991)
Increases in Self-Efficacy Related to Sexual Communication/ Negotiation	4/8	1. Bryan, Aiken, & West (1996) 2. J. D. Fisher, Fisher, Misovich, Kimble, & Malloy (1996) 3. Sanderson & Jemmott (1996) 4. Sikkema, Winett, & Lombard (1995)
Increases in Perceived Risk related to STI/ HIV	5/8	1. Bryan, Aiken, & West (1996) 2. Doherty & Low (2008) 3. Eitel & Friend (1999) 4. Sanderson & Jemmott (1996) 5. Wienhardt, Carey, & Carey (2000)
Increases in Protective Knowledge	4/5	1. Doherty & Low (2008) 2. Fisher, Fisher, Misovich, Kimble, & Malloy (1996) 3. Kiene & Bartha (2006) 4. Sanderson & Jemmott (1996)
Increases in Condom Carrying or Condom Purchasing	3/4	1. Bryan, Aiken, & West (1996) [condom carrying] 2. Kiene & Barta (2006) [condom carrying] 3. Weiss, Turbiasz, & Whitney (1995)[condom purchasing]

Table 11.1 (Continued)

Outcome	Significant Effects/ Assessed	Articles Demonstrating Positive Outcomes
Decreases in Number of Sexual Partners	2/3	1. Chernoff & Davison (2005) [women only] 2. Jaworski & Carey (2001)
Increases in Effective Contraceptive Use	2/2	1. Gerrard, McCann, & Fortini (1983) 2. Ingersoll et al. (2005)

The most common outcome revealed in the interventions included in this review was an increase in general STI/HIV knowledge (11/12; 92%). Although not assessed as frequently, four of the five studies (80%) that measured knowledge specific to sexual risk reduction found significant intervention effects for increasing this type of knowledge. While knowledge is a necessary first step in many behavior change models (e.g., information motivation behavior, AIDS risk reduction model), it alone is typically not sufficient to bring about behavior change.

The penultimate outcome for many sexual risk reduction interventions is increases in condom use. Although only 8 of the 14 studies that assessed condom use found a significant effect of the intervention for increasing condom use, there were several factors that are either directly or indirectly linked to condom use that did demonstrate an increase. Of the 11 studies that examined intentions to either use condoms or to engage in some other type of sexual risk reduction behavior, 8 demonstrated significant increases following the intervention (73%). In order for students to use condoms, they typically must have positive attitudes about using them and also have condoms in their possession during sexual encounters. Thus it was encouraging that four of the eight studies (50%) that assessed positive attitudes toward condoms found that their interventions did increase such viewpoints; and that three of the four studies (75%) that assessed condom carrying or condom purchasing found positive intervention effects for these behaviors.

Other perceptual factors that have been shown to be associated with increased condom use were also found to have been increased with some of the interventions. Increases in perceived risk for STIs/HIV was revealed in five of the eight studies (63%) that assessed it, whereas four of the eight studies (50%) that assessed self-efficacy beliefs related to sexual communication or sexual negotiation found a positive intervention effect. In addition to changes in condom use, two studies assessed increases in general contraceptive use and both found a positive intervention effect for this protective behavior. Studies revealed changes in other behavioral outcomes associated with sexual risk reduction, such as decreases in numbers of sexual partners (2/3; 67%).

The following sections of this chapter offer more detailed information regarding the various components of successful sexual risk reduction interventions for university/college students. The first set of interventions are those that were designed for delivery to general university/college student populations, followed by those specific to both female and male students. The last section addresses the lack of interventions specifically focused on LGB university/college students.

INTERVENTIONS FOR FEMALE AND MALE UNIVERSITY/ COLLEGE STUDENTS

As mentioned, young adults are disproportionately likely to acquire STIs (CDC, 2009). Given these statistics it is important for sexual health interventions to target both HIV and other STIs. Most general interventions for male and female university/college students involved in this review were focused on a specific STI, primarily HIV. Specifically, 10 of the interventions were HIV/ AIDS focused, 4 solely focused on STIs other than HIV, and only 5 focused on STIs or risk reduction, in general. Six of the interventions developed for male and female university/college students included in this review reported increases in participants' sexual risk reduction or prevention behaviors. These interventions utilized a variety of theoretical frameworks and designs.

J. D. Fisher, Fisher, Misovich, Kimble, and Malloy (1996) evaluated an intervention implemented with dormitory university students that was grounded in the IMB model. Seven hundred and forty-four students were assigned to either the intervention or a control condition. The intervention involved three two-hour workshops held one week apart. The workshops aimed to address deficits in AIDS risk reduction information, motivation, behaviors skills, and preventive behavior. A health educator and five peer educators conducted the workshops. The information component of the workshops involved a health educator presenting an "AIDS 101" slide show that used humor and illustrations to convey information on HIV transmission and prevention, sexual risk, effectiveness of condom use, HIV testing, and where to purchase condoms or get tested near campus. The presentation also addressed and corrected incorrect HIV/AIDS prevention heuristics.

The motivation component was facilitated in small groups held by peer educators and geared toward influencing students' attitudes towards performing HIV/AIDS preventive behaviors, their perceptions of normative support for performing preventive behaviors, and their perceptions of HIV vulnerability. After small-group sessions, larger group discussions were conducted by the health educator to reinforce attitude and normative change induced by the small-group discussions and to influence perceptions of social network expectations and support for safer sex. The motivation component also included a showing of a video that included interviews with HIV positive heterosexual young adults.

The behavioral component aimed to teach students to effectively initiate and maintain safer sex behavior by showing a video of couples that modeled safer sex behaviors. Intervention participants were also taught to correctly use a condom and participated in a condom demonstration. In addition, behavioral skills homework was assigned to reinforce behavior change.

Students in both the intervention and control conditions were assessed using surveys prior to the intervention, one month after the final workshop, and two months later. At the one-month follow-up, results confirmed that the intervention resulted in increases in AIDS risk reduction information, motivation, and behavioral skills, as well as significant increases in condom accessibility, safer sex negotiations, and condom use during sexual intercourse. At a long-term follow-up, the intervention again resulted in significant increases in HIV preventive behaviors.

Kiene and Barta (2006) investigated a computer-based HIV/AIDS risk reduction intervention based on the IMB model. One hundred and fifty-seven university students participated in the intervention or control conditions. The intervention consisted of two computer-based sessions held two weeks apart that ranged in duration from 10 to 40 minutes. The sessions were tailored to the individual, and each student received modules that addressed their IMB-related deficits.

Information content focused on condom effectiveness, correct usage, common problems and solutions, and accessibility. Participants were also quizzed and given correct feedback. Motivation involved narratives on the advantages of condoms, along with planning, negotiation of use, and norms related to condoms. Participants then had to pick and explain the most important advantage of condom use. The behavior component consisted of computer directed experimental activities related to condom negotiation and condom demonstrations.

Participants completed presession assessment and a follow-up assessment two weeks after the second session. Results indicated that intervention participants exhibited a significant increase in keeping condoms available and displayed greater condom-related knowledge at the follow-up assessment. Among sexually active participants, there was also a significant increase in self-reported condom use.

Eitel and Friend (1999) compared two interventions (cognitive or motivational) and a control condition. The motivational intervention aimed to decrease denial of HIV/STI risk, increase the purchase and intent to use condoms, and decrease sexual risk behaviors. One hundred and fifty-five students participated in the study. The motivation condition induced hypocrisy to reduce denial of HIV/STI risk. The motivation intervention participants were asked to make a video taking a public stand on the importance of condom use. Next, they were given a list of 15 situations that hamper condom use (e.g., "We forgot to buy condoms") and told to add any situations they had experienced in the past. In the cognitive condition participants were given information about their peers' risk behaviors in order to make them aware of their own risk behaviors compared to their peers. After either situation, participants were paid $3 and offered condoms for 10 cents after the experimenter left. Overall, the participants in the motivation condition reported significantly greater intent to use condoms in the future, lower levels of denial immediately after the intervention, and fewer risky sexual behaviors over time than participants in the other two conditions.

Sanderson and Jemmott (1996) examined two HIV prevention interventions on condom use and mediators of condom use that were based on social cognitive theory and the theory of planned behavior. University students were randomly assigned to a control condition or one of two interventions that were peer facilitated. The two intervention sessions were offered one week apart. The technical skills intervention included a series of activities designed to increase participants' belief that they could facilitate and use condoms correctly with partners. Participants were exposed to a variety of condoms and then asked to rate them on a variety of dimensions (e.g., texture, appearance, etc.). Participants also practiced putting condoms on models and discussed erotic aspects of condom use. The communication skills intervention included several activities designed to increase participants' beliefs that they could negotiate safer sex with their partners. Participants discussed effective methods of communication on issues such as HIV testing and inquiring about partners' sexual history. Participants then role-played scenes to increase confidence in safer sex and prevention negotiation with partners.

Participants were surveyed prior to the intervention, directly after the second session, and three months later. Participants in both interventions had greater condom use self-efficacy, more positive condom use attitudes, and stronger intentions to use condoms than controls. At three months, participants in either intervention who were not in a committed relationship reported more consistent condom use than did those in the control condition.

Sanderson (1999) examined the effectiveness of different HIV prevention videos. Two hundred and two college students were randomly assigned to watch one of three videos that focused on technical skills, communication skills, or combined skills. All three videos depicted: (1) a woman refusing to have sex without a condom and her partner then going to buy condoms, (2) a heterosexual man that had acquired HIV through sex, and (3) statistics on the prevalence of HIV and other STIs among young adults. The technical skills video focused on the skills and strategies related to condom use. The video also focused on eroticizing condom use, discussed the technical aspects of condom use, and demonstrated correct condom use. The communication skills video focused on skills and strategies to facilitate condom negotiation. The video focused on difficulties in discussing condom use and safer sex with partners. The video also involved two role-play sessions about initiating condom use between partners in committed relationships. The combined skills video focused on the importance of both technical and communication skills and incorporated aspects of both videos. Participants received pretests, posttests, and a three-month follow-up. Results indicated that participants exposed to the combined skills video and who were not in committed relationship were more likely to use condoms at follow-up.

Chernoff and Davison (2005) evaluated a 20-minute self-administered intervention that utilized normative feedback and goal setting to increase HIV/AIDS risk reduction among sexually active university students. The study involved 155 students that were assigned to either an intervention or control condition. The intervention was self-administered and participants were given two instruments containing the normative feedback and goal-setting components. The first instrument asked participants to assess their normative beliefs related to sexual behaviors. The second instrument provided the results of a college-wide survey and included findings related to the prevalence of condom use, number of sexual partners, safer-sex discussions, and substance use in conjunction with sexual activity to emphasize that safer sex was a prevailing social norm. Participants were then asked to compare their own behavior to the campus social norms and reflect on their willingness to change their behavior to reinforce normative feedback. Last, participants engaged in a goal-setting activity where they were given a list of behavior change goals and asked to select the behaviors they could commit to changing in the next 30 days (e.g., decreasing the number of sexual partners). Participants in all conditions were given a pretest and posttest to return 30 days later. Results indicated that males in the intervention group reported a significant increase in condom use during vaginal intercourse and women reported a significant reduction in their number of sexual partners.

INTERVENTIONS FOR HETEROSEXUAL FEMALE COLLEGE/ UNIVERSITY STUDENTS

This review included six interventions that targeted heterosexual women. The interventions for heterosexual college/university women were focused on preventing STI, HIV, or unintended pregnancy. Specifically, two of the interventions were focused on increasing contraceptive use, two focused solely on STI, one solely on HIV, and one on STI/HIV. Interventions utilized a variety of theoretical models and were found to have positive effects in a variety of areas including sexual risk and contraceptive use.

Bryan, Aiken, and West (1996) developed a health belief model-based intervention to prevent STIs in young women, with the goal of increasing condom use through skills-building condom use strategies. They developed a 45-minute multicomponent safer-sex intervention and compared it to a stress management control condition. The first component involved acceptance of sexuality by depicting a video of society's depictions of women's sexuality focusing on feelings of guilt related to planning for sex. The second component focused on the health belief model's constructs of perceived susceptibility by targeting beliefs about STIs and perceived severity by discussing the symptoms of STIs. The third component targeted self-efficacy for condom use by addressing participants' ability to obtain condoms, condom negotiation through emphasis on assertiveness communication, and condom use application. The specific strategies highlighted by the authors included video segments highlighting the previously mentioned issues, distribution of condoms, role-play activities, discussion, and condom use demonstrations and practice. The authors reported increased intentions to use condoms, increased affective attitudes toward condom use and condom users, and increased self-efficacy to negotiate condom use. The primary behavioral outcome that increased was condom carrying among participants in the intervention.

Sikkemma, Winett, and Lombard (1995) developed an HIV risk reduction program for female university students by conducting elicitation research, pilot testing the initial intervention, and then tailoring the final intervention based on data from the pilot and elicitation research. The formative research helped to target population-specific risk behaviors and to create tailored role plays. The emphasis was on integrating cognitive-behavioral skills training in the promotion of sexual assertiveness skills, self-efficacy, and perceived vulnerability for HIV infection. Specific strategies that were incorporated into the four 75- to 90-minute group intervention sessions included group discussion, modeling , and role playing, as well as demonstration and practice of condom-related skills. In the evaluation of the intervention, the authors compared different versions of the intervention and found increases in both the "education-only group" and the "skills-based group" on knowledge of HIV/AIDS, perceived vulnerability to HIV/AIDS, and self-efficacy to participate in lower-risk behaviors. Significant increases in self-efficacy related to ability to consistently practice lower-risk sexual behaviors was revealed only for participants in the "skills-based group" compared to those in the "education only group" at both postintervention and at the one-month follow-up. No other group differences were revealed.

Gerrard, McCann, and Fontini (1983) developed a cognitive restructuring intervention focused on increasing contraceptive use among female university students. The intervention was a one-hour structured lecture with both didactic presentation of materials and demonstrations of the actual use of contraceptives. The researchers developed the intervention to determine the efficacy of a specific cognitive restructuring lecture focused on common negative attitudes and beliefs about effective contraception and actively challenging these attitudes and beliefs.

The authors tested the intervention using a randomized controlled trial, and reported significant declines in inhibiting thoughts about contraceptives among those in the cognitive restructuring intervention. Increases in positive attitudes toward contraceptives were revealed in both the cognitive restructuring intervention and the information-only comparison condition, however, changes in negative beliefs about contraceptives were not revealed. The authors suggest that changes in thoughts, attitudes, and beliefs require a more complex approach toward understanding and predicting attitude changes. Additionally, the measures and sample size may not have been sensitive enough to measure differences between the groups.

The authors reported a marginally significant treatment effect for the cognitive restructuring intervention on changing participants' use of contraception. Although both the cognitive restructuring and information-only groups revealed initial changes in contraceptive use, only those in the cognitive restructuring condition maintained these differences at the three-month follow-up. These data suggest that for long-term changes, cognitive restructuring was more effective at sustaining these changes than the information-only group.

Gracia Jones, Patsdaughter, Jorda, Hamilton, and Malow (2008) developed an HIV/STI prevention intervention specifically for Latina female university/college students. The SENORITAS program used the IMB model to develop a culturally tailored intervention to promote HIV/STI preventive behaviors. The researchers incorporated the three-stage approach proposed by the IMB model. The first stage involved eliciting information from a subsample of the target population to define the deficits and assets in HIV prevention, information, and behavioral skills. In the second stage, the results obtained in the first stage guided the development and design of the targeted intervention by incorporating the deficits and assets. At the time of the publication, the authors had not completed the third stage of the evaluation to determine if the intervention obtained significant sustained effects.

The SENORITAS intervention was delivered in a three-hour single-session format. Due to the cultural tailoring of the intervention for Latina young women, it included peer educators and incorporated mini novellas (i.e. storytelling) as a teaching tool. The intervention involved teaching elements that incorporate the three IMB components. Another core component of the SENORITAS intervention was the peer educator one-day workshop. The peer educator workshop involved didactic and interactive sessions, and peer educators were expected to become competent in condom selection, application, removal, and negotiation skills in order to be able to teach these skills to other students. The use of peer educators to guide the specific prevention strategies helped to reduce a reliance on didactic materials, and increased the use of interactive strategies that maintain participants' attention without altering the theoretical aspects of the intervention.

Gracia Jones et al. (2008) reported selected outcome data for students that participated in the SENORITAS intervention. Overall, there were significant increases in knowledge about HIV/AIDS following participation in the intervention. Among those who participated in the eight-week follow-up, there were significant increases in knowledge as compared to preprogram assessments. Self-reports of condom application skills for a small subset of the participants were provided, suggesting that there were significant increases in the condom application skills postprogram. The authors also reported increases in comfort with teaching HIV prevention skills for the peer educators, suggesting that peer education is a cost-effective approach to campus-based HIV prevention.

Jaworski and Carey (2001) investigated the effects of a brief STI prevention program for female university/college students based in the IMB model. They randomized participants into a one-session 150-minute information-only intervention, or a one-session 150-minute IMB-based intervention, or a wait-list control group. The specific strategies in the IMB intervention included reflective listening, personalized feedback and information about HIV/AIDS, positive reinforcement for risk reduction strategies, as well as exercises to improve sexual communication skills.

Jaworski and Carey (2001) reported significant improvements in STI-related information at postintervention and at the two-month follow-up, for both the information-only and IMB groups. There were no reported differences in attitudes toward condom use, in behavioral intentions to use condoms, or in the decisional balance scale between the information-only and the IMB groups. Additionally, no differences in behavioral skills were reported. The authors compared the log odds of condom use during vaginal and oral sex encountered across the groups. No differences were found for condom use. However, participants in the IMB group reported a significant reduction in the number of sexual partners as compared to the wait-list control group. However, no differences in abstinence or number of sexual partners were detected across groups.

Ingersoll et al. (2005) developed a one-session motivational interviewing-based intervention to reduce binge drinking and pregnancy risk due to incorrect use of effective contraceptive methods among university/college women. This intervention was unique in its focus on the link between alcohol use and the incorrect use of contraceptive methods. The single 60- to 75-minute counseling session consisted of personalized feedback delivered using a motivational interviewing counseling style with a trained interventionist to reduce alcohol-exposed pregnancy risk. There were a series of motivational enhancement strategies that were part of the semistructured manual used by the interventionists. The strategies identified by the authors included a 90-day timeline follow-back, personalized feedback on risk, decisional balance, temptation exercises, confidence charts, and development of goal statements.

The authors found significant reductions in reports of risky-level drinking at the one-month follow-up among those in the control and intervention groups. However, the risk reductions were significantly greater among those in the intervention group. As compared to the control group, the intervention participants reduced their number of standard drinks by 2.2 drinks per day. Women in the intervention group also reduced their number of binges in the past month, whereas women in the control group slightly increased their number of binges in the past month. Significantly fewer women in the control condition used effective contraception at one-month follow-up as compared those in the intervention condition. The authors also developed an alcohol-exposed pregnancy risk outcome measure, which comprised potential mediators such as age, drinking factors, contraception factors, psychiatric risk, and personality variables. Their analysis revealed that only two factors predicted increased risk of continued alcohol-exposed pregnancy at one-month follow-up. The strongest predictor at one-month follow-up was being assigned to the control condition, suggesting that the intervention reduced alcohol-exposed pregnancy risk. The second predictor was number of drinks, although this contributed a smaller proportion of increased risk for alcohol-exposed pregnancy.

INTERVENTIONS FOR HETEROSEXUAL MALE COLLEGE/ UNIVERSITY STUDENTS

To the authors' knowledge, interventions targeting heterosexual men are sparse. This review included two effective interventions with heterosexual men, with one based on motivational interviewing and the other on an STI/AIDS risk reduction model developed by Solomon and DeJong (1986). Both interventions focused on increasing condom use and were found to have significant positive effects around specific risk reduction skill training strategies.

LaBrie, Pederson, Thompson, and Earleywine (2008) examined decisional balance, a component of motivational interviewing, as an intervention to promote condom use among heterosexual male university/college students. The decisional balance strategy involved having male participants complete a worksheet listing their own personal reasons for and reasons against using a condom every time they had sex in the past. Next, participants received additional reasons from a validated scale and rated all the reasons on a scale from 1 to 10. Finally, the interventionist engaged participants in 5- to 10-minute motivational interviewing-style conversations around reasons for using a condom for every sexual event. The brief decisional balance scale used by LaBrie et al. (2008) operates on Prochaska and Redding's (1994) theory that behavior change occurs when the reasons for changing a behavior outweigh the reasons for not changing. Therefore the decisional balance strategy can be seen as both an intervention and an outcome measure.

Three separate measures of motivation to change condom use increased significantly both immediately postintervention and at 30-day follow-up. The decisional balance scale also correlated significantly with the three measures of motivation to change scale, immediately postintervention. The correlation was moderately correlated at the 30-day follow-up, with effect sizes ranging from medium to large. The authors also reported significant increases in self-reported condom use, particularly with new sex partners and regular sex partners at the 30-day follow-up. Additionally, participants that reported lower levels of condom use at baseline reported using a condom every time at follow-up.

Weiss, Turbiasz, and Whitney (1995) designed a multifaceted HIV prevention intervention for university/college students based on principles of the Solomon and DeJong's (1986) STI/AIDS risk reduction model. The intervention was focused on reducing embarrassment to purchase condoms, encouraging positive attitudes about condoms, and promoting knowledge about AIDS. While the intervention was used with both men and women, Weiss et al. (1995) reported only how the workshop was tailored to meet the needs of young men because the barriers to using condoms varied for men and women. Participants received information concerning HIV/AIDS and participated in behavioral training experiences that familiarized them with proper condom use. In order to reduce embarrassment regarding accessing condoms, the intervention normalized condom purchasing anxieties through individual practice assignments and increasing peer acceptance.

At the one-month follow-up, the authors found that workshop participants reported greater intentions to use condoms, increased positive attitudes toward condoms, and increased knowledge about HIV/AIDs. However, these significant changes were not sustained at the three-month follow-up. After participating in the workshop, participants reported more condom purchases and more condom use as compared to the control condition. Workshop participants reported significantly less embarrassment over the purchase of condoms after the training session, and this effect became stronger with time, suggesting that specific skill training through behavioral training can produce long-term changes.

INTERVENTIONS FOR LGB COLLEGE/UNIVERSITY STUDENTS

None of the sexual risk reduction interventions included in this review were tailored specifically for LGB college/university student populations. As the only group in the United States with increasing annual numbers of new HIV infections (CDC, 2010a), gay and bisexual men in particular continue to be in need of interventions proven to reduce rates of HIV transmission. Of further concern is that among black and Latino gay/bisexual men, the majority of new HIV infections are occurring among those aged 13–29.

Given the lack of sexual risk reduction interventions developed specifically for LGB college/university students and the great need for such programs, we will discuss the Mpowerment Project (Kegeles, Hays, & Coates, 1996) since it is an intervention that has been developed for use with college-age gay and bisexual men, and was initially evaluated in two university communities.

The aim of the Mpowerment Project was to develop a process by which young gay men would exchange with each other the need for and virtue of sexual risk reduction, thereby making safer sex the social norm. Using the diffusion of innovation model (E. M. Rogers, 1995) as its guiding framework, the peer-led intervention has three components: outreach, small groups, and a publicity campaign. Two comparable communities with large state universities were chosen as study sites for the initial delivery and evaluation of the intervention.

Four young gay men were employed to serve as part-time project coordinators for the eight-month study, and the program was run by a core group of 12 to 15 young gay men. Outreach activities were conducted at bars and community events by young men with two main goals: (1) to diffuse safer sex messages and (2) to recruit more young men into the project. The intention was that new recruits would proceed to diffuse the safer sex messages to others within their social circles while then recruiting others into the project, thus creating a self-perpetuating process whereby men would join the project, learn about and adopt the messages around safer sex, and continue the recruitment process through their normal interactions within their social circles. The project also established what was called the Mpowerment Center, a physical setting designed to hold weekly meetings, to serve as a drop-in center, and to provide a location for various social activities.

"M-Groups" were small, onetime peer-led meetings that lasted three hours, were attended by 8 to 10 young men, and focused on different factors believed to contribute to unsafe sexual practices among young gay men. Topics included such issues as sexual communication, as well as misperceptions about and attitudes toward safer sex. Intervention outcomes were evaluated at the individual level through use of pre- and postintervention surveys delivered in the target communities. Among the young men in the intervention community, postintervention surveys showed a significant reduction in reports of unprotected anal intercourse. This included declines in reports of unprotected anal intercourse with nonprimary partners and boyfriends. There were no significant changes in unprotected anal intercourse among those in the comparison community.

CONCLUSIONS AND RECOMMENDATIONS

This overview of sexual risk reduction interventions for college and university students offers an array of interventions that have been shown to be effective at lowering the risk for negative sexual health outcomes (i.e., STIs, HIV, unplanned pregnancy) among college and university students. The most common significant outcome across the 27 studies that were reviewed was an increase in STI/HIV knowledge. Although knowledge is important, studies have demonstrated that it is not sufficient to create behavior change. For example, Reader, Carter, and Crawford (1988) conducted a study with 214 university students on their HIV/AIDS knowledge, attitudes, and behavior. Results of the study indicated that students were relatively well informed about HIV/AIDS prevention, but this was not reflected in their behavior. The authors inferred that targeted approaches, beyond solely educational ones focused on increasing knowledge, were needed to induce behavior change to reduce sexual risk.

Several interventions were able to demonstrate reductions in the frequency of sexual risk behaviors, most notably through increased condom use. Other interventions were able to demonstrate increases in various factors that are either directly or indirectly linked to condom use, such as intentions to use condoms, positive attitudes toward condoms, and carrying condoms. Yet other interventions impacted attitudes and beliefs associated with sexual risk reduction, such as perceived risk for STIs/HIV and self-efficacy beliefs related to sexual communication. Changes in other behavioral outcomes associated with sexual risk reduction, such as decreases in numbers of sexual partners, were also found.

The development of future sexual risk reduction interventions for university/college students should be guided by empirically validated health behavior change theories. The CDC has strongly advocated for theoretically based HIV and other STI interventions that target behavior change. With regard to theory, the CDC has noted that both IMB and social cognitive theory models have been most effective in changing high-risk HIV/STI behavior (CDC, n.d.). Our review revealed that the most commonly used theory/model in interventions that demonstrated significant effects on participants was the IMB model. The other theories and models that were used in successful interventions included social cognitive theory, the theory of planned behavior, the health belief model, and motivational enhancement. These represent some of the most widely used health behavior changes theories and models, and thus provide useful frameworks for colleges and universities wishing to develop theory-based interventions.

Given the predominance of the IMB model in creating successful risk reduction interventions for college and university students, an overview of this model is offered for those who may choose to use it to develop campus-based HIV/STI prevention interventions. The IMB model (J. D. Fisher & Fisher, 1992, 2000; W. A. Fisher & Fisher, 1993) was designed specifically to support the development of HIV prevention interventions, and details a three-step approach to promoting HIV preventive behaviors. In the first step, *elicitation research*, a subsample of a target population is queried to empirically identify that population's deficits and assets in HIV prevention information, motivation, behavioral skills, and behavior. In the second step, an *empirically targeted intervention* is designed based on the findings from the elicitation research and then it is delivered to address a population's HIV prevention information, motivation, and behavioral skills deficits. In addition, the intervention should be designed to capitalize on the population's strengths in these areas. In the third and final stage, *evaluation research* is independently conducted to determine whether the intervention has had significant sustained effects on the information, motivation, and behavioral skills precursors of HIV preventive behavior, as well as on the actual HIV preventive behaviors.

Given the disproportionate impact of HIV/STI/unplanned pregnancy among specific populations (e.g., gay and bisexual young men, African American young women), it is necessary to develop future sexual risk reduction interventions for those university/college students at greatest risk. Given the availability of efficacious prevention interventions and strategies for general university/college student samples, an examination of the appropriateness of these interventions for specific populations of students at greatest risk for negative sexual health outcomes is warranted. Existing interventions will need to be tailored to the needs of these populations to ensure that sexual risk reduction interventions are relevant and address population-specific risk and protective factors. For example, societal-level influences of heterosexism and racism have been shown to influence sexual risk behaviors among gay/bisexual young adults of color (G. Harper, 2007), but these issues were not addressed in any of the interventions included in the 27 articles we discovered in our systematic review. Alternatively, for ethnic minority or first-generation university/college students from underserved communities, health disparities and other socioeconomic factors that impact numerical minority populations may compound their risk of contracting HIV/STIs. Thus intervention efforts should be tailored to address these additional health-related risk factors. The SENORITAS intervention was the only successful intervention in our review that was ethnic specific, and provides examples of using participatory approaches that promote inclusion of relevant stakeholders and potential participants in developing, implementing and evaluating prevention interventions that are culturally tailored. The use of such participatory approaches to HIV/STI prevention intervention development has been used successfully with other populations of young people (G. W. Harper et al., 2004), and should be considered in the development of future sexual risk reduction interventions for university/college students.

In addition to future sexual risk reduction interventions for university/college students being guided by an understanding of the specific populations being served, the contexts under which students may be at increased risk for HIV/STI and/or unplanned pregnancy should also be explored. Although not explicitly detailed in the descriptions of the interventions in our review due to space limitations, some studies demonstrated differences in sexual risk-taking behaviors based on the type of sexual activities involved (i.e., oral, anal, vaginal), the type of sexual partners with whom they were having sex (casual vs. monogamous), and whether or not students were using alcohol and other substances during the sexual episode. With regard to types of sexual activity, students may use condoms during vaginal sex to avoid pregnancy, but not use them to protect against STIs when engaging in oral or anal sex. Future interventions should promote consistent condom use and other barrier methods when engaging in all types of sexual activity that present any risk for disease transmission and/or pregnancy, and explore reasons for differential condom use across sexual practices.

Although relationship status was explored in some of the reviews and found to influence participation in sexual risk reduction behaviors, a more nuanced exploration of relationship status is warranted in future interventions. Given that sexual relationships involve a dyadic interaction, it cannot be assumed that one partner's perception of the relationship status (e.g., casual, monogamous) is shared by both individuals. This has implications for sexual risk since some students may forgo the use of protective measures such as condoms based on an erroneous belief that both partners are monogamous, thus increasing their risk for STIs. Future interventions should also explore various characteristics of dating relationships within which sexual activity occurs, including the levels of commitment, love, intimacy, violence, and coercion that may be present in these relationships.

Additionally, future interventions should address the role of alcohol use in increasing negative sexual health outcomes given the high prevalence of binge drinking on college campuses. Coupling binge drinking prevention with sexual risk reduction strategies may require approaches that impact the social norms on college campuses surrounding alcohol use and sexual risk taking. Diffusion strategies that utilize peers to promote safer sex norms, such as those promoted by the Mpowerment Project, have been successful in reducing sexual risk taking among both primary and secondary partners. Other creative strategies for shifting social norms, perhaps through the use of social marketing, social media, and other technology-based platforms, should be explored.

Examining these varied contextual factors (i.e., types of sexual activity, relationship status, and alcohol use) will potentially lead to more effective interventions. More information is needed regarding whether these factors are moderators or mediators of risk, and under what conditions and with what populations they may have these influences. This will require increased research on the sexual activity of various groups of university/college students, and the multitude of cultural and contextual factors that may impact participation in risk and protective behaviors. In addition future research is needed on both existing and new interventions in order to promote the highest degree of sexual health among university and college students.

Future research efforts on sexual risk reduction interventions should allow for greater specificity regarding the effectiveness of the intervention theories, strategies, and intended outcomes. In the current review, interpretation of the study findings were limited since they often offered minimal information regarding the study sample socio-demographic characteristics, typically reported outcomes only for durations of less than six months, and relied heavily on self-reported measures of sexual risk. With regard to sample characteristics, it would be helpful in future studies to offer a broader range of information regarding the socio-demographics of the intervention populations, including race/ethnicity, sexual orientation, and educational status. Further, subgroup analyses that go beyond gender and sexual partnership status would be helpful to determine if there may be groups of students who are not successfully being reached by these interventions.

While there is some evidence that treatment effects were maintained over a follow-up period of up to three months for some of the interventions, in general the studies in this review did not examine long-term outcomes. Even less is known about the potential value of maintenance or booster sessions for maintaining reductions in sexual risk-taking knowledge, skills, and behaviors. Studies of prevention interventions should also consider triangulating outcome measures to determine the impact of these efforts above and beyond self-reports of knowledge, attitudes, and behavior. Such data may include results of STI/HIV/pregnancy serologic tests, or observations of sexual risk reduction skills. Campus-level data regarding sexual risk social norms could also be collected in order to determine the impact of interventions on the campus climate.

Chapter Twelve

SEXUAL PROBLEMS AND DYSFUNCTIONS AMONG COLLEGE STUDENTS

Peggy J. Kleinplatz

Since the 1980s, I have been teaching courses in human sexuality to a total of well over 10,000 university students to date. Each lecture, students are invited to submit anonymous questions to be answered aloud or as catalysts for class discussion. Of the 50,000 or so questions collected thus far, here are a few that seem to be especially frequent: What is the best position for intercourse? What is the right technique for "oral"? Why does my girlfriend not reach orgasm during sex? How can a guy stay hard longer? Which is the best birth control? Can you increase a person's sex drive? How do you stop the pain after sex? How do you get someone to quit being so jealous? How do you tell your boyfriend/girlfriend that you want to try a new fantasy? Among the commonalities notable in these questions is the assumption that there are objective and correct answers to these queries. The questions are strikingly out of context, as if there were some universally "right" ways to be sexual, to engage in sex, and to fix sexual problems and concerns—if only one knew what they were.

College students are relative sexual novices but are certain that they are at their peak and are eager for information so that they can perform as expected. It seems to surprise them that there is no best technique for this or that sexual act and that exploring personal preferences—which will require the dreaded act of communication and being comfortable with not knowing everything in advance—is the only way to discover what will bring pleasure in a particular individual or couple. It can be especially vexing that even after they master the skills with one partner, the next one is unique, too, and will require learning from scratch all over again. The pressure to perform smoothly while inexperienced, to operate skillfully despite a lack of imagined expertise and, for many young Americans, despite deliberately restricted sex education in high school leads many college students to feel inadequate, whether or not they qualify for formal diagnoses of sexual dysfunctions or disorders.

This chapter will discuss the major factors that lead to sexual difficulties. Some of the more common problems and their origins, as well as the context in which they come to be viewed as problematic among college students will be enumerated. Then the major male and female sexual problems will be discussed, followed by the major problem for couples, that is, differences in sexual desire.

WHAT CAUSES SEXUAL PROBLEMS AND OBSTACLES TO SEXUAL FULFILLMENT?

Sexual problems do not usually originate from one cause or type of factor alone; rather, they are more often multidetermined or multifactorial (Kaplan, 1974). Theoretically, obstacles to sexual fulfillment can be divided into the four broad categories of intrapsychic, sociocultural/economic/political, interpersonal, and biomedical causes, but there tends to be quite a bit of overlap in the actual origins of sexual difficulties in any given individual. For example, a young couple, both juniors in college, may complain of sexual desire discrepancy. They first met when both were sophomores living in residence and hit it off, having sex at every available opportunity. After six months, when they realized that they were starting to feel serious about each other, they quit using condoms. She went on oral contraceptives and was not warned about their often deleterious effects on desire. They also caused her to gain a few pounds and she is beginning to feel self-conscious when naked. When questioned as to when the problem began, they answer that they noticed it early in the semester. Last summer, her loan application was refused. His parents have helped him out with tuition and he offered to move in together off campus in hope of saving her some money. She is trying to keep up and increase her grades for a scholarship as well as having to work part-time outside school; she is so busy that she barely has time for assignments, let alone for their relationship; she is frustrated that he cannot seem to pick up the slack around the apartment. Both come from homes where conflict was managed poorly and do not know how to resolve their problems together without feeling threatened emotionally. As such, it is not surprising that these many factors lead to lack of sexual desire. This case also illustrates how many individuals/couples who come to have sexual problems actually have all manner of problems that are not necessarily "sexual" in nature (Kleinplatz, 2006). However, when these underlying problems are unresolved, eventually, they are manifest in the bedroom. It is at that point that such a couple may worry about how to resolve their "sexual" problem when what is really required is accurate information about contraceptive choices, attention to body image concerns, better funding for higher education, conflict resolution skills, and a more equitable division of labor around the house (Working Group for a New View of Women's Sexual Problems, 2001).

Although sexual problems generally cannot be broken down into one factor versus another, for purposes of this chapter, the following section breaks these factors down artificially as if they were separate when in fact, they are intertwined.

Intrapsychic Factors

Intrapsychic factors are those psychological elements within the individual that bear on his or her sexual expression. Many of these are related to early childhood experiences and the messages received in childhood about sexuality. For example, what was the nature of the parents' sexual relationship and how was it perceived within the family? Were the parents sexually open and expressive, affectionate and demonstrative, or more reserved? Did they seem loving to one another and to the children or cool and distant? Were they happily married, miserable together, or divorced? What did the parents teach about sex? What did the children learn from what the parents said or, more commonly, from what was never spoken about sexuality? How did the family deal with nudity, self-stimulation in childhood, privacy, questions about where babies come from, and about what to expect during puberty? The values learned about one's body and in particular the genitalia as well as about pleasure and sexuality overall have a tremendous impact on future sexual attitudes, comfort, or discomfort.

Clearly, childhood sexual abuse or incest can lead to feelings of shame, guilt, and fear around sexuality and generally diminished self-esteem (Bass & Davis, 2008; Finkelhor, 2008; Maltz, 2001, in press; Spiegel, 2003). Many survivors of sexual abuse do not feel entitled to consensual, mutually respectful, and loving sexual relations. Furthermore, they are often unable to imagine sex that is chosen freely and how that would look and feel, rather than sex occurring for someone else's sake—to fulfill another's needs. These are often contributing factors to the future development of sexual problems including low sexual desire, sexual aversion, and various sexual dysfunctions. Alternately, sometimes survivors of sexual abuse have no obvious difficulty with the "sexual" aspects of sexual relationships—it is the relationship part that is intimidating. That is, sometimes it can be hard to integrate the sexual and intimate aspects of relationships if one's history included sexual exploitation on the part of those one loved and trusted. Unfortunately, given that many people raised in "normal" homes contend with sex-negative environments, they too are subject to anxiety and discomfort regarding sexuality with similar consequences (Polonsky, 2010; Tolman, 2002), even if their concerns are not as intense as among those who were sexually abused. In other words, the notion that all sexual abuse survivors will develop sexual problems is an overstatement; correspondingly, in a sex-negative culture, "normal" sexual development may breed sexual problems.

Another common contributor to sexual problems is the focus on sex as performance rather than as a source of mutual pleasure. To the extent that one is observing one's body while in bed, concerned about getting or keeping an erection, reaching orgasm, or, more likely, reaching orgasm "soon enough" or delaying orgasm "long enough," one is typically unable to connect fully and joyfully with one's partner(s). Masters and Johnson (1970) referred to this as "spectatoring" and, indeed, it often feels as if one is off in the bleachers, watching and worrying from a distance, instead of being embodied within and present with one's partner(s). Thus performance anxiety interferes with sexual satisfaction even if it does not always technically impede "functioning."

Cultural Factors

Personal and sociocultural values have an enormous impact on sexuality. In North America, sexual values tend to be sex-negative and thus contribute to the development of sexual difficulties. In fact, growing up with our culture's "sex script" (i.e., social blueprints for sexual norms, values, beliefs, attitudes, practices, and their justifications) tends to instill sexual shame and guilt in many if not most people to some extent (Gagnon & Simon, 1973). It has been said that the major developmental task of adolescence is overcoming the shame-engendering messages internalized during childhood.

Another major contributor to sexual dissatisfaction is ignorance. An entire generation of American youth, many of whom are now in college, were raised under the Bush policy in which it was forbidden to offer comprehensive sexuality education in government-funded schools (J. Levine, 2002). By federal law, schools were to provide abstinence-only sex education, which taught the basics of reproductive biology. In such programs, many of which are continuing even under the current Obama administration, sex is equated with heterosexual intercourse. Conspicuously absent is any discussion of contraception or safer sex as ways of preventing unwanted pregnancies or sexually transmitted infections (STIs). Information about gay, lesbian, bisexual, and transgender sexuality is likely missing, too. By contrast, in Western countries where there are fewer restrictions on sex education, rates of unwanted pregnancies and STIs are significantly lower than they are in the United States (Advocates for Youth, 1999). More insidious perhaps is the exclusion of pleasure from sex education. As such, young people in abstinence-only sex education programs learn via silence that the ultimate taboo is not sex—it is discussion of pleasure.

The manifestations of ignorance and shame are pervasive when looking at sexual difficulties: Both men and women suffer from body image problems that contribute to discomfort with nudity and with being touched. The sense of being inadequate or perhaps even defective is ever-present. Talk of sex is everywhere in the media yet the capacity to express one's sexual wishes and preferences is limited by the taboo around asking for sexual pleasure. Many sexual problems could be prevented or at least dealt with simply and expediently if couples only felt free to show and tell what they find arousing. For many couples however, even saying "a little to the left, please" or "slower, gentler" is difficult enough; sharing one's deepest fantasies seems unimaginable.

By the time they reach college, many young adults have acquired a series of powerful messages in a vacuum of silence. These include: A man always wants and is always ready to have sex. Women's sexuality is more complicated than that of men's. Sex should be natural and spontaneous. You should not start anything you cannot finish. The ideal state is to be in a monogamous, lifelong, heterosexual relationship. On the other hand, a little "girl-on-girl" action is always fun to watch. Sexual satisfaction equals orgasm. And if you loved me, I would not have to tell you what I want; you would already know. Many of these myths could be cleared up if young adults were to talk to each other, but that remains another unspoken taboo.

The ubiquitous presence of Internet pornography combined with the absence of comprehensive sex education and open communication make it inevitable that college students will turn to this source to learn about sex. They are often unable to distinguish between fiction and reality. Unfortunately, Internet porn images area about as accurate as Saturday morning cartoons. Mainstream pornography portrays men and women with plastically perfect bodies, denuded of the hair that only recently had symbolized their reproductive maturity, engaging in seamless oral (female gives), vaginal, and anal sex (male gives), where the participants are always physically ready and emotional readiness is irrelevant; changing of positions always occurs gracefully, pregnancy prevention and safer sex are invisible and presumably unnecessary, interruptions are always an opportunity for a threesome, and there is no conversation but much screaming. Thus there is less focus on feelings during sex, communication, or intimacy than ever.

BECOMING A SEXUAL BEING IN THE AGE OF WEB 2.0?

One of the developmental tasks of youth is establishing one's sense of self as a sexual being and partner. This internal and, of necessity, interpersonal process has been characterized by a fair degree of ambiguity about what "normal" sexual intimacy means in college. It has probably always been the case and that murkiness allowed some latitude in experimentation; one of the complications in the course of establishing one's sense of self as an independent sexual being is the increasingly public and rapid nature of this process, to a degree that is without precedent. It is hard(er) to experiment privately with burgeoning identities, to try out new ways of being on for size, to delight and anguish in one's own tentativeness, to flirt slowly and surreptitiously, when one is expected to update the world on one's relationship status instantly on Facebook. The majority of college students send text messages as a way of making sexual overtures, as a way of communicating to prospective lovers what one dare not say face-to face and, later, immediately after hooking up. For better or for worse, this changes the nature of relationships.

The process for young adults has always been circumscribed by the norms of the day. At present, social conventions are bound by and enforced by technology. In a situation in which one is more public and therefore more exposed, one of the ways to protect oneself is to adhere more closely to convention, which may make it more difficult to choose one's unique path.

Interpersonal Factors

Interpersonal factors include all those elements that affect one's ability to be engaged in sexual relationships or for a couple to be mutually engaged. These factors include difficulties with trust, fears of rejection, power struggles, disappointment, and "goodness of fit" (i.e., the extent to which partners share compatible visions of sex, eroticism, pleasure, etc.). The most prominently reported interpersonal factor is communication difficulties, typically, "communicating about intimacy." Sometimes this phrase is a euphemism for fears of talking openly about sexual likes and dislikes, wishes, preferences, and fantasies. However, the difficulty is often with conflict resolution per se and its impact on the couple's willingness to risk emotional and sexual intimacy together. Couples who cannot really afford to get angry with another also cannot afford to feel much of anything, let alone to share passion.

Above and beyond these "communication difficulties" is the difficulty in literally talking about and defining sexual terms. Many people associate their Latinate sex vocabularies with physicians' offices and perhaps biology classes and thus claim such terms "sound clinical." In contrast, the slang terms for sexual parts and functions (in English) have derogatory connotations and make people uncomfortable, too. As such, people are often at a loss as to how to ask for what they want. The usual default, nonverbal communication, is an inadequate substitute for simple, clear requests. Furthermore, the seriousness of this seemingly trivial problem is exacerbated by the lack of consensus as to what constitutes "sex." It is fairly common for couples to use euphemisms that turn out to signify entirely different things to each partner. Partners who argue endlessly about wanting to "take more time in bed" may unknowingly have mistaken his self-doubts surrounding rapid ejaculation with her desire to receive more oral stimulation or their concerns about how frequently sex occurs.

Biomedical Factors

Any factor that affects the human body can affect sexuality. A wide variety of diseases or their treatments can affect sexual desire, arousal, and response directly, indirectly, or both. It is very useful for people to see their physicians and ask to be examined for any medical problems that might affect sexuality (Moser, 1999). STIs are exceedingly widespread among college students and can have a direct bearing on sexuality. Diagnoses of these conditions often make people feel defective immediately (Nack, 2008). People with STIs may describe feeling contaminated and untouchable.

A wide variety of drugs commonly used by college students affect sexual functioning. For example, most psychotropic drugs, that is, medications used for psychiatric purposes, tend to affect sexual functioning adversely. These certainly include drugs for attention deficit hyperactivity disorder, anxiety, and depression. A popular category of antidepressant medications, the selective serotonin reuptake inhibitors, which includes such drugs as Zoloft, Celexa, and Paxil, as well as its variant serotonin-norepinephrine reuptake inhibitors such as Effexor and Pristique, can diminish or prevent sexual arousal, orgasm, or even sexual desire itself. On the other hand, this very side effect has been used to assist men who have been diagnosed with rapid ejaculation to slow their responses (see below). Some commonly used drugs do not even "count" in patients' minds when giving a sexual/medical history. Over-the-counter drugs such as antihistamines and decongestants dry out mucous membranes in the nose and mouth; as such, they may well limit a woman's lubrication although it typically does not even occur to her that her allergy pills are making sex uncomfortable. Similarly, women using hormonal contraception, that is, oral contraceptive pills, "the patch," or "the shot", as in Depo-Provera, may not be aware of their possibly adverse effects on sexual desire in some women and, unfortunately, are not typically warned of such possibilities in advance.

Recreational drugs need to be considered as well. In particular, the increasing role of alcohol in the origin and exacerbation of the sexual dysfunctions in college students should not be underestimated. College students tend to think of alcohol as helping them to "loosen up" sexually and often use it deliberately for its disinhibiting effects. However, the same cautions that apply to drinking and driving are relevant for sex. Because alcohol depresses the central nervous system, it affects reflexes and judgment. Alcohol can impair the ability to make clear and consensual choices about sex, thereby contributing to unwanted sex or unsafe sex (which are covered in chapters 10, 11, and 13 in this book).

Enough alcohol will also impair the mechanisms involved in sexual excitement and orgasm. The consequences of frequent binge drinking on sexual functioning are barely noticed until they impair "performance," that is, the ability to engage in sexual intercourse (at least among heterosexuals). The deleterious effect of alcohol on erections is often referred to derisively as "whiskey dick." Delayed ejaculation tends to remain invisible because men who maintain their erections endlessly are regarded as sexual stalwarts rather than as dysfunctional. Correspondingly, to the extent that college students define "sex" as intercourse, the effects of alcohol on women's sexuality are easily overlooked even though they are similarly severe. Alcohol may impair vaginal lubrication, thus causing at least discomfort, if not pain and, subsequently, anorgasmia, but do not obstruct intercourse directly.

SEXUAL PROBLEMS IN MEN, WOMEN AND COUPLES

Men's Sexual Problems

Erectile Dysfunction

Of all male sexual dysfunctions, the one that has received the greatest attention in recent years has been erectile dysfunction largely because of the marketing of pharmacological treatments for this condition since the late 1990s.

Erections are triggered when men receive sexual stimulation, whether in the form of sexual thoughts and feelings or direct tactile contact. When men are young, mental stimulation is often sufficient to elicit an erection; typically, as men age, more direct physical stimulation is required to produce an erection. Sexual stimulation leads to an increase in blood flow into the arteries of the penis (more specifically, into highly vascular tissue in the chambers of the penis, especially the corpora cavernosa) faster than the veins can drain the blood back away. In fact, the now-expanding arteries compress the veins, making it difficult for the blood flow to return until either the erection subsides or the man reaches orgasm.

Many things can interfere with erections. The factors are so numerous, from nervousness with a new partner, fear of pregnancy, exam stress to recreational or prescribed drugs that virtually all men will have difficulties getting or maintaining erections from time to time. This is normal and does not require treatment. On the contrary, the problem sometimes occurs as a direct result of men, whether heterosexual or gay, worrying about what is normal (Polonsky, 2010). Young men often believe that their masculinity is tied directly to their abilities to get erections automatically, whenever even a prospective opportunity arises, and to keep them endlessly (Zilbergeld, 1978/1999). As such, occasional difficulties with getting or keeping erections can, itself, create the performance anxiety that then generates the self-fulfilling prophecy of erectile dysfunction. It is noteworthy that although many people think of erectile dysfunction strictly as a problem of getting erections, the more common difficulty is with maintaining a hard penis during sexual contact rather than simply getting the initial erection.

To the extent that the couple can broaden their sexual repertoire, they may be able to lift the pressure off the poor penis (not to mention the man attached to it!).

In some instances, what appear to mechanical difficulties in functioning can only be identified correctly as *appropriate* bodily responses to unsatisfactory sex or relationship issues when both partners are present (Kleinplatz, 2004, 2010b; Schnarch, 1991). For example, it is only when both are in the same room that one detects the simmering conflict between them—or even their outright dislike for one another—such that his "dysfunction" is more likely a solution than a problem. Perhaps rather than being problematic, the man's soft penis provides evidence of good judgment demonstrated via his body.

Rapid Ejaculation

Notwithstanding the greater public attention to erectile dysfunction, rapid ejaculation is probably the most common male sexual dysfunction (Polonsky, 2000) especially among young males. There has been considerable controversy in defining rapid ejaculation. How do you know when soon is too soon? All sorts of definitions have been proffered over the years with attempts at scientific objectivity. Some have focused on the number of minutes prior to ejaculation and others on the number of thrusts. There are several problems with such definitions: First, people who are enjoying sex rarely employ a stopwatch (fortunately!), so it is hard to ascertain what is "normal" and what is not. Second, much as scientist-clinicians seek objective criteria, how long sex lasts is only a problem when it creates distress. Surely, we can imagine the movie scene of lovers working feverishly to meet surreptitiously, ripping each other's clothes off in an empty corridor, and enjoying a "quickie" before they can even catch their breath. In such instances, the sex seems torrid—not problematic. Thus more recent approaches have focused on the man's or the couple's subjective experience. For example, Metz and McCarthy feel that the best professional description of this problem is when, "*. . . the man does not have voluntary, conscious control, or the ability to choose in most encounters when to ejaculate*" (2003, p. 1, emphasis in the original). On the other hand, the proposals for the *Diagnostic and Statistical Manual of Mental Disorders, 5th edition*, have suggested that the criterion of "how long" be changed to 60 seconds of penis-in-vagina (Segraves, 2010).

Typically, by the time men seek sex therapy for rapid ejaculation, they have already tried numerous delaying tactics regardless of the cost they may be paying. Common examples of "home remedies" include numbing creams, doubling up on condoms, and trying to think about disgusting things to turn themselves off. Unfortunately, these strategies "work" by depriving the man of pleasure and depriving the partners from feeling present with one another; their "success" inadvertently reinforces the notion that sex equals performing during intercourse.

Many men feel pressured to "last" as long as possible in the assumption that extensive thrusting is what it takes to satisfy female partners. Such men often feel quite relieved when they learn that most women prefer external, clitoral stimulation when seeking orgasm. As such, "lasting longer" becomes a choice for prolonging lovemaking when he or they desire it rather than an obligation.

Ideally, the emphasis is on increasing his tolerance for high levels of pleasure rather than reducing his sensitivity to partner stimulation. Bodily awareness exercises can help him learn how it feels to be highly aroused without "going over the edge" (Zilbergeld, 1978/1999).

More recently, pharmacological treatment of rapid ejaculation has been available. The side effects of selective serotonin reuptake inhibitor antidepressants such as Paxil on orgasmic response are so dramatic, diminishing or even preventing orgasm in many patients, that the drug has been prescribed for men concerned about rapid ejaculation. The selective serotonin reuptake inhibitors succeed in slowing down men's ejaculations and have been used as an adjunct to conventional sex therapy for rapid ejaculation (M. D. Waldinger, 2010).

Delayed Ejaculation

On the other end of the spectrum are men who are unable to reach orgasm with a partner. (Men who have never had an orgasm in their lives under any circumstances, including via masturbation, probably have underlying medical problems requiring evaluation.) Most people do not think of men capable of thrusting away endlessly during intercourse as having a problem. On the contrary, many would be envious of such a capacity. As such, it has been estimated that delayed ejaculation is the most underreported of male sexual problems, just as, correspondingly, rapid orgasm in women is probably the most underreported of women's sexual difficulties. Many people would just scratch their heads at hearing of such conditions and ask, "So what's the problem?" The assumption in our sex scripts is that no man can stay hard for too long and that no woman can reach orgasm too soon. However, Apfelbaum (2000) would respond that men who cannot ejaculate with a partner are the misunderstood "workhorses" of the sex world. Apfelbaum has argued that although such men have often been treated as if they were withholding during sex, on the contrary, they are giving too much. These are individuals who are trying so hard to please their partners that they continue to perform while subjectively feeling minimal arousal, numb, or even turned off. It seems that their desires are out of sync with their penises, which continue to remain erect despite lack of excitement (Apfelbaum, 2000). Why this should be the case is not clear.

The notion that delayed ejaculation could be a problem for young men seems surprising to many, especially college students themselves. The belief is that young men are ever ready for sex, any time, any place, with only logistical barriers (e.g., lack of a partner, lack of a bed) standing in the way. If anything, the image of young men is that they are all too ready, "too quick on the trigger," and need to slow down and to gain some measure of self-control. The idea that young men might actually have difficulty reaching orgasm or in letting go is counter to this image; it fits our stereotype of young women rather than their male counterparts. However, over the last 10 years, there have been numerous reports in the literature about men having difficulty with orgasm (Hartmann & Waldinger, 2007; C. J. Nelson, Ahmed, Valenzuela, Parker, & Mulhall, 2007; Perelman, 2008, 2010; Perelman & Rowland, 2006, 2008; M. D. Waldinger, 2010).

One interpretation of the increased prevalence of delayed ejaculation is that men are "performing" better sexually thanks to erectogenic drugs such as Viagra, but enjoying themselves less, thus the difficulty in male orgasm (Kleinplatz, 2011). The focus has been on performance at the expense of pleasure. Similarly, reports of young, heterosexual college men faking orgasm (Muehlenhard & Shippee, 2010) suggest that men pay the price for the confounding of minimal physiological readiness with subjective arousal. Or to put it another way, we can think of young men's and women's sexual problems as the inevitable manifestations of a sex script, "in which women should orgasm before men, and men are responsible for women's orgasms" (Muehlenhard & Shippee, 2010, p. 1). When one or the other feel the sex just is not "working" (i.e., will not conclude in orgasm) and does not feel comfortable—or in some instances, well acquainted—enough with the partner to talk it out, "faking it" becomes an easy way to make the sex end. The obvious solution is to tell the partner what might increase the pleasure, although that presupposes having sex only with partners with whom one can communicate openly. This commonsense idea strikes many college students as unrealistic and both too idealistic and unromantic simultaneously.

Pain Associated with Sex in Men—Dyspareunia

Most of the literature on pain associated with sex, known as dyspareunia, concentrates on female pain during intercourse. Unfortunately, there is insufficient attention to men's pain during or following various sexual acts. It is hard even to estimate just how prevalent such pain may be. Pain may occur anywhere in men's external or internal sexual and reproductive organs, that is, not only in the penis but also in the epididymis, vas deferens, prostate, etc. It may begin in the course of sexual arousal, orgasm, or thereafter. It can be related to anything from skin sensitivities and allergies to sexually transmitted or other infections, and injury. These problems are usually assessed and treated by a physician.

Women's Sexual Problems

Difficulties with Orgasm

Women's difficulties with arousal and orgasm have been the subject of much speculation and far too many myths. Problems with orgasm are sometimes called inhibited female orgasm or anorgasmia. Some would say that the term really should be "preorgasmic" rather than "anorgasmic" because all women are capable of orgasm, whether it has happened yet or not (Barbach, 2000).

Orgasm during sexual intercourse is the goal for many couples, notwithstanding our expanding knowledge of female genitalia and sexuality. The number and intensity of nerve endings in the clitoris far exceed those in the vagina and even those found in the vagina are located primarily near the entrance. (Any woman who has ever used tampons can remember her surprise upon first reading the package instructions; these indicated that once the tampon is inserted correctly, the woman will be unable to feel it in the course of normal activities.) It can be difficult for women to get enough direct clitoral stimulation during intercourse to bring about orgasm. Indeed, for some women the trick is to arrange enough external pressure and friction to trigger orgasm (almost) despite intercourse! Although this information is increasingly widespread, given a society that defines "sex" as intercourse—nothing else quite counts as "going all the way"—the objective of "climaxing during sex" endures. Even the obvious solution, for the woman or her partner to stimulate her clitoris manually during intercourse, strikes many people as "cheating," at least initially. It is as though the "hands-free orgasm" remains the cultural gold standard.

Couples who insist upon the woman achieving orgasm via sexual intercourse may need to learn enough about women's bodies to readjust their expectations and to expand their criteria for valid orgasm pathways (e.g., manual or oral sex). Alternately, they may be encouraged to use their hands or sex toys to provide direct clitoral stimulation during intercourse (Dodson, 2002).

It should not be surprising that difficulties with orgasm should be especially common among young women. The ability to experience orgasm is tied directly to an individual's knowledge of her (or his) body and what kinds of stimulation are pleasureful. In North American society, this knowledge is rather slow in coming and especially so for girls. In this culture, both boys and girls are generally chastised for "playing with themselves" and often learn to feel ashamed should their parents "catch them" in self-stimulation. However, at puberty gender differences emerge: in adolescence, young males learn that "boys will be boys" and it is seen as normative for them to begin self-stimulating. Movies like *American Pie* and its popular sequels illustrate that masturbatory ingenuity is an embarrassing if essential condition of male sexual development. By the age of 13, over 90 percent of boys will have self-stimulated to orgasm. In contrast, the uncomfortable silence surrounding female sexual development keeps young women from exploration and limits awareness of their own bodies (Tolman, 2002). Repeatedly, studies over the last 25 years have found that just over 50 percent of girls have begun to self-stimulate to orgasm by the age of 17 or so and only about 75 percent by 19 years of age.

This gender difference in orgasm experience by the late teens has major implications for difficulties with orgasm in female college students. College males come to sexual relationships knowing how it feels and what it takes to have an orgasm. They are equipped to seek out the kinds of genital stimulation that are most likely to produce pleasure. Female college students are in the awkward position during sexual contact with their partners, whether male or female, of hoping that their new partners will know more about their bodies than they do themselves.

The vast majority of women who self-stimulate focus on the clitoris rather than the vagina, but this information is beyond many college students. Obviously, if she is unable to teach her partner how to touch her genitals, she—and her partner—stands a good chance of being rather frustrated with the process. The explorations could potentially prove exciting and erotic in a different context (Kleinplatz, 1996).

Unfortunately, college students of the new millennium are subject to two influences, discussed above but crucial here, that militate against mutual fulfilment and toward female anorgasmia: The first is the traditional and enduring belief that "talking spoils the mood" or "ruins the mystery." Ironically, the verbal communication that could ameliorate their situation is taboo. The second is the ubiquitous access to Internet pornography throughout the development of current college students. Mainstream pornographic material increasingly conveys to viewers the expectation that women should reach orgasm as a result of intercourse alone to a degree that no one imagined possible 25 years ago. Viewers come to believe that women are dysfunctional for failing to reach orgasm when their partners have already followed all the steps to ensure that sex is enjoyable, as seen on the Internet (Kleinplatz, 2011). In other words, at least a generation or two has become accustomed to the idea that "sex" should consist of effortless penetration and thrusting. This depiction of "normal" sexuality prevails unchallenged, particularly in the absence of either interpersonal dialogue or comprehensive sex education to demystify the imagery seen on screen. This norm contributes not only to female anorgasmia but also to subsequent low desire for "sex." We may need to challenge this belief system and point out that when sex is barely subpar, partners are normal when they find it less than satisfying (Kleinplatz, 2010a, 2010b).

Most women who have never had an orgasm with a partner will probably find it easiest to experience it alone at first. Learning about one's own body and becoming aware of one's own sexual responses is crucial; sometimes, extra readings with accompanying exercises can be very helpful, (e.g., Barbach, 2000; Dodson, 2002; Heiman & LoPiccolo, 1988). The focused concentration on oneself makes it easier to discover one's own sensitivities and triggers to orgasm. It also seems safer to take all the time one needs alone; this is a serious consideration for many women (and their partners) who worry that, "It's taking too much time . . . I'm afraid [he/she] will get bored and give up on me." The implication that the couple should be able to rush through sex betrays their beliefs about sex and often the underlying fear of wanting more pleasure than entitled.

Once she has found out how to have orgasms alone, she will need to show and tell her partner what pleases her. Here, it is often literally a matter of teaching her partner about her desires and her body and demonstrating what kinds of stimulation she finds exciting. If they can communicate effectively and get over the initial awkwardness, this approach will usually allow her to begin having orgasms with a partner.

The pressure on women to perform corresponds to the pressure on men discussed earlier. If this theme is becoming repetitive, that is because its impact is ubiquitous. To the extent that sex must be heterosexual and that the ultimate end of sex is penis-in-vagina, we are creating obstacles to and "dysfunctions" in the way of sexual pleasure.

Female Sexual Arousal Problems

Traditionally, there has been little attention focused directly on women's sexual arousal difficulties, at least in part because of the confounding of arousal per se with orgasm. However, it is possible for a woman to feel aroused and to lubricate without reaching orgasm and, less commonly, for women to reach orgasm while lubricating and feeling minimal levels of sexual arousal.

Another reason for the lack of clinical or research attention to women's arousal difficulties is the conventional North American sexual script that emphasizes *functioning* over *subjective experience*. Men's difficulties with arousal may impede intercourse; therefore male arousal difficulties command the spotlight. Women's sexual arousal difficulties are manifest in terms of lack of vaginal lubrication and absent, minimal, or diminished subjective feelings of excitement. Neither of these difficulties necessarily obstructs intercourse per se, and therefore they are sometimes ignored.

Women who see their physicians for lack of lubrication often receive instructions on the use of lubricants. This treatment enables them to engage in intercourse whether or not they feel aroused. Lubricants are an important adjunct in helping women to engage in pain-free intercourse when their own, natural lubrication has been diminished by disease or by various prescription or over-the-counter medications (e.g., decongestants). However, such measures, when applied whenever women are slow to lubricate, are treating a symptom rather than what may be the underlying cause of the problem. It may simply be that she is not lubricating because the sex or her partner are not arousing to her. In such cases, the "treatment" may actually mask the problem—or the fact that there is no problem: it is healthy and normal *not* to be aroused if the sex or the relationship are not to one's liking or are actually a turn-off. The reasons that she is not lubricating or subjectively aroused warrant attention.

Vaginismus

Perhaps the ultimate obstacle to intercourse is vaginismus. Vaginismus has been described as an involuntary, reflexive spasm of the muscles of the outer third of the vagina and perineum, preventing vaginal penetration. It varies in severity from women who cannot tolerate vaginal penetration in any form to women who can insert tampons and perhaps a finger during sexual stimulation. Some can even weather a gynecological exam (albeit, with hesitation and discomfort) but still tighten up at the prospect of intercourse. Men who attempt penile penetration with women diagnosed with vaginismus report that as they try to get past the vaginal entrance, "It feels like I'm hitting a brick wall." If they endeavor to push farther, it will hurt the woman as well as the man's penile glans.

It is common for women with vaginismus to have orgasms via self-stimulation as well as manual and oral stimulation with a partner. What, then, brings them to therapy? Sometimes they seek treatment because they or their partners would like to be able to engage in intercourse. Sometimes they are referred for treatment by physicians unable to perform a pelvic exam. In many cases, the partners have developed a broad enough sexual repertoire such that they are able to satisfy one another (Hawton & Catalan, 1990; Pridal & LoPiccolo, 1993; Valins, 1992) with no particular desire for intercourse. It is striking that there is not a single case of vaginismus in lesbian couples reported in the literature.

There is extensive speculation about the origins of vaginismus. Certainly, any time a person feels tension or fear, the body responds accordingly: the muscles contract. Women diagnosed with vaginismus tend to have considerable anxiety about intercourse. More specifically, many are afraid of pain on intercourse, which results in the muscles at the vaginal opening tightening, making intercourse very difficult, if not impossible. Some, still virgins, have already attempted intercourse but the pain they have dreaded leads to a self-fulfilling prophecy; sure enough, attempting intercourse when terrified leads the body to shut down, the vaginal muscles to shut tightly, and then inevitably to pain. Sometimes, vaginismus results from a history of pain on intercourse, in which case it is important to evaluate the cause of this pain. Others are afraid because of a prior history of sexual abuse and assault. Almost inevitably, women diagnosed with vaginismus come from sex-negative backgrounds with little to no sex education. One cue mentioned in gynecological textbooks for diagnosing vaginismus is that the vaginal muscles are positioned just as lips might be in saying, “No.” Perhaps her body is sending a message about her reservations, which should be taken seriously rather than just trying, literally, to push past it.

Traditionally, experts have treated vaginismus using dilators for systematic desensitization. However, overriding her anxieties and fears in order to achieve mastery over her body may leave her feeling disconnected and alienated from her partner. It also ignores the possibility that she may simply not be willing to engage in sexual intercourse. Suggested alternatives help the woman to become centered and integrated enough to deal with her feelings openly and directly rather than through the symptom of the vaginal spasm (Kleinplatz, 1998; Shaw, 1994).

Pain Associated with Sex in Women—Dyspareunia

Whereas there is minimal attention to pain associated with sex in men, there is quite an extensive literature on dyspareunia in women. Occasional pain during sex and during sexual intercourse in particular is common. Continuing and persistent pain associated with sex is less so.

There are an enormous number of possible causes for genital pain. It is hard to determine the precise origin of the pain without a careful clinical assessment, including a pelvic examination. It is important and helpful for the woman to tell her physician in as much detail as possible what is bothering her; otherwise, it is very unlikely that the cause of her pain will be detected. Pain can be caused by anything from STIs to yeast infections, endometriosis, allergies, lack of arousal, and so on.

Unfortunately, one of the more common causes of pain in young women can be traced back to ignorance and myths about sexuality. Many women have been raised to believe that initial penile penetration will be painful—they are certain that, in fact, the pain and bleeding constitute proof of virginity with all the accompanying moral overtones. The widespread belief that "rupturing the hymen" (or "popping her cherry") when she "loses her virginity" is the inevitable consequence of the female heterosexual debut is enough to raise considerable anxiety in most women. It is, however, the anxiety and the bodily manifestation of that fear of pain that actually causes that pain. When people fear pain and bleeding they guard against it by contracting their muscles; it is precisely the tightening of the pubococcygeus muscle surrounding the vaginal opening that leads to pain on intercourse and sometimes even minor lacerations of the vaginal tissue. Of course, this is true not only for young virgins but also for sexually experienced wives and mothers who otherwise enjoy sex but are being raped at knifepoint—it is the fear that brings about the contraction of the muscles rather than her degree of sexual experience or lack thereof per se. A bit of information about female genital anatomy can prevent this outcome. The knowledge that the so-called intact hymen has been open long enough to allow menstrual fluid to pass through it can allay women's fears of having a foreign object tearing up their membranes. The further knowledge that manual or oral clitoral stimulation can create enough arousal and lubrication to further reduce the likelihood of pain on penetration often comes as a surprise to young women and their male partners.

The most common cause of pain on intercourse for women of all ages is lack of sexual arousal and with it, lack of lubrication. As mentioned above, women are often advised to circumvent this difficulty by adding some lubricant. Unfortunately, while that solution makes intercourse possible, it does not make it pleasureful. Furthermore, unless she is aroused, her vaginal walls will remain constricted and penetration will remain uncomfortable at best. Too many young women are convinced that sex is intended to satisfy male sexual needs anyway and their own pleasure is secondary. Ironically, the very rhetoric designed to keep women from heterosexual intercourse hardly dissuades them from it; instead it convinces them to engage in intercourse to keep their boyfriends but does prevent them from enjoying it.

The treatment of dyspareunia must, of course, be related to identifying the underlying cause of the pain. The ideal goal is to cure the source of the pain. When that is not possible and even when it is, to the extent that she is now suffering from chronic pain, treatment should be multifaceted.

Couples' Problems: Difficulties with Sexual Desire and Intimacy

The most common problem bringing couples of every age into sex therapy is low desire (known more formally as hypoactive sexual desire disorder). Actually, it is sexual desire discrepancy between the partners that brings couples into therapy more so than low (or high) levels of desire in the abstract. How low is too low? For that matter, how much is too much? And who is to make that determination? The context in which the problem arises is when one person wants more sex in that relationship than the other. In cases of sexual desire discrepancy, the couple assuredly has a problem, which may or may not be amenable to change, but whether or not the individuals in question require "treatment" is a complex matter.

It is important to understand the meaning of the problem in context. What precipitated the diminishing of desire? Is there low desire in all situations and in all relationships or only with the current partner? Is there desire for others? What about solo sex? Is the quality of the sex satisfactory to each partner? Is the type of sex they engage in mutually fulfilling? Sometimes people make assumptions based on the frequency of sex without considering the quality of the sex. How is the rest of the relationship? Sometimes the problems lie elsewhere but are manifest in the bedroom. Often when one is complaining of the other's low sexual desire, the other is dissatisfied with the relationship.

Many young people are justifiably disillusioned by their sex lives. After years of waiting for their sexual debut, many are disappointed, asking, in effect, "Is that all there is?" The couple may be technically proficient and there may be no mechanical failures. However, the sex may be lackluster enough that it is not really worth wanting (Kleinplatz, 1996; Schnarch, 1991). One or both may be having their required quota of orgasms yet disappointed at the absence of eroticism during sex. In such cases, the question is: "What would make it worth your while to get excited?" It is all too common for people to be perceived as having low sexual desire when, actually, they refuse to settle for mediocre sex and are geared toward ecstasy (Ogden, 1999).

Given the complexity of sexual desire complaints, dealing with them must be individualized to deal with the particular problems of each unique individual or couple. This is greatly disappointing to many of those who seek quick-fix solutions. The popular discourse in the media suggests that desire is just a matter of hormones. Although hormone levels are relevant, simply increasing them is rarely sufficient to solve desire problems. Sometimes the cause of the desire problems is primarily biochemical, as when a person's desire drops dramatically after starting to use certain drugs (e.g., selective serotonin reuptake inhibitors, sedatives, alcohol, cocaine).

Most of the time, sexual desire problems require high levels of honesty in order to tease out the interplay of contributing factors and to deal with each of them. These may be as diverse as history of incest, reluctance to engage in oral sex, or fear of getting pregnant. Thus a one-size-fits-all solution to these problems, all appearing as "low sexual desire," is unlikely to help.

CONCLUSION

Sexual difficulties in college students are remarkably prevalent. This seems inevitable in the current sociocultural context, given the paucity of accurate information and comprehensive sex education, in combination with the abundance of myths and fictional fantasy material, all mixed together in silence. Most sexual difficulties in young adults can be remedied given access to knowledge about sexuality, the awareness of cues from one's own body, and the skills and inclination to share openly with sexual partners. There are no universal answers, let alone "best" techniques or "right" positions to solve sexual problems. Even what constitutes a "problem" will never be understood in isolation but only in the context of lived, human experience.

Fortunately, the very complexity of sexual difficulties and the many reasons, meanings, and purposes underlying them remain an opportunity for individual and interpersonal growth and discovery. College students can seek out paint-by-numbers sex/solutions or can use their discomfort as a catalyst to developing their own, unique paths toward erotic intimacy (Kleinplatz, 1996, 2010b; Kleinplatz et al., 2009).

Chapter Thirteen

SEXUAL ASSAULT AMONG COLLEGE STUDENTS

Karen S. Calhoun, Emily R. Mouilso, and Katie M. Edwards

OVERVIEW

This chapter addresses a widespread problem on college campuses, one that remains under-acknowledged even by its victims. Sexual assault is an all-too-common accompaniment to campus life in spite of attempts by many colleges and universities at education and prevention. Sexual assault has numerous negative consequences for students impacted by it as well as their friends and family. In this chapter we will review definitions, rates, risk factors, consequences, intervention, and prevention efforts. The major focus is on sexual assaults perpetrated by college men against college women, since this constitutes the vast majority of research and women are far more likely to be victims of sexual assault than men. We briefly discuss the more limited literature on sexual assault among diverse groups.

Definitions

The term "sexual assault" refers to a wide range of sexual acts including fondling, kissing, and vaginal, oral, and anal penetration obtained through force, threat of force, or verbal coercion. The term "rape" is typically reserved for sexual acts that involve penetration obtained through force, threat of force, or verbal coercion or situations in which the victim is unable to give consent due to age, intoxication, or mental status (Bureau of Justice Statistics, 1995; Koss, 1992).

Characteristics of Typical College Sexual Assault

Although each act of sexual aggression is unique and has unique consequences for both the victim and the perpetrator, research over the past 30 years has identified several features that are common among many college students' sexual assault experiences. The perpetrator is almost always a man, while the victim is a woman (B. S. Fisher, Cullen, & Turner, 2001; Watkins, 1990). Typically, the victim and perpetrator know each other, at least casually, and they are often involved in a dating relationship or acquaintanceship (Abbey & McAuslan, 2004; Koss, Gidycz, & Wisniewski, 1987; Watkins, 1990). The perpetrator, the victim, or both have likely consumed alcohol prior to the assault (see Abbey, 2002; Abbey, Ross, McDuffie, & McAuslan, 1996b; Testa & Parks, 1996, for reviews). Further, the perpetrator likely uses verbal coercion or alcohol to obtain sex rather than physical force or a weapon (Carr & VanDuesen, 2004; Koss, Dinero, Seibel, & Cox, 1988; Muehlenhard & Linton, 1987). The perpetrator does not consider his action to be illegal (Koss et al., 1987), and the victim is unlikely to report the experience to the police (B. S. Fisher et al., 2000; Koss, 1998; Orchowski, Meyer, & Gidycz, 2009).

WOMEN VICTIMS

Rates

Rates of sexual victimization on college campuses are alarmingly high. In the first national study of sexual assault on college campuses, Koss et al. (1987) reported that 55 percent of college women reported some type of sexual victimization since the age of 14. Specifically, 15 percent of college women reported unwanted sexual contact victimization, 12 percent reported sexual coercion victimization, 12 percent reported attempted rape victimization, and 16 percent reported completed rape victimization. Despite increased research on and awareness of sexual violence, recent research documents similar rates of sexual victimization among college women (Edwards, Desai, Gidycz, & VanWynsberghe, 2009; Edwards, Kearns, Calhoun, & Gidycz, 2009; B. S. Fisher et al., 2000). Further, studies using longitudinal, prospective designs document that 17 to 29 percent of college women experience a sexual assault over a brief 10-week academic quarter (Edwards et al., 2009; Gidycz, Coble, Latham, & Layman, 1993; Turchik, Probst, Chau, Nigoff, & Gidycz, 2007). In fact, women are at greater risk of experiencing a sexual assault during college than during any other life period (B. S. Fisher et al., 2000; Rickert, Vaughan, & Wiemann, 2002). Also, research evidence demonstrates that risk changes across the college period with women being at the greatest risk to experience a sexual assault during their freshman year (Humphrey & White, 2000; Kimble, Neacsiu, Flack, & Horner, 2008).

Risk Factors for Sexual Victimization

Although perpetrators are always responsible for all acts of sexual violence, research suggests that certain factors increase women's likelihood of experiencing a sexual assault. Of all risk factors, a history of sexual victimization has been consistently found to be the strongest predictor of future sexual victimization in studies of college students (Gidycz et al., 1993; Koss & Dinero, 1989), community (Wyatt, Guthrie, & Notgrass, 1992), and clinical (Stermac, Reist, Addison, & Millar, 2002) samples. Several explanations have been used for women's experiences of sexual revictimization as well as initial sexual victimization. These include deficits in global and situational risk recognition, barriers to responding assertively to a sexual assault situation, and engagement in behaviors that increase exposure to perpetrators, which are discussed below. Of note, given that most research shows that personality and attitudinal variables (e.g., acceptance of rape myths and hyperfemininity) do not increase women's likelihood of experiencing a sexual assault (Amick & Calhoun, 1987; Breitenbecher, 2000; Koss, 1985; Rich, Combs-Lane, Resnick, & Kilpatrick, 2004), these variables are not discussed further.

Risk Recognition

One theory suggests that women who fail to recognize their general vulnerability to sexual assault may engage in less self-protective behaviors and thus increase their likelihood of experiencing a sexual assault (see Gidycz, McNamara, & Edwards, 2006, for a review). This is consistent with research that demonstrates that college women underestimate their likelihood of experiencing a sexual assault (Cue, George, & Norris, 1996; Hickman & Muehlenhard, 1997; Norris, Nurius, & Graham, 1999; Nurius, Norris, Dimeff, & Graham, 1996), a phenomenon known as the optimistic bias (Weinstein, 1989).

Norris et al. (1999) found that college women, on average, rated themselves below the risk perception scale midpoint and other women above it, indicating that they viewed other women at a considerably higher risk than themselves of experiencing a sexual assault. Research also shows that women with sexual victimization histories perceive themselves at greater risk for sexual assault than women without sexual victimization histories (Brown, Messman-Moore, Miller, & Stasser, 2005). Similarly, Gidycz, Loh, Lobo,

Rich, and Lynn (2007) found that perceived vulnerability to experience a sexual assault was significantly related (although not as strongly as a history of victimization and alcohol use) to women's subsequent reports of sexual victimization. Although it has been previously hypothesized that experiences of sexual victimization would be related to lower perceived risk (because of less engagement in self-protective behaviors), this is often confounded by the fact that most college women who are sexually victimized over a follow-up period report experiences of sexual victimization at the initial survey session (Gidycz, McNamara et al., 2006; Gidycz et al., 2007).

In addition to global risk recognition, there is some research to suggest that deficits in the ability to recognize situational risk increase college women's likelihood of sexual victimization (Gidycz, McNamara et al., 2006). However, the research to support this idea of situational risk recognition is mixed. Whereas some studies suggest that women's inability to recognize risk in audiotaped or written vignettes relates to sexual victimization (Marx, Calhoun, Wilson, & Meyerson, 2001; A. E. Wilson, Calhoun, & Bernat, 1999; Yeater, Treat, Viken, & McFall, 2010), other studies find no such relationships (Breitenbecher, 1999; Messman-Moore & Brown, 2006; VanZile-Tamsen, Testa, & Livingston, 2005). These discrepant findings are likely due to (1) varying definitions of sexual assault (i.e., studies with more restricted and severe definitions of sexual assault document stronger relationships between situational risk recognition and sexual victimization than studies with more inclusive definitions) and (2) varying methodological designs (i.e., retrospective studies document stronger relationships between situational risk recognition and sexual victimization than do prospective studies) (see Gidycz, McNamara et al., 2006, for a discussion). Additionally, vignettes used in risk recognition studies vary across studies and are often criticized for suspected lack of external validity. That is, vignettes administered in research laboratories may not accurately capture real-life situations in which women are confronted with a potential sexual assault.

Several mechanisms have been proposed to explain why some women demonstrate deficits in situational risk recognition. One theory used to explain this phenomenon is the alcohol myopia theory (C. M. Steele & Josephs, 1990), which suggests that intoxicated individuals are more likely to focus on salient, situational cues in their environment as opposed to other potentially important cues. According to this theory, when a woman is intoxicated within a social setting, the focus of her attention would be on various aspects of the social setting and socialization. Her attention would not likely be given to potential danger or assault cues. Potential consequences of this myopic focus may include a decreased ability to recognize situational risk. Although there is some conflicting evidence (e.g., Livingston & Testa, 2000), several studies have found that self-reports of global alcohol use as well as alcohol administered as a part of the research study negatively affect women's abilities to detect risk in a sexual assault situation (Norris et al., 1999; Testa & Livingston, 2000).

Additionally, psychological distress, particularly posttraumatic stress disorder (PTSD) and dissociation, is believed to increase women's risk to experience sexual assault via deficits in risk recognition. More specifically, dissociative and numbing symptoms of PTSD may render women less able to perceive danger in their environment and are thus more likely to be sexually revictimized (Chu, 1992). Cloitre, Scarvalone, and Difede (1997) further suggested that dissociative women have difficulty recognizing and classifying emotional states and therefore may not recognize internally produced warning signs when confronted with risky situations. Multiple studies have demonstrated that PTSD symptoms mediate the relationship between childhood sexual abuse and subsequent victimization in adolescence or adulthood (Arata, 2000; Fortier et al., 2009), and one study (i.e., A.E. Wilson et al., 1999) has assessed specifically how PTSD symptoms relate to actual risk recognition among college students. A. E. Wilson et al. (1999) found that PTSD and dissociative symptoms were not related to deficits in risk recognition. In fact, sexually revictimized women with greater PTSD-related arousal symptoms showed risk recognition abilities similar to those of nonvictims, suggesting that certain PTSD symptoms may actually increase women's ability to detect risk.

Behavioral Responding

Despite some conflicting evidence, women's primary appraisal of risk is believed to guide their responses to sexual assault situations (Gidycz et al., 2007; Macy, Nurius, & Norris, 2006; Nurius, Norris, Young, Graham, & Gaylord, 2000). Women's responses to a sexual assault situation are often referred to as behavioral responding or resistance tactics. Research shows that women who utilize nonforceful resistance tactics (e.g., freezing or turning cold to resist) are less likely to thwart a sexual assault than women who utilize assertive resistance tactics (e.g., screaming or physical fighting back) (Ullman & Knight, 1993; Zoucha-Jensen & Coyne, 1993). Similarly, both retrospective and prospective laboratory research demonstrates that sexual victimization is related to lower sexual assertiveness and less intention to use assertive resistance tactics in a hypothetical sexual assault situation/vignette (Messman-Moore & Brown, 2006; VanZile-Tamsen et al., 2005).

Given the importance of assertive resistance tactics in responding to a sexual assault, several studies have been conducted with college women in order to explore the factors related to women's use of these tactics. In a prospective study of college women, Gidycz, VanWynsberghe, and Edwards (2008) found that women's intentions to use assertive resistance tactics predicted their increased utilization of these strategies in a subsequent sexual assault experience. Utilization of assertive resistance tactics was also predicted by increased perpetrator aggression, whereas a history of sexual victimization significantly predicted women's utilization of nonforceful resistance tactics. In another prospective study of college students, Turchik et al. (2007) found that women's use of verbally assertive resistance tactics was predicted by their intention to use verbally assertive tactics, concern about injury, greater confidence, and feelings of being isolated or controlled. Women's use of physically assertive resistance tactics was predicted by greater severity of the assault, greater confidence, and feelings of being isolated or controlled. The use of nonforceful tactics was predicted by women's intentions to use nonforceful tactics, increased self-consciousness, fears of losing the relationship with the perpetrator, and knowing the perpetrator. These findings are consistent with previous research and theory, suggesting that college women often face multiple relational and psychological barriers to responding assertively to a sexual assault situation (Nurrius & Norris, 1995).

Engagement in Behaviors that Increase Exposure to Perpetrators

In addition to deficits in risk recognition and use of nonforceful resistance tactics, engagement in behaviors that increase contact with perpetrators is believed to place women at increased risk for sexual victimization. For example, high levels of substance use are associated with other high-risk behaviors and tendencies toward sensation seeking (e.g., engaging in unprotected sex, high number of sexual partners) that render women more vulnerable to experiencing a sexual assault (Abbey, Ross, McDuffie, & McAuslan, 1996a; Koss & Dinero, 1989; Lam & Roman, 2009; Testa, Hoffman, & Livingston, 2010). Also, high levels of global alcohol use increase women's risk for sexual victimization given that this drinking often occurs in high-risk environments (i.e., bars), which increases women's likelihood of coming in contact with a potential perpetrator. In fact, research shows that binge drinking is a particularly risky behavior that increases women's risk for experiencing a sexual victimization (McCauley, Calhoun, & Gidycz, in press; Mohler-Kuo, Dowdall, Koss, & Wechsler, 2004). It is possible that binge drinking (or engagement in other risky behaviors) places women at increased risk not only due to increased exposure to perpetrators but because perpetrators view intoxicated women as particularly vulnerable. Taken together, both global and situational alcohol use are related to women's experiences of sexual victimization because alcohol use occurs in environments that increase women's contact with perpetrators as well as reduces their ability to recognize risk and respond assertively.

Consequences of Sexual Victimization

There are many insidious consequences of sexual victimization. In fact, research with college women demonstrates that sexual victimization leads to various psychological and physical health consequences, as well as increased risk for sexual revictimization.

Psychological Consequences

There is a range of both short-term and long-term psychological consequences associated with sexual victimization. Short-term psychological consequences of sexual assault include fear, anger, withdrawal, shock, denial, guilt, confusion, anxiety, nervousness, and distrust of others (Centers for Disease Control and Prevention [CDC], 2004; Lloyd & Emery, 2000). Also, there are numerous long-term psychological consequences, depression, suicidal ideation and behaviors, lowered self-esteem, heightened mistrust of men and other interpersonal problems, sexual dysfunction, substance abuse, and PTSD (CDC, 2004; Lloyd & Emery, 2000; Messman-Moore & Long, 2003). In fact, women who are victims of sexual assault have higher rates and more severe PTSD than survivors of accidents and natural disasters (Kessler, 2000; Resnick, Kilpatrick, Dansky, Saunders, & Best, 1993). Indeed, research shows that between 17 and 65 percent of women sexually assaulted develop PTSD (see Campbell, Dworkin, & Cabral, 2009, for a review). Additionally, 13 to 51 percent of sexual assault victims develop depression, 13 to 49 percent develop alcohol abuse, 23 to 44 percent report suicidal ideation, and 2 to 19 percent attempt suicide (Campbell et al., 2009).

Research has identified risk and resiliency factors related to the development (or nondevelopment) of sexual assault-related psychological sequelae. Certain victim characteristics—such as demographics, personality, preexisting mental health, coping, and previous victimization—increase the likelihood of negative psychological outcomes associated with a sexual assault (see Campbell et al., 2009, for a review). Additionally, assault characteristics (e.g., assault severity, perpetrator aggression, victim-perpetrator relationship) and postassault attributions (e.g., labeling, blame) are predictive of various forms of psychological distress (Atkeson, Calhoun, Resick, & Ellis, 1982; Littleton & Breikopf, 2006). Further, sociocultural attitude and beliefs, such as rape myths, negatively impact victims' recovery from sexual assault (Campbell et al., 2009; Orchowski, Uhlin, Probst, Edwards, & Anderson, 2009)

There is a growing body of research suggesting that social reactions to women's disclosure of sexual assault impact psychological recovery. A small percentage (5% and 13%) of college women report experiences of attempted or completed rape to the police (B. S. Fisher et al., 2000; Koss, 1988), which is considerably lower than reporting rates among noncollege populations

(Tjaden & Thoennes, 2000). Although college women are unlikely to report experiences of sexual assault to police or other authorities, research suggests that the majority of college women tell informal supports (most commonly friends) about their experiences (Ahrens, Campbell, Ternier-Thames, Wasco, & Sefl, 2007; Baumer, 2004; B. S. Fisher, Diagle, Cullen, & Turner, 2003; Golding, Siegel, Sorenson, Burnam, & Stein, 1989). However, the consequences of women's disclosures to informal supports are not always positive. Indeed, between 25 and 75 percent of women who disclose experiences of sexual victimization are refused help, blamed for the assault, or receive other negative responses (Campbell & Raja, 1999; Campbell, Wasco, Ahrens, Sefl, & Barnes, 2001). These negative responses are related to a host of negative psychological outcomes, such as depression and PTSD (R. C. Davis, Brickman, & Baker, 1991; Ullman, 1996a, 1996b, 1996c). The evidence regarding positive responses to social disclosure (e.g., providing emotional support, believing the victim) is equivocal. Whereas some studies find a significant relationship between positive social reactions and psychological adjustment (Borja, Callahan, & Long, 2006; Ullman & Siegel, 1995), other studies find no relationships between these variables (R. C. Davis et al., 1991; Ullman, 1996c). Given that social reactions to women's disclosure of sexual assault impact the recovery process, it is critical that we educate others—especially other college students since they are the most likely source of their friends' disclosures—on how to respond to the disclosure of sexual assault. In fact, some programs (e.g., Black & Wiesz, 2008; Foshee et al., 1998) are beginning to address how adolescents and college students can help their friends who experience a sexual assault or other form of dating violence.

Physical Consequences

Research has also documented the physical health sequelae of sexual assault in college, community, and national samples. There are health consequences directly related to experiencing a sexual assault, such as physical injuries, vaginal tearing, and contraction of sexually transmitted infections (CDC, 2004; Wingood, DiClemente, & Raj, 2000). Additionally, sexual assault survivors also evidence higher rates of physical health complaints (e.g., gastrointestinal, gynecological), poorer health perceptions, and an increase in medically unexplained symptomatology, including somatization (Demaris & Kaukinen, 2005; Tansill, Edwards, Kearns, Calhoun, & Gidycz, 2010). Studies with college women suggest that a history of interpersonal victimization is related to more negative menstrual/premenstrual and greater physical and somatic symptomatology (Fillingim, Wilkinson, & Powell, 1999; Runtz, 2002; Tansill et al., 2010).

One hypothesis has been proposed to explain the relationships between traumatic experiences and physical health symptomatology. Clum, Nishith, and Resick (2001) suggest that the constant state of arousal as well as negative health behaviors associated with posttraumatic symptomatology lead to an increase in physical health symptomatology due to a decrease in individual's immunological functioning. In a partial test of this hypothesis with college women, Tansill et al. (2010) found that PTSD symptoms mediated the relationship between a history of sexual victimization in adolescence/young adulthood (but not in childhood) and the development of somatic and physical health problems.

Sexual Revictimization

Perhaps one of the most devastating consequences of sexual violence is women's increased risk to experience a subsequent sexual assault, termed sexual revictimization. Research demonstrates that college women who are sexually abused in childhood or adolescence are up to 20 times more likely to be assaulted again than women without sexual victimization histories (Gidycz, Hanson, & Layman, 1995; Humphrey & White, 2000; Testa et al., 2010). As previously discussed, deficits in risk recognition, failure to use assertive resistance tactics in a sexual assault situation, and engagement in behaviors that increase women's contact with perpetrators are believed to contribute to sexual revictimization (Abbey et al., 1996b; Gidycz et al., 2008; Testa et al., 2010; Turchik et al., 2007; Yeater et al., 2010). Furthermore, there is growing evidence to suggest that 31 to 85 percent of victim-perpetrator relationships continue for some time following a sexual assault (Edwards, Kearns, Gidycz, & Calhoun, in press; I. M. Johnson & Sigler, 1996; Katz, Kuffel, & Brown, 2006; Sappington, Pharr, Tunstall, & Rickert, 1997), which likely increases women's risk for revictimization. Research has identified several predictors of college women's decisions to remain in the relationship with a perpetrator following a sexual assault, including a history of childhood sexual abuse, sexual assault severity, greater trauma symptomatology, less perpetrator blame, nondisclosure of the assault, and greater relationship investment and commitment (Edwards et al., in press; Katz et al., 2006).

Intervention and Risk Reduction Efforts for Victims/Women

Intervention

Although the majority of sexual assault survivors do not seek help from mental health professionals (Orchowski et al., 2009), there are various psychological interventions designed to help women recover from experiences of sexual assault. Given that initial distress level predicts later psychological adjustment and outcomes, several interventions have been developed to assist women in the immediate aftermath of a sexual assault. For example, Foa, Hearst-Ikeda, and Perry (1995) developed a brief four-session cognitive-behavioral intervention for women who recently experienced a sexual assault. Although the intervention was successful in reducing PTSD symptoms immediately following the intervention, the impact dissipated over the five-month follow-up period. In a more recent study, Resnick, Acierno, Amstadter, Self-Brown, and Kilpatrick (2007) tested the efficacy of a video intervention for women undergoing a medical examination within 72 hours of a sexual assault. Results suggested that for women with previous histories of sexual assault, the video intervention was associated with lower levels of PTSD and depression six weeks postassault and lower levels of depression six months postassault.

In addition to brief treatments to assist women in the immediate aftermath of a sexual assault, there are effective treatments for women who develop PTSD. Cognitive-behavioral interventions, specifically those that involve an exposure component, are the most effective treatments for PTSD. One of these treatments is prolonged exposure therapy (Foa & Rothbaum, 1998) in which individuals repeatedly confront fearful images and memories of their sexual assault in order to decrease fear and anxiety. This is done by *imaginable* exposure where victims recount the trauma memories and detail to the therapist (Falsetti, 1997). Prolonged exposure therapy has been shown to be effective in decreasing PTSD and depressive symptoms among rape survivors (Foaet al., 1995). Cognitive processing therapy (CPT), another treatment for sexual assault-related PTSD, is based on information processing theory and combines exposure therapy and cognitive restructuring (Resick & Schnicke, 1993). The exposure element is accomplished by having clients write about their rape and reading it aloud in session and for homework. Cognitive distortions in the rape narrative are identified and cognitive restructuring is utilized. CPT also includes psychoeducation and discussion of safety, trust, power, esteem, and intimacy. Research shows that CPT is an effective treatment for PTSD and depression among sexual assault survivors (Resick & Schnicke, 1993). In a study that compared PE to CPT in the treatment of rape survivors, similar, positive outcomes were demonstrated. However, CPT produced greater reductions in sexual trauma-related guilt, most likely because, unlike prolonged exposure therapy, there is a cognitive restructuring component to CPT (Resick, Nishith, Weaver, Astin, & Feuer, 2002).

As well as traditional exposure psychotherapies, several recent studies have assessed the effectiveness of a writing intervention on ameliorating psychological and physical distress among sexual assault survivors. These writing interventions for sexual assault survivors are based on Pennebaker's written emotional disclosure paradigm that involves having individuals write about various traumatic or upsetting experiences over three to four short writing sessions of approximately 15 to 30 minutes in duration (for a discussion, see Pennebaker, 1997). In an effort to test the applicability of Pennebaker's paradigm with sexual assault survivors, Kearns, Edwards, Calhoun, and Gidycz (2010) had college women with a history of sexual assault write about their most severe sexual victimization or about how they spend their time. Overall, results indicated that the writing intervention did not lead to reductions in psychological or physical distress immediately after the final writing session or at the one-month follow-up. The findings from the Kearns et al. (2010) study are consistent with findings from other studies with college (E. J. Brown & Heimberg, 2001) and community (Batten, Follette, Rasmussen Hall, & Palm, 2002; Freyd, Klest, & Allard, 2005) women that generally find null results for this paradigm with interpersonal violence survivors. It is possible that writing about sexual assault is ineffective because the modality does not provide sufficient exposure to the trauma or opportunities for cognitive restructuring.

Risk Reduction Programming

Perpetrators are solely responsible for all acts of sexual aggression, and primary prevention efforts with boys and men are critical. Ultimately, boys and men must prevent sexual violence, but it is vital that we use research to help women reduce their risk of experiencing a sexual assault. The most comprehensive research and development of sexual assault risk reduction programming for women has been conducted by Gidycz and her colleagues, who have worked for over a decade to systematically develop and evaluate a sexual assault risk reduction program for women (i.e., Breitenbecher & Gidycz, 1998; Gidycz et al., 2001; Gidycz, Rich, Orchowski, King, & Miller, 2006; K. A. Hanson & Gidycz, 1993; Marx et al., 2001; Orchowski,Gidycz, & Raffle, 2008). The goals of sexual assault risk reduction programming for women include increasing women's use of self-protective behaviors, providing women with the necessary skills to communicate their intents assertively, and, most important, reducing women's risk of experiencing a sexual assault. Critical components of women's programming are as follows: defining rape and sexual assault; giving statistics on frequency of rape and sexual assault; discussing societal pressures and causes of rape; discussing common characteristics of perpetrators; teaching risk reduction techniques, including self-defense; provision of information about rape aftereffects; and providing information about victim assistance resources.

Several rigorous outcome evaluation studies have assessed the effectiveness of risk reduction programming in reducing sexual assault among women. In one of the earlier studies, K. A. Hanson and Gidycz (1993) found that the sexual assault risk reduction program was effective in increasing knowledge about sexual assault and reducing risky dating behaviors compared to control group participants. Most importantly, the program was effective in reducing rates of sexual victimization for program participants, but only for those without a previous history of victimization. Given the significant role that previous victimization plays on subsequent sexual victimization, researchers have focused on the development of risk reduction programs specifically for women with sexual victimization histories. Results from both a pilot study (Marx et al., 2001) and a large, multisite study (Calhoun et al., 2002) found that a risk reduction program designed for women with sexual assault histories was successful in reducing rates of subsequent sexual revictimization.

Although there have been some promising results from evaluations of risk reduction programs, not all studies document reductions in sexual victimization rates. For example, Gidycz, Rich, et al., (2006) found that the risk reduction program was not effective in reducing rates of sexual victimization; however, women who participated in the program reported significant increases in self-protective behaviors, and women who were victimized during the two-month follow-up reported less self-blame compared to the wait-list control group. In a revision of Gidycz's risk reduction curriculum that added a self-defense component, Orchowski, Gidycz, and Raffle (2008) found that relative to the placebo control group, program participants increased self-protective behaviors, self-efficacy in resisting attack, and use of assertive communication over four-month follow-up. Additionally, there was a 50 percent reduction in incidence of rape among program participants over two-month follow-up.

PERPETRATORS

Rates

Although sexual aggression can be perpetrated by anyone, males perpetrate the majority of sexual violence against both male and female victims (Bureau of Justice Statistics, 1995; Tjaden & Thoennes, 1998). Between 25 and 60 percent of college men self-report a history of sexual assault perpetration, while 8 to 14 percent report a history of rape perpetration (Abbey & McAuslan, 2004; Koss et al., 1987; Loh, Gidycz, Lobo, & Luthra, 2005; J. W. White & Smith, 2004; Zawacki, Abbey, Buck, McAuslan, & Clinton-Sherrod, 2003). Over a one-year period, approximately 13 percent of college men report perpetrating at least one sexual assault (Abbey & McAuslan, 2004; J. W. White & Smith, 2004). Longitudinal studies that follow individuals from adolescence into adulthood suggest that the percentage of men who report engaging in sexually aggressive behavior peaks in late adolescence (Ageton, 1983; Teten, Hall, & Capaldi, 2009). Similarly, the percentage of college men who report perpetrating sexually aggressive behavior decreases across the college years, and within individuals the severity of perpetration consistently decreases over time (J. W. White & Smith, 2004).

Rape-Supportive Attitudes

Rape is fostered by a cultural system that is supportive of rape in particular and violence against women in general (Baron & Straus, 1989; Funk, 1993). Cross-cultural variation in rates of rape and sexual aggression against women prompted Sanday (1981) to designate societies as "rape-prone" or "rape-free." Rape-prone societies are notable in that men and women are segregated from each other, women are less powerful (e.g., economically, socially, politically), and rates of physical violence against women are higher than in rape-free societies. Societies that differ in incidence of violence against women also differ in basic values or attitudes (Nayak, Byrne, Martin, & Abraham, 2003). For example, societies with more traditional gender roles, especially when male dominance and female subordination are emphasized, exhibit the highest rates of aggression directed at women (Heise, Ellsberg, & Gottemoeller, 1999; Nayak et al., 2003; Rozee, 1993).

Societal attitudes governing interpersonal interactions permeate all aspects of life; however, individuals differ in the extent to which they internalize and act upon dominant cultural attitudes. Attitudes associated with sexual assault, like other attitudes, are both explicitly taught and modeled in families, at schools, in the media, and by peers (Senn, Desmarais, Verberg, & Wood, 2000). Therefore attitudes supportive of rape are, at least partially, the result of the socialization process in rape-prone societies (Berkowitz, Burkhart, & Bourg, 1994). Individual differences in levels of several rape-supportive attitudes are associated with differences in the likelihood of sexual assault perpetration among college students. For example, hypermasculinity or "macho" personality traits consist of extreme adherence to the masculine gender role, including the beliefs that violence is "manly" and that danger is exciting (D. L. Mosher & Sirkin, 1984). Hypermasculine men are more likely to report sexual assault perpetration (Koralewski & Conger, 1992; Lisak, 1991; Lisak & Roth, 1990; D. L. Mosher & Anderson, 1986; Warkentin & Gidycz, 2007) and are less disgusted, ashamed, or distressed when asked to imagine committing a sexual assault (D. L. Mosher & Anderson, 1986; J. P. Sullivan & Mosher, 1990). Malamuth and colleagues proposed a related construct, hostile masculinity, which combines a controlling and domineering interpersonal style, particularly in relation to women, and an insecure, defensive, and distrustful orientation toward women (Malamuth, Sockloskie, Koss, & Tanaka, 1991; Malamuth & Thornhill, 1994). Men high in hostile masculinity are also more likely to report sexual assault perpetration (Malamuth, Linz, Heavey, Barnes, & Acker, 1995; Malamuth et al., 1991; Wheeler, George, & Dahl, 2002).

College men who are more accepting of violence against women are also more likely to perpetrate a sexual assault (Abbey & McAuslan, 2004;

Loh et al., 2005), and perpetrators report more callous attitudes toward women (Abbey & McAuslan, 2004). Lack of empathy for rape victims is associated with perpetration likelihood (Deitz, Blackwell, Daley, & Bentley, 1982; Wheeler et al., 2002), and in their longitudinal study of college sexual assault perpetrators, Abbey and McAuslan (2004) found that men who expressed remorse about a past sexual victimization were less likely to assault again.

Rape myths are "prejudicial, stereotyped, or false beliefs about rape, rape victims, and rapists" that encourage and excuse men's sexually aggressive behavior toward women (M. R. Burt, 1980, p. 217). Examples of common rape myths include statements such as "only bad girls get raped" and "women ask to be raped by dressing provocatively." Some degree of acceptance of rape myths is common in our society and seems to be present from an early age. For example, more than half of the high school boys interviewed by Goodchilds and Zellman (1984) agreed that it was acceptable for a man to force sex on a women if she "led him on," changed her mind, or sexually aroused him. While Cook (1995) found lower agreement rates in a college sample, sexual aggression was perceived as most justifiable in circumstances similar to those endorsed by younger students. In general between 25 and 35 percent of college students (both male and female) agreed with the majority of rape myths to which they were presented (Lonsway & Fitzgerald, 1994), and 43 percent of college women agreed with at least one rape myth (M. R. Burt, 1980). College men who are more accepting of rape myths are also more likely to report having perpetrated a sexual assault (Byers & Eno, 1991; Christopher, Owens, & Stecker, 1993; S. R. Gold & Clegg, 1990; Hersh & Gray-Little, 1998; Malamuth et al., 1995; Muehlenhard & Linton, 1987). Although the goal of an interaction may be to have sex, through the acceptance of rape myths, aggression or coercion is deemed excusable and may be used to achieve this goal (G. C. N. Hall, 1996). Rape myths also allow sexually aggressive men to deny the impact of their crime and to excuse their behavior (Scully & Morolla, 1984).

The different types of rape supportive beliefs outlined above are strongly related to each other so that men who report one type often report all (Koss, Leonard, Beezley, & Oros, 1985; Lisak & Roth, 1990). A recent meta-analysis suggests that, although all types of rape supportive attitudes are positively associated with perpetration, hypermasculinity demonstrates the strongest association, followed by hostile masculinity, acceptance of interpersonal violence, and, finally, rape myth acceptance (Murnen, Wright, & Kaluzny, 2002). While these rape-supportive attitudes are an important risk factor for perpetration, it is important to remember that a person's behavior is not always consistent with their attitudes (Ageton, 1983). Even when consistent, attitudes often account for only a small amount of variance in behavior

(Metts & Spitzberg, 1996; Senn et al., 2000). It seems likely that rape-supportive attitudes constitute a necessary, but not sufficient, condition for the perpetration of sexually aggressive behavior (J. W. White & Koss, 1993).

Sociosexuality

Sociosexuality refers to one's willingness to engage in sexual relations without closeness or commitment (Gangestad & Simpson, 1990; Simpson & Gangestad, 1991). Sociosexuality is characterized as either unrestricted (i.e., having sex earlier in relationships, having more than one concurrent sexual relationship, having had sex with many different partners, having had sex with partners on only one occasion, foreseeing many different partners in the future) or restricted (i.e., likely to insist on the development of closeness and commitment before engaging in sex). In general, perpetrators report having started dating and having sex at an earlier age (Abbey, McAuslan, Zawacki, Clinton, & Buck, 2001; Byers & Eno, 1991). Perpetrators also report a greater number of sexual partners (Byers & Eno, 1991; S. R. Gold & Clegg, 1990; Kanin, 1985; Koss & Dinero, 1988; Koss et al., 1985) and a greater preference for partner variety, uncommitted sex, and less intimate relationships (Comett & Shuntich, 1991) as well as a desire to have more sexual activity in general (Kanin, 1983, 1985). Finally, perpetrators report that they talk about sex with their friends more often than do nonperpetrators (Lisak & Roth, 1988).

The male gender role typically includes a desire for frequent sexual encounters and de-emphasis of love and commitment in sexual encounters, and therefore unrestricted sociosexuality is consistent with hypermasculinity (Kanin, 1985). In fact, men with unrestricted sociosexuality are more likely to endorse rape-supportive attitudes (Yost & Zurbriggen, 2006). Given the link between rape-supportive attitudes and perpetration, it is not surprising that sociosexuality is associated with perpetration. The association has also been explained in terms of increased opportunities to commit an assault and individual differences in sexual interest and motivation (Kanin, 1985; Malamuth et al., 1991). As sexual interest and motivation increases, a "predatory" mind-set may develop in which a man attempts to engage in sex at every opportunity, through any means necessary (Abbey et al., 1996b; Kanin, 1985; Malamuth et al., 1991). In fact, sexual arousal in situations that involve forced or coerced sex distinguishes perpetrators from nonperpetrators. For example, self-reported arousal while reading an acquaintance rape script is positively associated with self-reported likelihood of committing an acquaintance rape (Check & Malamuth, 1983), and men who report a history of sexual assault perpetration also report more sexual arousal when asked to imagine committing a rape (D. L. Mosher & Anderson, 1986). Therefore the combination of sociosexuality (i.e., intense sexual interest and motivation), sexual arousal in situations that involve forced or coerced sex, and rape-supportive attitudes may predispose men to sexual aggression.

Antisocial and Delinquent Behavior

The perpetration of a sexual assault is an antisocial and potentially criminal act. Research suggests that men who perpetrate acts of sexual aggression are also likely to have a history of delinquent behavior in adolescence and to perpetrate other types of antisocial behavior in adulthood. For example, among boys in grades 8 through 11, individuals who reported sexual assault perpetration were more likely to report other delinquent behavior, including drinking alcohol, using illegal drugs, starting fights, and running away from home (Lacasse & Mendelson, 2007). College sexual assault perpetrators report engaging in other types of antisocial behavior (Petty & Dawson, 1989; Rapaport & Burkhart, 1984), and attraction to sexual aggression is related to attraction to criminality among college men (Voller, Long, & Aosved, 2009).

In addition, personality traits and attitudes associated with antisocial behavior have been found in college perpetrators. For example, psychopathy is comprised of affective and interpersonal features including callousness, lack of remorse, lack of empathy, egocentricity, superficial charm, willingness to con or manipulate others, grandiosity, impulsivity, and irresponsibility (Hare, 1991). Psychopathy is predictive of criminal behavior (T. D. Fisher & Walters, 2003; R. K. Hanson & Bussiere, 1998; Walters, 2003; Harpur & Hare, 1994), particularly violent criminal behavior (Salekin, Rogers, & Sewell, 1996). Although research on psychopathy in nonincarcerated samples is still in its infancy (Nicholls, Ogloff, Brink, & Spidel, 2005), college perpetrators display many of the affective, interpersonal, and behavioral characteristics of psychopathy (Hersh & Gray-Little, 1998) and score higher on measures of trait psychopathy than nonperpetrators (Kosson, Kelly, & White, 1997; Mouilso, 2010). Interestingly, men who perpetrate more severe acts of sexual aggression (e.g., rape, attempted rape) display more psychopathic traits (Hersh & Gray-Little, 1998).

Narcissism is characterized by an exaggerated sense of self-importance and uniqueness, an unreasonable sense of entitlement, an intense need for admiration, a willingness to exploit others, deficient empathy, and arrogance (American Psychiatric Association, 1994). Narcissism is associated with the perpetration of many forms of aggression, including domestic violence perpetration (Raskin & Terry, 1988; Rhodewalt & Morf, 1995; K. M. Ryan, Weikel, & Sprechini, 2008; Wink, 1991). Among college students, sexual assault perpetrators score higher on trait narcissism (Kosson et al., 1997), and narcissism is associated with greater acceptance of rape myths, less empathy for rape victims, and greater enjoyment of a film depicting rape (Bushman, Bonacci, Van Dijk, & Baumeister, 2003). Recently, college perpetrators were also found to score higher on trait measures of narcissism than nonperpetrators (Mouilso, 2010). Taken together, perpetration of sexual assault among college students seems to be only one part of larger constellation of personality traits, attitudes, and behaviors associated with general antisocial tendencies.

Misperceptions of Sexual Interest

Communication of sexual interest or lack of interest is a complicated, dynamic social process, which consists of interpreting both nonverbal and verbal cues (Fichten, Tagalakis, Judd, Wright, & Amsel, 2001). It should come as no surprise that this process is vulnerable to errors in interpretation and can be confusing for both men and women (Abbey, 1982). Misperception of a partner's sexual communication most often results in embarrassment (Byers & Lewis, 1988); however, among some individuals, sexual misperception increases the probability of sexual aggression. When compared with women, men perceive women as having more sexual interest (Abbey, Cozzarelli, McLaughlin, & Harnish, 1987; Abbey & Melby, 1986; Abbey, Zawacki, & McAuslan, 2000). Men who endorse rape-supportive beliefs are especially likely to misperceive women's friendliness as sexual interest (Abbey & Harnish, 1995; Vrij & Kirby, 2002; Willand & Pollard, 2003). A recent review concluded that several situational factors increase the likelihood that college men will misperceive a women's sexual interest, including her clothing style (i.e., those that are more revealing or provocative), her dating behaviors (i.e., returning to an apartment after a date), and alcohol use by either the perceiver or the perceived (Farris, Treat, Viken, & McFall, 2008).

One interpretation of the link between sexual misperception and sexual assault perpetration is that men who misinterpret their partner's refusal cues may expect that she will respond to their advances with consent, and when they instead receive nonambiguous refusal cues, this unexpected outcome may seem arbitrary and hostile (Farris et al., 2008). In fact, many sexually coercive men report that this series of the events (i.e., that their partner "led them on") occurred prior to their aggressive behavior (Muehlenhard & Linton, 1987). As described above, the rape myth that sexual coercion or force is justified if a man is "led on" (Cook, 1995; Goodchilds & Zellman, 1984) may increase the likelihood that a man will choose to aggress against his partner in such a situation. Without the early misperception of sexual intent, nonconsent may be more likely to be respected. Additionally, men who are generally socially unskilled may have deficits in the decoding of interest as well as consent so that men who misperceive sexual interest also misperceive consent to sexual intercourse and perpetrate a sexual assault. Therefore misperception of sexual interest is a fairly common phenomenon and, combined with rape supportive attitudes, can result in perpetration of sexual aggression.

Alcohol

Alcohol use is widespread on college campuses (Vicary & Karshin, 2002) and rates of alcohol consumption have remained high despite numerous intervention efforts (Wechsler, Lee, Nelson, & Kuo, 2002). Laboratory studies suggest that, after consuming alcohol, college men are more tolerant of sexual aggression (Marx, Gross, & Adams, 1999; Marx, Gross, & Juergens, 1997) and indicate greater willingness to behave in a sexually aggressive manner (Norris & Kerr, 1993; Norris, Martell, & George, 2001). Researchers estimate that between 50 and 75 percent of sexual assaults are perpetrated by men who have recently consumed alcohol (Abbey, 2002; Koss, 1988; Pernanen, 1991; Testa, 2002). For example, among men who reported an attempted or completed sexual assault, 81 percent report that they had been drinking before the incident, and of these men, 94 percent report being drunk before the assault occurred (C. P. Krebs, Lindquist, Warner, Fisher, & Martin, 2007).

Assaults that involve alcohol seem to result in more negative outcomes for victims, relative to assaults that do not involve alcohol. For example, assaults in which the perpetrator has consumed alcohol are more likely to result in completed rapes (Brecklin & Ullman, 2002; Ullman, Karabatsos, & Koss, 1999) and more physical injury to the victim (Abbey et al., 2002; Ullman et al., 1999). Completed rapes and victim injury are especially common when the perpetrator, but not the victim, has consumed alcohol (Brecklin & Ullman, 2002; Ullman & Brecklin, 2000; Testa, Vanzile-Tamsen, & Livingston, 2004). This association may result from the perpetrator being unable to take advantage of the victim's intoxication and therefore resorting to force to subdue her. Intoxicated men are also less able to modulate the amount of aggression they use, and lack of intoxication may increase victims' resistance (Abbey et al., 2002).

Perpetrators of assaults that involved alcohol are more likely to report believing that alcohol enhances their sex drive and that women's drinking signifies their sexual interest (Zawacki et al., 2003). College perpetrators also report that alcohol is an effective tactic to gain sex (Kanin, 1985) and that women who drink are "fair game" for sexual aggression (Abbey et al., 1996b). These beliefs may be used to excuse sexually aggressive behavior (Abbey et al.,1996b; George & Norris, 1991).

Alcohol consumption is also related to the misperception of sexual interest. For example, the belief that women consume alcohol to communicate sexual interest may increase men's misperception of women's friendliness. Alcohol consumption also impairs cognitive abilities such as selective attention (Abroms & Fillmore, 2004) and cognitive control (Fillmore, Marczinski, & Bowman, 2005) that are necessary for accurate decoding of communications of sexual interest. Therefore it is not surprising that acute alcohol intoxication increases the likelihood that men misperceive friendliness as sexual interest (Abbey, Zawacki, & Buck, 2005). One possible source of error may be an increased reliance on universal cues (i.e., cues visible to all individuals such as clothing, youthfulness, hair style) to make decisions about a woman's sexual interest rather than person-specific cues (i.e., cues directed to one individual such as facial expressions, verbal cues, posture, and physical proximity) when individuals have consumed alcohol (Farris, Treat, & Viken, 2010). Alcohol consumption also results in a reduced capacity to attend to multiple cues and to look beyond the most salient aspects of a situation (Bushman, 1997; Taylor & Leonard, 1983). According to the alcohol myopia theory, alcohol intoxication restricts cognitive capacity so that individuals attend only to the most salient environmental cues (C. M. Steele & Josephs, 1990). Applied to sexual aggression, an intoxicated man may be aware of the salient universal cues indicating sexual interest but have difficulty perceiving and interpreting less salient and ambiguous person-specific refusal cues (Abbey, Ross, & McDuffie, 1994; Norris & Kerr, 1993). Attending to universal cues rather than personal-specific cues may predispose a man to misinterpret sexual interest and therefore predispose him to sexual assault perpetration as described above.

It is unlikely that alcohol causes a man to become sexually aggressive if he does not already possess such tendencies (Seto & Barbaree, 1995). It is more likely that alcohol consumption aids the perpetrator in overcoming personal inhibitions by decreasing perceived responsibility for his actions (Abbey et al., 1996b). The disinhibiting effect of alcohol may explain why laboratory analog studies show that men's consumption of alcohol results in increased acceptance of and intentions to engage in sexually aggressive behavior (Gross, Bennett, Sloan, Marx, & Juergens, 2001; J. D. Johnson, Noel, & Sutter- Hernandez, 2000; Marx et al., 1999; Marx et al., 1997; Norris, Davis, George, Martell, & Heiman, 2002). Furthermore, situations conducive to sexual aggression often include alcohol (e.g., bars or large parties; Lackie & de Man, 1997). Given the association between sexual aggression and other antisocial behavior, it is also likely that alcohol use and sexual aggression co-occur in men who lead a generally deviant lifestyle (Swartout & White, 2010). Taken together, results suggest that the relation between alcohol consumption and sexual assault perpetration is complex, and alcohol likely confers risk via many pathways.

Although alcohol is the most common drug associated with sexual assault (Hindmarch, El Sohly, Gambles, & Salamone, 2001), substances such as

Rohypnol, gamma hydroxybutyrate (GHB), and Ketamine have also been implicated in sexual assaults. These so-called date rape drugs are used to incapacitate and silence potential victims, heightening vulnerability and increasing the likelihood that victims will be unable to remember the assault. For example, GHB is a colorless, odorless liquid with a slightly salty taste that is easily masked by any beverage (Chin, Sporere, Cullison, Dyer, & Wu, 1998; R. H. Schwartz, Milteer, & LeBeau, 2000). Intoxication results from ingestion of as little as one teaspoon of GHB liquid and occurs within 10–15 minutes (R. H. Schwartz et al., 2000). GHB acts as a central nervous system depressant, causing muscles to relax and inducing a coma-like state lasting approximately five hours (Chin et al., 1998). GHB also produces anterograde amnesia so that the victim has no memory of events that occur after ingestion (R. H. Schwartz et al., 2000). Effects of these drugs are potentiated, and in some cases made lethal, by alcohol (Payne-James, 2002).

Prevalence rates for drug-facilitated sexual assault among college students are difficult to estimate because detection of drugs such as GHB requires a toxicology screening performed within hours after ingestion (LeBeau et al., 1999) and the majority of college victims do not report the experience to the police (B. S. Fisher et al., 2000; Koss, 1998; Orchowski et al., 2009). Among a community of sample of women reporting a sexual assault to the police, toxicology analyses indicated that approximately 40 percent were victims of a drug-facilitated sexual assault (i.e., had ingested a drug that could have reduced their ability to give consent within 72 hours of the reported sexual assault; Juhascik et al., 2007). Some research suggests that drug-facilitated sexual assaults are becoming more common on college campuses (Dyer, 2000).

Witnessing and Experiencing Abuse

Witnessing abuse and direct experiences of abuse and neglect occur more frequently among college perpetrators than among other college men (Koss & Dinero, 1989; Lisak, Hopper, & Song, 1996; J. W. White & Smith, 2004). For example, 70 percent of college perpetrators report some form of childhood sexual or physical abuse (Lisak et al., 1996). However, the vast majority of childhood abuse victims do not use aggression in adulthood (H. R. White & Widom, 2003), and many perpetrators report no experience of childhood victimization (Koss & Dinero, 1989; Lisak et al., 1996; J. W. White & Smith, 2004). A nationally representative survey of more than 20,000 youth from 132 schools identified via stratified random sampling recently explored the developmental pathway from childhood victimization to perpetration (Casey, Beadnell, & Lindhorst, 2008). Results suggest that boys who experienced childhood physical abuse were at 43 percent greater risk of perpetrating a sexual assault in late adolescence or early adulthood than nonabused boys. Those reporting both childhood physical and sexual victimization were at 450 percent greater risk. Child sexual abuse conferred risk via age at first sexual encounter (i.e., boy who were sexually abused began having sex at an earlier age) and number of sex partners (i.e., boy who were sexually abused reported having had more sexual partners). Child physical abuse conferred risk via delinquent behavior and the co-occurrence of sex and alcohol consumption. Although the experience of abuse in childhood is associated with perpetration during the college years, childhood abuse is neither a necessary nor sufficient factor for adult perpetration.

Perceived Social Norms and Peer Influences

According to social norms theory, individuals tend to behave in a manner that they believe is consistent with behavioral norms of their group (Berkowitz, 2003). Therefore men who believe that others are using aggression or coercion to obtain sex are theorized to be more likely to engage in these behaviors themselves. In fact, relative to themselves, college men believe that their peers are more accepting of rape myths and are more comfortable and less likely to intervene in situations where women are being mistreated (Loh et al., 2005). Perceived peer approval of forced sex is greater among perpetrators than among nonperpetrators (Abbey et al., 2001), and peer support can encourage sexual assault perpetration (Boeringer, Shehan, & Akers, 1991; Kanin, 1985).

Peer encouragement may be overt or covert. For example, a man who belongs to a peer group that emphasizes sexual "conquest" and dominance over women may feel more comfortable committing a sexual assault (Malamuth et al., 1991). Some men and boys report experiencing pressure from peers to engage in sexual behaviors (Malamuth, 1996; Malamuth et al., 1991), and perceived pressure to have sex can result in an increased likelihood of perpetrating a sexual assault (Malamuth, 1996; Malamuth et al., 1991). Sexually aggressive peer groups can also facilitate perpetration via informational support and creating opportunities (e.g., parties with copious drinking) to engage in sexually aggressive behaviors (DeKeseredy & Schwartz, 1993).

The effect of membership in all-male peer groups (e.g., fraternity, athletic team) on sexual assault perpetration has received a great deal of attention. A recent meta-analysis of more than 50 studies concluded that, compared to nonmembers, both fraternity and athletic team members are more accepting of rape myths and higher in hypermasculinity (Murnen & Kohlman, 2007). One rape myth that is particularly associated with fraternities is the idea that forcing a drunk woman to have sex is acceptable (Sanday, 1990). Fraternity members are more likely to report that they have friends who had gotten women drunk or high to have sex and to report having friends who approve of this practice (Boeringer, 1996). All-male peer groups are, therefore, associated both with rape supportive attitudes and with perceived peer support for sexual aggression. It is not surprising that membership in such a group results in increased likelihood of sexual assault perpetration (Murnen & Kohlman, 2007).

An individual's peer group can mediate the link between witnessing intrafamily violence in childhood and perpetrating violence in adulthood. Witnessing domestic violence in childhood affects attitudes that favor violence against women, which, in turn, predict associating with peers who endorsed similar attitudes, and indirectly increases the likelihood that boys will go on to perpetrate aggression against women themselves (Williamson & Silverman, 2001). However, having strong social bonds in childhood (including bonds with peers) significantly lessens the likelihood that men who witnessed violence in their families will later perpetrate violence (Lackey & Williams, 1995). The relationship between witnessing intrafamily violence in childhood and perpetration of violence during a later dating relationship is weaker among individuals who perceive that their friends disapproved of violence (Williamson & Silverman, 2001). Relationships with peers and perceived social norms can strongly impact sexual assault perpetration in college, as both risk and protective factors depending on the characteristics of the peer group.

Prevention Programming with College Men

Whereas risk reduction programming on college campuses aims to reduce college women's likelihood of experiencing a sexual assault, prevention programming aims to prevent men from perpetrating sexual assault. Although programming with men focuses on primary prevention, which is of critical importance, most program development and evaluation has not focused on men, but rather women (Morrison, Hardison, Mathew, & O'Neil, 2004). Furthermore, although some primary prevention programs for men have been developed, very few programs have undergone rigorous outcome evaluation and there is no compelling evidence to date that these programs lead to long-term reduction in sexual violence (Foubert, Newberry, & Tatum, 2007; Gidycz, Orchowski, & Edwards, in press).

Components of prevention programming for men generally include discussions of prevalence of violence against women, definition of sexual assault, gender role ideology, rape myths, obtaining consent, and how to support a survivor of sexual assault. Program developers and researchers are also beginning to stress the importance of social norms (encouraging men to question and challenge gender-based norms that foster violence against women) and bystander behavior (teaching men assertiveness strategies to intervene when they witness inappropriate social and dating situations) as components of effective sexual assault prevention programming with men (Banyard, Moynihan, & Plante, 2007; Berkowitz, 2003, 2004; Foubert, 2000). Additionally, programs that are peer facilitated, multisession, single-sex, and culturally sensitive as well as programs with interactive formats that include multimedia presentations and role plays are likely to be most effective in changing attitudes and behaviors among men (Gidycz et al., in press; Weisz & Black, 2001). One of the most critical areas for future research is the development, refinement, and evaluation of sexual assault prevention programming for boys and men.

Sexual Assault among Diverse Groups

Homosexual Individuals

Very few studies have investigated victimization or perpetration among homosexual individuals (S. D. Gold, Dickstein, Marx, & Lexington, 2009). Community samples suggest that between 30 and 65 percent of gay men (S. D. Gold, Marx, & Lexington, 2007; Heidt, Marx, & Gold, 2005; Hickson, Davies, Hunt, & Weatherburn, 1994) and between 20 and 40 percent of lesbians report having experienced a sexual assault (S. D. Gold et al., 2009; Heidt et al., 2005). However, victimization rates among homosexual college students may be somewhat lower (i.e., 12%; Waterman, Dawson, & Bologna, 1989).

Relative to lesbians, gay men and bisexual individuals seem to be at increased risk of experiencing a sexual victimization (Heidt et al., 2005). Similarly, compared to heterosexual men, homosexual men are more likely to report a sexual victimization (Stermac, Sheridan, Davidson, & Dunn, 1996). Having male sexual partners seems to be a risk factor for victimization (Heidt et al., 2005), which makes sense in light of the fact that men perpetrate the majority of sexual assaults (Bureau of Justice Statistics, 1995; Tjaden & Thoennes, 1998). Among gay men, risk factors for experiencing a sexual assault are similar to risk factors among heterosexual women, including a childhood abuse history, acceptance of money for sex, and younger age at first sexual contact (Krahe, Scheinberger-Olwig, & Schutze, 2001).

Our knowledge of perpetration among homosexual individuals is still in its infancy. In a community sample of German homosexual men, Krahe, Schiitze, Fritsche, and Waizenhofer (2000) found that 5 percent of respondents indicated that they had used, or threatened to use, physical force to make an unwilling man comply with their sexual demands; 16 percent reported exploiting a person's inability to resist due to alcohol or drug intoxication; and 6 percent admitted to the use of verbal coercion. Of the sample, 35 percent reported both victimization and perpetration of sexual aggression while only 7 percent reported perpetration only. Results suggest that perpetration rates are similar among homosexual and heterosexual men; however, overlap between perpetration and victimization seems to be more common relative to samples of heterosexual females. Results are certainly preliminary at this time and it is unclear whether these findings will generalize to samples of American college students.

As in the general population, sexual victimization is associated with increased depression, substance abuse and dependence, and PTSD symptomatology among homosexual individuals (Garnets, Herek, & Levy, 1990; Heidt et al., 2005; T. L. Hughes, Johnson, & Wilsnack, 2001; Otis & Skinner, 1996), and revictimized individuals report significantly greater psychological distress than do single-incident victims (Heidt et al., 2005). Although results suggest that outcomes are generally similar to outcomes for heterosexual women, several unique factors are associated with victimization for homosexual victims. For example, survivors may have more difficulty recovering due to the chronic stress associated with their minority status (T. L. Hughes et al., 2001; Meyer, 1995). In addition, homophobic myths related to sexual assault permeate mainstream society (S. D. Gold et al., 2007), including the belief that sexual assault causes homosexuality (Balsam, 2003) and that homosexual individuals deserve to be victimized because they are immoral and deviant (Arey, 1995; Garnets et al., 1990).

Perhaps as a result of these beliefs, homosexual victims tend to be viewed negatively by others. For example, gay male victims of rape tend to be blamed more for their assault (Mitchell, Hirschman, & Hall, 1999; Wakelin & Long, 2003) and the significance of the assault is more likely to be minimized (S. White & Yamawaki, 2009). Highly homophobic respondents and those who ascribe to traditional gender roles are more likely to blame homosexual victims and minimize their victimization (D. L. Burt & DeMello, 2002; S. White & Yamawaki, 2009). In addition to the impact of others' negative beliefs, internalized homophobia (i.e., the acceptance of negative stereotypes and myths about homosexuality in others and in oneself; Shidlo, 1994) has been found to predict negative outcomes following a sexual assault. Internalized homophobia is associated with both depressive and PTSD symptom severity in gay men and lesbian women (S. D. Gold et al., 2007, 2009). Thus homosexual individuals may experience more negative outcomes relative to heterosexual individuals, and those who have internalized homophobic attitudes may experience outcomes that are particularly negative.

Diverse Racial and Ethnic Groups

Growing awareness of the shifting ethnic demographics of the U.S. population and sensitivity to impact of ethnic differences has stimulated interest in exploring the relationship between race/ethnicity and sexual aggression. Although research on sexual assault is conducted with predominately Caucasian samples, victimization rates seem to be similar in African American (Koss et al., 1987; Rouse, 1988), Hispanic (Hannon, Hall, Kuntz, Van Laar, &

Williams, 1995; Kiernan & Taylor, 1990; Koss et al., 1987; Rouse, 1988), and Asian (Koss et al., 1987; Mills & Granoff, 1992) college women. Furthermore, those differences that are reported (i.e., that Asian American women experience victimization less frequently) are likely due to cultural influences on the identification and acknowledgment of sexual assault rather than differences in incidence rates (Mills & Granoff, 1992). Although national crime statistics suggest that African American men perpetrate a disproportionately high percentage of rapes (Federal Bureau of Investigation, 1994), perpetration rates seem to be roughly equivalent in ethnically diverse groups of college men (Koss et al., 1987). This discrepancy is likely due to the confounding of ethnicity and socioeconomic status in national crime data while socioeconomic status is relatively constant among college students (G. C. N. Hall & Barongan, 1997).

Experiencing a sexual assault is associated with increased psychological distress for women of diverse racial and ethnic backgrounds (Neville & Heppner, 1999; Neville & Pugh, 1997; J. E. Williams & Holmes, 1982; Wyatt, 1992). Although diverse survivors do not differ on levels of long-term psychological and sexual functioning (Wyatt, 1992), significant differences in the levels of postassault distress have been reported among African American, Hispanic, and Caucasian women (J. E. Williams & Holmes, 1982). Specifically, Hispanic women report the most distress and African American women report the least. In addition, African American and Caucasian college women differ on their explanations for being assaulted and for not reporting the crime to police (Neville ,Heppner, Oh, Spanierman, & Clark, 2004; Neville & Pugh, 1997). African American women report expectations of experiencing nonsupportive reactions or no response (Wyatt 1992). Relative to Caucasian women, African American and Hispanic women seem to be less likely to seek mental health services fallowing a sexual assault (Sorenson & Siegel, 1992).

These discrepancies can be understood in the context of cultural difference in the rules that govern interpersonal interactions (Goodwin, 1994) and the impact of ethnicity on individuals' experiences (A. White, 1995). For example, African American victims' expectation of experiencing nonsupportive reactions makes sense given that individuals tend to be less supportive of African American victims. For example, participants are less empathic toward African American victims, relative to Caucasian victims (Varelas & Foley, 1998; Willis, 1992), and harsher sentences are imposed when Caucasian women are raped, relative to African American women, regardless of perpetrator's characteristics (A. White, 1995). African American perpetrators are also viewed as more responsible for their actions, relative to Caucasian perpetrators (Varelas & Foley, 1998; Willis, 1992).

African Americans have long been thought to be less sympathetic to rape victims and more accepting of rape myths than are Caucasians (M. R. Burt,

1980; Giacopassi & Dull, 1986). However, socioeconomic status and education modulate these ethnic differences (Giacopassi & Dull, 1986; Nagel, Matsuo, McIntyre, & Morrison, 2005) so that levels of rape myth acceptance are similar between African American and Caucasian college students (Carmody & Washington, 2001). In contrast Asian American college students are more accepting of rape myths and have more negative attitudes toward rape victims (J. Lee, Pomeroy, Yoo, & Rheinboldt, 2005; Mori, Bernat, Glenn, Selle, & Zarate, 1995). The prevalence of rape-supportive attitudes has been attributed to Asian cultural traditions that endorse a patriarchal structure in which the status of women is low (Shon & Ja, 1982) and male dominance and female submission are emphasized (Kim & Ward, 2007; Mills & Granoff, 1992; Okazaki, 2002; Tang, Wong, & Cheung, 2002). Furthermore, many Asian cultures include a sexual double standard. Women, but not men, are expected to maintain chastity as a direct reflection of their family's honor (Espiritu, 2001; Gupta, 1999; Inman, Ladany, Constantine, & Morano, 2001). J. Lee et al. (2005) speculated that this sexual double standard results in rape victims being blamed for failing to remain chaste. The suggestion that traditional Asian culture is associated with negative attitudes toward rape victims is supported by research on the role of acculturation (i.e., adoption of the values and practices of mainstream U.S. culture). Asian American individuals who are highly acculturated report more positive views of rape victims and women and are less accepting of rape myths than their less acculturated peers (Mori et al., 1995).

Similar to findings with Asian American individuals, Hispanic individuals are more accepting of rape myths and less sympathetic toward rape victims than their Caucasian peers (Jimenez & Abreu, 2003; Lefley, Scott, Llabre, & Hicks, 1993). In Hispanic cultures, women are often considered inferior to men and considerable emphasis is placed on virginity as the proof of a woman's honor (Espin, 1985). The dominant culture standards of *decente* (i.e., that a woman must be pure) and *marianismo* (i.e., ennoblement of female chastity in emulation of the Virgin Mary) suggest that Hispanic women experiencing a sexual assault may come to be viewed as tainted, blameworthy, or promiscuous (Espin, 1985; J. A. Hamilton, 1989; Holzman, 1996; Lira, Koss, & Russo, 1999). These aspects of Hispanic culture may contribute to the finding that Hispanic women have greater difficulty recovering from rape than do Caucasian women. For Hispanic (and perhaps Asian) rape victims, the personal trauma of a sexual assault may be compounded by cultural values that are less supportive of rape victims. Taken together, results suggest that, although commonalities exist, cultural differences must be considered to understand individuals' experiences with sexually aggressive behavior.

REFERENCES

Note: * denotes studies included in the literature review of chapter 11, *Empirically Based Sexual Risk Reduction Interventions for University and College Students.*

Abbey, A. (1982). Sex differences in attributions for friendly behavior: Do males misperceive females' friendliness? *Journal of Personality and Social Psychology*, *42*, 830–838.

Abbey, A. (2002). Alcohol-related sexual assault: A common problem among college students. *Journal of Studies on Alcohol*, *14*, 118–128.

Abbey, A., Cozzarelli, C., McLaughlin, K., & Harnish, R. J. (1987). The effects of clothing on dyad sex composition on perceptions of sexual intent: Do women and men evaluate these cues differently? *Journal of Applied Social Psychology*, *17*, 108–126.

Abbey, A., & Harnish, R. J. (1995). Perceptions of sexual intent: The role of gender, alcohol consumption, and rape supportive attitudes. *Sex Roles*, *32*, 297–313.

Abbey, A., & McAuslan, P. (2004). A longitudinal examination of male college students' perpetration of sexual assault. *Journal of Consulting and Clinical Psychology*, *72*(5), 747–756.

Abbey, A., McAuslan, P., Zawacki, T., Clinton, A. M., & Buck, P. O. (2001). Attitudinal, experiential, and situational predictors of sexual assault perpetration. *Journal of Interpersonal Violence*, *16*, 784–807.

Abbey, A., & Melby, C. (1986). The effects of nonverbal cues on gender differences in perceptions of sexual intent. *Sex Roles*, *15*, 283–297.

Abbey, A., Ross, L. T., & McDuffie, D. (1994). Alcohol's role in sexual assault. In R. R. Watson (Ed.), *Drug and alcohol abuse reviews: Vol. 5. Addictive behaviors in women* (pp. 97–123). Totowa, NJ: Humana Press.

Abbey, A., Ross, L. T., McDuffie, D., & McAuslan, P. (1996a). Alcohol and dating risk factors for sexual assault among college women. *Psychology of Women Quarterly*, *20*, 147–169.

Abbey, A., Ross, L. T., McDuffie, D., & McAuslan, P. (1996b). Alcohol, misperception, and sexual assault: How and why are they linked? In D. M. Buss & N. M. Malamuth

(Eds.), *Sex, power, conflict: Evolutionary and feminist perspectives* (pp. 138–161). New York, NY: Oxford University Press.

Abbey, A., Zawacki, T., & Buck, P. O. (2005). The effects of past sexual assault perpetration and alcohol consumption on men's reactions to women's mixed signals. *Journal of Social and Clinical Psychology, 24*, 129–155.

Abbey, A., Zawacki, T., Buck, P. O., Testa, M., Parks, K., Norris, J., . . . Martell, J. (2002). How does alcohol contribute to sexual assault? Explanations for laboratory and survey data. *Alcoholism: Clinical and Experimental Research, 26*, 575–581.

Abbey, A., Zawacki, T., & McAuslan, P. (2000). Alcohol's effect on sexual perception. *Journal of Studies on Alcohol, 61*, 688–697.

Abroms, B. D., & Fillmore, M. T. (2004). Alcohol-induced impairment of inhibitory mechanisms involved in visual search. *Experimental and Clinical Psychopharmacology, 12*(4), 243–250.

Adams, H. E., Wright, L. W., Jr., & Lohr, B. A. (1996). Is homophobia associated with homosexual arousal? *Journal of Abnormal Psychology, 105*, 440–445.

Adams, J., Kottke, J., & Padgitt, J. (1983). Sexual harassment of university students. *Journal of College Student Personnel, 24*, 484–490.

Adimora, A. A., Schoenbach, V. J., Bonas, D., Martinson, F. E. A., Donaldson, K. H., & Stancil, T. R. (2002). Concurrent partnerships among women in the United States. *Epidemiology, 14*, 155–160.

Advocates for Youth. (1999). *European approaches to adolescent sexual behavior and responsibility*. Washington, DC: Author.

Afifi, W. A., Falato, W. L., & Weiner, J. L. (2001). Identity concerns following a severe relational transgression: The role of discovery method for the relational outcomes of infidelity. *Journal of Social and Personal Relationships, 18*(2), 291–308.

Afifi, W. A., & Faulkner, S. L. (2000). On being "just friends": The frequency and impact of sexual activity in cross-sex friendships. *Journal of Social and Personal Relationships, 17*, 205–222.

Afifi, W. A., & Lucas, A. A. (2008). Information seeking in the initial stages of relationship development. In S. Sprecher, A. Wenzel, & J. Harvey (Eds.), *Handbook of relationship initiation* (pp. 135–151). New York: Psychology Press.

Ageton, S. S. (1983). *Sexual assault among adolescents*. Lexington, MA: Lexington Books.

Ahrens, C. E., Campbell, R., Ternier-Thames, K. N., Wasco, S. M., & Tracy, S. (2007). Deciding whom to tell: Expectations and outcomes of rape survivors' first disclosures. *Psychology of Women Quarterly, 31*, 38–49.

Ahrold, T. K., & Meston, C. M. (2010). Ethnic differences in sexual attitudes of U.S. college students: Gender, acculturation, and religiosity factors. *Archives of Sexual Behavior, 39*, 190–202.

Ajzen, I. (1991). The theory of planned behavior. *Organizational Behavior and Human Decision Processes, 50*, 179–211.

Ajzen, I., & Fishbein, M. (1977). Attitude-behavior relations: A theoretical analysis and review of empirical research. *Psychological Bulletin, 84*, 888–918.

Albarracin, D., Johnson, B. T., Fishbein, M., & Muellerleile, P. A. (2001). Theories of reasoned action and planned behavior as models of condom use: A meta-analysis. *Psychological Bulletin, 127*(1), 142–161.

Albarracin, D., Kumkale, G. T., & Johnson, B. T. (2004). Influences of social power and normative support on condom use decisions: A research synthesis. *AIDS CARE, 16*(6), 700–723.

Alexander, M. G., & Fisher, T. D. (2003). Truth and consequences: Using the bogus pipeline to examine sex differences in self-reported sexuality. *The Journal of Sex Research*, *40*, 27–35.

Allen, E. S., & Baucom, D. H. (2004). Adult attachment and patterns of extradyadic involvement. *Family Process*, *23*(4), 467–488.

Allen, E. S., & Baucom, D. H. (2006). Dating, marital, and hypothetical extradyadic involvements: How do they compare? *The Journal of Sex Research*, *43*, 307–317.

Allen, E. S., & Rhoades, G. K. (2008). Not all affairs are created equal: Involvement with an extradyadic partner. *Journal of Sex and Marital Therapy*, *34*, 51–65.

Allen, E. S., Rhoades, G. K., Stanley, S. M., Markman, H. J., Williams, T., Melton, J., & Clements, M. L. (2008). Premarital precursors of marital infidelity. *Family Process*, *47*(2), 243–259.

Allgeier, E. R., & Wiederman, M. W. (1991). Love and mate selection in the 1990s. *Free Inquiry*, *11*, 25–27.

Amar, A. F. (2006). College women's experiences of stalking: Mental health symptoms and changes in routine. *Archives of Psychiatric Nursing*, *20*, 108–116.

Amaro, H. (1995). Considering women's realities in HIV prevention. *American Psychologist*, *50*(6), 437–447.

Amato, P. R. (2011). Relationship sequences and trajectories: Women's family formation pathways in emerging adulthood. In F. D. Fincham & M. Cui (Eds.), *Romantic relationships in emerging adulthood* (pp. 27–43). New York, NY: Cambridge University Press.

Amato, P. R., Booth, A., Johnson, D. R., & Rogers, S. J. (2007). *Alone together: How marriage in America is changing*. Cambridge, MA: Harvard University.

Amato, P. R., Landale, N., Habasevich, T., Booth, A., Eggebeen, D., McHale, S., & Schoen, R. (2008). Precursors of young women's family formation trajectories. *Journal of Marriage and the Family*, *70*, 1271–1286.

American College Health Association. (2010). *American College Health Association-National College Health Assessments II: Reference Group Data, Report Fall 2009*. Baltimore: Author.

American Psychiatric Association. (1994). *Diagnostic and statistical manual of mental disorders* (4th ed.). Washington, DC: Author.

American Psychological Association. (2009). *Resolution on appropriate affirmative responses to sexual orientation distress and change efforts*. Washington, DC: Author.

Amick, A. E., & Calhoun, K. S. (1987). Resistance to sexual aggression: Personality, attitudinal, and situational factors. *Archives of Sexual Behavior*, *16*, 153–163.

Anderson, E. (2002). Openly gay athletes: Contesting hegemonic masculinity in a homophobic environment. *Gender & Society*, *16*, 860–877.

Anderson, E. (2010). "At least with cheating there is an attempt at monogamy": Cheating and monogamism among undergraduate heterosexual men. *Journal of Social and Personal Relationships*, *27*(7) 851–872.

Apfelbaum, B. (2000). Retarded ejaculation: A much misunderstood syndrome. In S. R. Leiblum & R. C. Rosen (Eds.), *Principles and practice of sex therapy* (3rd ed., pp. 205–241). New York, NY: Guilford.

Arafat, I. S., & Yorburg, B. (1973). On living together without marriage. *The Journal of Sex Research*, *13*, 97–106.

Arata, C. M. (2000). From child victim to adult victim: A model for predicting sexual revictimization. *Child Maltreatment*, 5, 28 –38.

Arata, C. M. (2002). Child sexual abuse and sexual revictimization. *Clinical Psychology: Science & Practice*, *9*, 135–164.

Arey, D. (1995). Gay males and sexual child abuse. In L. A. Fontes (Ed.), *Sexual abuse in nine North American cultures* (pp. 200–235). Thousand Oaks, CA: Sage.

Arnett, J. J. (1997). Young people's conceptions of the transition to adulthood. *Youth & Society*, *29*, 1–23.

Arnett, J. J. (1998). Learning to stand alone: The contemporary American transition to adulthood in cultural and historical context. *Human Development*, *41*, 295–315.

Arnett, J. J. (2000a). Emerging adulthood: A theory of development from the late teens through the twenties. *American Psychologist*, *55*, 469–480.

Arnett, J. J. (2000b). High hopes in a grim world: Emerging adults' views of their futures and "Generation X." *Youth & Society*, *31*, 267–286.

Arnett, J. J. (2001). Conceptions of the transition to adulthood: Perspectives from adolescence to midlife. *Journal of Adult Development*, *8*, 133–143.

Arnett, J. J. (2003). Conceptions of the transition to adulthood among emerging adults in American ethnic groups. In J. J. Arnett & N. L. Galambos (Eds.), *New directions for child and adolescent development: Vol. 100. Exploring cultural conceptions of the transitions to adulthood* (pp. 63–75). San Francisco, CA: Jossey-Bass.

Arnett, J. J. (2004). *Emerging adulthood: The winding road from the late teens through the twenties*. New York, NY: Oxford University.

Arnett, J. J. (2006). *Emerging adulthood: Understanding the new way of coming of age*. In J. J. Arnett & J. L. Tanner (Eds.), *Emerging adults in America: Coming of age in the 21st century* (pp. 3–19). Washington, DC: American Psychological Association.

Arnett, J. J., & Tanner, J. L. (Eds.) (2006). *Emerging adults in America: Coming of age in the 21st century*. Washington, DC: American Psychological Association.

Arias, D. F., & Hernandez, A. M. (2007). Emerging adulthood in Mexican and Spanish Youth: Theories and realities. *Journal of Adolescent Research*, *22*, 476–503.

Associated Press. (2010). Germany to make forced marriage a crime. Retrieved from http://www.foxnews.com/world/2010/10/27/germany-make-forced-marriage-crime/

Atkeson, B. M., Calhoun, K. S., Resick, P. A., & Ellis, E. M. (1982). Victims of rape: Repeated assessment of depressive symptoms. *Journal of Consulting and Clinical Psychology*, *50*, 96–102.

Atkins, D. C. Baucom, D. H., & Jacobson, N. S. (2001). Understanding infidelity: Correlates in a national random sample. *Journal of Family Psychology*, *15*(4), 735–749.

Atkins, D. C., & Kessel, D. E. (2008). Religiousness and infidelity: Attendance, but not faith and prayer, predict marital infidelity. *Journal of Marriage and Family*, *70*, 407–418.

Ault, L. K., & Philhower, C. (2001, July). *Allergen avoidance: Qualities in romantic partners that are shunned by lovers and their parents*. Paper presented at the joint conference of the International Network on Personal Relationships and the International Society for the Study of Personal Relationships, Prescott, AZ.

Auslander, B. A., Rosenthal, S. L., Fortenberry, D., Biro, F. M., Berenstein, D. I., & Zimet, G. D. (2007). Predictors of sexual satisfaction in an adolescent and college population. *Journal of Pediatric and Adolescent Gynecology*, *20*, 25–28.

Bailey, B. L. (1988). *From front porch to back seat: Courtship in twentieth-century America*. Baltimore, MD: Johns Hopkins University Press.

Bailey, J. M. (2008). What is sexual orientation and do women have one? In D. A. Hope (Ed.), *Contemporary perspectives on lesbian, gay, and bisexual identities* (pp. 43–64). Nebraska Symposium on Motivation. New York, NY: Springer-Verlag.

Bailey, J. M., Gaulin, S., Agyei, Y., & Gladue, B. A. (1994). Effects of gender and sexual orientation on evolutionarily relevant aspects of human mating psychology. *Journal of Personality and Social Psychology*, *66*, 1081–1093.

Bailey, J. M., & Zucker, K. J. (1995). Childhood sex-typed behavior and sexual orientation: A conceptual analysis and quantitative review. *Developmental Psychology*, *31*, 43–55.

Baldwin, M. W., & Holmes, J. G. (1987). Salient private audiences and awareness of the self. *Journal of Personality and Social Psychology*, *52*, 1087–1098.

Balsam, K. F. (2003). Traumatic victimization in the lives of lesbian and bisexual women: A contextual approach. *Journal of Lesbian Studies*, *7*, 1–14.

Bancroft, J., Janssen, E., Strong, D., Carnes, L., Vukadinovic, Z., & Long, J. S. (2003). Sexual risk-taking in gay men: The relevance of sexual arousability, mood and sensation seeking. *Archives of Sexual Behavior*, *32*(6), 555–572.

Bandura, A. (1994). Social cognitive theory and exercise of control over HIV infection. In R. DiClemente & J. Peterson (Eds.), *Preventing AIDS: Theories, methods, and behavioral interventions* (pp. 25–60). New York, NY: Plenum.

Banyard, V. L., Moynihan, M. M., & Plante, E. G. (2007). Sexual violence prevention through bystander education: An experimental evaluation. *Journal of Community Psychology*, *35*, 463–481.

Banyard, V. L., Ward, S., Cohn, E. S., Plante, E. G., Moorhead, C., & Walsh, W. (2007). Unwanted sexual contact on campus: A comparison of women's and men's experiences. *Violence and Victims*, *22*(1), 52–70.

Barbach, L. (2000). *For yourself: The fulfillment of female sexuality*. New York, NY: Signet Books.

Barber, N. (1999). Women's dress fashions as a function of reproductive strategy. *Sex Roles*, *40*, 459–471.

Barickman, R. B., Paludi, M. A., & Rabinowitz, V. C. (1991). Sexual harassment of students: Victims of the college experience. In E. C. Viano (Ed.) *Critical issues in victimology: International perspectives* (pp. 153–165). New York: Springer.

Baron, L. & Straus, M. A. (1989). *Four theories of rape in American society: A state-level analysis*. New Haven, CT: Yale University Press.

Barr, V., Rando, R., Krylowicz, B., & Winfield, E. (2009). *The Association for University and College Counseling Center Directors Annual Survey*. Retrieved from http://aucccd.org/img/pdfs/directors_survey_2009_nm.pdf

Barta, W. D., & Kiene, S. M. (2005). Motivations for infidelity in heterosexual dating couples: The roles of gender, personality differences, and sociosexual orientation. *Journal of Social and Personal Relationships*, *22*, 339–360.

Bartz, J. A., & Lydon, J. E. (2006). Navigating the interdependence dilemma: Attachment goals and the use of communal norms with potential close others. *Journal of Personality and Social Psychology*, *91*, 77–96.

Basow, S. A., & Johnson, K. (2000). Predictors of homophobia in female college students. *Sex Roles*, *42*, 391–404.

Bass, E., & Davis, L. (2008). *The courage to heal*. New York, NY: Harper & Row.

Batten, S. V., Follette, V. M., Rasmussen Hall, M. L., & Palm, K. M. (2002). Physical and psychological effects of written disclosure among sexual abuse survivors. *Behavior Therapy*, *33*, 107–122.

Bauman, K. E., & Wilson, R. R. (1974). Sexual behavior of unmarried university students in 1968 and 1972. *The Journal of Sex Research*, *10*, 327–333.

Bauman, L. J., & Berman, R. (2005). Adolescent relationships and condom use: Trust, love and commitment. *AIDS and Behavior*, *9*(2), 211–222.

Baumeister, R. F. (2000). Gender differences in erotic plasticity: The female sex drive as socially flexible and responsive. *Psychological Bulletin, 126*, 347–374.

Baumeister, R. F., Catanese, K. R., & Vohs, K. D. (2001). Is there a gender difference in strength of sex drive? Theoretical views, conceptual distinctions, and a review of relevant evidence. *Personality and Social Psychology Review, 5*, 242–273.

Baumeister, R. F., Catanese, K. R., & Wallace, H. M. (2002). Conquest by force: A narcissistic reactance theory of rape and sexual coercion. *Review of General Psychology, 6*, 92–135.

Baumeister, R. F., Maner, J. K., & DeWall, C. N. (2006). Theories of human sexuality. In R. D. McAnulty & M. M. Burnette (Eds.), *Sex and sexuality* (Vol. 1, pp. 17–34). Westport, CT: Praeger.

Baumeister, R. F., & Tice, D. M. (2001). *The social dimension of sex*. Boston, MA: Allyn & Bacon.

Baumeister, R. F., & Twenge, J. M. (2002). Cultural suppression of female sexuality. *Review of General Psychology, 6*, 166–203.

Baumeister, R. F., & Vohs, K. D. (2004). Sexual economics: Sex as female resource for social exchange in heterosexual interactions. *Personality and Social Psychology Review, 8*, 339–363.

Baumeister, R. F., & Wotman, S. R. (1992). *Breaking hearts: The two sides of unrequited love*. New York, NY: Guilford.

Baumeister, R. F., Wotman, S. R., & Stillwell, A. M. (1993). Unrequited love: On heartbreak, anger, guilt, scriptlessness, and humiliation. *Journal of Personality and Social Psychology, 64*, 377–394.

Baumer, E. P. (2004). *Temporal variation in the likelihood of police notification by victims of rapes, 1973–2000.* U.S. Department of Justice, Report no. NCJ207497. Washington, DC: U.S. Government Printing Office.

Baxter, L. A., & Wilmot, W. W. (1985). Taboo topics in close relationships. *Journal of Social and Personal Relationships, 2*, 253–269. doi:10.1177/0265407585023002

Beaudoin, S. (2003). *Industrial revolution*. Boston, MA: Houghton Mifflin.

Beck, L. A., & Clark, M. S. (2009). Choosing to enter or avoid diagnostic social situations. *Psychological Science, 20*, 1175–1181.

Beckman, L. J., Harvey, S. M., & Tiersky, L. A. (1996). Attitudes about condoms and condom use among college students. *Journal of American College Health, 44*, 243–249. doi:10.1080/07448481.1996.9936851

Beemyn, B., Curtis, B., Davis, M., Tubbs, N. J. (2005). Transgender issues on college campuses. *New Directions for Student Services, 111*, 49–60.

Bem, D. J. (1972). Self-perception theory. In L. Berkowitz (Ed.), *Advances in experimental social psychology* (Vol. 6, pp. 1–62). New York, NY: Academic Press.

Bem, D. J. (1996). Exotic becomes erotic: A developmental theory of sexual orientation. Psychological Review, 103, 320–335.

Benedict, R. F. (1946). *The chrysanthemum and the sword*. Boston: Houghton Mifflin.

Bennett, K. (1992). Feminist bisexuality: A both/and option for an either/or world. In E. R. Weise (Ed.), *Close to home: Bisexuality and feminism* (pp. 205–231). Seattle: Seal Press.

Berdahl, J. L. (2007). The sexual harassment of uppity women. *Journal of Applied Psychology, 92*(2), 425–437.

Berger, P. L., & Luckmann, T. (1967). *The social construction of reality: A treatise in the sociology of knowledge*. Garden City, NJ: Anchor.

Berkowitz, A. D. (2003). Applications of social norms theory to other health and social justice issues. In W. Perkins (Ed.)*The social norms approach to preventing school and college age substance abuse: A handbook for educators, counselors, and clinicians* (pp. 259–279). San Francisco, CA: Jossey-Bass.

Berkowitz, A. D. (2004). *Working with men to prevent violence against women: Program Modalities and formats (part two)*. Violence Against Women Network, Applied Research Forum, National Electronic Network on Violence Against Women. Retrieved from http://www.vawnet.org/DomesticViolence/Research/VAWnet Docs/AR_MenPreventVAW2.php

Berkowitz, A. D., Burkhart, B. R., & Bourg, S. E. (1994). Research on college men and rape. In A. D. Berkowitz (Ed.), *Men and rape: Theory, research, and prevention programs in higher education* (Vol. 65, pp. 3–19). San Francisco, CA: Jossey-Bass.

Berman, M. I., & Frazier, P. A. (2005). Relationship power and betrayal experience as predictors of reactions to infidelity. *Personality and Social Psychology Bulletin*, *31*(12), 1617–1627.

Besharov, D. J. (1999). *America's disconnected youth*. Washington, DC: Child Welfare League of America.

Bettor, L., Hendrick, S. S., & Hendrick, C. (1995). Gender and sexual standards in dating relationships. *Personal Relationships*, *2*, 359–369. doi:10.1111/j.1475-6811 .1995.tb00098.x

Birenbaum, A. (1970). Revolution without the revolution: Sex in contemporary America. *The Journal of Sex Research*, *6*, 257–267.

Bisson, M. A., & Levine, T. R. (2009). Negotiating a friends with benefits relationship. *Archives of Sexual Behavior*, *38*, 66–73.

Black, B. M., & Weisz, A. M. (2008). Effective interventions with dating violence and domestic violence. In C. Franklin, M. B. Harris, & P. Allen-Meares (Eds.), *The school practitioner's concise companion to preventing violence and conflict* (pp. 127–139). New York, NY: Oxford University Press.

Blau, P. N. (1964). *Exchange and power in social life*. New York, NY: Wiley.

Bloom, H. S., Thompson, S. L., Unterman, R., Herlihy, C., & Payne, C. F. (2010). *Transforming the high school experience: How New York City's schools are boosting achievement and graduation rates*. New York, NY: MDRC. Retrieved from http://www.mdrc.org/publications/560/overview.html

Blow, A. J., & Hartnett, K. (2005a). Infidelity in committed relationships I: A methodological review. *Journal of Marital and Family Therapy*, *31*, 183–216.

Blow, A. J., & Hartnett, K. (2005b). Infidelity in committed relationships II: A substantive review. *Journal of Marital and Family Therapy*, *31*, 217–234.

Blumenfeld, W. J. (1992). *Homophobia: How we all pay the price*. Boston, MA: Beacon Press.

Blumstein, P., & Schwartz, P. (1983). *American couples: Money, work, and sex*. New York, NY: Morrow.

Blumstein, P. W., & Schwartz, P. (1997). Bisexuality: Some social psychological issues. *Journal of Social Issues*, *33*, 33–45.

Bobrow, D., & Bailey, M. (2001). Is homosexuality maintained via kin selection? *Evolution and Human Behavior*, *22*, 361–368.

Boeringer, S. B. (1996). Influences of fraternity membership, athletics, and male living arrangements on sexual aggression. *Violence Against Women*, *2*, 134–147.

Boeringer, S. B., Shehan, C. L., & Akers, R. L. (1991). Social contexts and social-learning in sexual coercion and aggression: Assessing the contribution of fraternity membership. *Family Relations*, *40*(1), 58–64.

Bogaert, A. F. (2006). Toward a conceptual understanding of asexuality. *Review of General Psychology, 20*, 241–250.

Bogaert, A. F., & Sadava, S. (2002). Adult attachment and sexual behavior. *Personal Relationships, 9*, 191–204.

Bogart, L. M., Cecil, H., Wagstaff, D. A., Pinkerton, S. D., & Abramson, P. R. (2000). Is it "sex"?: College students' interpretations of sexual behavior terminology. *The Journal of Sex Research, 37*, 108–117.

Bogle, K. (2007). The shift from dating to hooking up in college: What scholars have missed. *Sociology Compass, 1*, 775–788.

Bogle, K. A. (2008). *Hooking up: Sex, dating, and relationships on campus*. New York, NY: New York University Press.

Bond, B. J., Hefner, V., & Drogos, K. L. (2009). Information-seeking practices during the sexual development of lesbian, gay, and bisexual individuals: The influence and effects of coming out in a mediated environment. *Sexuality & Culture, 13*, 32–50.

Borja, S. E., Callahan, J. L., & Long, P. (2006). Positive and negative adjustment and social support of sexual assault survivors. *Journal of Traumatic Stress, 19*, 905–914.

Bowen, A. M., & Bourgeois, M. J. (2001). Attitudes toward lesbian, gay and bisexual college students: The contribution of pluralistic ignorance, dynamic social impact and contact theories. *Journal of American College Health, 50*(2), 91–96.

Bowlby, G., & Jennings, P. (1999). Youth employment: A lesson on its decline. *Educational Quarterly Review, 5*, 36–42.

Boyd, B., & Wandersman, A. (1991). Predicting undergraduate condom use with Fishebein and Ajzen and the Triandis attitude behavior models: Implications for public health interventions. *Journal of Applied Social Psychology, 21*, 1810–1830.

Braithwaite, S. R., Delevi, R., & Fincham, F. D. (2010). Romantic relationships and the physical and mental health of college students. *Personal Relationships, 17*, 1–12.

Braithwaite, S., Lambert, N., Fincham, F., & Pasley, K. (2010). Does college-based relationship education decrease extradyadic involvement in relationships? *Journal of Family Psychology, 24*, 740–745.

Brecklin, L. R., & Ullman, S. E. (2002). The roles of victim and offender alcohol use in sexual assaults: Results from the National Violence Against Women Survey. *Journal of Studies on Alcohol*, 63, 57–63.

Brehm, J. W. (1966). *A theory of psychological reactance*. New York: Academic Press.

Breitenbecher, K. H (1999). The association between the perception of threat and dating situation and sexual victimization. *Violence and Victims, 14*, 135–146.

Breitenbecher, K. H. (2000). Sexual assault on college campuses: Is an ounce of prevention enough? *Applied & Preventive Psychology, 9*, 23–52.

Breitenbecher, K. H., & Gidycz, C. A. (1998). An empirical evaluation of a program designed to reduce the risk of multiple sexual victimization. *Journal of Interpersonal Violence, 13*, 472–488.

Brewster, M. P. (2003). Power and control dynamics in prestalking and stalking situations. *Journal of Family Violence, 18*, 207–217.

Brown, A. L., Messman-Moore, T. L., Miller, A. G., & Stasser, G. (2005). Sexual victimization in relation to perceptions of risk: Mediation, generalization, and temporal stability. *Personality and Social Psychology Bulletin, 31*, 963–976.

Brown, E. J., & Heimberg, R. G. (2001). Effects of writing about rape: Evaluating Pennebaker's paradigm with a severe trauma. *Journal of Traumatic Stress, 14*, 781–790.

Brown, J. D., Keller, S., & Stern, S. (2009). Sex, sexuality, sexting, and sexed: Adolescents and the media. *Prevention Research*, *16*, 12–16.

Brown, N. R., & Sinclair, R. C. (1999). Estimating numbers of lifetime partners: Men and women do it differently. *The Journal of Sex Research*, *36*, 292–297.

Brown, R. D., Clarke, B., Gortmaker, V. & Robinson-Keilig, R. (2004). Assessing the campus climate for gay, lesbian, bisexual, and transgender (GLBT) students using a multiple perspectives approach. *Journal of College Student Development*, *45*(1), 8–26.

Brownmiller, S. (1975). *Against our will: Men, women, and rape*. New York, NY: Simon & Schuster.

Brunswig, K. A., & O'Donohue, W. (2008). *Relapse prevention for sexual harassers*. New York, NY: Plenum.

*Bryan, A. D., Aiken, L. S., & West, S. G. (1996). Increasing condom use: Evaluation of a theory-based intervention to prevent sexually transmitted diseases in young women. *Health Psychology*, *15*, 371–382.

Bullough, V. L. (1994). *Science in the bedroom: A history of sex research*. New York, NY: Basic Books.

Bumpass, L. L., & Liu, H. H. (2000). Trends in cohabitation and implications for children's family contexts in the United States. *Population Studies*, *54*, 29–41.

Bureau of Justice Statistics. (1995). *Criminal victimization in the United States*. Washington, DC: U.S. Department of Justice.

Burdette, A. M., Ellison, C. G., Hill, T. D., & Glenn, N. D. (2009). "Hooking up" at college: Does religion make a difference?*Journal for the Scientific Study of Religion*, *48*(3), 535–551.

Burdette, A. M., Ellison, C. G., Sherkat, D. E., & Gore, K. A. (2007). Are there religious variations in marital infidelity?*Journal of Family Issues*, *28*(12), 1553–1581.

Burn, S. M. (2000). Heterosexuals' use of "fag" and "Queer": Contributor to heterosexism and stigma. *Journal of Homosexuality*, *40*, 1–11.

Burn, S. M., Kadlec, K., & Rexer, R. (2005). Effects of subtle heterosexism on gays, lesbians, and bisexuals. *Journal of Homosexuality*, *49*, 23–48.

Burt, D. L., & DeMello, L. R. (2002). Attribution of rape blame as a function of victim's gender and sexuality, and perceived similarity to the victim. *Journal of Homosexuality*, 43(2), 39–57.

Burt, M. R. (1980). Cultural myths and supports for rape. *Journal of Personality and Social Psychology*, 38, 217–230.

Bushman, B. J. (1997). Effects of alcohol on human aggression: Validity of proposed explanations. In M. Galanter (Ed.), *Recent advances in alcoholism* (pp. 227–243). New York, NY: Plenum.

Bushman, B. J., Bonacci, A. M., Van Dijk, M., & Baumeister, R. F. (2003). Narcissism, sexual refusal, and aggression: Testing a narcissistic reactance model of sexual coercion. *Journal of Personality and Social Psychology*, *84*(5), 1027–1040.

Buss, D. M. (1989a). Love acts: The evolutionary biology of love. In R. J. Sternberg & M. L. Barnes (Eds.), *The psychology of love* (pp. 100–118). New Haven, CT: Yale University Press.

Buss, D. M. (1989b). Sex differences in human mate-preferences: Evolutionary hypotheses tested in 37 cultures. *Behavioral and Brain Sciences*, *12*, 1–49.

Buss, D. M. (1998). Sexual strategies theory: Historical origins and current status. *The Journal of Sex Research*, *35*, 19–31.

Buss, D. M., Larsen, R. J., Westen, D., & Semmelroth, J. (1992). Sex differences in jealousy: Evolution, physiology, and psychology. *Psychological Science*, *3*, 251–255.

Buss, D. M., & Schmitt, D. P. (1993). Sexual strategies theory: An evolutionary perspective on human mating. *Psychological Review*, *100*, 204–232. doi:10.1017/S0140525X00023992

Byers, E. S., Demmons, S., & Lawrance, K. (1998). Sexual satisfaction within dating relationships: A test of the interpersonal exchange model of sexual satisfaction. *Journal of Social and Personal Relationships*, *15*, 257–267.

Byers, E., & Eno, R. (1991). Predicting men's sexual coercion and aggression from attitudes, dating history, and sexual response. *Journal of Psychology and Human Sexuality*, *4*(3), 55–69.

Byers, E. S., Henderson, J., & Hobson, K. M. (2009). University students' definitions of sexual abstinence and having sex. *Archives of Sexual Behavior*, *38*, 665–674. doi: 10.1007/s10508–007–9289–6

Byers, E. S., & Lewis, K. (1988). Dating couples' disagreements over the desired level of sexual intimacy. *The Journal of Sex Research*, *24*, 15–29.

Byne, W. (2007). Biology and sexual minority status. In I. H. Meyer & M. E. Northridge (Eds.), *The health of sexual minorities: Public health perspectives on lesbian, gay, bisexual and transgender populations* (pp. 65–90). New York, NY: Springer.

Byrne, D. (1971). *The attraction paradigm*. New York, NY: Academic Press.

Calhoun, K. S., et al. (2002, November). Long-term evaluation of a group risk reduction program for sexual revictimization. Poster presented at the 36th annual meeting of the Association for Advancement of Behavior Therapy, Reno, NV.

Calzo, J. P., & Ward, L. M. (2009). Media exposure and viewers' attitudes toward homosexuality: Evidence for mainstreaming or resonance? *Journal of Broadcasting and Electronic Media*, *53*(2), 280–299.

Campbell, R., Dworkin, E., & Cabral, G. (2009). An ecological model of the impact of sexual assault on women's mental health. *Trauma, Violence, and Abuse*, *10*, 225–246.

Campbell, R., & Raja, S. (1999). Secondary victimization of rape victims: Insights from mental health professionals who treat survivors of violence. *Violence and Victims*, *14*, 261–275.

Campbell, R., Wasco, S. M., Ahrens, C. E., Sefl, T., & Barnes, H. E. (2001). Preventing the "second rape": Rape survivors' experiences with community service providers. *Journal of Interpersonal Violence*, *16*, 1239–1259.

Camperio-Ciani, A., Corna, F., & Capiluppi, C. (2004). Evidence for maternally inherited factors favouring male homosexuality and promoting female fecundity. *Proceedings of the Royal Society of London: Biological Sciences*, *271*, 2217–2221.

Cannon, K. D., & Dirks-Linhorst, P. A. (2006) How will they understand if we don't teach them?: The status of criminal justice education on gay and lesbian issues. *Journal of Criminal Justice Education*, *17*, 263–278.

Carmody, D. C. & Washington, L. M. (2001). Rape myth acceptance among college women : The impact of race and prior victimization. *Journal of Interpersonal Violence*, *16*(5), 424–436.

Caron, S. L. (1998). *Cross-cultural perspectives on human sexuality*. Needham Heights, MA: Allyn & Bacon.

Carpenter, C. S. (2009). Sexual orientation and outcomes in college. *Economics of Education Review*, *28*(6), 693–703.

Carpenter, L. M. (2001). The ambiguity of "having sex": The subjective experience of virginity loss in the United States. *The Journal of Sex Research*, *38*, 127–139.

Carr, J. L., & VanDuesen, K. M. (2004). Risk factors for male sexual aggression on college campuses. *Journal of Family Violence*, *19*, 279–289.

Carr, R. A. (1991). Addicted to power: Sexual harassment and the unethical behaviour of university faculty. *Canadian Journal of Counseling*, *25*, 447–461.

Carroll, J. S., Willoughby, B., Badger, S., Nelson, L. J., Barry, C. M., & Madsen, S. D. (2007). So close, yet so far away: The impact of varying marital horizons on emerging adulthood. *Journal of Adolescent Research*, *22*, 219–247.

Casey, E. A., Beadnell, B., & Lindhorst, T. P. (2008). Predictors of sexually coercive behavior in a nationally representative sample of adolescent males. *Journal of Interpersonal Violence*, *24*(2), 1129–1147.

Caspi, A., Roberts, B. W., & Shiner, R. L. (2005). Personality development: Stability and change. *Annual Review of Psychology*, *56*, 453–484.

Cate, R. M., Koval, J., Lloyd, S. A., & Wilson, G. (1995). Assessment of relationship thinking in dating relationships. *Personal Relationships*, *2*, 77–95.

Cate, R. M., Lloyd, S. A., Henton, J. M., & Larson, J. H. (1982). Fairness and reward level as predictors of relationship satisfaction. *Social Psychology Quarterly*, *45*, 177–181.

Cavan, R. S. (1969). *The American family* (3rd ed.). New York, NY: Thomas Y. Crowell.

Cavazos-Rehg, P. A., Krauss, M. J., Spitznagel, E. L., Schootman, M., Bucholz, K. K., Peipert, J., & Bierut, L. J. (2009). Age of sexual debut among US adolescents. *Contraception*, *80*(2), 158–162.

Cengage, G. (2003). Sexual harassment. In S. Phelps (Ed.), *Encyclopedia of Everyday Law*. eNotes.com. 2006. Retrieved from http://www.enotes.com/everyday-law-encyclopedia/sexual-harassment

Centers for Disease Control and Prevention. (2002). *Sexually transmitted disease surveillance, 2001*. Atlanta, GA: Author.

Centers for Disease Control and Prevention (2003). Advancing HIV prevention: New strategies for a changing epidemic – United States, 2003. *Morbidity and Mortality Weekly Report, 52*(15): 329–332.

Centers for Disease Control and Prevention. (2004). Sexual violence facts. Retrieved from http://www.cdc.gov/ncipc/factsheets/svfacts.htm

Centers for Disease Control and Prevention. (2007). Trends in reportable sexually transmitted diseases in the United States, 2006. Atlanta, GA; U.S. Department of Health and Human Services. Retrieved from http://www.cdc.gov/STI/stats06/trends2006.htm

Centers for Disease Control and Prevention. (2009). *Sexually transmitted disease surveillance, 2008*. Atlanta, GA: U.S. Department of Health and Human Services.

Centers for Disease Control and Prevention. (2010a). Prevalence and awareness of HIV infection among men who have sex with men—21 cities, United States, 2008. *Morbidity and Mortality Weekly Report (MMWR)*, *59*(37), 1201–1207.

Centers for Disease Control and Prevention (2010b). Sexually transmitted disease surveillance 2009. Atlanta, GA: U.S. Department of Health and Human Services. Retrieved from http://www.cdc.gov/STI/stats09/default.htm

Centers for Disease Control and Prevention. (2011). Estimates of new HIV infections in the United States, 2006–2009. Retrieved from http://www.cdc.gov/nchhstp/newsroom/docs/HIV-Infections-2006-2009.pdf

Centers for Disease Control and Prevention. (n.d.). *Program operations guidelines for STD prevention: Community and individual behavior change interventions*. Retrieved from http://www.cdc.gov/std/program/community.pdf

Chan, D. K-S., Lan, C. B., Chow, S. Y., & Cheung, S. F. (2008). Examining the job-related, psychological, and physical outcomes of workplace sexual harassment: A meta-analytic review. *Psychology of Women Quarterly*, *32*, 362–376.

Chandra, A., Mosher, W. D., Copen, C., & Sionean, C. (2011). Sexual behavior, sexual attraction, and sexual identity in the United States: Data from the 2006–2008 National Survey of Family Growth. *National Health Statistics Reports*, *36*, 1–36.

Charny, I. W., & Parnass, S. (1995). The impact of extramarital relationships on the continuation of marriages. *Journal of Sex & Marital Therapy*, *20*, 101–115.

Check, J. V. P., & Malamuth, N. M. (1983). Sex role stereotyping and reactions to depictions of stranger versus acquaintance rape. *Journal of Personality and Social Psychology*, *45*, 344–356.

*Chernoff, R. A., & Davison, G. C. (2005). An evaluation of a brief HIV/AIDS prevention intervention for college students using normative feedback and goal setting. *AIDS Education & Prevention*, *17*(2), 91–104.

Chin, R. L., Sporere, K. A., Cullison, B., Dyer, I. E., & Wu, T. D. (1998). Clinical course of gamma-hydroxybutyrate overdose. *Annals of Emergency Medicine*, *31*, 716–722.

Chivers, M. L., Rieger, G., Latty, E., & Bailey, J. M. (2004). A sex difference in the specificity of sexual arousal. *Psychological Science*, *15*, 736–744.

Chng, C. L., & Moore, A. (1991). Can attitudes of college students toward AIDS and homosexuality be change in six weeks? The effects of a gay panel. *Health Values*, *15*, 41–49.

Christensen, H. T. (1947). Student views on mate selection. *Marriage and Family Living*, *9*, 85–88.

Christopher, F. S., & Cate, R. M. (1984). Factors involved in premarital sexual decision-making. *The Journal of Sex Research*, *20*, 363–376.

Christopher, F. S., & Cate, R. M. (1985). Premarital sexual pathways and relationship development. *Journal of Social and Personal Relationships*, *2*, 271–288.

Christopher, F. S., & Frandsen, M. M. (1990). Strategies of influence in sex and dating. *Journal of Social and Personal Relationships*, *7*, 89–105.

Christopher, F. S., Owens, L. A., & Stecker, H. L. (1993). Exploring the darkside of courtship: A test of a model of male premarital sexual aggressiveness. *Journal of Marriage and the Family*, *55*(2), 469–479.

Christopher, F. S., & Sprecher, S. (2000). Sexuality in marriage, dating, and other relationships: A decade review. *Journal of Marriage and the Family*, *62*, 999–1017.

Chu, J. A. (1992). The revictimization of adult women with histories of childhood abuse. *Journal of Psychotherapy Practice and Research*, *1*, 259–269.

Clark, M. S., & Beck, L. A. (2011). Initiating and evaluating close relationships: A task central to emerging adults. In F. D. Fincham, & M. Cui (Eds.), *Romantic relationships in emerging adulthood* (pp. 190–212). New York, NY: Cambridge University Press.

Clark, R. D., & Hatfield, E. (1989). Gender differences in receptivity to sexual offers. *Journal of Psychology and Human Sexuality*, *2*, 39–55.

Cline, R. J. W., & Johnson, S. J. (1992). Mosquitoes, doorknobs, and sneezing: Relationships between homophobia and AIDS mythology among college students. *Health Communication*, *4*, 273–289.

Clodfelter, T. A., Turner, M. G., Hartman, J. L., & Kuhns, J. B. (2010). Sexual harassment victimization during emerging adulthood, *Crime and Delinquency*, *56*, 455–481.

Cloitre, M., Scarvalone, P., & Difede, J. (1997). Post-traumatic stress disorder, self and interpersonal dysfunction among sexually revictimized women. *Journal of Traumatic Stress*, *10*(3), 437–452.

Clum, G. A., Nishith, P., & Resick, P. A. (2001) Trauma-related sleep disturbance and self-reported physical health symptoms in treatment-seeking female rape victims. *The Journal of Nervous and Mental Disease*, *189*, 618 –622.

Cohen, L. L., & Shotland, R. L. (1996). Timing of first sexual intercourse in a relationship: Expectations, experiences, and perceptions of others. *The Journal of Sex Research*, *33*, 291–299.

Cohen, P., Kasen, S., Chen, H., Hartmark, C., & Gordon, K. (2003). Variations in patterns of developmental transitions in the emerging adulthood period. *Developmental Psychology*, *39*, 657–669.

Coleman, F. L. (1997). Stalking behavior and the cycle of domestic violence. *Journal of Interpersonal Violence*, *12*, 420–432.

Collins, W. A. (2003). More than myth: The developmental significance of romantic relationships during adolescence. *Journal of Research on Adolescence*, *13*, 1–24.

Collins, W. A., & Van Dulmen, M. (2006). Friendships and romance in emerging adulthood: Assessing distinctiveness in close relationships. In In J. J. Arnett & J. L. Tanner (Eds.), *Emerging adults in America: Coming of age in the 21st century* (pp. 219–234). Washington, DC: American Psychological Association.

Comett, M. B., & Shuntich, R. (1991). Sexual aggression: Perceptions of its likelihood of occurring and some correlates of self-admitted perpetration. *Perceptual and Motor Skills*, *73*, 499–507.

Cook, S. L. (1995). Acceptance and expectation of sexual aggression in college students. *Psychology of Women Quarterly*, 19, 181–194.

Cooper, A., McLoughlin, I. P., & Campbell, K. M. (2000). Sexuality in cyberspace: Update for the 21st century. *CyberPsychology & Behavior*, *3*(4), 521–536.

Cooper, M. L. (2002). Alcohol use and risky sexual behavior among college students and youth: Evaluating the evidence. *Journal of Studies on Alcohol, Supplement*, *14*, 101–117.

Cooper, M. L., Shapiro, C. M., & Powers, A. M. (1998). Motivations for sex and risky sexual behavior among adolescents and young adults: A functional perspective. *Journal of Personality and Social Psychology*, *75*, 1528–1558.

Corbin, W. R., & Fromme, K. (2002). Alcohol use and serial monogamy as risk for sexually transmitted diseases in young adults. *Health Psychology*, *21*, 229–236.

Cortina, L. M., Swan, S., Fitzgerald, L. F., & Waldo, C. (1998). Sexual harassment and assault: Chilling the climate for women in academia. *Psychology of Women Quarterly*, *27*(3), 419–441.

Cosmides, L., & Tooby, J. (1992). Cognitive adaptations for social exchange. In J. Barkow, L. Cosmides, & J. Tooby (Eds.), *The adapted mind* (pp. 163–228). New York, NY: Oxford University Press.

Côté, J. E. (1997). An empirical test of the identity capital model. *Journal of Adolescence*, *20*, 577–597.

Côté, J. E. (2000). *Arrested adulthood: The changing nature of maturity and identity*. New York, NY: New York University Press.

Côté, J. E. (2002). The role of identity capital in the transition to adulthood: The individualization thesis examined. *Journal of Youth Studies*, *5*, 117–134.

Côté, J. E. (2006). Emerging adulthood as institutionalized moratorium: Risks and benefits to identity formation. In J. J. Arnett & J. L. Tanner (Eds.), *Emerging adults in America: Coming of age in the 21st century* (pp. 85–116). Washington, DC: American Psychological Association.

Côté, J. E., & Levine, C. (2002). *Identity formation, agency, and culture.* Hillsdale, NJ: Erlbaum.

Crawford, M., & Popp, D. (2003). Sexual double standards: A review and methodological critique of two decades of research. *The Journal of Sex Research, 40,* 13–26. doi:10.1080/00224490309552163

Cress, C. M. (2008). Creative inclusive learning communities: The role of student-faculty relationships in mitigating negative campus climate. *Learning Inquiry, 2,* 95–111.

Crouter, A. C., & Booth, A. (Eds.). (2006). *Romance and sex in adolescence and emerging adulthood: Risks and opportunities.* New York, NY: Erlbaum.

Cue, K. L., George, W. H., & Norris, J. (1996). Women's appraisals of sexual-assault risk in dating situations. *Psychology of Women Quarterly, 20,* 487–504.

Cunningham, M. R., Barbee, A. P., & Druen, P. B. (1996). Social allergens and the reactions that they produce: Escalation of annoyance and disgust in love and work. In R. M. Kowalski (Ed.), *Aversive interpersonal behaviors* (pp. 189–214). New York, NY: Plenum.

Cunningham, M. R., Druen, P. B., & Barbee, A. P. (1997). Angels, mentors, and friends: Trade-offs among evolutionary, social, and individual variables in physical appearance. In J. A. Simpson & D. T. Kenrick (Eds.), *Evolutionary social psychology* (pp. 109–140). Mahwah, NJ: Lawrence Erlbaum.

Cunningham, M. R., Shamblen, S. R., Barbee, A. P., & Ault, L. K. (2005). Social allergies in romantic relationships: Behavioral repetition, emotional sensitization, and dissatisfaction in dating couples. *Personal Relationships, 12,* 273–295.

Cupach, W. R., & Metts, S. (1995). The role of sexual attitude similarity in romantic heterosexual relationships. *Personal Relationships, 2,* 287–300. doi:10.1111/j.1475-6811.1995.tb00093.x

Cupach, W. R., & Spitzberg, B. H. (1998). Obsessive relational intrusion and stalking. In B. H. Spitzberg & W. R. Cupach (Eds.), *The dark side of close relationships* (pp. 233–263). Mahwah, NJ: Erlbaum.

Cupach, W. R., & Spitzberg, B. H. (2004). *The dark side of relational pursuit: From attraction to obsession and stalking.* Mahwah, NJ: Erlbaum.

Cupach, W. R., & Spitzberg, B. H. (2008). "Thanks, but no thanks . . . ": The occurrence and management of unwanted relationship pursuit. In S. Sprecher, A. Wenzel, & J. Harvey (Eds.), *Handbook of relationship initiation* (pp. 409–424). New York, NY: Psychology Press.

Dainton, M. (1991, May). *Relational maintenance revisited: The addition of physical affection measures to a maintenance typology.* Paper presented at the meeting of the International Communication Association, Chicago, IL.

Daley, S. E., & Hammen, C. (2002). Depressive symptoms and close relationships during the transition to adulthood: Perspectives from dysphoric women, their best friends, and their romantic partners. *Journal of Consulting and Clinical Psychology, 70,* 129–1414.

Daneback, K., Månsson, S-A., & Ross, M. W. (2007). Using the Internet to find offline sex partners. *CyberPsychology & Behavior, 10*(1): 100–107.

Darwin, C. (1871). *The descent of man, and selection in relation to sex.* London, England: John Murray.

Darwin, C. (1964). *On the origin of species*. Cambridge, MA: Harvard University Press. (Original work published 1859)

D'Augelli, A. R. (1989). Lesbians' and gay men's experiences of discrimination and harassment in a university community. *American Journal of Community Psychology*, *17*, 317–321.

D'Augelli, A. R. (1992). Lesbian and gay male undergraduates' experiences of harassment and fear on campus. *Journal of Interpersonal Violence*, *7*, 383–395.

D'Augelli, A. R., & Rose, M. L. (1990). Homophobia in a university community: Attitudes and experiences of heterosexual freshmen. *Journal of College Student Development*, *31*, 484–491.

Davies, A. P. C., Shackelford, T. K., & Hass, G. (2007). When a "poach" is not a poach: Re-defining human mate poaching and re-estimating its frequency. *Archives of Sexual Behavior*, *36*(5), 702–716.

Davies, M. (2004). Correlates of negative attitudes toward gay men: Sexism, male role norms, and male sexuality. *The Journal of Sex Research*, *42*, 259–266.

Davies, S., Katz, J., & Jackson, J. L. (1999). Sexual desire discrepancies: Effects on sexual and relationship satisfaction in heterosexual dating couples. *Archives of Sexual Behavior*, *28*, 553–567.

Davila, J. (2011). Romantic relationships and mental health in emerging adulthood. In F. D. Fincham & M. Cui (Eds.), *Romantic relationships in emerging adulthood* (pp. 275–292). New York, NY: Cambridge University Press.

Davis v. Monroe County Board of Education, 526 U.S. 629 (1999).

Davis, J., & Bauman, K. (2008). School enrollment in the United States: 2006. *U.S. Census*. Retrieved from http://www.census.gov/prod/2008pubs/p20–559.pdf

Davis, J. A., & Smith, T. W. (1991). *General Social Surveys, 1972–1991: Cumulative code book*. Chicago, IL: National Opinion Research Center.

Davis, J. A., Smith, T. W., & Marsden, P. V. (2003). *General Social Surveys, 1972–2002: Cumulative code book*. Chicago, IL: National Opinion Research Center.

Davis, K. E., Ace, A., & Andra, M. (2000). Stalking perpetrators and psychological maltreatment of partners: Anger-jealousy, attachment insecurity, need for control, and break-up context. *Violence and Victims*, *15*, 407–425.

Davis, K. E., & Latty-Mann, H. (1987). Love styles and relationship quality: A contribution to validation. *Journal of Social and Personal Relationships*, *4*, 409–428.

Davis, R. C., Birckman, R., & Baker, T. (1991). Supportive and unsupportive responses of others to rape victims: Effects on concurrent adjustment. *American Journal of Community Psychology*, *19*, 443–451.

De Becker, G. (1998). *The gift of fear: Survival signals that protect us from violence*. New York, NY: Dell.

DeGenova, M. K. (2006). *Intimate relationships, marriages, and families*. New York, NY: McGraw-Hill.

DeGenova, M. K., & Rice, F. P. (2005). *Intimate relationships, marriages, and families* (6th ed.). Boston, MA: McGraw Hill.

Deitz, S. R., Blackwell, K. T., Daley, P. C., & Bentley, B. J. (1982). Measurement of empathy towards rape victims and rapists. *Journal of Personality and Social Psychology*, *43*(2), 372–384.

DeKeseredy, W. S. & Schwartz, M. D. (1993). Male peer support and women abuse: An expansion of DeKeseredy model. *Sociological Spectrum*, *13*(4), 393–413.

DeLamater, J. D. (1989). The social control of human sexuality. In K. McKinney & S. Sprecher (Eds.), *Human sexuality: The societal and interpersonal context* (pp. 30–62). Norwood, NJ: Ablex.

DeLamater, J. D., & Hyde, J. S. (1998). Essentialism vs. social constructionism in the study of human sexuality. *The Journal of Sex Research*, *35*, 10–18.

DeLamater, J., & MacCorquodale, P. (1979). *Premarital sexuality*. Madison, WI: University of Wisconsin Press.

Delgado, M. (2007). *Youth led community organizing: Theory and action*. New York, NY: Oxford University Press.

DeMaris, A., & Kaukinen, C. (2005). Violent victimization and women's mental and physical health: Evidence from a national sample. *Journal of Research in Crime and Delinquency*, *42*, 384–411.

D'Emilio, J., & Freedman, E. B. (1997). *Intimate matters: A history of sex in America*. Chicago, IL: University of Chicago Press.

Dempsey, D., Hillier, L., & Harrison, L. (2001). Gendered (s)explorations among same-sex attracted young people in Australia. *Journal of Adolescence*, *24*, 67–81.

Desiderato, L. L., & Crawford, H. J. (1995). Risky sexual behavior in college students: Relationship between number of sex partners, disclosure of previous risky behavior, and alcohol use. *Journal of Youth and Adolescence*, *24*, 55–67.

Devine, P. G., Evett, S. R., & Vasquez-Suson, K. A. (1996). Exploring the interpersonal dynamics of intergroup interactions. In R. M. Sorrentino & E. T. Higgins (Eds.), *Handbook of motivation and cognition: The interpersonal context* (Vol. 3, pp. 423–464). New York, NY: Guilford.

Devor, A. H. (1999). Witnessing and mirroring. A fourteen stage model of transsexual identity formation. *Journal of Gay and Lesbian Psychotherapy*, *8*(1/2), 41–67.

Diamant, A. L., Schuster, M. A., McGuigan, K., & Lever, J. (1999). Lesbians' sexual history with men: Implications for taking a sexual history. *Archives of Internal Medicine*, *159*, 2730–2736.

Diamant, A. L., & Wold, C. (2003). Sexual orientation and variation in physical and mental health status among women. *Journal of Women's Health*, *12*(1), 41–49.

Diamond, L. M. (2007). A dynamical systems approach to the development and expression of female same-sex sexuality. *Perspectives on Psychological Science*, *2*(2), 142–161.

Diamond, L. M. (2008). Female bisexuality from adolescence to adulthood: Results from a 10-year longitudinal study. *Developmental Psychology*, *44*(1), 5–14.

DiClemente, R. J., & Wingood, G. M. (1995). A randomized controlled trial of an HIV sexual risk-reduction intervention for young African-American women. *Journal of the American Medical Association*, *274*(16), 1271–1276.

DiClemente, R. J., Wingood, G. M., Vermund, S. H., & Steward, K. E. (1999). Prevention of HIV/AIDS. In J. M. Raczynski & R. J. DiClemente (Eds.), *Handbook of health promotion and disease prevention* (pp. 371–394). New York: Kluwer Academic.

Dion, K. L., & Dion, K. K. (1993). Gender and ethnocultural comparisons in styles of love. *Psychology of Women Quarterly*, *17*, 463–473.

Docan-Morgan, T., & Docan, C. A. (2007). Internet infidelity: Double standards and the differing views of women and men. *Communication Quarterly*, *55*(3), 317–342.

Dodge, B., & Sandfort, T. G. M. (2007). A review of mental health research on bisexual individuals when compared to homosexual and heterosexual individuals. In B. A. Firestein (Ed.), *Becoming visible: Counseling bisexuals across the lifespan* (pp. 28–51). New York, NY: Columbia University.

Dodson, B. (2002). *Orgasms for two*. New York, NY: Harmony.

*Doherty, K, & Low, K. G. (2008). The effects of a web-based intervention on college students' knowledge of human papillomavirus and attitudes toward vaccination. *International Journal of Sexual Health*, *20*(4), 223–232.

Drigotas, S. M., & Barta, W. (2001). The cheating heart: Scientific explorations of infidelity. *Current Directions in Psychological Science, 10*(5), 177–180.

Drigotas, S. M., Safstrom, A., & Gentilia, T. (1999). An investment model prediction of dating infidelity. *Journal of Personality and Social Psychology, 77*, 509–524.

Duncan, L. E., Peterson, B. E., & Winter, D. G. (1997). Authoritarianism and gender roles: Toward a psychological analysis of hegemonic relationships. *Personality and Social Psychology Bulletin, 23*, 41–49.

Dunn, M. P. (2002). Sampling considerations. In M. W. Wiederman & B. E. Whitley Jr. (Eds.), *Handbook for conducting research on human sexuality* (pp. 85–112). Mahwah, NJ: Erlbaum.

Dutton, L. B., & Winstead, B. A. (2006). Predicting unwanted pursuit: Attachment, relationship satisfaction, relationship alternatives, and break-up distress. *Journal of Social and Personal Relationships, 23*, 565–586.

Dyer, J. E. (2000). Evolving abuse of GHB in California: Bodybuilding drugs to date rape drug. *Journal of Toxicology, 38*, 184.

Eagly, A. H., Eastwick, P. W., & Johannesen-Schmidt, M. C. (2009). Possible selves in marital roles: The impact of the anticipated division of labor on the mate preferences of women and men. *Personality and Social Psychology Bulletin, 35*, 403–414.

Edgar, T., Freimuth, V. S., Hammond, S. L., McDonald, D. A., & Fink, E. L. (1992). Strategic sexual communication: Condom use resistance and response. *Health Communication, 4*, 83–104.

Edwards, K. M., Desai, A. D., Gidycz, C. A., & VanWynsberghe, A. (2009). College women's aggression in relationships: The role of childhood and adolescent victimization. *Psychology of Women Quarterly, 33*, 255–265.

Edwards, K. M., Kearns, M. C., Calhoun, K. S., & Gidycz, C. A. (2009). College women's reactions to participating in sexual assault research: Is it distressing? *Psychology of Women Quarterly, 33*, 225–234.

Edwards, K. M., Kearns, M. C., Gidycz, C. A., & Calhoun, K. S. (in press). Predictors of relationship stability following a sexual assault. *Violence and Victims.*

Ehrenreich, B., Hess, E., & Jacobs, G. (1986). *Re-making love: The feminization of sex.* Garden City, NJ: Doubleday Anchor.

Ehrmann, W. (1959). *Premarital dating behavior.* New York, NY: Holt.

Eisenberg, M. E. (2002). The association of campus resources for gay, lesbian, and bisexual students with college students' condom use. *Journal of American College Health, 51* (3), 109–116.

Eisenberg, M. E., Ackard, D. M., Resnick, M. D., & Neumark-Sztainer, D. (2009). Casual sex and psychological health among young adults: Is having "friends with benefits" emotionally damaging? *Perspectives on Sexual & Reproductive Health, 41*, 231–237.

Eisenberg, M. E., & Wechsler, H. (2003). Social influences on substance-use behaviors of gay, lesbian, and bisexual college students: Findings from a national study. *Social Science & Medicine, 57*(10), 1913–1923.

*Eitel, P, & Friend, R. (1999). Reducing denial and sexual risk behaviors in college students: A comparison of a cognitive and a motivational approach. *Annals of Behavioral Medicine, 21*(1), 12–19.

El-Bassel, N., Gilbert, L., Rajah, V., Foleno, A., & Frye, V. (2000). Fear and violence: Raising the HIV stakes. *AIDS Education and Prevention, 12*, 154–170.

Elias, M. (2007, February 7). Gay teens coming out earlier to peers and family. *USA Today.* Retrieved from http://www.usatoday.com/news/nation/2007-02-07-gay-teens-cover_x.htm

Eliason, M. J. (1995). Accounts of sexual identity formation in heterosexual students. *Sex Roles*, *32*(11/12), 821–833.

Eliason, M. J., & Schope, R. (2007). Shifting sands or solid foundation? Lesbian, gay, bisexual, and transgender identity formation. In I. H. Meyer & M. E. Northridge (Eds.), *The health of sexual minorities: Public health perspectives on lesbian, gay, bisexual and transgender populations* (pp. 1–26). New York, NY: Springer.

Ellis, L., Robb, B., & Burke, D. (2005). Sexual orientation in United States and Canadian college students. *Archives of Sexual Behavior*, *34*(5), 569–581.

Emerson, R. M., Ferris, K. O., & Gardner, C. B. (1998). On being stalked. *Social Problems*, *45*, 289–314.

Emory University. (n.d.). LGBT life. Retrieved from http://www.emory.edu/CAMPUS_LIFE/LGBTOFFICE/index.php

England, P., Shafer, E. F., & Fogarty, A. C. K. (2010). Hooking up and forming romantic relationships on today's college campuses. In M. Kimmel & A. Aronson (Eds.), *The gendered society reader* (4th ed., pp. 578–591). New York: Oxford University.

Erikson, E. H. (1968). *Identity: Youth and crisis*. New York, NY: Norton.

Erikson, E. H. (1982). *The life cycle completed: A review*. New York, NY: Norton.

Erikson, E. H. (1994). *Identity: Youth and crisis*. New York: Norton.

Eshbaugh, E. M., & Gute, G. (2008). Hookups and sexual regret among college women. *Journal of Social Psychology*, *148*, 77–89.

Espin, O. M. (1985). Psychotherapy with Hispanic women: Some considerations. In P. Pederson (Ed.), *Handbook of cross cultural counseling and therapy* (pp. 165–171). Westport, CT: Greenwood Press.

Espinosa-Hernandez, G., & Lefkowitz, E. S. (2009). Sexual behaviors and attitudes and ethnic identity during college. *The Journal of Sex Research*, *46*, 471–482. doi: 10.1080/00224490902829616.

Espiritu, Y. L. (2001). "We don't sleep around like white girls do": Family, culture, and gender in Filipina American lives. *Signs: Journal of Women in Culture and Society*, *26*, 415–440.

*Evans, A. E., Edmunson-Drane, E. W., & Harris, K. K. (2000). Computer-assisted instruction: An effective instructional method for HIV prevention education?. *Journal of Adolescent Health*, *26*, 244–251.

Eysenck, H. J. (1976). *Sex and personality*. Austin, TX: University of Texas Press.

Facio, A., & Micocci, E. (2003). Emerging adulthood in Argentina. In J. J. Arnett & N. L. Galambos (Eds.), *New directions for child and adolescent development: Vol. 100. Exploring cultural conceptions of the transitions to adulthood* (pp. 21–31). San Francisco, CA: Jossey-Bass.

Falsetti, S. (1997). The decision-making process of choosing a treatment for patients with civilian trauma-related PTSD. *Cognitive and Behavioral Practice*, *4*, 99–121.

Farley, L. (1978). *Sexual shakedown: The sexual harassment of women on the job*. New York, NY: McGraw-Hill.

Farrer, J., Tsuchiya, H., & Bagrowicz, B. (2008). Emotional expression in *tsukiau* dating relationships in Japan. *Journal of Social and Personal Relationships*, *25*, 169–188.

Farrington, D. P. (1995). The development of offending and antisocial behavior from childhood: Key findings from the Cambridge study in delinquent development. *Journal of Child Psychology and Psychiatry and Allied Disciplines*, *360*, 929–964.

Farrington, D. P., & West, D. J. (1995). Effects of marriage, separation and children on offending by adult males. In J. Hagan (Ed.), *Current perspectives on aging and the life course* (Vol. 4, pp. 249–281). Greenwich, CT: JAI Press.

Farris, C., Treat, T. A., & Viken, R. J. (2010). Alcohol alters men's perceptual and decisional processing of women's sexual interest. *Journal of Abnormal Psychology, 119*(2), 427–432.

Farris, C., Treat, T. A., Viken, R. J., & McFall, R. M. (2008). Sexual coercion and the misperception of sexual intent. *Clinical Psychology Review, 28*, 48–66.

Federal Bureau of Investigation. (1994). *Uniform crime reports for the United States, 1993.* Washington, DC: U.S. Government Printing Office.

Fehr, B. (1988). Prototype analysis of the concepts of love and commitment. *Journal of Personality and Social Psychology, 55*, 557–579.

Fehr, B. (1994). Prototype-based assessment of layperson's views of love. *Personal Relationships, 1*, 309–331.

Fehr, B., & Russell, J. A. (1991). The concept of love viewed from a prototype perspective. *Journal of Personality and Social Psychology, 60*, 425–438.

Feldman, M. B., & Meyer, I. H. (2007). Eating disorders in diverse lesbian, gay, and bisexual populations. *International Journal of Eating Disorders, 40*, 218–226.

Feldman, S. S., & Cauffman, E. (1999a). Sexual betrayal among late adolescents: Perspectives of the perpetrator and the aggrieved. *Journal of Youth and Adolescence, 28*, 235–258.

Feldman, S. S., & Cauffman, E. (1999b). Your cheatin' heart: Attitudes, behaviors, and correlates of sexual betrayal in late adolescents. *Journal of Research on Adolescence, 9*, 227–252.

Felmlee, D., Sprecher, S., & Bassin, E. (1990). The dissolution of intimate relationships: A hazard model. *Social Psychology Quarterly, 53*, 13–30.

Felson, R. B. (2002). *Violence and gender reexamined.* Washington, DC: American Psychological Association.

Fernandez, A. M., Vera-Villaroel, P., Sierra, J. C., & Zubeidat, I. (2007). Distress in response to emotional and sexual infidelity: Evidence of evolved gender differences in Spanish students. *The Journal of Psychology, 141*(1), 17–24.

Fichten, C. S., Tagalakis, V., Judd, D., Wright, J., & Amsel, R. (2001). Verbal and nonverbal communication cues in daily conversations and dating. *Journal of Social Psychology, 132*, 751–769.

Fielder, R. L., & Carey, M. P. (2010). Prevalence and characteristics of sexual hookups among first-semester female college students. *Journal of Sex and Marital Therapy, 36*, 346–359.

Fillingim, R. B., Wilkinson, C. S., & Powell, T. (1999). Self-reported abuse history and pain complaints among young adults. *Clinical Journal of Pain, 15*, 85–91.

Fillmore, M. T., Marczinski, C. A., & Bowman, A. M. (2005). Acute tolerance to alcohol effects on inhibitory and activational mechanisms of behavioral control. *Journal of Studies on Alcohol, 66*(5), 663–672.

Fincham, F. D., & Cui, M. (2011). *Romantic relationships in emerging adulthood.* New York, NY: Cambridge University Press.

Fincham, F. D., Lambert, N. M., & Beach, S. R. H. (2010). Faith and unfaithfulness: Can praying for your partner reduce infidelity? *Journal of Personality and Social Psychology, 99*(4), 649–659.

Fincham, F. D., Stanley, S. M., & Rhoades, G. K. (2011). Relationship education in emerging adulthood: Problems and prospects. In F. D. Fincham & M. Cui (Eds.), *Romantic relationships in emerging adulthood* (pp. 293–316). New York, NY: Cambridge University Press.

Finer, L. (2007). Trends in premarital sex in the United States, 1954–2003. *Public Health Reports, 122*, 73–78.

Finkelhor, D. (2008). *Childhood victimization*. New York, NY: Oxford University Press.

Fischer, K. W., Shaver, P. R., & Carnochan, P. (1990). How emotions develop and how they organise development. *Cognition and Emotion*, *4*, 81–127.

Fisher, B. S., Cullen, F. T., & Turner M. G. (2000). *The sexual victimization of college women*. Retrieved from http://www.ncjrs.org/txtfiles1/nij/182369.txt

Fisher, B. S., Daigle, L. E., Cullen, F. T., & Turner, M. G. (2003). Reporting sexual victimization to the police and others: Results from a national-level study of college women. *Criminal Justice and Behavior*, *30*, 6–38.

Fisher, J. D., & Fisher, W. A. (1992). Changing AIDS-risk behavior. *Psychological Bulletin*, *111*, 455–474.

Fisher, J. D., & Fisher, W. A. (2000). Theoretical approaches to individual-level change in HIV-risk behavior. In J. Peterson & R. J. DiClemente (Eds.), *HIV prevention handbook* (pp. 3–55). New York: Kluwer Academic/Plenum Press.

*Fisher, J. D., Fisher, W. A., Misovich, S. J., Kimble, D. L., & Mallory, T. E. (1996). Changing AIDS risk behavior: Effects of an intervention emphasizing aids risk reduction information, motivation, and behavioral skills in a college student population. *Health Psychology*, *15*(2), 114–123.

Fisher, T. D. & Walters, A. S. (3003). Variables in addition to gender that help to explain differences in perceived sexual interest. *Psychology of Men & Masculinity*, *4*(2), 154–162.

Fisher, W. A., & Fisher, J. D. (1993). A general social psychological model for changing AIDS risk behavior. In J. Pryor & G. Reeder (Eds.), *The social psychology of HIV infection* (pp. 127–153). Hillsdale, NJ: Erlbaum.

Fitzgerald, L. F. (1993). Sexual harassment: Violence against women in the workplace. *American Psychologist*, *48*, 1070–1076.

Foa, E. B., Hearst-Ikeda, D. E., & Perry, K. (1995). Evaluation of a brief cognitive behavioral program for the prevention of chronic PTSD in recent assault victims. *Journal of Consulting and Clinical Psychology*, *63*, 948–955.

Foa, E. B., & Rothbaum, B. O. (1998). *Treating the trauma of rape: Cognitive behavioral therapy for PTSD*. New York: Guilford.

Folkman, S., Chesney, M. A., Pollack, L., & Phillips, C. (1992). Stress, coping, and high-risk sexual behavior. *Health Psychology*, *11*, 218–222.

Forste, R., & Tanfer, K. (1996). Sexual exclusivity among dating, cohabitating, and married women. *Journal of Marriage and the Family*, *58*, 33–47.

Forte, J. A. (2007). *Human behavior and the social environment: Models, metaphors, and maps for applying theoretical perspectives to practice*. Belmont, CA: Brookes Thompson.

Fortier, M. A., DiLillo, D., Messman-Moore, T. L., Peugh, J., DeNardi, K. A., & Gaffey, K. J. (2009). Severity of child sexual abuse and revictimization: The mediating role of coping and trauma symptoms. *Psychology of Women Quarterly*, 33, 308–320.

Foshee, V. A., Bauman, K. E., Arriaga, X. B., Helms, R. W., Koch, G. G., & Linder, G. F. (1998). An evaluation of Safe Dates, an adolescent dating violence prevention program. *American Journal of Public Health*, *88*(1), 45–50

Foubert, J. D. (2000). The longitudinal effects of a rape-prevention program on fraternity men's attitudes, behavioral intent, and behavior. *Journal of American College Health*, *48*, 158–163.

Foubert, J. D., Newberry, J. T., & Tatum, J. L. (2007). Behavior differences seven months later: Effects of a rape prevention program on first-year men who join fraternities. *NASPA Journal*, *44*(4), 728–749.

Fradella, J. F., Owen, S. S., & Burke, T. W. (2009). Integrating gay, lesbian, bisexual, and transgender issues into the undergraduate criminal justice curriculum. *Journal of Criminal Justice Education*, *20*, 127–156.

Franklin v. Gwinnett County Public Schools, 503 U.S. 60 (1992).

Franklin, K. (2000). Antigay behaviors among young adults: Prevalence, patterns, and motivators in a noncriminal population. *Journal of Interpersonal Violence*, *15*, 339–362.

Frayser, S. (1985). *Varieties of sexual experience: An anthropological perspective on human sexuality*. New Haven, CT: Human Relations Area File Press.

Freitas, D. (2008). *Sex and the soul: Juggling sexuality, spirituality, romance, and religion on America's college campuses*. Oxford, England: Oxford University Press.

Freyd, J. J., Klest, B., & Allard, C. B. (2005). Betrayal trauma: Relationship to physical health, psychological distress, and a written disclosure intervention. *Journal of Trauma and Dissociation*, *6*(3), 83–104.

Fricker, J., & Moore, S. (2002). Relationship satisfaction: The role of love styles and attachment styles. *Current Research in Social Psychology*, *7*, 182–204.

Friedman, E. (2010). Victim of secret dorm sex tape posts Facebook goodbye, jumps to his death: Rutgers University freshman jumped from the George Washington Bridge. Retrieved from: http://abcnews.go.com/US/victim-secret-dorm-sex-tape-commits-suicide/story?id=11758716

Friere, P. (1970). *Pedagogy of the oppressed*. New York, NY: Seabury Press.

Frisbie, S. H. (2002). *Sexual harassment: A comparison of online versus traditional training methods*. Unpublished doctoral dissertation, Texas Tech University, Lubbock.

Funk, R. E. (1993). *Stopping rape: A challenge for men*. Philadelphia, PA: New Society.

Furlong, A., & Cartmel, F. (1997). *Young people and social change: Individualism and risk in late modernity*. Buckingham, England: Open University Press.

Furman, W., & Shaffer, L. (2011). Romantic partners, friends, friends with benefits, and casual acquaintances as sexual partners. *The Journal of Sex Research*, *48*, 554–564.

Gagnon, J. H., & Simon, W. (1973). *Sexual conduct: The social sources of human sexuality*. Chicago, IL: Aldine.

Galliher, R. V., Rostosky, S. S., Welsh, D. P., & Kawaguchi, M. C. (1999). Power and psychological well-being in late adolescent relationships. *Sex Roles*, *40*, 689–710.

Gangestad, S. W., & Simpson, J. A. (2000). The evolution of human mating: Trade-offs and strategic pluralism. *Behavioral and Brain Sciences*, *23*, 573–644.

Gao, G. (2001). Intimacy, passion, and commitment in Chinese and US American romantic relationships. *International Journal of Intercultural Relations*, *25*, 329–342.

Garcia, L. T., & Markey, C. (2007). Matching in sexual experience for married, cohabiting, and dating couples. *The Journal of Sex Research*, *44*, 250–255.

Garcia-Moreno, C., & Watts, C. (2000). Violence against women: Its importance for HIV/AIDS. *AIDS*, *14* (Supplement 3): S235–265.

Garnets, L., Herek, G. M., & Levy, B. (1990). Violence and victimization of lesbians and gay men: Mental health consequences. *Journal of Interpersonal Violence*, *5*(3), 366–383.

Gencoz, T., & Yuksel, M. (2006). Psychometric properties of the Turkish version of the Internalized Homophobia Scale. *Archives of Sexual Behavior*, *35*, 597–602.

George, W. H. & Norris, J. (1991). Alcohol, disinhibition, sexual arousal, and deviant sexual behavior. *Alcohol Health & Research World, 15*(2), 133–138.

George, W. H., Stoner, S. A., Norris, J., Lopez, P. A., & Lehman, G. I. (2000). Alcohol expectancies and sexuality: A self-fulfilling prophecy analysis of dyadic perceptions and behavior. *Journal of Studies on Alcohol*, *61*, 168–176.

*Gerrard, M., McCann, L., & Fortini, M. (1983). Prevention of unwanted pregnancy. *American Journal of Community Psychology, 11*, 153–167.

Getz, C., & Kirkley, E. (2006). Shaking up the status quo: Challenging intolerance of the lesbian, gay and bisexual community at a private Roman Catholic university. *College Student Journal, 40*(4), 857–869.

Giacopassi, D. J. & Dull, R. T. (1986). Gender and racial differences in the acceptance of rape myths within a college population. *Sex Roles, 15*(1–2), 63–75.

Gidycz, C. A., Coble, C. N., Latham, L., & Layman, M. J. (1993). Sexual assault experience in adulthood and prior victimization experiences: A prospective analysis. *Psychology of Women Quarterly, 17*, 151–168.

Gidycz, C. A., Hanson, K., & Layman, M. J. (1995). A prospective analysis of the relationships among sexual assault experiences. *Psychology of Women Quarterly, 19*, 5–29.

Gidycz, C. A., Loh, C., Lobo, T., Rich, C., & Lynn, S. J. (2007). Reciprocal relationships among alcohol use, risk perception, and sexual victimization: A prospective analysis. *Journal of American College Health, 56*, 5–14.

Gidycz, C. A., Lynn, S. J., Rich, C. L., Marioni, N. L., Loh, C., Marmelstein, L., Stafford, J., & Fite, R. (2001). The evaluation of a sexual assault risk reduction program: A multisite investigation. *Journal of Consulting and Clinical Psychology, 69*, 1073–1078.

Gidycz, C. A., McNamera, J. R., & Edwards, K. M. (2006). Women's risk perception and sexual victimization: A review of the literature. *Aggression and Violent Behavior: A Review Journal, 11*, 441–456.

Gidycz, C. A., Orchowski, L. M., & Edwards, K. M. (in press). Sexual violence: Primary prevention. In J. White, M. Koss, & A. Kazdin (Eds.), *Violence against women and children: Consensus, critical analysis, and emergent priorities*. Washington, DC: American Psychological Association.

Gidycz, C. A., Rich, C. L., Orchowski, L., King, C., & Miller, A. (2006). The evaluation of a sexual assault self-defense and risk-reduction program for college women: A prospective study. *Psychology of Women Quarterly, 30*, 173–186.

Gidycz, C. A., VanWynsbergh, A., & Edwards, K. M. (2008). Prediction of women's utilization of resistance strategies in a sexual assault situation: A prospective study. *Journal of Interpersonal Violence, 23*, 571–588.

Gifford, R. (2010). In China, looking for Mr. Right (enough). Retrieved from http://www.npr.org/templates/story/story.php?story Id=130833495&sc=emaf

Gilligan, C. (1979). Woman's place in man's life cycle. *Harvard Educational Review, 49*, 431–446.

Glass, S. P., & Wright, T. L. (1992). Justifications for extramarital relationships: The associations between attitudes, behaviors, and gender. *The Journal of Sex Research, 29*, 361–387.

Glenn, N., & Marquardt, E. (2001). *Hooking up, hanging out, and hoping for Mr. Right: College women on dating and mating today*. New York, NY: Institute for American Values.

Glenn, N. D., & Weaver, C. N. (1979). Attitudes toward premarital, extramarital, and homosexual relations in the U.S. in the 1970s. *The Journal of Sex Research, 15*, 108–118. doi:10.1080/00224497909551029

Gold, R. S. (2000). AIDS education for gay men: Towards a more cognitive approach. *AIDS Care, 12*, 267–272.

Gold, S. D., Dickstein, B. D., Marx, B P., & Lexington, J. M. (2009). Psychological outcomes among lesbian sexual assault survivors: An examination of the roles of internalized homophobia and experiential avoidance. *Psychology of Women Quarterly, 33*, 54–66.

Gold, S. D., Marx, B. P., & Lexington, J. M. (2007). Gay male sexual assault survivors: The relations among internalized homophobia, experiential avoidance, and psychological symptom severity. *Behaviour Research and Therapy, 45*, 549–562.

Gold, S. R. & Clegg, C. L. (1990). Sexual fantasies of college students with coercive experiences and coercive attitudes. *Journal of Interpersonal Violence, 5*, 464–473.

Golding, J. M., Siegel, J. M., Sorenson, S. B., Burnam, M. A., & Stein, J. A. (1989). Social support following sexual assault. *Journal of Community Psychology, 17*, 92–107.

Goldscheider, F., & Goldscheider, C. (1999). *The changing transition to adulthood: Leaving and returning home*. Thousand Oaks, CA: Sage.

Gomez, C., & Marin, B. (1996). Gender, culture, and power: Barriers to HIV-prevention strategies for women. *The Journal of Sex Research, 33*, 355–362.

Goodchilds, J. D., & Zellman, G. L. (1984). Sexual signalling and sexual aggression in adolescent relationships. In N. M. Malamuth & E. Donnerstein (Eds.), *Pornography and sexual aggression* (pp. 233–243). San Diego: Academic Press.

Goodman, M. B., & Moradi, B. (2008). Attitudes and behaviors toward lesbian and gay persons: Critical correlates and mediated relations. *Journal of Counseling Psychology, 55*, 371–384.

Goodwin, R. (1994). Putting relationship aggression in its place. In J. Archer (Ed.), *Male violence*. London, England: Routledge.

Gordon, M. (1978). *The American family: Past, present, and future*. New York, NY: Random House.

Gore, S., Aseltine, R., Colton, M. E., & Lin, B. (1997). Life after high school: Development stress and well-being. In I. H. Gotlib & B. Wheaton (Eds.), *Stress and adversity over the life course* (pp. 197–214). New York, NY: Cambridge University Press.

Gould, J. L., & Gould, C. G. (1997). *Sexual selection: Mate choice and courtship in nature*. New York, NY: Freeman/Scientific American.

Gowen, L. K., Feldman, S. S., Diaz, R., & Yisrael, D. S. (2004). A comparison of the sexual behaviors and attitudes of adolescent girls with older vs. similar-aged boyfriends. *Journal of Youth and Adolescence, 33*(2), 167–175.

*Gracia Jones, S., Patsdaughter, C. A., Jorda, M. L., Hamilton, M., & Malow, R. (2008). SENORITAS: An HIV/sexually transmitted infection prevention project for Latina college students at a Hispanic-serving university. *Journal of the Association of Nurses in AIDS Care, 19*, 311–319.

Green, A. I. (2003). "Chem friendly": The institutional basis of "club drug" use in a sample of urban gay men. *Deviant Behavior, 24*, 427–447.

Greenberg, B. S., & Busselle, R. (1996). Soap operas and sexual activity: A decade later. *Journal of Communication, 46*, 153–160.

Greenberg, B. S., Sherry, J. L., Busselle, R. W., Rampoldi-Hnilo, L., & Smith, S. W. (1997). Daytime television talk shows: Guests, content, and interactions. *Journal of Broadcasting and Electronic Media, 41*, 412–426.

Greenberg, B. S., & Woods, M. G. (1999). The soaps: Their sex, gratification, and outcomes. *The Journal of Sex Research, 36*, 250–257.

Greenberg, J. S., Bruess, C. E., & Conklin, S. C. (2011). *Exploring the dimensions of human sexuality* (4th ed.). Boston, MA: Jones and Bartlett.

Greer, G. (1999). *The whole woman*. New York, NY: Knopf.

Gregersen, E. (1986). Human sexuality in cross-cultural perspective. In Byrne, D., & Kelly, K. (eds.), *Alternative approaches to the study of sexual behavior* (pp. 87–102) Hillsdale, NJ: Erlbaum.

Grello, C. M., Welsh, D. P., & Harper, M. S. (2006). No strings attached: The nature of casual sex among college students. *The Journal of Sex Research*, *43*, 255–267.

Groothof, H. A. K., Djkstra, P., & Barelds, D. P. H. (2009). Sex differences in jealousy: The case of Internet infidelity. *Journal of Social and Personal Relationships*, *26*(8), 1119–1129.

Gross, A. M., Bennett, T., Sloan, L., Marx, B. P., & Juergens, J. (2001). The impact of alcohol and alcohol expectancies on male perception of female sexual arousal in a date rape analog. *Experimental and Clinical Psychopharmacology*, *9*(4), 380–388.

Grossman, L. (2005, January 24). Grow up? Not so fast. *Time*, *165*, 42–54.

Grov, C., Bimbi, D. S., Nanín, J. E., & Parsons, J. T. (2006). Race, ethnicity, gender, and generational factors associated with the coming-out process among gay, lesbian, and bisexual individuals. *The Journal of Sex Research*, *43*(2), 115–121.

Gruber, J. E., & Fineran, S. (2008). Comparing the impact of bullying and sexual harassment on the mental and physical health of adolescents. *Sex Roles*, *59*, 1–13.

Gruendel, J., & Aber, J. L. (2007). Bridging the gap between research and child policy change: The role of strategic communications in policy advocacy. In J. L. Aber et al. (Eds.), *Bridging the gap between research and child policy change: The role of strategic communications in policy advocacy* (pp. 43–58). Washington, DC: American Psychological Association.

Gunderson, P. R., & Ferrari, J. R. (2008). Forgiveness of sexual cheating in romantic relationships: Effects of discovery method, frequency of offense and presence of apology. *North American Journal of Psychology*, *10*(1), 1–14.

Gupta, S. R. (1999). *Emerging voices: South Asian American women redefine self, family, and community*. Walnut Creek, CA: AltaMira Press.

Guth, L. J., Lopez, D. F., Rojas, J., Clements, K. D., & Tyler, J. M. (2004). Experiential versus rational training: A comparison of student attitudes toward homosexuality. *Journal of Homosexuality*, *48*, 83–102.

Guttentag, M., & Secord, P. F. (1983). *Too many women? The sex ratio question*. Beverly Hills, CA: Sage.

Hall, G. C. N. (1996). *Theory-based assessment, treatment, and prevention of sexual aggression*. New York, NY: Oxford University Press.

Hall, G. C. N., & Barongan, C. (1997). Prevention of sexual aggression: Sociocultural risk and protective factors. *American Psychologist*, *52*, 5–14.

Hall, G. S. (1904). *Adolescence: Its psychology and its relation to physiology, anthropology, sociology, sex, crime, religion, and education (Vols. I & II)*. Englewood Cliffs, NJ: Prentice-Hall.

Hall, J. H., & Fincham F. D. (2009). Psychological distress: Precursor or consequence of dating infidelity? *Personality and Social Psychology Bulletin*, *35*(2), 143–159.

Halperin, S. (Ed.). (1998). *The forgotten half revisited: American youth and young families, 1988–2008*. Washington, DC: American Youth Policy Forum.

Hamer, D. H., & Copeland, P. (1994). *The science of desire: The search for the gay gene and the biology of behavior*. New York, NY: Simon & Schuster.

Hamilton, J. A. (1989). Emotional consequences of victimization and discrimination in "special populations" of women. *Psychiatric Clinics of North America*, *12*, 35–51.

Hamilton, L. (2007). Trading on heterosexuality: College women's gender strategies and homophobia. *Gender & Society*, *21*(2), 145–172.

Hammack, P. L. (2005). The life course development of human sexual orientation: An integrative paradigm. *Human Development*, *48*, 267–290.

Hamon, R. R., & Ingoldsby, B. B. (Eds.). (2003). *Mate selection across cultures*. Thousand Oaks, CA: Sage.

Hannon, R., Hall, D. S. Kuntz, T., Van Laar, S., & Williams, J. (1995). Dating characteristics leading to unwanted vs. wanted sexual behavior. *Sex Roles*, *33*(11/12), 767–783.

Hansen, G. L. (1987). Extradyadic relations during courtship. *The Journal of Sex Research*, *23*, 382–390.

Hanson, K. A., & Gidycz, C. A. (1993). Evaluation of a sexual assault prevention program. *Journal of Consulting and Clinical Psychology*, *61*, 1046–1052.

Hanson, R. K., & Bussiere, M. T. (1998). Predicting relapse: A meta-analysis of sexual offender recidivism studies. *Journal of Consulting and Clinical Psychology*, *66*(2), 348–362.

Harding, D. J., & Jencks, C. (2003). Changing attitudes toward premarital sex. *Public Opinion Quarterly*, *67*, 211–226.

Hare, R. D. (1991). *The Hare Psychopathy Checklist-Revised*. Toronto, Canada: Multi-Health Systems.

Hareven, T. K. (Ed.). (1977). *Family and kin in American urban communities, 1700–1930*. New York, NY: Franklin Watts.

Harper, G. (2007). Sex isn't simple: Culture and context in HIV prevention interventions for gay and bisexual male adolescents. *American Psychologist*, *62*, 806–819.

Harper, G. W., Bangi, A. K., Contreras, R., Pedraza, A., Tolliver, M., & Vess, L. (2004). Diverse phases of collaboration: Working together to improve community-based HIV interventions for youth. *American Journal of Community Psychology*, *33*(3/4), 193–204.

Harper, S. R., & Gasman, M. (2008). Consequences of conservatism: Black male undergraduates and the politics of historically black colleges and universities. *Journal of Negro Education*, *77*(4): 336–351.

Harpur, T. J., & Hare, R. D. (1994). Assessment of psychopathy as a function of age. *Journal of Abnormal Psychology*, *103*(4), 604–609.

Harrell, J., & Wright, L. W., Jr. (1998). Development of a multicomponent scale assessing AIDS-phobia. *Journal of Psychopathology and Behavioral Assessment*, *20*, 201–216.

Harris v. Forklift Systems, 510 U.S. 17 (1993).

Harris, C. R. (2002). Sexual and romantic jealousy in heterosexual and homosexual adults. *Psychological Science*, *13*, 7–12.

Harris, C. R. (2003). A review of sex differences in jealousy, including self-report data, psychophysiological responses, interpersonal violence, and morbid jealousy. *Personality and Social Psychology Review*, *7*, 102–128.

Harris, K. M., Halpern, C. T., Whitsel, E., Hussey, J., Tabor, J., Entzel, P., & Udry, J. R. (2009). The National Longitudinal Study of Adolescent Health: Research design. Retrieved from http://www.cpc.unc.edu/projects/addhealth/design

Hart, T., Peterson, J. L., & the Community Intervention Trial for Youth Study Team (2004). Predictors of risky sexual behavior among young African-American men who have sex with men. *American Journal of Public Health*, *94*(7), 1122–1123.

Hartmann, U., & Waldinger, M. D. (2007). Treatment of delayed ejaculation. In S. R. Leiblum (Ed)., *Principles and practice of sex therapy* (4th ed., pp. 241–276). New York, NY: Guilford.

Hartrup, W. W., & Stevens, N. (1999). Friendships and adaptation across the life span. *Current Issues in Psychological Science*, *8*, 76–79.

Haselton, M., & Buss, D. (2000). Error management theory: A new perspective on biases in cross-sex mind reading. *Journal of Personality and Social Psychology*, *78*, 81–91.

Hastings Christian Fellowship v. Martinez et al., 561 U.S. 08-1371 (2010). Retrieved from http://www.supremecourt.gov/opinions/09pdf/08–1371.pdf

Hatano, Y. (1991). Changes in sexual activities of Japanese youth. *Journal of Sex Education and Therapy*, *17*, 1–14.

Hatfield, E., & Rapson, R. L. (2005). *Love and sex: Cross-cultural perspectives*. Lanham, MD: University Press of America.

Hatfield, E., & Rapson, R. L. (2006). Passionate love, sexual desire, and mate selection: Cross-cultural and historical perspectives. In P. Noller & J. A. Feeney (Eds.), *Close relationships: Function, forms, and processes* (pp. 227–243). Hove, England: Psychology Press.

Hatfield, E., & Sprecher, S. (1995). Men's and women's preferences in marital partners in the United States, Russia, and Japan. *Journal of Cross-Cultural Psychology*, *26*, 728–750.

Haugaard, J. J., & Seri, L. G. (2003). Stalking and other forms of intrusive contact after the dissolution of adolescent dating or romantic relationships. *Violence and Victims*, *18*, 279–297.

Hawton, K., & Catalan, J. (1990). Sex therapy for vaginismus: Characteristics of couples and treatment outcome. *Sexual and Marital Therapy*, *5*(1), 39–48.

Hays, R. B., Kegeles, S. M., & Coates, T. J. (1997). Unprotected sex and HIV risk-taking among young gay men within boyfriend relationships. *AIDS Education and Prevention*, *9*, 314–329.

Hazan, C., & Shaver, P. (1987). Romantic love conceptualized as an attachment process. *Journal of Personality and Social Psychology*, *52*, 511–524.

Heidenry, J. (1997). *What wild ecstasy: The rise and fall of the sexual revolution*. New York, NY: Simon & Schuster.

Heidt, J. M., Marx, B. P., & Gold, S. D. (2005). Sexual revictimization among sexual minorities: A preliminary study. *Journal of Traumatic Stress*, *18*, 533–540.

Heiman, J. & LoPiccolo, J. (1988). *Becoming orgasmic: A sexual and personal growth program for women*. New York, NY: Prentice Hall.

Heise, L., Ellsberg, M., & Gottemoeller, M. (1999). Violence against women. *Population Reports*, *27*, 1–43.

Hekma, G. (1998). "As long as they don't make an issue of it . . .": Gay men and lesbians in organized sports in the Netherlands. *Journal of Homosexuality*, *35*, 1–23.

Helderman, R. S. (2010, March 6). Virginia attorney general to colleges: End gay protections. *Washington Post*. Retrieved from http://www.washingtonpost.com/wp-dyn/content/article/2010/03/05/AR2010030501582.html

Hendrick, C., & Hendrick, S. S. (1986). A theory and method of love. *Journal of Personality and Social Psychology*, *50*, 392–402.

Hendrick, C., & Hendrick, S. S. (1988). Lovers wear rose colored glasses. *Journal of Social and Personal Relationships*, *5*, 161–183.

Hendrick, C., & Hendrick, S. (1990). A relationship-specific version of the Love Attitudes Scale. *Journal of Social Behavior and Personality*, *5*, 239–254.

Hendrick, C., & Hendrick, S. S. (2006). Styles of romantic love. In R. J. Sternberg & K. Weis (Eds.), *The new psychology of love* (pp. 149–170). New Haven, CT: Yale University Press.

Hendrick, C., Hendrick, S. S., & Dicke, A. (1998). The Love Attitudes Scale: Short form. *Journal of Social and Personal Relationships*, *15*, 147–159.

Hendrick, C., Hendrick, S. S., Foote, F. H., & Slapion-Foote, M. J. (1984). Do men and women love differently? *Journal of Social and Personal Relationships*, *1*, 177–195.

Hendrick, S. S., & Hendrick, C. (1987). Multidimensionality of sexual attitudes. *The Journal of Sex Research*, *23*, 502–526. doi:10.1080/00224498709551387

Hendrick, S. S., & Hendrick, C. (1995). Gender differences and similarities in sex and love. *Personal Relationships*, *2*, 55–65.

Hendrick, S. S., & Hendrick, C. (2002). Linking romantic love with sex: Development of the Perceptions of Love and Sex Scale. *Journal of Social and Personal Relationships*, *19*, 361–378.

Hendrick, S. S., Hendrick, C., & Adler, N. L. (1988). Romantic relationships: Love, satisfaction, and staying together. *Journal of Personality and Social Psychology*, *54*, 980–988.

Hendry, J. (1995). *Understanding Japanese society*. London, England: Routledge.

Henig, R. M. (2010, August 18). What is it about 20-somethings?: Why are so many people in their 20s taking so long to grow up? *New York Times*.

Henline, B. H., Lamke, L. K. & Howard, M. D. (2007). Exploring perceptions of online infidelity. *Personal Relationships*, *14*, 113–128.

Henning-Stout, M., James, S., & Macintosh, S. (2000). Reducing harassment of lesbian, gay, bisexual, transgender, and questioning youth in schools. *School Psychology Review*, *29*, 180–191.

Herbenick, D., Reece, M., Schick, V., Sanders, S. A., Dodge, B., & Fortenberry, J. D. (2010). Sexual behavior in the United States: Results from a national probability sample of men and women ages 14–94. *The Journal of Sexual Medicine*, *7*, 255–265. doi: 10.1111/j.1743-6109.2010.02012.x

Herdt, G. H., & McClintock, M. (2000). The magical age of 10. *Archives of Sexual Behavior*, *29*, 587–606.

Herek, G. M. (1988). Heterosexuals' attitudes toward lesbians and gay men: Correlates and gender differences. *The Journal of Sex Research*, *25*, 451–477.

Herek, G. M. (1989). Hate crimes against lesbian and gay men: Correlates and gender differences. *American Psychologist*, *44*, 948–955.

Herek, G. M. (1991). Stigma, prejudice, and violence against lesbians and gay men. In J. C. Gonsiorek & J. D. Weinrich (Eds.), *Homosexuality: Research, implications for public policy* (pp. 60–80). Newbury Park, CA: Sage.

Herek, G. M. (2002). Heterosexuals' attitudes toward bisexual men and women in the United States. *The Journal of Sex Research*, *39*(4), 264–274.

Herek, G. M. (2004). Beyond "homophobia": Thinking about sexual prejudice and stigma in the twenty-first century. *Sexuality Research and Social Policy*, *1*, 6–24.

Herek, G. M. (2009). Hate crimes and stigma-related experiences among sexual minority adults in the United States: Prevalence estimates from a national probability sample. *Journal of Interpersonal Violence*, *24*, 54–74.

Herek, G. M., & Capitanio, J. P. (1995). Black heterosexuals' attitudes toward lesbians and gay men in the United States. *The Journal of Sex Research*, *32*, 95–105.

Herek, G. M., Chopp, R., & Strohl, D. (2007). Sexual stigma: Putting sexual minority health issues in context. In I. H. Meyer & M. E. Northridge (Eds.), *The health of sexual minorities: Public health perspectives on lesbian, gay, bisexual and transgender populations* (pp. 171–208). New York, NY: Springer.

Herek, G. M., & Gonzalez-Rivera, M. (2006). Attitudes toward homosexuality among U.S. residents of Mexican descent. *The Journal of Sex Research*, *43*, 122–135.

Herold, E. S., Mantle, D., & Zemitis, O. (1979). A study of sexual offenses against females. *Adolescence*, *14*, 65–72.

Hersh, K. & Gray-Little, B. (1998). Psychopathic traits and attitudes associated with self-reported sexual aggression in college men. *Journal of Interpersonal Violence*, 13, 456–471.

Hickman, S. E., & Muehlenhard, C. L. (1997). College women's fears and precautionary behaviors relating to acquaintance rape and stranger rape. *Psychology of Women Quarterly*, *21*, 527–547.

Hicks, T. V., & Leitenberg, H. (2001). Sexual fantasies about one's partner versus someone else: Gender differences in incidence and frequency. *The Journal of Sex Research*, *38*(1), 43–50.

Hickson, F. C. I., Davies, P. M., Hunt, A. J., & Weatherburn, P. (1994). Gay men as victims of nonconsensual sex. *Archives of Sexual Behavior*, 23(3), 281–294.

Hill, C., & Silva, E. (2005). *Drawing the line: Sexual harassment on campus*. Washington, DC: American Association of University Women Educational Foundation.

Hill, R. (1945). Campus values in mate-selection. *Journal of Home Economics*, *37*, 554–558.

Hillier, L., & Harrison, L. (2007). Building realities less limited than their own: Young people practising same-sex attraction on the internet. *Sexualities*, *10*, 82–100.

Hindmarch, I., ElSohly, M., Gambles, J., & Salamone, S. (2001). Forensic urinalysis of drug use in cases of alleged sexual assault. *Journal of Clinical Forensic Medicine*, *8*, 197–205.

Hinrichs, D. W., & Rosenberg, P. J. (2002). Attitudes toward gay, lesbian, and bisexual persons among heterosexual liberal arts college students. *Journal of Homosexuality*, *43*(1), 61–84.

Holzman, C. G. (1996). Counseling adult women rape survivors: Issues of race, ethnicity, and class. *Women & Therapy*, *19*(2), 47–62.

Homans, G. C. (1950). *The human group*. New York, NY: Harcourt, Brace, & World.

Homans, G. C. (1961). *Social behavior: Its elementary forms*. New York, NY: Harcourt, Brace, & World.

Hornblower, M. (1997, June 9). Great xpectations. *Time*, *129*, 58–68.

Hou, S. I. (2009). HIV-related behaviors among black students attending historically black colleges and universities (HBCU) versus white students attending a traditionally white institution (TWI). *AIDS Care*, *21*(8), 1050–1057.

Hoyle, R. H., Fejfar, M. C., & Miller, J. D. (2000). Personality and sexual risk taking: A quantitative review. *Journal of Personality*, *68*(6), 1203–1231.

Hoyt, L. L., & Hudson, J. W. (1981). Personal characteristics important in mate preference among college students. *Social Behavior and Personality*, *9*, 93–96. doi:10.2224/sbp.1981.9.1.93

Hsu, F. L. K. (1985). The self in cross-cultural perspective. In A. J. Marsella, G. DeVos, & F. L. K. Hsu (Eds.), *Culture and the self: Asian and Western perspectives* (pp. 24–55). London, England: Tavistock.

Huang, K., & Uba, L. (1992). Premarital sexual behavior among Chinese college students in the United States. *Archives of Sexual Behavior*, *21*, 227–240.

Hudson, J. W., & Henze, L. F. (1969). Campus values in mate selection: A replication. *Journal of Marriage & the Family*, *31*, 772–775.

Hudson, L., Aquillino, S., & Kienzi, G. (2005). *Postsecondary participation rates by sex and race/ethnicity: 1974 – 2003* (NCES 2005-028). U.S. Department of Education. Washington, DC: National Center for Education Statistics.

Huerta, M., Cortina, L. M., Pang, J. S., Torges, C. M., & Magley, V. J. (2006). Sex and power in the academy: Modeling sexual harassment in the lives of college women. *Personality and Social Psychology Bulletin*, *32*, 616–628.

Hugelshofer, D. S. (2006). *The effectiveness of lesbian, gay, and bisexual speaker panels in facilitating attitude and behavior change among heterosexual university students.* Unpublished doctoral dissertation, Washington State University, Pullman.

Hughes, M., Morrison, K., & Asada, K. J. K. (2005). What's love got to do with it? Exploring the impact of maintenance rules, love attitudes, and network support on friends with benefits relationships. *Western Journal of Communication, 69*, 49–66.

Hughes, T. L., Johnson, T., & Wilsnack, S. C. (2001). Sexual assault and alcohol abuse: A comparison of lesbians and heterosexual women. *Journal of Substance Abuse, 13*, 515–532.

Humphrey, J. A., & White, J. W. (2000). "Women's vulnerability to sexual assault from adolescence to young adulthood." *Journal of Adolescent Health, 27*, 419–424.

Humphreys, T., & Newby, J. (2007). Initiating new sexual behaviours in heterosexual relationships. *Canadian Journal of Human Sexuality, 16*, 77–88.

Hyde, J. S., & DeLamater, J. D. (1997). *Understanding human sexuality* (6th ed.). New York, NY: McGraw-Hill.

Impett, E. A., & Peplau, L. A. (2003). Sexual compliance: Gender, motivational, and relationship perspectives. *The Journal of Sex Research, 40*, 87–100.

*Ingersoll, K. S., Ceperich, S. D., Nettleman, M. D., Karanda, K., Brocksen, S., & Johnson, B. A. (2005). Reducing alcohol-exposed pregnancy risk in college women: Initial outcomes of a clinical trial of a motivational intervention. *Journal of Substance Abuse and Treatment, 29*, 173–180.

Ingoldsby, B. B., & Smith, S. (1995). *Families in multicultural perspective.* New York, NY: Guilford.

Inman, A. G., Ladany, N., Constantine, M. G., & Morano, C. K. (2001). Development and preliminary validation of the cultural values conflict scale for South Asian women. *Journal of Counseling Psychology, 48*, 17–27.

Istvan, J., & Griffitt, W. (1980). Effects of sexual experience on dating desirability and marriage desirability: An experimental study. *Journal of Marriage and the Family, 42*, 377–385. doi:10.2307/351235

Jakubowski, S. F., Milne, E. P., Brunner, H., & Miller, B. (2004). A review of empirically supported marital enrichment programs. *Family Relations, 53*, 528–536.

James, W. (1950). *The principles of psychology.* New York, NY: Dover. (Original work published 1890)

Janssen, E. (2002). Psychophysiological measurement of sexual arousal. In M. W. Wiederman & B. E. Whitley Jr. (Eds.), *Handbook for conducting research on human sexuality* (pp. 139–171). Mahwah, NJ: Erlbaum.

Japanese Association for Sex Education (JASE). (2006). Modern sex education research Monthly, *24* (10). Retrieved from http://www.jase.or.jp/. Cited in Farrer, J., Tsuchiya, H., & Bagrowicz, B. (2008). Emotional expression in *tsukiau* dating relationships in Japan. *Journal of Social and Personal Relationships, 25*, 169–188.

Jason, L. A., Reichler, A., Easton, J., Neal, A., & Wilson, M. (1984). Female harassment after ending a relationship: A preliminary study. *Alternative Lifestyles, 6*, 259–269.

*Jaworski, B. C. & Carey, M. P. (2001). Effects of a brief, theory-based STD-prevention program for female college students. *Journal of Adolescent Health, 29*, 417–425.

Jenkins, M., Lambert, E. G., & Baker, D. N. (2009). The attitudes of black and white college students toward gays and lesbians. *Journal of Black Studies, 39*(4), 589–613.

Jessor, R. (1991). Risk behavior in adolescence: A psychosocial framework for understanding and action. *Journal of Adolescent Health, 12*(8), 597–605.

Jessor, R., Donovan, J. E., & Costa, F. M. (1991). *Beyond adolescence: Problem behavior and young adult development*. New York, NY: Cambridge University Press.

Jimenez, J. A., & Abreu, J. M. (2003). Race and sex effects on attitudinal perceptions of acquaintance rape. *Journal of Counseling Psychology, 50*, 252–256.

Johnson, I. M., & Sigler, R. T. (1996). Forced sexual intercourse on campus: Crime or offensive behavior? *Journal of Contemporary Criminal Justice, 12*, 54–68.

Johnson, J. D., Noel, N. E., & Sutter-Hernandez, J. (2000). Alcohol and male acceptance of sexual aggression: The role of perceptual ambiguity. *Journal of Applied Social Psychology, 30*(6), 1186–1200.

Johnston, L. D., O'Malley, P. M., Bachman, J. G., & Schulenberg, J. E. (2004). *Monitoring the future national survey results on drug use, 1975–2003: Volume II: College students and adults ages 19–45* (NIH Publication No. 04-5508). Bethesda, MD: National Institute on Drug Abuse.

Jonason, P. K., Li, N. P., & Cason, M. J. (2009). The "booty call": A compromise between men's and women's ideal mating strategies. *The Journal of Sex Research, 46*, 460–470.

Juhascik, M. P., Negrusz, A., Faugno, D., Ledray, L., Greene, P., Lindner, A., . . . Gennsslen, R. E. (2007). An estimate of the proportion of drug-facilitation of sexual assault in four U.S. localities. *Journal of Forensic Science, 52*(6), 1396–1400.

Jurgens, J. C., Schwitzer, A. M., & Middleton, T. (2004). Examining attitudes toward college students with minority sexual orientations: Findings and suggestions. *Journal of College Student Psychotherapy, 19*(1): 57–75.

Kaestle, C. E., & Halpern, C. T. (2007). What's love got to do with it? Sexual behaviors of opposite-sex couples through emerging adulthood. *Perspectives on Sexual and Reproductive Health, 39*, 134–140.

Kalichman, S. C., Benotsch, E., Rompa, D., Gore-Felton, C., Austin, J., Webster, L., . . . Simpson, D.. (2001). Unwanted sexual experiences and sexual risk in gay and bisexual men: Associations among revictimization, substance use, and psychiatric symptoms. *The Journal of Sex Research, 38*(1), 1–9.

Kalichman, S. C., Cain, D., Zweben A., & Geoff, S. (2003). Sensation seeking, alcohol use and sexual risk behaviors among men receiving services at a clinic for sexually transmitted infections. *Quarterly Journal of Studies on Alcohol, 64*(4), 564–569.

Kalichman, S. C., & Rompa, D. (1995). Sexually coerced and noncoerced gay and bisexual men: Factors relevant to risk for human immunodeficiency virus (HIV) infection. *The Journal of Sex Research, 32*, 45–50.

Kalof, L., & Cargill, T. (1991). Fraternity and sorority membership and gender dominance attitudes. *Sex Roles, 25*(7–8), 417–423.

Kalof, L., Eby, K. K., Matheson, J. L., & Kroska, R. J. (2001). The influence of race and gender on student self-reports of sexual harassment by college professors. *Gender and Society, 15*, 282–302.

Kamen, P. (2000). *Her way: Young women remake the sexual revolution*. New York, NY: New York University Press.

Kamerman, S. B. (1996). Child and family policies: An international perspective. In E. F. Zigler, S. L. Kagan, & N. W. Hall (Eds.), *Children, families, and government: Preparing for the twenty-first century* (pp. 31–48). New York, NY: Cambridge University Press.

Kanin, E. J. (1983). Rape as a function of relative sexual frustration. *Psychological Reports, 52*, 133–134.

Kanin, E. J. (1985). Date rapists: Differential sexual socialization and relative deprivation. *Archives of Sexual Behavior, 14*, 219–231.

Kaplan, H. S. (1974). *The new sex therapy*. New York, NY: Brunner/Mazel.

Katz, J., Kuffel, S. W., & Brown, F. A. (2006). Leaving a sexually coercive dating partner: A prospective application of the investment model. *Psychology of Women Quarterly*, *30*, 267–275.

Kauth, M. R. (2000). *True nature: A theory of sexual attraction*. New York, NY: Kluwer Academic/Plenum.

Kauth, M. R. (2005). Revealing assumptions: Explicating sexual orientation and promoting conceptual integrity. *Journal of Bisexuality*, *5*(4), 79–105.

Kauth, M. R. (2006). Epilogue: Implications for conceptualizing human sexuality. *Journal of Psychology & Human Sexuality*, *18*(4), 371–385.

Kearns, M. E., Edwards, K. M., Calhoun, K. S., & Gidycz, C. A (2010). Disclosure of sexual victimization: The effects of Pennebaker's emotional disclosure paradigm on physical and psychological distress. *Journal of Trauma and Dissociation*, *11*, 193–209.

Kegeles, S. M., Hays, R. B., & Coates, T. J. (1996). The Mpowerment Project: A Community-Level HIV Prevention Intervention for Young Gay Men. *American Journal of Public Health*, *86*(8), 1129–1136.

Kelley, M. L., & Parsons, B. (2000). Sexual harassment in the 1990s: A university-wide survey of female faculty, administrators, staff, and students. *The Journal of Higher Education*, *71*, 548–568.

Kelly, G. F. (2011). *Sexuality today* (10th ed.). New York: McGraw-Hill.

Kelly, J. A., & Kalichman, S. C. (1995). Increased attention to human sexuality can improve HIV-AIDS prevention efforts: Key research issues and directions. *Journal of Consulting and Clinical Psychology*, *63*(6), 907–918.

Kelly, J. A., & Kalichman, S. C. (2002). Behavioral research in HIV/AIDS primary and secondary prevention: Recent advances and future Directions. *Journal of Consulting and Clinical Psychology*, *70*(3), 626–639.

Kenrick, D. T., Maner, J. K., Butner, J., Li, N. P., Becker, D. V., & Schaller, M. (2002). Dynamical evolutionary psychology: Mapping the domains of the new interactionist paradigm. *Personality and Social Psychology Review*, *6*, 347–356.

Kenrick, D. T., Sundie, J. M., Nicastle, L. D., & Stone, G. O. (2001). Can one ever be too wealthy or too chaste? Searching for nonlinearities in mate judgement. *Journal of Personality and Social Psychology*, *80*, 462–471.

Kenyatta, J. (1953). *Facing Mount Kenya: The tribal life of the Gikuu*. London, England: Secher & Warburg.

Kephart, W. M. (1967). Some correlates of romantic love. *Journal of Marriage & the Family*, *29*, 470–474.

Kershaw, T. S., Niccolai, L. M., Ethier, K. A., Lewis, J. B., & Ickovics, J. R. (2003). Perceived susceptibility to pregnancy and sexually transmitted disease among pregnant and nonpregnant adolescents. *Journal of Community Psychology*, *31*(4). 419–434.

Kessler, R. C. (2000). Posttraumatic stress disorder: The burden to the individual and to society. *Journal of Clinical Psychiatry*, *61*[suppl. 5], 4–12.

*Kiene, S. M., & Barta, W. D. (2006). A brief individualized computer-delivered sexual risk reduction intervention increases HIV/AIDS preventive behavior. *Journal of Adolescent Health*, *39*(3), 404–410.

Kiernan, J. E., & Taylor, V. L. (1990). Coercive sexual behavior among Mexican-American college students. *Journal of Sex & Marital Therapy*, *16*(1), 44–50.

Kim, J. L., & Ward, L. M. (2007). Silence speaks volumes: Parental sexual communication among Asian American emerging adults. *Journal of Adolescent Research*, *22*, 3–31.

Kimble, M., Neacsiu, A. D., Flack, W. F., & Horner, J. (2008). Risk of unwanted sex for college women: Evidence for a red zone. *Journal of American College Health*, *57*, 331–337.

Kimmel, M. (2008). *Guyland: The perilous world where boys become men: Understanding the critical years between 16 and 26*. New York, NY: Harper.

Kinsey, A. C., Pomerory, W. B., & Martin, C. E. (1948). *Sexual behavior in the human male*. Philadelphia, PA: Saunders.

Kinsey, A. C., Pomerory, W. B., Martin, C. E., & Gebhard, P. H. (1953). *Sexual behavior in the human female*. Philadelphia, PA: Saunders.

Kinsman, S. B., Romer, D., Furstenberg, F. F., & Schwarz, D. F. (1998). Early sexual initiation: The role of peer norms. *Pediatrics*, *102*(5), 1185–1192.

Kisch, J., Leino, V., & Silverman, M. M. (2005). Aspects of suicidal behavior, depression, and treatment in college students: Results from the Spring 2000 National College Health Assessment Survey. *Suicide and Life-Threatening Behavior*, *35*(1), 3–13.

Kite, M. E., & Whitley, B. E., Jr. (1996). Sex differences in attitudes towards homosexual persons, behaviour, and civil rights: A meta-analysis. *Personality and Social Psychology Bulletin*, *22*, 336–353.

Kito, M. (2005). Self-disclosure in romantic relationships and friendships among American and Japanese college students. *Journal of Social Psychology*, *145*, 127–140.

Klassen, A. D., Williams, C. J., & Levitt, E. E. (1989). *Sex and mortality in the U.S.: An empirical enquiry under the auspices of the Kinsey Institute*. Middletown, CT: Wesleyan University Press.

Kleinke, C. L. (1978). *Self-perception: The psychology of personal awareness*. San Francisco, CA: Freedman.

Kleinplatz, P. J. (1996). The erotic encounter. *Journal of Humanistic Psychology*, *36*(3), 105–123.

Kleinplatz, P. J. (1998). Sex therapy for vaginismus: A review, critique and humanistic alternative. *Journal of Humanistic Psychology*, *38*(2), 51–81.

Kleinplatz, P. J. (2004). Beyond sexual mechanics and hydraulics: Humanizing the discourse surrounding erectile dysfunction. *Journal of Humanistic Psychology*, *44*(2), 215–242.

Kleinplatz, P. J., (2006). Sex therapy: How do sex therapists think about and deal with sexual problems? In R. D. McAnulty & M. M. Burnette (Eds.) *Sex and sexuality* (Vol 2, pp.179–211). Westport, CT: Praeger.

Kleinplatz, P. J. (2010a). "Desire disorders" or opportunities for optimal erotic intimacy. In S. R. Leiblum (Ed.), *Treating sexual desire disorders: A clinical casebook* (pp. 92–113). New York, NY: Guilford.

Kleinplatz, P. J. (2010b). Lessons from great lovers. In S. Levine, S. Althof, & C. Risen (Eds.), *Handbook of adult sexuality for mental health professionals* (2nd ed., pp. 57–72). New York, NY: Brunner-Routledge.

Kleinplatz, P. J. (2011). Arousal and desire problems: Conceptual, research and clinical considerations or the more things change the more they stay the same. *Sex and Relationship Therapy*, *26*(1), 1–13.

Kleinplatz, P. J., Ménard, A. D., Paquet, M.-P., Paradis, N., Campbell, M., Zuccarini, D., & Mehak, L. (2009). The components of optimal sexuality: A portrait of "great sex." *Canadian Journal of Human Sexuality*, *18*(1–2), 1–13.

Knox, D., Schacht, C., & Zusman, M. E. (1999). Love relationships among college students. *College Student Journal*, *33*, 149–151.

Knox, D., Zusman, M. E., Kaluzny, M., & Sturdivant, L. (2000). Attitudes and behavior of college students toward infidelity. *College Student Journal*, *34*, 162–164.

Koralewski, M. A., & Conger, J. C. (1992). The assessment of social skills among sexually coercive college males. *The Journal of Sex Research*, *29*(2), 169–188.

Koss, M. P. (1985). The hidden rape victim: Personality, attitudinal, and situational characteristics. *Psychology of Women Quarterly*, *9*, 193–212.

Koss, M. P. (1988). Hidden rape: Sexual aggression and victimization in a national sample of students in higher education. In A. W. Burgess (Ed.), *Rape and sexual assault* (pp. 3–25). New York, NY: Garland.

Koss, M. P. (1992). The underdetection of rape: Methodological choices influence incidence estimates. *Journal of Social Issues*, *48*, 61–75.

Koss, M. P., & Dinero, T. E. (1988). Predictors of sexual aggression among a national sample of male college students. *Annals of the New York Academy of Sciences*, *528*, 133–147.

Koss, M. P., & Dinero, T. E. (1989). Discriminant analysis of risk factors for sexual victimization among a national sample of college women. *Journal of Consulting & Clinical Psychology*, *57*, 242–250.

Koss, M. P., Dinero, T. E., Seibel, C. A., & Cox, S. L. (1988). Stranger and acquaintance rape. *Psychology of Women Quarterly*, *12*, 1–24.

Koss, M. P., Gidycz, C A., & Wisniewski, N. (1987). The scope of rape: Incidence and prevalence of sexual aggression and victimization in a national sample of higher education students. *Journal of Consulting and Clinical Psychology*, *55*, 162–170.

Koss, M. P., Leonard, K. E., Beezley, D. A., & Oros, C. J. (1985). Non stranger sexual aggression: A discriminant analysis of the psychological characteristics of undetected offenders. *Sex Roles*, *12*, 981–992.

Kosson, D. S., Kelly, J. C., & White, J. W. (1997). Psychopathy-related traits predict self-reported sexual aggression among college men. *Journal of Interpersonal Violence*, *12*(2), 241–254.

Koumans, E. H., Sternberg, M. R., Motamed, C., Kohl, K., Schillinger, J. A., & Markowitz, L. E. (2005). Sexually transmitted disease services at US colleges and universities. *Journal of American College Health*, *53*(5), 211–217.

Krahe, B., Scheinberger-Olwig, R., & Schutze, S. (2001). Risk factors of sexual aggression and victimization among homosexual men. *Journal of Applied Social Psychology*, *31*(7), 1385–1408.

Krahe, B., Schiitze, S., Fritsche, I., & Waizenhofer, E. (2000). The prevalence of sexual aggression and victimization among homosexual men. *The Journal of Sex Research*, *37*(2), 142–150.

Krane, V. (1996). Lesbians in sport: Toward acknowledgement, understanding, and theory. *Journal of Sport and Exercise Psychology*, *18*, 237–246.

Krane, V., & Barber, H. (2005). Identity tensions in lesbian intercollegiate coaches. *Research Quarterly in Exercise and Sport*, *76*(1), 67–81.

Krebs, C. P., Lindquist, C. H., Warner, T. D., Fisher, B. S., & Martin, S. L. (2007). *The campus sexual assault (CSA) study*. Washington, DC: U.S. National Institute of Justice.

Krebs, D. L. (2003). Fictions and facts about evolutionary approaches to human behavior: Comment on Lickliter and Honeycutt (2003). *Psychological Bulletin*, *129*, 842–847.

Ku, L., Sonestein, F. L., & Pleck, J. H. (1994). The dynamics of young men's condom use during and across relationships. *Family Planning Perspectives*, *26*, 246–251.

*Kyes, K. B. (1995). Using fear to encourage safer sex. *Journal of Psychology and Human Sexuality*, *7*(3), 21–73.

*LaBrie, J. W., Pedersen, E. R., Thompson, A. D., & Earleywine, M. (2008). A brief decisional balance intervention increases motivation and behavior regarding condom use in high-risk heterosexual college men. *Archives of Sexual Behavior*, *37*, 330–339.

Lacasse, A., & Mendelson, M. J. (2007). Sexual coercion among adolescents: Victims and perpetrators. *Journal of Interpersonal Violence*, *22*(4), 424–437.

Lacey, R. S., Reifman, A., Scott, J. P., Harris, S. M., & Fitzpatrick, J. (2004). Sexual-moral attitudes, love styles, and mate selection. *The Journal of Sex Research*, *41*, 121–128.

Lackey, C., & Williams, K. R. (1995). Social bonding and the cessation of partner violence across generations. *Journal of Marriage & the Family*, *57*(2), 295–305.

Lackie, L., & de Man, A. E. (1997). Correlates of sexual aggression among male university students. *Sex Roles*, *37*, 451–457.

LaGreca, A. M., & Harrison, H. M. (2005). Adolescent peer relations, friendships, and romantic relationships: Do they predict social anxiety and depression? *Journal of Clinical Child and Adolescent Psychology*, *34*, 49–61.

Lam, C., & Roman, B. (2009). When granny is the wolf: Understanding and approaching college-aged female victims of acquaintance rape. *Psychiatry*, *6*, 18–26.

Lamanna, M. A., & Reidman, A. (2008). *Marriages and families: Making choices in a diverse society* (8th ed.). Belmont, CA: Wadsworth.

*Lambert, E. C. (2001). College students' knowledge of human papillomavirus and effectiveness of a brief educational intervention. *Journal of the American Board of Family Practice*, *14*(3), 178–183.

Lambert, E. G., Ventura, L. A., Hall, D. E., & Cluse-Tolar, T. (2006). College students' views on gay and lesbian issues: Does education make a difference? *Journal of Homosexuality*, *50*(4), 1–30.

Lambert, T. A., Kahn, A. S., & Apple, K. J. (2003). Pluralistic ignorance and hooking up. *The Journal of Sex Research*, *40*, 129–133.

Lance, L. M. (2008). Social inequality on the college campus: A consideration of homosexuality. *College Student Journal*, *42*, 789–794.

Lang, A. R. (1985). The psychology of drinking and human sexuality. *Journal of Drug Issues*, *15*, 273–289.

Larson, R. (1990). The solitary side of life: An examination of the time people spend alone from childhood to old age. *Developmental Review*, *10*, 155–183.

LaSala, M. C. (2004a). Extradyadic sex and gay male couples: Comparing monogamous and nonmonogamous relationships. *Families in Society: The Journal of Contemporary Social Services*, *85*(3), 405–412.

LaSala, M. C. (2004b). Monogamy of the heart: Extradyadic sex and gay male couples. *Journal of Gay & Lesbian Social Services*, *17*(3), 1–24.

Laumann, E. O., Gagnon, J. H., Michael, R. T., & Michaels, S. (1994). *The social organization of sexuality: Sexual practices in the United States*. Chicago, IL: University of Chicago Press.

Lawrence, A. A. (2007). Transgender health concerns. In I. H. Meyer and M. E. Northridge (Eds.), *The health of sexual minorities: Public health perspectives on lesbian, gay, bisexual and transgender populations* (pp. 473–505). New York, NY: Springer.

Le, T. N. (2005). Narcissism and immature love as mediators of vertical individualism and ludic love style. *Journal of Social and Personal Relationships*, *22*, 543–560.

LeBeau, M., Andollo, W., Hearn, W. L. Baselt, R., Cone, E., Finkle, B., . . . Saady, J. (1999). Recommendations for toxicological investigations of drug-facilitated sexual assaults. *Journal of Forensic Science*, *44*, 227–230.

Lee, J., Pomeroy, E. C., Yoo, S. K., & Rheinboldt, K. T. (2005). Attitudes toward rape: A comparison between Asian and Caucasian college students. *Violence Against Women*, *11*, 177–196.

Lee, J. A. (1973). *Colours of love: An exploration of the ways of loving*. Toronto, Canada: New Press.

Lee, J. A. (1977). A typology of styles of loving. *Personality and Social Psychology Bulletin*, *3*, 173–182.

Lee, J. A. (1988). Love-styles. In R. J. Sternberg & M. L. Barnes (Eds.), *The psychology of love* (pp. 38–67). New Haven, CT: Yale University Press.

Lefkowitz, E. S., Gillen, M. M., Shearer, C. L., & Boone, T. L. (2004). Religiosity, sexual behaviors, and sexual attitudes during emerging adulthood. *The Journal of Sex Research*, *41*, 150–159. doi:10.1080/00224490409552223

Lefkowitz, E. S., Gillen, M. M., & Vasilenko, S. A. (2011). Putting the romance back into sex: Sexuality in romantic relationships. In F. D. Fincham & M. Cui (Eds.), *Romantic relationships in emerging adulthood* (pp. 213–233). New York, NY: Cambridge University Press.

Lefley, H. P., Scott, C. S., Llabre, M., & Hicks, D. (1993). Cultural beliefs about rape and victims' response in three ethnic groups. *American Journal of Orthopsychiatry*, *63*, 623–632.

Lehmiller, J. L., VanderDrift, L. E., & Kelly, J. R. (2011). Sex differences in approaching friends with benefits relationships. *The Journal of Sex Research*, *48*, 275–284

Leitz-Spitz, M. A. (2003). Stalking: Terrorism at our doors—how social workers can help victims fight back. *Social Work*, *48*, 504–512.

LeVay, S. (2010). *Gay, straight, and the reason why: The science of sexual orientation*. Oxford, England: Oxford University Press.

LeVay, S., & Valente, S. M. (2006). *Human sexuality* (2nd ed.). Sunderland, MA: Sinauer Associates.

Lever, J., Grov, C., Royce, T., & Gillespie, B. J. (2008). Searching for love in all the "write" places: Exploring Internet personals use by sexual orientation, gender, and age. *International Journal of Sexual Health*, *20*(4), 233–246.

Levine, A., & Cureton, A. (1998). *When hope and fear collide: A portrait of today's college student*. San Francisco, CA: Jossey-Bass.

Levine, J. (2002). *Harmful to minors: The perils of protecting children from sex*. Minneapolis, MN: University of Minnesota Press.

Levine, R., Sato, S., Hashimoto, T., & Verma, J. (1995). Love and marriage in eleven cultures. *Journal of Cross-Cultural Psychology*, *26*, 554–571.

Levinson, D. J., with Darrow, C. N., Klein, E. B., Levinson, M. H. & McKee, B. (1978). *The seasons of a man's life*. New York: Knopf.

Lewandowski, G. W., & Ackerman, R. A. (2006). Something's missing: Need fulfillment and self-expansion as predictors of susceptibility of infidelity. *Journal of Social Psychology*, *146*, 389–403.

Lewis, G. B. (2003). Black-white differences in attitudes toward homosexuality and gay rights. *Public Opinion Quarterly*, *67*, 245–257.

Li, N. P., Bailey, J. M., Kenrick, D. T., & Linsenmeier, J. A. (2002). The necessities and luxuries of mate preferences: Testing the trade-offs. *Journal of Personality & Social Psychology*, *82*, 947–955.

Liang, C. T. H., & Alimo, C. (2005). The impact of white heterosexual students' interactions on attitudes toward gay, lesbian, and bisexual people: A longitudinal study. *The Journal of College Student Development*, *46*(3), 237–250.

Liberty Counsel. (2010, February 3). *LU law school hosts conference on same-gender attraction*. Retrieved from http://www.lc.org/index.cfm?PID=14100&PRID=903

Lickliter, R., & Honeycutt, H. (2003). Developmental dynamics: Toward a biologically plausible evolutionary psychology. *Psychological Bulletin*, *129*, 819–835.

Lieberman, B. (1988). Extrapremarital intercourse: Attitudes toward a neglected sexual behavior. *The Journal of Sex Research*, *24*, 291–298.

Lindley, L. L., Nicholson, T. J., Kerby, M. B., & Lu, N. (2003). HIV/STI associated risk behaviors among self-identified lesbian, gay, bisexual, and transgender college students in the United States. *AIDS Education and Prevention*, *15*(5), 413–429.

Lingiardi, V., Falanga, S., & D'Augelli, A. R. (2005). The evaluation of homophobia in an Italian sample. *Archives of Sexual Behavior*, *34*, 81–93.

Lippa, R. A. (2005). *Gender, nature, and nurture* (2nd ed.). Mahwah, NJ: Erlbaum.

Lippa, R. A., & Tan, F. D. (2001). Does culture moderate the relationship between sexual orientation and gender-related personality traits? *Cross-Cultural Research*, *35*, 65–87.

Lira, L. R., Koss, M. P., & Russo, N. F. (1999). Mexican American women's definitions of rape and sexual abuse. *Hispanic Journal of Behavioral Sciences*, *21*, 236–265.

Lisak, D. (1991). Sexual aggression, masculinity, and fathers. *Signs*, *16*, 238–262.

Lisak, D., Hopper, J., & Song, P. (1996). Factors in the cycle of violence: Gender rigidity and emotional constriction. *Journal of Traumatic Stress*, *9*(4), 721–743.

Lisak, D., & Roth, S. (1988). Motivational factors in non-incarcerated sexually aggressive men. *Journal of Personality and Social Psychology*, *55*, 795–802.

Lisak, D., & Roth, S. (1990). Motives and psychodynamics of self-reported, unincarcerated rapists. *American Journal of Orthopsychiatry*, *60*, 268–280.

Littleton, H. L., & Breitkopf, R. C. (2006). Coping with experiences of rape. *Psychology of Women Quarterly*, *30*, 106–116.

Livingston, J. A., & Testa, M. (2000). Qualitative analysis of women's perceived vulnerability to sexual aggression in a hypothetical dating context. *Journal of Social and Personal Relationships*, *17*, 729–741.

Lloyd, S. A., & Emery, B. C. (2000). *The dark side of courtship: Physical and sexual aggression*. Thousand Oaks, CA: Sage.

LoConte, J., O'Leary, A., & Labouvie, E. (1997). Psychosocial correlates of HIV-related sexual behavior in an inner-city STI clinic. *Psychology and Health*, *12*, 589–601.

Logan, T. K., Cole, J., & Leukefeld, C. (2002). Women, sex, and HIV: Social and contextual factors, meta-analysis of published interventions, and implications for practice and research. *Psychological Bulletin*, *128*, 851–885.

Logan, T. K., Leukefeld, C., & Walker, B. (2000). Stalking as a variant of intimate violence: Implications from a young adult sample. *Violence & Victims*, *15*, 91–111.

Loh, C., Gidycz, C. A., Lobo, T. R., & Luthra, R. (2005). A prospective analysis of sexual assault perpetration: Risk factors related to perpetrator characteristics. *Journal of Interpersonal Violence*, *20*, 1325–1348.

Long, W., & Millsap, C. A. (2008). Fear of AIDS and Homophobia Scales in an ethnic population of university students. *Journal of Social Psychology*, *148*, 637–640.

Longerbeam, S. D., Inkelas, K. K., Johnson, D. R., & Lee, Z. S. (2007). Lesbian, gay, and bisexual college student experiences: An exploratory study. *Journal of College Student Development*, *48*(2), 215–230.

Lonsway, K. A., & Fitzgerald, L. F. (1994). Rape myths: In review. *Psychology of Women Quarterly*, *18*, 133–164.

Lottes, I., Weinberg, M., & Weller, I. (1993). Reactions to pornography on a college campus: For or against? *Sex roles: A Journal of Research*, *29*, 69–90.

Love, P., Bock, M., Jannarone, A., & Richardson, P. (2005). Identity interaction: Exploring the spiritual experiences of lesbian and gay college students. *Journal of College Student Development*, *46*(2), 193–209.

Lovell, A. (1998). "Other students always used to say, 'look at the dykes' ": Protecting students from peer sexual orientation harassment. *California Law Review*, *86*, 617–654.

MacDonald, A. P. (1981). Bisexuality: Some comments on research and theory. *Journal of Homosexuality*, *6*, 21–35.

Macgillivray, I. K., & Jennings, T. (2008). A content analysis exploring lesbian, gay, bisexual, and transgender topics in foundations of education textbooks. *Journal of Teacher Education*, *59*, 170–188.

MacKinnon, C. (1979). *Sexual harassment of working women: A case of discrimination*. New Haven, CT: Yale University Press.

Macy, R. J., Nurius, P. S., & Norris, J. (2006). Responding in their best interests: Contextualizing women coping with acquaintance sexual assault. *Violence Against Women*, *12*(5), 478–500.

Malamuth, N. M. (1996). The confluence model of sexual aggression: Feminist and evolutionary perspectives. In D. Buss & N. Malamuth (Eds.), *Sex, power, conflict* (pp. 269–295). New York, NY: Oxford University Press.

Malamuth, N. M., Linz, D., Heavey, C. L., Barnes, G., & Acker, M. (1995). Using the confluence model of sexual aggression to predict men's conflict with women: A 10-year follow-up. *Journal of Personality and Social Psychology*, *69*, 353–369.

Malamuth, N. M., Sockloskie, R. J., Koss, M. P., & Tanaka J. S. (1991). Characteristics of aggressors against women: Testing a model using a national sample of college students. *Journal of Consulting and Clinical Psychology*, *59*, 670–681.

Malamuth, N. M., & Thornhill, N. W. (1994). Hostile masculinity, sexual aggression, and gender-biased domineeringness in conversations. *Aggressive Behavior*, *20*(3), 185–193.

Maltz, W. (2001). *The sexual healing journey: A guide for survivors of sexual abuse*. New York, NY: Harper Paperbacks.

Maltz, W. (in press). Sex therapy with survivors of sexual abuse. In P. J. Kleinplatz (Ed.), *New directions in sex therapy: Innovations and alternatives* (2nd ed.). New York: Routledge.

Maner, J. K., Kenrick, D. T., Becker, D. V., Delton, A. W., Hofer, B., Wilbur, C., & Neuberg, S. (2003). Sexually selective cognition: Beauty captures the mind of the beholder. *Journal of Personality and Social Psychology*, *85*, 1107–1120.

Maner, J. K., Kenrick, D. T., Becker, D. V., Robertson, T., Hofer, B., Neuberg, S., . . . Schaller, M. (2005). Functional projection: How fundamental social motives can bias interpersonal perception. *Journal of Personality and Social Psychology*, *88*, 63–78.

Manning, W. D., Giordano, P. C., & Longmore, M. A. (2006). Hooking up: The relationship contexts of "non-relationship" sex. *Journal of Adolescent Research*, *21*(5), 459–483.

Manning, W. D., Giordano, P. C., Longmore, M. A., & Hocevar, A. (2011). Romantic relationships and academic/career trajectories in emerging adulthood. In F. D. Fincham, & M. Cui (Eds.), *Romantic relationships in emerging adulthood* (pp. 317–333). New York, NY: Cambridge University Press.

Manning, W. D., Longmore, M. A., & Giordano, P. C. (2005). Adolescents' involvement in non-romantic sexual activity. *Social Science Research*, *34*, 384–407.

Marcia, J. E. (1994). The empirical study of ego identity. In H. A. Bosma, T. G. Graafsma, H. D. Grotevant, & D. J. de Levita (Eds.), *Identity and development: An interdisciplinary approach* (pp. 67–79). Thousand Oaks, CA: Sage.

Markus, H. R., & Kitayama, S. (1991). Culture and self: Implications for cognition, emotion, and motivation. *Psychological Review*, *98*, 224–253.

Marx, B. P., Calhoun, K. S., Wilson, A. E., & Meyerson, L. A. (2001). Sexual revictimization prevention: An outcome evaluation. *Journal of Consulting and Clinical Psychology*, *69*, 25–32.

Marx, B. P., Gross, A. M., & Adams, H. E. (1999). The effect of alcohol on the responses of sexually coercive and noncoercive men to an experimental rape analogue. *Sexual Abuse*, *11*, 131–145.

Marx, B. P., Gross, A. M., & Juergens, J. P. (1997). The effects of alcohol consumption and expectancies in an experimental date rape analogue. *Journal of Psychopathology and Behavioral Assessment*, *19*, 281–302.

Masten, A. S., Coatsworth, J. D., Neemann, J., Gest, S. D., Tellegen, A., Garmezy, N., & Ramirez, M. L. (1999). Competence in the context of adversity: Pathways to resilience and maladaptation from childhood to late adolescence. *Development & Psychopathology*, *11*, 143–169.

Masters, W. H., & Johnson, V. E. (1970). *Human sexual inadequacy*. New York, NY: Bantam Books.

Mathewes-Green, F. (1997). Free love didn't come cheap. *Christianity Today*, *41*, 68–69.

Maticka-Tyndale, E., Herold, E. S., & Mewhinney, D. (1998). Casual sex on spring break: Intentions and behaviors of Canadian students. *The Journal of Sex Research*, *35*, 254–264.

Mattingly, B. A., Wilson, K., Clark, E. M., Bequette, A. W, & Weidler, D. J. (2010). Foggy faithfulness: Relationship quality, religiosity, and the Perceptions of Dating Infidelity Scale in an adult sample. *Journal of Family Issues*, *31*(11), 1465–1484.

Mayseless, O., & Scharf, M. (2003). What does it mean to be an adult?: The Israeli experience. *New Directions in Child and Adolescent Development*, *100*, 5–20.

McAlister, A. R., Pachana, N., & Jackson, C. J. (2005). Predictors of young dating adults' inclination to engage in extradyadic sexual activities: A multi-perspective study. *British Journal of Psychology*, *96*, 331–350.

McCabe, S. E., Boyd, C., Hughes, T. L., & D'Arcy, H. (2003). Sexual identity and substance use among undergraduate students. *Substance Abuse*, *24*, 77–91.

McCandless, S. R., & Sullivan, L. P. (1991, May 6). Two courts adopt new standard to determine sexual harassment. *National Law Journal*, 18–20.

McCauley, J., Calhoun, K. S., & Gidycz, C. A. (in press). Binge drinking and rape: A prospective examination in college women with a history of previous sexual victimization. *Journal of Interpersonal Violence*.

McClintock, M. K., & Herdt, B. (1996). Rethinking puberty: The development of sexual attraction. *Current Directions in Psychological Science*, *5*(6), 173–183.

McCormick, N. B. (1979). Come-ons and put-offs: Unmarried students' strategies for having and avoiding sexual intercourse. *Psychology of Women Quarterly*, *4*(2), 194–211. doi:10.1111/j.1471-6402.1979.tb00708.x

McGinnis, R. (1958). Campus values in mate selection: A repeat study. *Social Forces*, *36*, 368–373.

McKinney, K., & Sprecher, S. (Ed.). (1991). Introduction. In K. McKinney & S. Sprecher (Eds.), *Sexuality in close relationships* (pp. 1–8). Hillsdale, NJ: Erlbaum.

McKirnan, D. J., Ostrow, D. G., & Hope, B. (1996). Sex, drugs and escape: A psychological model of HIV-risk sexual behaviors. *AIDS Care*, *8*, 655–669.

Mead, M. (1928). *Coming of age in Samoa*. New York, NY: Morrow.

Mead, M. (1961). Cultural determinants of sexual behavior. In W. C. Young (Ed.), *Sex and internal secretions* (pp. 1433–1479). Baltimore, MD: Williams and Wilkins.

Medora, N. P., Larson, J. H., Hortaçsu, N., & Dave, P. (2002). Perceived attitudes toward romanticism: A cross-cultural study of American, Asian-Indian, and Turkish young adults. *Journal of Comparative Family Studies*, *33*, 155–178.

Meeks, B. S., Hendrick, S. S., & Hendrick, C. (1998). Communication, love and relationship satisfaction. *Journal of Social and Personal Relationships*, *15*, 755–773.

Meeus, W., Iedema, J., Helsen, M., & Vollebergh, W. (1999). Patterns of adolescent identity development: Review of the literature and longitudinal analysis. *Developmental Review*, *19*, 419–461.

Meier, A., & Allen, G. (2008). Intimate relationship development during the transition to adulthood: Differences by social class. In J. T. Mortimer (Ed.), *Social class and transitions to adulthood: New directions for child and adolescent development* (Vol. 199, pp. 25–39). San Francisco, CA: Jossey-Bass.

Meloy, J. R. (2007). Stalking: The state of the science. *Criminal Behaviour and Mental Health*, *17*, 1–7.

Ménard, K. S., Hall, G. N., Phung, A. H., Ghebrial, M. E. & Martin, L. (2003). Gender differences in sexual harassment and coercion in college students: Developmental, individual, and situational determinants. *Journal of Interpersonal Violence*, *18*, 1222–1239.

Meritor Savings Bank v. Vinson, 477 U.S. 57 (1986).

Messman-Moore, T. L., & Brown, A. L. (2006). Risk perception, rape and sexual revictimization: A prospective study of college women. *Psychology of Women Quarterly*, *30*(2), 159–172.

Messman-Moore, T. L., & Long, P. J. (2000). Child sexual abuse and revictimization in the form of adult sexual abuse, adult physical abuse, and adult psychological maltreatment. *Journal of Interpersonal Violence*, *15*(5), 489–502.

Messman-Moore, T. L., & Long, P. J. (2003). The role of childhood sexual abuse sequelae in the sexual revictimization of women: An empirical review and theoretical reformulation. *Clinical Psychology Review*, 23, 537–571.

Metts, S. (2004). First sexual involvement in romantic relationships: An empirical investigation of communicative framing, romantic beliefs, and attachment orientation in the passion turning point. In J. H. Harvey, A. Wenzel, & S. Sprecher (Eds.), *The handbook of sexuality in close relationships* (pp. 135–158). Mahwah, NJ: Erlbaum.

Metts, S., & Cupach, W. R. (1989). The role of communication in human sexuality. In K. McKinney & S. Sprecher (Eds.), *Human sexuality: The societal and interpersonal context* (pp. 139–161). Norwood, NJ: Ablex.

Metts, S., & Spitzberg, B. H. (1996). Sexual communication in interpersonal contexts: A script-based approach. In B. R. Burleson (Ed.), *Communication yearbook 19* (pp. 49–91). Thousand Oaks, CA: Sage.

Metz, E. M., & McCarthy, B. W. (2003). *Coping with premature ejaculation: How to overcome P. E., please your partner & have great sex*. Oakland, CA: New Harbinger.

Meyer, I. H. (1995). Minority stress and mental health in gay men. *Journal of Health and Social Behavior, 36*(1), 38–56.

Michael, R. T., Gagnon, J. H., Laumann, E. O., & Kolata, G. (1994). *Sex in America: A definitive survey*. New York, NY: Warner Books.

Middleton, D. R. (2002). *Exotics and erotics: Human cultural and sexual diversity*. Prospect Heights, IL: Waveland Press.

*Miller, J. A., & Gilman, D. A. (1996). *Effects of peer health facilitator HIV/AIDS intervention with university students*. Terre Haute, IN: Indiana State University. Retrieved from ERIC databse (ED 397 374).

Miller, K. S., Forehand, R., & Kotchick, B. A. (2000). Adolescent sexual behavior in two ethnic minority groups: A multisystem perspective. *Adolescence, 35*(138), 313–333.

Miller, R. S., & Perlman, D. (2009). *Intimate relationships* (5th ed.). Boston, MA: McGraw-Hill.

Millhausen, R. R., & Herold, E. S. (1999). Does the sexual double standard still exist? Perceptions of university women. *The Journal of Sex Research, 36*, 361–368.

Mills, C. S., & Granoff, B. J. (1992). Date and acquaintance rape among a sample of college students. *Social Work, 37*, 504–509.

Ministry of Health, Labor, and Welfare. (2006). Vital statistics survey. Tokyo: Statistics and Information Department. Cited in Farrer, J., Tsuchiya, H., & Bagrowicz, B. (2008). Emotional expression in *tsukiau* dating relationships in Japan. *Journal of Social and Personal Relationships, 25*, 169–188.

Misovich, S., Fisher, J., & Fisher, W. (1997). Close relationships and elevated HIV risk behavior: Evidence and possible underlying psychological processes. *Review of General Psychology, 1*, 72–107.

Mitchell, D., Hirschman, R., & Hall, G. C. N. (1999). Attributions of victim responsibility, pleasure, and trauma in male rape. *The Journal of Sex Research, 36*(4), 369–373.

Mohler-Kuo, M., Dowdall, G. W., Koss, M. P., & Wechsler, H. (2004). Correlates of rape while intoxicated in a national sample of college women. Journal of Studies on Alcohol, 65(1), 37–45.

Mohr, J. J., & Sedlacek, W. E. (2000). Perceived barriers to friendships with lesbians and gay men among university students. *Journal of College Student Development, 41*, 70–80.

Molitor, F., Facer, M., & Ruiz, J. D. (1999). Safer sex communication and unsafe sexual behavior among young men who have sex with men in California. *Archives of Sexual Behavior, 28*(4), 335–343.

Mongeau, P. A., Hale, J. L., & Alles, M. (1994). An experimental investigation of accounts and attributions following sexual infidelity. *Communication Monographs, 61*, 326–343.

Mongeau, P. A., Ramirez, A., & Vorell, M. (2003, February). *Friends with benefits: Initial exploration of sexual, non-romantic relationships*. Paper presented at the meeting of the Western States Communication Association, Salt Lake City, UT.

Mongeau, P. A., & Schulz, B. E. (1997). What he doesn't know won't hurt him (or me): Verbal responses and attributions following sexual infidelity. *Communication Reports, 10*, 143–152.

Mori, L. Bernat, M. L., Glenn, J. A., Selle, P. A., & Zarate, M. G. (1995). Attitudes toward rape: Gender and ethnic differences across Asian and Caucasian college students. *Sex Roles, 32*(7/8), 457–467.

Morrison, S., J. Hardison, A. Mathew, and J. O'Neil. (2004). *An evidence-based review of sexual assault preventive intervention programs*. Washington, DC: U.S. Department of Justice.

Morrow, G. D., Clark, E. M., & Brock, K. F. (1995). Individual and partner love styles: Implications for the quality of romantic involvements. *Journal of Social and Personal Relationships, 12*, 363–387.

Mosher, D. L., & Anderson, R. D. (1986). Macho personality, sexual aggression, and reactions to guided imagery of realistic rape. *Journal of Research in Personality, 20*, 77–94.

Mosher, D. L., & Sirkin, M. (1984). Measuring a macho personality constellation. *Journal of Research in Personality, 18*, 150–163.

Mosher, W. D., Chandra, A., & Jones, J. (2005). Sexual behavior and selected health measures: Men and women 15–44 years of age, United States, 2002. *Advance Data from Vital and Health Statistics*, no. 362. Hyattsville, MD: National Center for Health Statistics.

Mouilso, E. R. (2010). *Narcissism and psychopathy explain the relationship between sociosexuality and sexual assault perpetration*. Manuscript in preparation.

Muehlenhard, C. L., & Falcon, P. L. (1990). Men's heterosocial skill and attitude toward women as predictors of verbal and sexual coercion and forceful rape. *Sex Roles, 23*, 241–259.

Muehlenhard, C. L., & Linton, M. A. (1987). Date rape and sexual aggression in dating situations: Incidence and risk factors. *Journal of Counseling Psychology, 34*, 186–196.

Muehlenhard, C., & Shippee, S. (2010). Men's and women's reports of pretending orgasm. *The Journal of Sex Research, 46*, 1–16.

Mueller, J. A., & Cole, J. C. (2009). A qualitative examination of heterosexual consciousness among college students. *Journal of College Student Development, 50*, 320–336.

Mulick, P. S., & Wright, L. W., Jr. (2002). Examining the existence of biphobia in the heterosexual and homosexual populations. *Journal of Bisexuality, 2*, 45–64.

Murnen, S. K., & Kohlman, M. H. (2007). Athletic participation, fraternity membership, and sexual aggression among college men: A meta-analytic review. *Sex Roles, 57*(1–2), 145–157.

Murnen, S. K., Wright, C., & Kaluzny, G. (2002). If "boys will be boys," then girls will be victims? A meta-analytic review of the research that relates masculine ideology to sexual aggression. *Sex Roles, 46*(11–12), 359–375.

Murray, C. I., & Kimura, N. (2003). Multiplicity of paths to couple formation in Japan. In R. R. Hamon & B. B. Ingoldsby (Eds.), *Mate selection across cultures* (pp. 247–268). Thousand Oaks, CA: Sage.

Muscarella, F. (2000). The evolution of homoerotic behavior in humans. *Journal of Homosexuality, 40*(1), 51–77.

Nack, A. (2008). *Damaged goods? Women living with incurable sexually transmitted diseases*. Philadelphia, PA: Temple University Press.

Nagel, B., Matsuo, H., McIntyre, K. P., & Morrison, N. (2005). Attitudes toward victims of rape: Effects of gender, race, religion, and social class. *Journal of Interpersonal Violence, 20*, 725–737.

Nannini, D. K., & Meyers, L. S. (2000). Jealousy in sexual and emotional infidelity: An alternative to the evolutionary explanation. *The Journal of Sex Research, 37*, 117–122.

National Campaign to Prevent Teen and Unplanned Pregnancy. (2008). *Unplanned Pregnancy Among 20-Somethings: The Full Story*. Retrieved from http://www.thenationalcampaign.org/resources/pdf/briefly-unplanned-pregnancy-among-20somethings-the-full-story.pdf

National Institute of Population and Social Security Research. (2005). *Attitudes toward marriage and the family among married couples: Thirteenth Japanese national fertility survey*. Tokyo: Author. Cited in Farrer, J., Tsuchiya, H., & Bagrowicz, B. (2008). Emotional expression in *tsukiau* dating relationships in Japan. *Journal of Social and Personal Relationships*, *25*, 169–188.

The National Student Genderblind Campaign. (2010). *Statement on recent events*. Retrieved from http://www.genderblind.org/

Nayak, M. B., Byrne, C. A., Martin, M. K., & Abraham, A. G. (2003). Attitudes toward violence against women: A cross-nation study. *Sex Roles*, *49*(7–8), 333–342.

Negy, C., & Eisenman, R. (2005). A comparison of African American and white college students' affective and attitudinal reactions to lesbian, gay, and bisexual individuals: An exploratory study. *The Journal of Sex Research*, *42*, 291–298.

Nelson, C. J., Ahmed, A., Valenzuela, R., Parker, M., & Mulhall, J. P. (2007). Assessment of penile vibratory stimulation as a management strategy in men with secondary retarded orgasm. *Urology*, *69*(2, 552–555.

Nelson, E. S., & Krieger, S. L. (1997). Changes in attitudes toward homosexuality in college students: Implementation of a gay men and lesbian peer panel. *Journal of Homosexuality*, *33*, 63–81.

Nelson, G., & Prilleltensky, I. (2010). The foundations of community research. In G. Nelson & I. Prilleltensky (Eds.), *Community psychology: In pursuit of liberation and well-being* (pp. 251–273). Houndmills, Basingstoke, England: Palgrave Macmillan.

Neville, H. A., & Heppner, M. J. (1999) Contextualizing rape: Reviewing sequelae and proposing a culturally inclusive ecological model of sexual assault recovery. *Applied and Preventive Psychology*, *8*, 41–62.

Neville, H. A., Heppner, M. J., Oh, E., Spanierman, L. B., & Clark, M. K. (2004). General and cultural-specific factors influencing Black and White women rape survivors' self-esteem. *Psychology of Women Quarterly*, *28*, 83–94.

Neville, H. A., & Pugh, A. O. (1997). General and culture-specific factors influencing African American women's reporting patterns and perceived social support following sexual assault: An exploratory investigation. *Violence Against Women*, *3*, 361–381.

Nicholls, T. L., Ogloff, J. R. P., Brink, J., & Spidel, A. (2005). Psychopathy in women: A review of its clinical usefulness for assessing risk for aggression and criminality. *Behavioral Sciences and the Law*, *23*, 779–802.

Norris, J., Davis, K. C., George, W. H., Martell, J., & Heiman, J. R. (2002). Alcohol's direct and indirect effects on men's self-reported sexual aggression likelihood. *Journal of Studies on Alcohol*, *63*(6), 688–695.

Norris, J., & Kerr, K. L. (1993). Alcohol and violent pornography: Responses to permissive and nonpermissive cues. *Journal of Studies on Alcohol* (Suppl. 11), 118–127.

Norris, J., Martell, J., & George, W. H. (2001). Men's judgments of a sexual assailant in an eroticized rape: The role of rape myth attitudes and contextual factors. In M. Martinez (Ed.), *Prevention and control of aggression and the impact on its victims* (pp. 249–254). New York, NY: Kluwer Academic/Plenum.

Norris, J., Nurius, P. A., & Graham, T. L. (1999). When a date changes from fun to dangerous: Factors affecting women's ability to distinguish. *Violence Against Women*, *5*, 230–250.

Nurius, P. S., & Norris, J. (1995). A cognitive ecological model of women's responses to male sexual coercion in dating. *Journal of Psychology and Human Sexuality*, *8*, 117–139.

Nurius, P. S., Norris, J., Dimeff, L. A., & Graham, T. L. (1996). Expectations regarding acquaintance sexual aggression among sorority and fraternity members. *Sex Roles*, *35*, 427–444.

Nurius, P. S., Norris, J., Young, D. S., Graham, T. L., & Gaylord, J. (2000). Interpreting and defensively responding to threat: Examining appraisals and coping with acquaintance sexual aggression. *Violence and Victims*, *15*, 187–208.

Ochs, E. P., & Binik, Y. M. (1999). The use of couple data to determine the reliability of self-reported sexual behavior. *The Journal of Sex Research*, *36*, 374–384.

Ochs, R. (1996). Biphobia: It goes more than two ways. In B. A. Firestein (Ed.), *Bisexuality: The psychology and politics of an invisible minority* (pp. 217–239). Thousand Oaks, CA: Sage.

Odets, W. (1994). AIDS education and harm reduction for gay men: Psychological approaches for the 21st century. *AIDS and Public Policy Journal*, *9*, 1–18.

Ogden, G. (1999). *Women who love sex*. Boston, MA: Womanspirit Press.

*O'Grady, M. A., Wilson, K, & Harman, J. J. (2009). Preliminary findings from a brief, peer-led safer sex intervention for college students living in residence halls. *Journal of Primary Prevention*, *30*, 716–731.

Okazaki, S. (2002). Influences of culture on Asian American sexuality. *The Journal of Sex Research*, *39*, 34–41.

O'Leary, A. (2000). Women at risk for HIV from a primary partner: Balancing risk and intimacy. *Annual Review of Sex Research*, *11*, 191–234.

O'Leary, D. K., Wooden, E. M., & Fritz, P. (2006). Can we prevent hitting? Recommendations for preventing intimate partner violence between young adults. *Journal of Aggression, Maltreatment, & Trauma*, *13*, 121–178.

Oliver, M. B., & Hyde, J. S. (1993). Gender differences in sexuality: A meta-analysis. *Psychological Bulletin*, *114*, 29–51.

Oliver, M. B., & Sedikides, C. (1992). Effects of sexual permissiveness on desirability of partner as a function of low and high commitment to relationship. *Social Psychology Quarterly*, *55*, 321–333. doi:10.2307/2786800

O'Malley, P. M., & Johnston, L. D. (2002). Epidemiology of alcohol and other drug use among American college students. *Journal of Studies on Alcohol*, *14*, 23–29.

Oncale v. Sundowner Offshore Services, Inc., 523 U.S. 75 (1998).

Orchowski, L. M., Gidycz, C. A., & Raffle, H. (2008). Evaluation of a sexual assault risk reduction and self-defense program: A prospective analysis of a revised protocol. *Psychology of Women Quarterly*, *32*, 204–218.

Orchowski, L. M., Meyer, D., & Gidycz, C. A. (2009). College women's likelihood to report unwanted sexual victimization to campus agencies: Trends and correlates. *Journal of Aggression, Maltreatment, and Trauma*, *18*(8), 839–858.

Orchowski, L. M., Uhlin, B., Probst, D., Edwards K. M., & Anderson, T. (2009). An assimilation analysis of clinician-assisted emotional disclosure therapy with survivors of intimate partner sexual assault. *Psychotherapy Research*, *19*, 293–311.

Orlofsky, J. L. (1993). Intimacy status: Theory and research. In J. Marcia (Ed.), *Ego identity: A handbook for psychosocial research* (pp. 111–133). New York, NY: Springer-Verlag.

ORU Online Campus Degree-Seeking Application. (n.d.). Retrieved from http://www.oru.edu/academics/online_campus/pdfs/Degree_seeking_app_online.pdf

Orzeck, T., & Lung, E. (2005). Big-five personality differences of cheaters and non-cheaters. *Current Psychology*, *24*, 274–286.

Osgood, D. W., Foster, E. M., Flanagan, C., & Ruth, G. R. (2005). Introduction: Why focus on the transition to adulthood for vulnerable populations? In D. W. Osgood, E. M. Foster, C. Flanagan, & G. R. Ruth (Eds.), *On your own without a net: The transition to adulthood for vulnerable populations* (pp. 1–26). Chicago, IL: University of Chicago Press.

Ostrow, D. G. (2000). The role of drugs in the sexual lives of men who have sex with men: Continuing barriers to researching this question. *AIDS and Behavior*, *4*, 205–219.

O'Sullivan, L. F. (1995). Less is more: The effects of sexual experience on judgments of men's and women's personality characteristics and relationship desirability. *Sex Roles*, *33*, 159–181. doi:10.1007/BF01544609

O'Sullivan, L. F., & Byers, E. S. (1992). College students' incorporation of initiator and restrictor roles in sexual dating interactions. *The Journal of Sex Research*, *29*, 435–446. doi:10.1080/00224499209551658b

O'Sullivan, L. F., Udell, W., Montrose, V. A., Antoniello, P., & Hoffman, S. (2010). A cognitive analysis of college students' explanations for engaging in unprotected sexual intercourse. *Archives of Sexual Behavior*, *39*, 1121–1131.

Otis, M. D., & Skinner, W. F. (1996). The prevalence of victimization and its effect on mental well-being among lesbian and gay people. *Journal of Homosexuality*, *30*(3), 93–121.

Owen, J., Rhoades, G. K., Stanley, S. M., & Finchman, F. D. (2010). "Hooking up" among college students: Demographic and psychosocial correlates. *Archives of Sexual Behavior*, *39*, 653–663.

Page, R. M., Hammermeister, J. J., & Scanlan, A. (2000). Everybody's not doing it: Misperceptions of college students' sexual activity. *American Journal of Health Behavior*, *24*, 387–394.

Palmer, C. T. (1988). Twelve reasons why rape is not sexually motivated: A skeptical examination. *The Journal of Sex Research*, *25*, 512–530.

Paludi, M. A. (1996). Editor's notes. In M. A. Paludi (Ed.), *Sexual harassment on college campuses: Abusing the ivory power* (rev. ed.). Albany, NY: State University of New York Press.

Pan, S. (1993). A sex revolution in current China. *Journal of Psychology & Human Sexuality*, *6*, 1–14.

Parrott, D. J., & Zeichner, A. (2008). Determinants of anger and physical aggression based on sexual orientation: An experimental examination of hypermasculinity and exposure to male gender role violations. *Archives of Sexual Behavior*, *37*, 891–901.

Parson, J. T., Halkitis, P. N., Bimbi, D., & Borkowski, T. (2000). Perceptions of the benefits and costs associated with condom use and unprotected sex among late adolescent college students. *Journal of Adolescence, 2000*, 23*(4)* 377–391.

Pascarella, E. T., & Terenzini, P. T. (1991). *How college affects students: Findings and insights from twenty years of research*. San Francisco, CA: Jossey-Bass.

Patrick, M. E., & Maggs, J. L. (2009). Does drinking lead to sex? Daily alcohol-sex behaviors and expectancies among college students. *Psychology of Addictive Behaviors*, *23*, 472–481.

Paul, E. L., & Hayes, K. A. (2002). The casualties of "casual" 'sex: A qualitative exploration of the phenomenology of college students' hookups. *Journal of Social and Personal Relationships*, *19*, 639–661.

Paul, E. L., McManus, B., & Hayes, A. (2000). "Hookups": Characteristics and correlates of college students' spontaneous and anonymous sexual experiences. *The Journal of Sex Research*, *37*(1), 76–88

Paul, E. L., Wenzel, A., & Harvey, J. (2008). Hookups: A facilitator or a barrier to relationship initiation and intimacy development? In S. Sprecher, A. Wenzel, & J. Harvey (Eds.), *Handbook of relationship initiation* (pp. 375–390). New York, NY: Taylor & Francis.

Payne-James, J. (2002). Drug-facilitated sexual assault, "ladettes" and alcohol. *Journal of the Royal Society of Medicine*, *95*, 326–327.

Pearson, M., Stanley, S. M., & Rhoades, G. K. (2008). *Within My Reach instructor manual.* Denver, CO: PREP.

Penhollow, T., Young, M., & Bailey, W. (2007). Relationship between religiosity and "hooking up" behavior. *American Journal of Health Education*, *38*, 338–345.

Pennebaker, J. W. (1997). Writing about emotional experiences as a therapeutic process. *Psychological Science*, *8*(3), 162–166.

Peplau, L. A., Rubin, Z., & Hill, C. T. (1977). Sexual intimacy in dating relationships. *Journal of Social Issues*, *33*(2), 86–109. doi:10.1111/j.1540-4560.1977.tb02007.x

Perelman, M. A. (2008). Understanding and treating retarded ejaculation: A sex therapist's perspective. *Newsletter of the International Society of Sexual Medicine*, *27*, 17–20.

Perelman, M. A. (2010). Comments on "Considerations for a better definition of male orgasmic disorder in DSM V." *Journal of Sexual Medicine*, 7(2, Pt. 1), 697–699.

Perelman, M. A., & Rowland, D. L. (2006). Retarded ejaculation. *World Journal of Urology*, *24*, 645–652.

Perelman, M. A., & Rowland, D. L. (2008). Retarded and inhibited ejaculation. In D. L. Rowland & L. Incrocci (Eds.), *Handbook of sexual and gender identity disorders* (pp. 100–121.) Hoboken, NJ: Wiley.

Peril, L. (2006). *College girls: Bluestockings, sex kittens, and co-eds, then and now.* New York, NY: Norton.

Perkins, D. D., Crim, B., Silberman, P., & Brown, B. B. (2004). Community development as a response to community-level adversity: Ecological theory and research and strengths-based policy. In K. I. Maton, C. J. Schellenbach, B. J. Leadbeater, & A. L. Solarz (Eds.), *Investing in children, youth, families, and communities: Strengths-based research and policy* (pp. 321–340). Washington, DC: American Psychological Association.

Perlman, D., & Campbell, S. (2004). Sexuality in close relationships: Concluding commentary. In J. H. Harvey, A. Wenzel, & S. Sprecher (Eds.), *The handbook of sexuality in close relationships* (pp. 613–635). Mahwah, NJ: Erlbaum.

Pernanen, K. (1991). *Alcohol in human violence.* New York, NY: Guilford.

Petersen, J. L., & Hyde, J. S. (2010). A meta-analytic review of research on gender differences in sexuality, 1993–2007. *Psychological Bulletin*, *136*, 21–38. doi:10.1037/a0017504

Petersen, J. R. (1999). *The century of sex.* New York, NY: Grove Press.

Pettijohn, T. F., & Walzer, A. S. (2008). Reducing racism, sexism, and homophobia in college students by completing a psychology of prejudice course. *College Student Journal*, *42*, 459–468.

Petty, G. M. & Dawson, B. (1989). Sexual aggression in normal men: Incidence, beliefs, and personality characteristics. *Personality and Individual Differences*, 10, 355–362.

Pinkerton, S. D., & Abramson, P. R. (1995). Decision making and personality factors in sexual risk-taking for HIV/AIDS: A theoretical integration. *Personality and Individual Differences*, *19*(5), 713–723.

Pinkerton, S. D., Bogart, L. M., Cecil, H., & Abramson, P. R. (2002). Factors associated with masturbation in a collegiate sample. *Journal of Psychology and Human Sexuality*, *14*(2/3), 103–121.

Pinkerton, S. D., Cecil, H., Bogart, L. M., & Abramson, P. R. (2003). The pleasures of sex: An empirical investigation. *Cognition and Emotion*, *17*, 341–353. doi:10.1080/02699930302291

Planned Parenthood Federation of America. (2001). *White paper: Adolescent sexuality.* Retrieved from http://www.plannedparenthood.org/files/PPFA/adsex_01-01.pdf

Polonsky, D. C. (2000). Premature ejaculation. In S. R. Leiblum & R. C. Rosen (Eds.), *Principles and practice of sex therapy* (3rd ed., pp. 305–332). New York, NY: Guilford.

Polonsky, D. C. (2010). The sexual challenges and dilemmas of young single men. In S. B. Levine, C. B. Risen, & S. E. Althof (Eds.), *Handbook of clinical sexuality for mental health professionals* (2nd ed., pp.231–250). New York, NY: Routledge/Taylor & Francis.

Popenoe, D., & Whitehead, B. D. (2001). Who wants to marry a soul mate? In D. Popenoe & B. D. Whitehead (Eds.), *The state of our unions: The social health of marriage in America* (pp. 6–16). Piscataway, NJ: National Marriage Project.

Poulson, R. L., Eppler, M. A., Satterwhite, T. N., Wuensch, K. L., & Bass, L. A. (1998). Alcohol consumption, strength of religious beliefs and risky sexual behavior among college students in the Bible Belt. *Journal of American College Health*, *46*, 227–232.

Poynter, K. J., & Tubbs, N. J. (2008). Safe zones: Creating LGBT Safe Space ally programs. *Journal of LGBT Youth*, *5*(1), 121–132.

Prause, N., & Graham, C. A. (2007). Asexuality: Classification and characterization. *Archives of Sexual Behavior*, *36*, 341–356.

Prejean, J., Song, R., Hernandez, A., Ziebell, R., Green, T., Walker, F., . . . HIV Incidence Surveillance Group. (2011). Estimated HIV incidence in the United States, 2006–2009. *PLoS ONE*, *6*, e17502. doi: 10.1371/journal.pone.0017502

Price, M. (2000). *Rugby as a gay men's game*. Unpublished doctoral dissertation. University of Warwick, Coventry, England.

Pridal, C. G., & LoPiccolo, J. (1993). Brief treatment of vaginismus. In R. A. Wells & V. J. Gianetti (Eds.), *Casebook of the brief psychotherapies* (pp. 329–345). New York, NY: Plenum.

Prins, K. S., Buunk, B. P., & VanYperen, N. W. (1993). Equity, normative disapproval and extramarital relationships. *Journal of Social and Personal Relationships*, *10*, 39–53.

Prochaska, J. O., & Redding, C. A. (1994). The transtheoretical model of change and HIV prevention: A review. *Health Education Quarterly*, *21*, 471–487.

Puentes, J., Knox, D., & Zusman, M. E. (2008). Participants in "friends with benefits" relationships. *College Student Journal*, *42*, 176–180.

Pulerwitz, J., Gortmaker, S., & DeJong, W. (2000). Measuring sexual relationship power in HIV/STI research. *Sex Roles*, *42*, 637–660.

Quinton, D., Pickles, A., Maughan, B., & Rutter, M. (1993). Partners, peers, and pathways: Assortive pairing and continuities in conduct disorder. *Development & Psychopathology*, *5*, 763–783.

Randall, H. E., & Byers, E. S. (2003). What is sex? Students' definitions of having sex, sexual partner, and unfaithful sexual behavior. *Canadian Journal of Human Sexuality*, *12*, 87–96.

Randolph, M. E., Torres, H., Gore-Felton, C., Lloyd, B., & McGarvey, E. L. (2009). Alcohol use and sexual risk behavior among college students: Understanding gender and ethnic differences. *The American Journal of Drug and Alcohol Abuse*, *35*, 80–84.

Rankin, S. (2003, May 1). *Campus climate for gay, lesbian, bisexual, and transgender people: A national perspective*. Retrieved from http://www.thetaskforce.org/reports_and_research/campus_climate

Rankin, S., Weber, G., Blumenfeld, W., & Frazer. S. (2010). *2010 state of higher education for lesbian, gay, bisexual & transgender people*. Charlotte, NC: Campus Pride.

Rapaport, K., & Burkhart, B. R. (1984). Personality and attitudinal characteristics of sexually coercive college males. *Journal of Abnormal Psychology*, *93*, 216–221.

Raskin, R., & Terry, H. (1988). A principle components analysis of the Narcissistic Personality Inventory and further evidence of its construct validity. *Journal of Personality and Social Psychology, 54*, 890–902.

*Reader, E. G., Carter R. P., & Crawford A. (1988). AIDS—knowledge, attitudes and behaviour: A study with university students. *Health Education Journal, 47*,125–127.

Reason, R. D., & Rankin, S. R. (2006). College students' experiences and perceptions of harassment on campus: An exploration of gender differences. *College Student Affairs Journal, 26*(1), 7–29.

Reece, M., Herbenick, D., Schick, V., Sanders, S. A., Dodge, B., & Fortenberry, J. D. (2010). Condom use rates in a national probability sample of males and females aged 14 to 94 in the United States. *The Journal of Sexual Medicine, 7*, 266–276. doi: 10.1111/j.1743-6109.2010.02017.x

Regan, P. C. (2008). *The mating game: A primer on love, sex, and marriage* (2nd ed.). Thousand Oaks, CA: Sage.

Regan, P. C., & Berscheid, E. (1997). Gender differences in characteristics desired in a potential sexual and marriage partner. *Journal of Psychology and Human Sexuality, 9*, 25–37.

Regan, P. C., Durvasula, R., Howell, L., Ureño, O., & Rea, M. (2004). Gender, ethnicity, and the developmental timing of first sexual and romantic experiences. *Social Behavior and Personality, 32*, 667–676.

Regan, P. C., Levin, L., Sprecher, S., Christopher, F. S., & Cate, R. (2000). Partner preferences: What characteristics do men and women desire in their short-term sexual and long-term romantic partners? *Journal of Psychology & Human Sexuality, 12*, 1–21.

Regnerus, M., & Uecker, J. (2011). *Premarital sex in America: How young Americans meet, mate, and think about marrying*. New York, NY: Oxford University.

Reifman, A. (2011). Romantic relationships in emerging adulthood: Conceptual foundations. In F. D. Fincham, & M. Cui (Eds.), *Romantic relationships in emerging adulthood* (pp. 15–26). New York, NY: Cambridge University Press.

Reifman, A., Arnett, J. J., & Colwell, M. J. (2006). Emerging adulthood: Theory, assessment, and application. *Journal of Youth Development, 1*, 1–12.

Reis, H. T., Collins, W. A., & Bescheid, E. (2000). The relationship context of human behavior and development. *Psychological Bulletin, 126*, 844–872.

Reis, H. T., Lin, Y.-C, Bennet, M. E., & Nezlak, J. B. (1993). Change and consistency in social participation during early adulthood. *Developmental Psychology, 29*, 633–645.

Reiss, I. L. (1960). *Premarital sexual standards in America*. New York, NY: Free Press.

Reiss, I. L. (1964). The scaling of premarital sexual permissiveness. *Journal of Marriage and the Family, 26*, 188–198.

Reiss, I. L. (1967). *The social context of premarital sexual permissiveness*. New York, NY: Holt, Rinehart & Winston.

Reiss, I. L. (1986). *Journey into sexuality: An exploratory voyage*. Englewood Cliffs, NJ: Prentice-Hall.

Reiss, I. L. (1989). Society and sexuality: A sociological explanation. In K. McKinney & S. Sprecher (Eds.), *Human sexuality: The society and interpersonal context* (pp. 3–29). Norwood, NJ: Ablex.

Reiss, I. L., & Miller, B. C. (1979). Heterosexual permissiveness: A theoretical analysis. In W. R. Burr, R. Hill, F. I. Nye, & I. L. Reiss (Eds.), *Contemporary theories about the family* (pp. 57–100). New York, NY: Free Press.

Remafedi, G. (1994). *Death by denial: Studies of suicide in gay and lesbian teenagers.* Boston, MA: Alyson Publications.

Resick, P. A., Nishith, P., Weaver, T. L., Astin, M. C., & Feuer, C. A. (2002). A comparison of cognitive-processing with prolonged exposure and a waiting condition for the treatment of chronic posttraumatic stress disorder in female rape victims. *Journal of Consulting and Clinical Psychology, 70,* 867–879.

Resick, P. A., & Schnicke, M. K. (1993). *Cognitive processing therapy for rape victims: A treatment manual.* Thousand Oaks, CA: Sage.

Resnick, H. S., Acierno, R., Amstadter, A. B., Self-Brown, S., & Kilpatrick, D. G. (2007). An acute post-sexual assault intervention to prevent drug abuse: Updated findings. *Addictive Behaviors, 32,* 2032–2045.

Resnick, H. S., Kilpatrick, D. G., Dansky, B. S., Saunders, B. E., & Best, C. L. (1993). Prevalence of civilian trauma and posttraumatic stress disorder in a representative national sample of women. *Journal of Consulting and Clinical Psychology, 61,* 984–991.

Rhoads, R. (1994). *Coming out in college: The struggle for a queer identity.* Westport, CN: Bergin & Garvey.

Rhodewalt, F., & Davison, J. (1983). Reactance and coronary-phone behavior pattern: The role of self-attribution in responses to reduced behavioral freedom. *Journal of Personality and Social Psychology, 44,* 220–228.

Rhodewalt, F., & Morf, C. (1995). Self and interpersonal correlates of the narcissistic personality inventory: A review and new findings. *Journal of Research in Personality, 29,* 1–23.

Rich, C. L., Combs-Lane, A. M., Resnick, H. S. , & Kilpatrick, D. G. (2004). Child sexual abuse and adult sexual revictimization. In L. J. Koenig, L. S. Doll, & A. O'Leary (Eds), *From child sexual abuse to adult sexual risk: Trauma, revictimization, and intervention* (pp. 49–68). Washington, DC: American Psychological Association.

Rich, M. (2008). Virtual sexuality: The influence of entertainment media on sexual attitudes and behavior. In J. Brown (Ed.), *Managing the media monster: The influence of media (from television to text messages) on teen sexual behavior and attitudes* (pp. 18–38.). Washington, DC: National Campaign to Prevent Teen and Adolescent Pregnancy.

Rickert, V. I., Vaughan, R. D., & Wiemann, C. M. (2004). Adolescent dating violence and date rape. *Current Opinion in Obstetrics and Gynecology, 14,* 495–500.

Ridley, M. (1993). *The red queen: Sex and evolution in human nature.* New York, NY Penguin.

Rieger, G., Chivers, M., & Bailey, J. M. (2005). Sexual arousal patterns of bisexual men. *Psychological Science, 16*(8), 579–584.

Rieger, G., Linsenmeier, J. A. W., Gygax, L., & Bailey, J. M. (2008). Sexual orientation and childhood gender nonconformity: Evidence from home videos. *Developmental Psychology, 44,* 46–58.

Riger, S. (1992). Epistemological debates, feminist voices. *American Psychologist, 47,* 730–740.

Rimsza, M. E. (2005). Sexually transmitted infections: New guidelines for an old problem on the college campus. *Pediatric Clinics of North America, 51*(1), 217–228.

Risman, B., & Schwartz, P. (2002). After the sexual revolution: Gender politics in teen dating. *Contexts, 1,* 16–24.

Ritter, K. Y., & O'Neill, C. W. (1989). Moving through loss: The spiritual journal of gay men and lesbian women. *Journal of Counseling and Development, 68*(1), 9–15.

Robin, L., Dittus, P., Whitaker, D., Crosby, R., Ethier, K. A., Mezoff, J., . . . Pappas-Deluca, K. (2004). Behavioral interventions to reduce incidence of HIV, STD, and pregnancy among adolescents: A decade in review. *Journal of Adolescent Health*, *34*, 3–26.

Roche, J. P., & Ramsbey, T. W. (1993). Premarital sexuality: A five-year follow-up study of attitudes and behavior by dating stage. *Adolescence*, *28*, 67–80.

Rogers, E. M. (1995). *Diffusion of innovations* (4th ed.). New York, NY: Free Press.

Rogers, R. W. (1983). A protection motivation theory of fear appeals and attitude change. In J. Cacioppo & R. Petty (Eds.), *Social psychology: A sourcebook* (pp. 153–176). New York, NY: Guilford.

Roisman, G. I., Aguilar, B., & Egeland, B. (2004). Antisocial behavior in the transition to adulthood: The independent and interactive roles of developmental history and emerging developmental tasks. *Development & Psychopathology*, *16*, 857–872.

Roper, E. A., & Halloran, E. (2007). Attitudes toward gay men and lesbians among heterosexual male and female student-athletes. *Sex Roles*, *57*, 919–928.

Rosch, E. H. (1973). On the internal structure of perceptual and semantic categories. In T. E. Moore (Ed.), *Cognitive development and the acquisition of language* (pp. 111–144). New York, NY: Academic Press.

Rosch, E. (1975). Cognitive representations of semantic categories. *Journal of Experimental Psychology*, *104*, 192–233.

Rosch, E. (1978). Principles of categorization. In E. Rosch & B. B. Lloyd (Eds.), *Cognition and categorization* (pp. 27–48). Hillsdale, NJ: Erlbaum.

Roscoe, B., Cavanaugh, L. E., & Kennedy, D. R. (1988). Dating infidelity: Behaviors, reasons, and consequences. *Adolescence*, *23*, 35–43.

Rosenthal, R. (1994). Science and ethics in conducting, analyzing, and reporting psychological research. *Psychological Science*, *5*, 127–134.

Rosentock, I. M., Strecher, V. J., & Becker, M. H. (1994). The health belief model and HIV risk behavior change. In R. J. DiClemente & J. L. Peterson (Eds.), *Preventing AIDS: Theories and methods of behavioral interventions* (pp. 5–24). New York, NY: Plenum.

Ross, M. W., & Kauth, M. R. (2002). Men who have sex with men and the Internet: Emerging clinical issues and their management. In A. Cooper (Ed.), *Sex and the Internet: A guidebook for clinicians* (pp. 47–69). Philadelphia, PA: Brunner-Routledge.

Ross, M. W., & Williams, M. L. (2001). Sexual behavior and illicit drug use. *Annual Review of Sex Research*, *12*, 290–310.

Rosser, B. R. S., Bockting, W. O., Ross, M. W., Miner, M. H., & Coleman, E. (2008). The relationship between homosexuality, internalized homonegativity, and mental health in men who have sex with men. *Journal of Homosexuality*, *55*, 185–203.

Rotella, R. J., & Murray, M. (1991). Homophobia, the world of sport, and sport psychology consulting. *The Sport Psychologist*, *5*, 355–364.

Rotenberg, K. J., & Korol, S. (1995). The role of loneliness and gender in individuals' love styles. *Journal of Social Behavior and Personality*, *10*, 537–546.

Rothbaum, F., Pott, M., Azuma, H., Miyake, K., & Weisz, J. (2000). The development of close relationships in Japan and the United States: Paths of symbiotic harmony and generative tension. *Child Development*, *71*, 1121–1142.

Rotheram-Borus, M. J., Hunter, J., & Rosario, M. (1994). Suicidal behavior and gay related stress among gay and bisexual male adolescents. *Journal of Adolescent Research*, *9*, 498–508.

Rotheram-Borus, M. J., Reid, H., Rosario, M., & Kasen, S. (1995). Determinants of safer sex patterns among gay/bisexual male adolescents. *Journal of Adolescence, 9*, 498–508.

Rouse, L. P. (1988). Abuse in dating relationships: A comparison of Blacks, Whites, and Hispanics. *Journal of College Student Development*, *29*, 312–319.

Rowatt, T. J., Cunningham, M. R., Rowatt, W. C., Miles, S. S., Ault-Gauthier, L. K., Georgiana, J., & Shamblin, S. (1997, July). *Men and women are from Earth: Life-span strategy dynamics in mate choices*. Paper presented at the meeting of the International Network on Personal Relationships, Oxford, OH.

Rozee, P. (1993). Forbidden or forgiven: Rape in cross-cultural perspective. *Psychology of Women Quarterly*, *17*, 499–514.

Rubin, Z., Hill, C. T., Peplau, L. A., & Dunkel-Schetter, C. (1980). Self-disclosure in dating couples: Sex roles and the ethic of openness. *Journal of Marriage and the Family*, *42*, 305–317.

Runtz, M. (2002). Health concerns of university women with a history of child physical and sexual maltreatment. *Child Maltreatment*, *7*, 241–253.

Ruppel, H. J., Jr. (1994). *Publication trends in the sexological literature: A comparison of two contemporary journals*. Unpublished doctoral dissertation. Institute for the Advanced Study of Human Sexuality, San Francisco, CA.

Ruscombe-King, R. (2009). Homophobia, prejudice, and attitudes to gay men and lesbians. AVERT (an international AIDS charity). Retrieved from: http://www.avert.org/homophobia.htm

Ryan, C., & Futterman, D. (1998). *Lesbian & gay youth: Care and counseling*. New York, NY: Columbia University Press.

Ryan, K. M., Weikel, K., & Sprechini, G. (2008). Gender differences in narcissism and courtship violence in dating couples. *Sex Roles*, *58*, 802–813.

Saad, L. (2008, June 18). Americans evenly divided on morality of homosexuality. *Gallup*. Retrieved from: http://www.gallup.com/poll/108115/americans-evenly-divided-morality-homosexuality.aspx

Saad, L. (2010, May 10). Americans' acceptance of gay relations crosses 50% threshold. *Gallup*. Retrieved from http://www.gallup.com/poll/135764/americans-acceptance-gay-relations-crosses-thresold.aspx

Sabini, J., & Green, M. C. (2004). Emotional responses to sexual and emotional infidelity: Constants and differences across genders, samples and methods. *Personality and Social Psychology Bulletin*, *30*, 1375–1388.

Sabini, J., & Silver, M. (2005). Gender and jealousy: Stories of infidelity. *Cognition and Emotion*, *19*(5), 713–727.

Sadalla, E. K., Kenrick, D. T., & Vershure, B. (1987). Dominance and heterosexual attraction. *Journal of Personality and Social Psychology*, *52*, 730–738.

Sadker, D., & Zittleman, K. (2005). Gender bias lives, for both sexes. *Education Digest, 70*, 27–30.

Sadler, A. G., Booth, B. M., Cook, B. L., & Doebbeling, B. N. (2003). Factors associated with women's risk of rape in the military environment. *American Journal of Industrial Medicine, 43*, 262–273.

Salekin, R. T., Rogers, R., & Sewell, K. W. (1996). A review and meta-analysis of the psychopathy checklist and psychopathy checklist-revised: Predictive validity of dangerousness. *Clinical Psychology—Science and Practice*, *3*(3), 203–215.

Sanday, P. R. (1981). The socio-cultural context of rape: A cross-cultural study. *Journal of Social Issues*, *37*, 5–27.

Sanday, P. R. (1990). *Fraternity gang rape: Sex, brotherhood, and privilege on campus.* New York, NY: New York University.

Sanders, S. A., & Reinisch, J. M. (1999). Would you say you "had sex" if . . . ? *Journal of the American Medical Association, 281*, 275–277.

*Sanderson, C. A. (1999). Role of relationship context influencing college students' responsiveness to HIV-prevention videos. *Health Psychology, 18*(3), 295–300.

*Sanderson, C. A., & Jemmott, J. B., III. (1996). Moderation and mediation of HIV prevention interventions: Relationship status, intentions, and condom use among college students. *Journal of Applied Social Psychology, 26*(23), 2076–2099.

Sappington, A. A., Pharr, R., Tunstall, A., & Rickert, E. (1997). Relationships among child abuse, date abuse, and psychological problems. *Journal of Clinical Psychology, 53*, 319–329.

Savin-Williams, R. C. (1994). Verbal and physical abuse as stressors in the lives of lesbian, gay male, and bisexual youths: Associations with school problems, running away, substance abuse, prostitution, and suicide. *Journal of Consulting and Clinical Psychology, 62*, 261–269.

Savin-Williams, R. C. (2005). *The new gay teenager.* Cambridge, MA: Harvard University Press.

Savin-Williams, R. C., & Cohen, K. M. (2007). Development of same-sex attracted youth. In I. H. Meyer & M. E. Northridge (Eds.), *The health of sexual minorities: Public health perspectives on lesbian, gay, bisexual and transgender populations* (pp. 27–47). New York, NY: Springer.

Schaefer, M. T., & Olson, D. H. (1981). Assessing intimacy: The PAIR inventory. *Journal of Marital and Family Therapy, 7*, 47–60.

Schmitt, D. P., & Buss, D. M. (2001). Human mate poaching: Tactics and temptations for infiltrating existing mateships. *Journal of Personality and Social Psychology, 80*, 894–917.

Schmitt, D. P., & 121 Members of the International Sexuality Description Project. (2004). Patterns and universals of mate poaching across 53 nations: The effects of sex, culture, and personality on romantically attracting another person's partner. *Journal of Personality and Social Psychology, 86*, 560–584.

Schnarch, D. (1991). *Constructing the sexual crucible: An integration of sexual and marital therapy.* New York, NY: Norton.

Scholly, K., Katz, A. R., Gascoigne, J., & Holck, P. S. (2005). Using social norms theory to explain perceptions and sexual health behaviors of undergraduate college students. *Journal of American College Health, 53*, 159–166.

Schuetze, H. G., & Slowey, M. (2002). Participation and exclusion: A comparative analysis of non-traditional students and lifelong learners in higher education. *Higher Education, 44*, 309–327.

Schulenburg, J. E., O'Malley, P. M., Bachman, J. G., & Johnston, L. D. (2005). Early adult transitions and their relation to well-being and substance use. In R. Setterstein, F. Furstenburg, & R. Rumbault (Eds.), *On the frontier of adulthood: Theory, research, and public policy* (pp. 417–453). Chicago, IL: University of Chicago Press.

Schwartz, B. (2000). The tyranny of freedom. *American Psychologist, 55*, 79–88.

Schwartz, J. (2010, October 2). Bullying, suicide, punishment. *New York Times.* Retrieved from http://www.nytimes.com/2010/10/03/weekinreview/03schwartz.html

Schwartz, N. (1999). Self-reports: How the questions shape the answers. *American Psychologist, 54*, 93–105.

Schwartz, R. H., Milteer, R., & LeBeau, M. A. (2000). Drug facilitated sexual assault. *Southern Medical Journal, 93*, 558–561.

Scully, D., & Marolla, J. (1984). Convicted rapists' vocabulary of motive: Excuses and justifications. *Social Problems, 31*, 530–544.

Seal, D. W., Agostinelli, G., & Hannett, C. A. (1994). Extradyadic romantic involvement: Moderating effects of sociosexuality and gender. *Sex Roles, 31*, 1–22.

Segraves, R. T. (2010). Considerations for an evidence-based definition of premature ejaculation in the DSM-V. *Journal of Sexual Medicine, 7*(2, Pt. 1), 679–689.

Senn, C. Y., Desmarais, S., Verberg, N., & Wood, E. (2000). Predicting coercive sexual behavior across the lifespan in a random sample of Canadian men. *Journal of Social and Personal Relationships, 17*(1), 95–113.

Seto, M. C., & Barbaree, H. E. (1995). The role of alcohol in sexual aggression. *Clinical Psychology Review, 15*, 545–566.

Shaver, P., Schwartz, J., Kirson, D., & O'Connor, C. (1987). Emotion knowledge: Further exploration of a prototype approach. *Journal of Personality and Social Psychology, 52*, 1061–1086.

Shaver, P. R., Wu, S., & Schwartz, J. C. (1991). Cross-cultural similarities and differences in emotion and its representation: A prototype approach. In M. S. Clark (Ed.), *Review of personality and social psychology* (Vol. 13, pp. 175–212). Newbury Park, CA: Sage.

Shaw, J. (1994). Treatment of primary vaginismus: A new perspective. *Journal of Sex & Marital Therapy, 20*(1), 46–55.

Sheppard, V. J., Nelson, E. S., & Andreoli-Mathie, V. (1995). Dating relationships and infidelity: Attitudes and behaviors. *Journal of Sex and Marital Therapy, 21*, 202–212.

Sherfey, M. J. (1966). The evolution and nature of female sexuality in relation to psychoanalytic theory. *Journal of the American Psychoanalytic Association, 14*, 28–128.

Sherwin, R., & Corbett, S. (1985). Campus sexual norms and dating relationships: A trend analysis. *The Journal of Sex Research, 21*, 258–274.

Shon, S. & Ja, D. (1982). Asian families. In M. McGoldrick, J. Pearce, & J. Giordano (Eds.), *Ethnicity and family therapy* (2nd ed., pp. 208–228). New York, NY: Guilford Press.

*Shulkin, J. J., Mayer, J. A., Wessel, L. G., de Moor, C, Elder, J. P., & Franzini, L. R., (1991). Effects of a peer-led AIDS intervention with university students. *Journal of College Health, 40*(2), 75–78.

Sikkema, K. J., Kelly, J. A., Winett, R. A., Solomon, L. J., Cargill, V. A., Roffman, R. A., . . . Mercer, M. B. (2000). Outcomes of a randomized community-level HIV prevention intervention for women living in 18 low-income housing developments. *American Journal of Public Health, 90*, 57–63.

*Sikkema, K. J., Winett, R. A., & Lombard, D. N. (1995). Development and evaluation of an HIV-risk reduction program for female college students. *AIDS Education and Prevention, 7*, 145–159.

Simon, R. (1995). Gender, multiple roles, role meaning, and mental health. *Journal of Health and Social Behavior, 36*, 182–194.

Simpson, J. A. (1987). The dissolution of romantic relationships: Factors involved in relationship stability and emotional distress. *Journal of Personality and Social Psychology, 53*, 683–692.

Simpson, J. A., Campbell, B., & Berscheid, E. (1986). The association between romantic love and marriage: Kephart (1967) twice revisited. *Personality and Social Psychology Bulletin*, *12*, 363–372.

Simpson, J. A., & Gangestad, S. W. (1991). Individual differences in sociosexuality: Evidence for convergent and discriminant validity. *Journal of Personality and Social Psychology*, *60*, 870–883.

Simpson, J. A., & Gangestad, S. W. (1992). Sociosexuality and romantic partner choice. *Journal of Personality*, *60*, 31–51. doi:10.1111/j.1467-6494.1992.tb00264.x

Simpson, J. A., Wilson, C. L., & Winterheld, H. A. (2004). Sociosexuality and romantic relationships. In J. H. Harvey, A. Wenzel, & S. Sprecher (Eds.), *The handbook of sexuality in close relationships* (pp. 87–112). Mahwah, NJ: Erlbaum.

Sinclair, H. C., & Frieze, I. H. (2002). Initial courtship behavior and stalking: How should we draw the line? In K. E. Davis, I. H. Frieze, & R. D. Maiuro (Eds.), *Stalking: Perspectives on victims and perpetrators* (pp. 186–211). New York, NY: Springer.

Sinclair, H. C., & Frieze, I. H. (2005). When courtship persistence becomes intrusive pursuit: Comparing rejecter and pursuer perspectives of unrequited attraction. *Sex Roles*, *52*, 839–852.

Smith, P. D., & Roberts, C. M. (2009). American College Health Association annual Pap test and sexually transmitted infection survey: 2006. *Journal of American College Health*, *57*(4), 389–394.

Smith, T. W. (1990). The polls—a report: The sexual revolution? *The Public Opinion Quarterly*, *54*, 415–435.

Smith, T. W. (1994). Attitudes toward sexual permissiveness: Trends, correlates, and behavioral connections. In A. S. Rossi (Ed.), *Sexuality across the life course* (pp. 63–97). Chicago, IL: University of Chicago Press.

Smith, T. W. (2006). Sexual behavior in the United States. In R. D. McAnulty & M. M. Burnette (Eds.), *Sex and sexuality* (Vol. 1, pp. 103–132). Westport, CT: Praeger.

Snyder, M., Simpson, J. A., & Gangestad, S. (1986). Personality and sexual relations. *Journal of Personality and Social Psychology*, *51*, 181–190. doi:10.1037/0022-3514.51.1.181

Sobo, E. (1995). Women and AIDS in the United States. In E. Sobo (Ed.), *Choosing unsafe sex: AIDS-risk denial among disadvantaged inner city women* (pp. 9–24). Philadelphia, PA: University of Pennsylvania Press.

Solomon, M. Z., & DeJong, W. (1986). Sexually transmitted disease prevention efforts and their implications for AIDS health education. *Health Education Quarterly*, *13*, 301–316.

Sommers, C. H. (1994). *Who stole feminism?: How women have betrayed women*. New York, NY: Simon & Schuster.

Sorenson, S. B., & Siegel, J. M. (1992). Gender, ethnicity, and sexual assault: Findings from a Los Angeles study. *Journal of Social Issues*, *48*(1), 93–104.

Spiegel, J. (2003). *Sexual abuse of males*. New York, NY: Brunner-Routledge.

Spitzberg, B. H. (1998). Sexual coercion in courtship relations. In B. H. Spitzberg & W. R. Cupach (Eds.), *The dark side of close relationships* (pp. 179–232). Mahwah, NJ: Erlbaum.

Spitzberg, B. H., & Cupach, W. R. (1996, July). *Obsessive relational intrusion: Victimization and coping*. Paper presented at the meeting of the International Society for the Study of Personal Relationships, Banff, Alberta, Canada.

Spitzberg, B. H., & Cupach, W. R. (2001). Paradoxes of pursuit: Toward a relational model of stalking-related phenomena. In J. A. Davis (Ed.), *Stalking crimes and victim protection: Prevention, intervention, and threat assessment* (pp. 97–136). Boca Raton, FL: CRC Press.

Spitzberg, B. H., & Cupach, W. R. (2002). The inappropriateness of relational intrusion. In R. Goodwin & D. Cramer (Eds.), *Inappropriate relationships: The unconventional, the disapproved, and the forbidden* (pp. 191–219). Mahwah, NJ: Erlbaum.

Spitzberg, B. H., & Cupach, W. R. (2003). What mad pursuit? Obsessive relational intrusion and stalking related phenomena. *Aggression and Violent Behavior, 8*, 345–375.

Spitzberg, B. H., & Cupach, W. R. (2007). The state of the art of stalking: Taking stock of an emerging literature. *Aggression and Violent Behavior, 12*, 64–86.

Spitzer, R. L. (2003). Can some gay men and lesbians change their sexual orientation? 200 participants reporting a change from homosexual to heterosexual orientation. *Archives of Sexual Behavior, 32*(5), 403–417.

Sprecher, S. (1988). Investment model, equity and social support determinants of relationship commitment. *Social Psychology Quarterly, 51*, 318–328.

Sprecher, S. (1989). Premarital sexual standards for different categories of individuals. *The Journal of Sex Research, 26*, 232–248. doi:10.1080/00224498909551508

Sprecher, S. (1992). How men and women expect to feel and behave in response to inequity in close relationships. *Social Psychology Quarterly, 55*, 57–69.

Sprecher, S. (1998). Social exchange theories and sexuality. *The Journal of Sex Research, 35*, 32–43.

Sprecher, S. (2002). Sexual satisfaction in premarital relationships: Associations with satisfaction, love, commitment, and stability. *The Journal of Sex Research, 3*, 1–7.

Sprecher, S., & Hatfield, E. (1996). Premarital sexual standards among U.S. college students: Comparisons with Russian and Japanese students. *Archives of Sexual Behavior, 25*, 261–288. doi:10.1007/BF02438165

Sprecher, S., & McKinney, D. (1993). *Sexuality*. Newbury Park, CA: Sage.

Sprecher, S., McKinney, K., & Orbuch, T. L. (1991). The effect of current sexual behavior on friendship, dating, and marriage desirability. *The Journal of Sex Research, 28*, 387–408.

Sprecher, S., McKinney, K., Walsh, R., & Anderson, C. (1988). A revision of the Reiss Premarital Sexual Permissiveness Scale. *Journal of Marriage and the Family, 50*, 821–828. doi:10.2307/352650

Sprecher, S., & Metts, S. (1989). Development of the "Romantic Beliefs Scale" and examination of the effects of gender and gender-role orientation. *Journal of Social and Personal Relationships, 6*, 387–411.

Sprecher, S., & Metts, S. (1999). Romantic beliefs: Their influence on relationships and patterns of change over time. *Journal of Social and Personal Relationships, 16*, 834–851.

Sprecher, S., & Regan, P. C. (1996). College virgins: How men and women perceive their sexual status. *The Journal of Sex Research, 33*, 3–15. doi:10.1080/00224499609551810

Sprecher, S., & Regan, P. C. (1998). Passionate and companionate love in courting and young married couples. *Sociological Inquiry, 68*, 163–185.

Sprecher, S., & Regan, P. C. (2002). Liking some things (in some people) more than others: Partner preferences in romantic relationships and friendships. *Journal of Social and Personal Relationships, 19*, 436–481. doi:10.1177/0265407502019004048

Sprecher, S., Regan, P. C., McKinney, K., Maxwell, K., & Wazienski, R. (1997). Preferred level of sexual experience in a date or mate: The merger of two methodologies. *The Journal of Sex Research, 34*, 327–337. doi:10.1080/00224499709551901

Sprecher, S., & Toro-Morn, M. (2002). A study of men and women from different sides of earth to determine if men are from Mars and women are from Venus in their beliefs about love and romantic relationships. *Sex Roles, 46*, 131–147.

Sroufe, L. A., Egeland, B., Carlson, E. A., & Collins, W. A. (2005). *The development of the person*. New York, NY: Guilford.

Stall, R. D., & Purcell, D. W. (2000). Intertwining epidemics: A review of research on substance use among men who have sex with men and its connection to the AIDS epidemic. *AIDS and Behavior, 4*, 181–192.

Steele, C. M., & Josephs, R. A. (1990). Alcohol myopia: Its prized and dangerous effects. *American Psychologist*, 45*(8)*, 921–933.

Steele, L. S., Ross, L. E., Dobinson, C., Veldhuizen, S., & Tinmouth, J. M. (2009). Women's sexual orientation and health: Results from a Canadian population-based study. *Women & Health, 49*(5), 353–367.

Steinberg, L. (2004). Risk taking in adolescence: What changes, and why? *Annals of the New York Academy of Sciences, 1021*, 51–58.

Steinberg, M., & Schnall, M. (2000). *The stranger in the mirror: Dissociation—the hidden epidemic*. New York, NY: Cliff Street Books.

Stephenson, K. R., & Sullivan, K. T. (2009) Social norms and general sexual satisfaction: The cost of misperceived descriptive norms. *Canadian Journal of Human Sexuality, 18*, 89–105.

Stepp, L. S. (2007). *Unhooked: How young women pursue sex, delay love and lose at both*. New York, NY: Riverhead Books.

Stermac, L., Reist, D., Addison, M., & Millar, G. M. (2002). Childhood risk factors for women's sexual victimization. *Journal of Interpersonal Violence, 17*, 647–670.

Stermac, L. Sheridan, P. M., Davidson, A., & Dunn, S. (1996). Sexual assault of adult males. *Journal of Interpersonal Violence, 11*(1), 52–64.

Sternberg, R. J. (1986). A triangular theory of love. *Psychological Review, 93*, 119–135.

Sternberg, R. J. (1987). *The triangle of love: Intimacy, passion, commitment*. New York, NY: Basic Books.

Sternberg, R. J. (1997). Construct validation of a triangular love scale. *European Journal of Social Psychology, 27*, 313–335.

Sternberg, R. J. (1998). *Cupid's arrow: The course of love through time*. Cambridge, England: Cambridge University Press.

Sternberg, R. J. (2006). A duplex theory of love. In R. J. Sternberg & K. Weis (Eds.), *The new psychology of love* (pp. 184–199). New Haven, CT: Yale University Press.

Stevens, R. A. (2004). Understanding gay identity development within the college environment. *Journal of College Student Development, 45*(2), 185–206.

Stinson, R. D. (2010). Hooking up in young adulthood: A review of factors influencing the sexual behavior of college students. *Journal of College Student Psychotherapy, 24*, 98–115.

St. Lawrence, J., Eldridge, G., Reitman, D., Little, C., Shelby, M., & Brasfield, T. (1998). Factors influencing condom use among African American women: Implications for risk reduction interventions. *American Journal of Community Psychology, 26*, 7–28.

Stokes, J. P., Miller, R. L., & Mundhenk, R. (1998). Toward an understanding of behaviourally bisexual men: The influence of context and culture. *The Canadian Journal of Human Sexuality*, 7(2), 101–113.

Sturaro, C., Denissen, J. J. A., van Aken, M. A. G., & Asendorpf, J. B. (2008). Person-environment transactions during emerging adulthood: The interplay between personality characteristics and social relationships. *European Psychologist, 13*, 1–11.

Sullivan, H. S. (1953). *The interpersonal theory of psychiatry*. New York, NY: Norton.

Sullivan, J. P., & Mosher, D. L. (1990). Acceptance of guided imagery of marital rape as a function of macho personality. *Violence and Victims*, *5*(4), 275–286.

Surra, C. (1990). Research and theory on mate selection and premarital relationships in the 1980s. *Journal of Marriage and the Family*, *52*, 844–865.

Swartout, K. M., & White, J. W. (2010). The relationship between drug use and sexual aggression in men across time. *Journal of Interpersonal Violence*, *25*(9), 1716–1735.

Tang, C. S. K., Wong, D., & Cheung, F. M. C. (2002). Social construction of women as legitimate victims of violence in Chinese societies. *Violence Against Women*, 8, 968–996.

Tanner, J. L. (2006). Recentering during emerging adulthood: A critical turning point in life span human development. In J. J. Arnett & J. L. Tanner (Eds.), *Emerging adults in America: Coming of age in the 21st century* (pp. 21–55). Washington, DC: American Psychological Association.

Tansill, E. C., Edwards, K. M., Kearns, M. C., Calhoun, K. S., & Gidycz, C. A. (2010). *Sexual victimization, trauma symptomatology, and physical health symptomatology*. Manuscript in preparation.

Taylor, H. (1994). Thirty-one percent of women workers and seven percent of male workers say they were sexually harassed at work. *The Harris Poll*, *18*, 1–7.

Taylor, S. P., & Leonard, K. E. (1983). Alcohol and human physical aggression. In R. G. Green & E. I. Donnerstein (Eds.), *Aggression: Theoretical and empirical reviews* (pp. 77–101). San Diego, CA: Academic Press.

Tedeschi, J. T., & Felson, R. B. (1994). *Violence, aggression, and coercive actions*. Washington, DC: American Psychological Association.

Testa, M. (2002). The impact of men's alcohol consumption on perpetration of sexual aggression. *Clinical Psychology Review*, *22*, 1239–1263.

Testa, M., Hoffman, J. H., & Livingston, J. A. (2010). Alcohol and sexual risk behaviors as mediators of the sexual victimization-revictimization relationship. *Journal of Consulting and Clinical Psychology*, *78*, 249–259.

Testa, M., & Livingston, J. A. (2000). The role of women's alcohol consumption in evaluation of vulnerability to sexual aggression. *Experimental and Clinical Psychopharmacology*, *8*, 185–191.

Testa, M., & Parks, K. A. (1996). The role of women's alcohol consumption in sexual victimization. *Aggression & Violent Behavior*, *1*, 217–234.

Testa, M., VanZile-Tamsen, C., Livingston, J. A., & Koss, M. P. (2004). Assessing women's experiences of sexual aggression using the Sexual Experiences Survey: Evidence for validity and implications for research. *Psychology of Women Quarterly*, *28*, 256–265.

Teten, A. L., Hall, G. C. N., &. Capaldi, D. M. (2009). Use of coercive sexual tactics across 10 years in at-risk young men: Developmental patterns and co-occurring problematic dating behaviors. *Archives of Sex Behavior*, *38*, 574–582.

Thibaut, J. W., & Kelley, H. H. (1959). *The social psychology of groups*. New York, NY: Wiley.

Thornhill, R., & Palmer, C. T. (2000). *A natural history of rape: Biological bases of sexual coercion*. Cambridge, MA: MIT Press.

Thornton, A., & Young-DeMarco, L. (2001). Four decades of trends in attitudes toward family issues in the United States: The 1960s through the 1990s. *Journal of Marriage and the Family*, *63*, 1009–1037.

Thurlow, C. (2001). Naming the "outsider within": Homophobic pejoratives and the verbal abuse of lesbian, gay, and bisexual high-school pupils. *Journal of Adolescence, 24, 25–38.*

Tiefer, L. (1995). *Sex is not a natural act and other essays.* Boulder, CO: Westview Press.

Till, F. (1980). *Sexual Harassment: A report on the sexual harassment of students.* Washington, DC: National Advisory Council on Women's Educational Programs.

Tjaden, P. & Thoennes, N. (1998). *Prevalence, incidence, and consequences of violence against women: Findings from the National Violence Against Women survey.* Washington, DC: National Institute of Justice.

Tjaden, P. & Thoennes, N. (2000). Prevalence and consequences of male-to-female and female-to-male intimate partner violence as measured by the National Violence Against Women Survey. *Violence Against Women, 6*(2), 142–161.

Tolman, D. L. (2002). *Dilemmas of desire: Teenage girls talk about sexuality.* Cambridge, MA: Harvard University Press.

Toyama, M. (2002). Positive illusions in close relationships among college students. *Japanese Journal of Social Psychology, 18,* 51–60.

Træen, B., Holmen, K., & Stigum, H. (2007). Extradyadic sexual relationships in Norway. *Archives of Sexual Behavior, 36,* 55–65.

Træen, B., & Martinussen, M. (2008). Extradyadic activity in a random sample of Norwegian couples. *The Journal of Sex Research, 45*(4), 319–328.

Treas, J., & Giesen, D. (2000). Sexual infidelity among married and cohabitating Americans. *Journal of Marriage and the Family, 62,* 48–60.

Triandis, H. C. (1995). *Individualism and collectivism.* Boulder, CO: Westview Press.

Triandis, H. C. (2001). Individualism-collectivism and personality. *Journal of Personality, 69,* 907–924.

Trivers, R. L. (1972). Parental investment and sexual selection. In B. Campbell (Ed.), *Sexual selection and the descent of man: 1871–1971* (pp. 136–179). Chicago, IL: Aldine.

Trotter, E. C., & Alderson, K. G (2007). University students' definitions of having sex, sexual partner, and virginity loss: The influence of participant gender, sexual experience, and contextual factors. *The Canadian Journal of Human Sexuality, 16*(1–2), 11–29.

Turchik, J. A., & Garske, J. P. (2009). Measurement of sexual risk taking among college students. *Archives of Sexual Behavior, 38,* 936–948.

Turchik, J. A., Probst, D. R., Chau, M., Nigoff, A., & Gidycz, C. A. (2007). Factors predicting the type of tactics used to resist sexual assault: A prospective study of college women. *Journal of Consulting and Clinical Psychology, 75,* 605–614.

Turmanis, S. A., & Brown, R. I. (2006). The Stalking and Harassment Behaviour Scale: Measuring the incidence, nature, and severity of stalking and relational harassment and their psychological effects. *Psychology and Psychotherapy: Theory, Research and Practice, 79,* 183–198.

Turner, J. S. (2003). *Dating and sexuality in America.* Santa Barbara, CA: ABC-CLIO.

Uecker, J. E., & Stokes, C. E. (2008). Early marriage in the United States. *Journal of Marriage and the Family, 70,* 835–846.

Ullman, S. E. (1996a). Correlates and consequences of adult sexual assault disclosure. *Journal of Interpersonal Violence, 11,* 554–571.

Ullman, S. E. (1996b). Do social reactions to sexual assault victims vary by support provider? *Violence and Victims, 11,* 143–156.

Ullman, S. E. (1996c). Social reactions, coping strategies, and self-blame attributions in adjustment to sexual assault. *Psychology of Women Quarterly, 20,* 505–526.

Ullman, S. E., & Brecklin, L. R. (2000). Alcohol and adult sexual assault in a national sample of women. *Journal of Substance Abuse, 11*, 405–420.

Ullman, S. E., Karabatsos, G., & Koss, M. P. (1999). Alcohol and sexual aggression in a national sample of college men. *Psychology of Women Quarterly, 23*, 673–689.

Ullman, S. E. & Knight, R. A. (1993). The efficacy of women's resistance strategies in rape situations. *Psychology of Women Quarterly, 17*, 23–38.

Ullman, S. E., & Siegel, J. M. (1995). Sexual assault, social reactions and physical health. *Women's Health, 1*, 289–308.

University of California at Berkeley. (n.d.). *Unity house.* Retrieved from http://themeprograms.berkeley.edu/unity.html

University of Illinois at Chicago. (n.d.). *Safe zone.* Retrieved from http://www.housing.uic.edu/current/safe-zone.php#how

University of North Dakota. (2010). *Affirmative action.* Retrieved from http://www.und.edu/dept/aao/newharrassment.htm

University of San Diego. (2010). *Rainbow educators.* Retrieved from http://www.sandiego.edu/unitedfront/re/

U.S. Census. (2010). Family and living arrangements. U.S. Census Bureau. Retrieved from http://www.census.gov/population/www/socdemo/hh-fam.html

U.S. Equal Employment Opportunity Commission. Final amendment to guidelines on discrimination because of sex under Title VII of Civil Rights Act of 1964, as amended. 29 C.F.R., pt. 1604. 45 Fed. Reg. 74, 74675-74677 (Nov. 10, 1980).

Valins, L. (1992). *When a woman's body says no to sex: Understanding and overcoming vaginismus.* New York, NY: Viking.

Vanable, P. A., McKirnan, D. J., Buchbinder, S. P., Bartholow, B. N., Douglas, J. M., Judson, F. N., & MacQueen, K. M. (2004). Alcohol use and high-risk sexual behavior among men who have sex with men: The effects of consumption level and partner type. *Health Psychology, 23*(5), 525–532.

van Dulmen, M. H. M., Goncy, E. A., Haydon, K. C., & Collins, W. A. (2008). Distinctiveness of adolescent and emerging adult relationship features in predicting externalizing behavior problems. *Journal of Youth and Adolescence, 37*, 336–345.

van Hoof, A. (1999). The identity status field re-reviewed: An update of unresolved and neglected issues with a view on some alternative approaches. *Developmental Review, 19*, 497–556.

Van Zile-Tamsen, C., Testa, M., & Livingston, J. A. (2005). The impact of sexual assault history and relationship context on appraisal of and responses to acquaintance sexual assault risk. *Journal of Interpersonal Violence, 20*, 813–832.

Varelas, N. & Foley, L. A. (1998). Blacks' and whites' perceptions of interracial and intraracial date rape. *Journal of Social Psychology, 138*, 392–400.

Vasey, P. L., & VanderLaan, D. P. (2010). Avuncular tendencies and the evolution of male androphilia in Samoan *fa'afafine*. *Archives of Sexual Behavior, 39*, 821–830.

Vesely, S. K., Wyatt, V. H., Oman, R. F., Aspy, C. B., Kegler, M. C., Rodine, S., Marshall, L., & Mcleroy, K. R. (2004). The potential protective effects of youth assets from adolescent sexual risk behaviors. *Journal of Adolescent Health, 34*, 356–365.

Vicary, J. R., & Karshin, C. M. (2002). College alcohol abuse: A review of the problems, issues, and prevention approaches. *The Journal of Primary Prevention, 22*(3), 299–331.

Voller, E. K., Long, P. J., & Aosved, A. C. (2009). Attraction to sexual violence towards women, sexual abuse of children, and non-sexual criminal behavior: Testing the Specialist vs. Generalist models in male college students. *Archives of Sexual Behavior, 38*(2), 235–243.

Vrij, A., & Kirby, E. (2002). Sex differences in interpreting male-female dyad interactions: Males' predominance in perceiving sexual intent. *International Review of Victimology*, *9*(3), 289–297.

Wakelin, A., & Long, K. M. (2003). Effects of victim gender and sexuality on attributions of blame to rape victims. *Sex Roles*, *49*(9–10), 477–487.

Waldinger, M. D. (2010). Premature ejaculation and delayed ejaculation. In S. B. Levine, C. B. Risen and S. E. Althof (Eds.). *Handbook of clinical sexuality for mental health professionals* (2nd ed., pp. 267–292). New York, NY: Routledge/Taylor & Francis.

Waldinger, R. J., Diguer, L., Guastealla, F., Lefebvre, R., Allen, J. P., Luborsky, L., & Hauser, S. T. (2002). The same old song? Stability and change in relationship schemas from adolescence to young adulthood. *Journal of Youth and Adolescence*, *31*, 17–44.

Waldner, L. K., Sikka, A., & Baig, S. (1999). Ethnicity and sex differences in university students' knowledge of AIDS, fear of AIDS, and homophobia. *Journal of Homosexuality, 37*, 117–133.

Waldo, C. R. (1998). Out on campus: Sexual orientation and academic climate in a university context. *American Journal of Community Psychology*, *26*(5): 745–774.

Wallace, S. G. (2007, March/April). Hooking up, losing out. *Camping Magazine*, *80*, 27–30.

Wallen, K. (1989). Mate selection: Economics and affection. *Behavioral and Brain Sciences*, *12*, 37–38.

Waller, W., & Hill, R. (1951). *The family: A dynamic interpretation*. New York, NY: Dryden. (Original work published 1938)

Walters, G. D. (1993). Predicting institutional adjustment and recidivism with the Psychopathy Checklist factor scores: A meta-analysis. *Law and Human Behavior*, *27*, 541–558.

Warkentin, J. B., & Gidycz, C. A. (2007). The use and acceptance of sexually aggressive tactics in college men. *Journal of Interpersonal Violence*, *22*(7), 829–850.

Waterman, C. K., Dawson, L. J., & Bologna, M. J. (1989). Sexual coercion in gay male and lesbian relationships: Predictors and implications for support services. *The Journal of Sex Research*, *26*(1), 118–124.

Watkins, C. E. (1990). Psychiatric epidemiology: II. The prevalence and aftermath of sexual assault. *Journal of Counseling & Development*, *68*(3), 341–343.

Weaver, S. E., & Ganong, L. H. (2004). The factor structure of the Romantic Beliefs Scale for African Americans and European Americans. *Journal of Social and Personal Relationships*, *21*, 171–185.

Wechsler, H., Lee, J. E., Nelson, T. F., & Kuo, M. (2002). Underage college students' drinking behavior, access to alcohol, and the influence of deterrence policies: Findings from the Harvard School of Public Health College Alcohol Study. *Journal of American College Health*, *50*(5), 203–217.

Weeks, J. (1991). *Against nature: Essays on history, sexuality and identity*. London, England: Rivers Oram Press.

Weinberg, G. (1972). *Society and the healthy homosexual*. New York: St. Martin's Press.

Weinberg, M. S., Williams, C. J., & Pryor, D. W. (1994). *Dual attraction: Understanding bisexuality*. New York, NY: Oxford University Press.

Weinhardt, L. S., & Carey, M. P. (2000). Does alcohol lead to sexual risk behavior? Findings from event-level research. *Annual Review of Sex Research*, *11*, 125–157.

Weinhardt, L. S., Carey, K. B., & Carey, M. P. (2000). HIV-risk-sensitization following a detailed sexual behavior interview: A preliminary investigation. *Journal of Behavioral Medicine*, *23*, 393–398.

Weinstein, N. D. (1989). Effects of personal experience on self-protective behavior. *Psychological Bulletin, 105*, 31–50.

Weinstock, H., Berman, S., & Cates, W. (2004). Sexually transmitted diseases among American youth: Incidence and prevalence estimates, 2000. *Perspectives on Sexual and Reproductive Health, 36*, 6–10.

Weis, D. L. (1998). Conclusion: The state of sexual theory. *The Journal of Sex Research, 35*, 100–114.

Weis, D. L., Rabinowitz, B., & Ruckstuhl, M. F. (1992). Individual changes in sexual attitudes and behavior within college-level human sexuality courses. *The Journal of Sex Research, 29*, 43–59. doi:10.1080/00224499209551633

*Weiss, C. S., Turbiasz, A. A., & Whitney, D. J. (1995). Behavioral training and AIDS risk reduction: Overcoming barriers to condom use. *AIDS Education and Prevention, 7*(1), 50–59.

Weisz, A., & Black, B. (2001). Sexual assault and dating violence prevention with urban youth: Assessing effectiveness. *Social Work Research, 25*, 89–102.

Wells, B. E., & Twenge, J. M. (2005). Changes in young people's sexual behavior and attitudes, 1943–1999: A cross-temporal meta-analysis. *Review of General Psychology, 9*, 249–261. doi:10.1037/1089-2680.9.3.249

Westefeld, J. S., Maples, M. R., Buford, B., & Taylor, S. (2001). Gay, lesbian, and bisexual college students: The relationship between sexual orientation and depression, loneliness, and suicide. *Journal of College Student Psychotherapy, 15*(3), 71–82.

Wetherill, R. R., Neal, D. J., & Fromme, K. (2010). Parents, peers, and sexual values influence sexual behavior during the transition to college. *Archives of Sexual Behavior, 39*, 682–694.

Wharton, D. (2007, July 28). Young gay athletes find a place on the field. *Los Angeles Times*. Retrieved from http://articles.latimes.com/2007/jul/28/sports/sp-gay28

Wheeler, J. G., George, W. H., & Dahl, B. J. (2002). Sexually aggressive college males: Empathy as a moderator in the "Confluence Model" of sexual aggression. *Personality and Individual Differences, 33*(5), 759–776.

Whisman, M. A., & Snyder, D. K. (2007). Sexual infidelity in a national survey of American women: Differences in prevalence and correlates as a function of method of assessment. *Journal of Family Psychology, 21*(2), 147–154.

White, A. (1995). *Social-psychological factors related to the prevention of male sexual violence: An anti-sexist African American profile*. St. Louis, MO: Missouri Institute of Mental Health.

White, H. R., & Widom, C. S. (2003). Intimate partner violence among abused and neglected children in young adulthood: The mediating effects of early aggression, antisocial personality, hostility and alcohol problems. *Aggressive Behavior, 29*(4), 332–345.

White, J. W., & Koss, M. P (1993). Adolescent sexual aggression within heterosexual relationships: Prevalence, characteristics, and causes. In H. E. Barbaree, W. L. Marshall, & S. M. Hudson (Eds.), *The juvenile sex offender* (pp. 182–202). New York, NY: Guilford.

White, J. W., & Smith, P. H. (2004). Sexual assault perpetration and reperpetration: From adolescence to young adulthood. *Criminal Justice and Behavior, 31*, 182–202.

White, M. I. (1993). *The material child: Coming of age in Japan and America*. New York, NY: Free Press.

White, S., & Yamawaki, N. (2009). The moderating influence of homophobia and gender-role traditionality on perceptions of male rape victims. *Journal of Applied Social Psychology, 39*(5), 1116–1136.

Whitty, M. T. (2003). Pushing the wrong buttons: Men's and women's attitudes toward online and offline infidelity. *CyberPsychology*, *6*(3), 569–579.

Whitty, M. T. (2005). The realness of cybercheating: Men's and women's representations of unfaithful internet relationships. *Social Science Computer Review*, *23*(1), 57–67.

Widmer, E. D., Treas, J., & Newcomb, R. (1998). Attitudes toward nonmarital sex in 24 countries. *The Journal of Sex Research*, *35*, 349–358. doi:10.1080/00224499809551953

Wiederman, M. W. (1997a). Extramarital sex: Prevalence and correlates in a national survey. *The Journal of Sex Research*, *34*, 167–174.

Wiederman, M. W. (1997b). The truth must be in here somewhere: Examining the gender discrepancy in lifetime number of sexual partners. *The Journal of Sex Research*, *34*, 375–386.

Wiederman, M. W. (1999). Volunteer bias in sexuality research involving college student participants. *The Journal of Sex Research*, *36*, 59–66.

Wiederman, M. W. (2002). Reliability and validity of measurement. In M. W. Wiederman & B. E. Whitley Jr. (Eds.), *Handbook for conducting research on human sexuality* (pp. 25–50). Mahwah, NJ: Erlbaum.

Wiederman, M. W., & Dubois, S. L. (1998). Evolution and sex differences in preferences for short-term mates: Results from a policy capturing study. *Evolution and Human Behavior*, *19*, 153–170. doi:10.1016/S1090-5138(98)00006-3

Wiederman, M. W., & Hurd, C. (1999). Extradyadic involvement during dating. *Journal of Social and Personal Relationships*, *16*, 265–274.

Wiederman, M. W., & LaMar, L. (1998). "Not with him you don't": Gender and emotional reactions to sexual infidelity during courtship. *The Journal of Sex Research*, *35*, 288–297.

Wiederman, M. W., & Whitley, B. E., Jr. (Eds.). (2002). *Handbook for conducting research on human sexuality*. Mahwah, NJ: Erlbaum.

Wilder, J. A., Mobasher, Z., & Hammer, M. F. (2004). Genetic evidence for unequal effective population sizes of human females and males. *Molecular Biology and Evolution*, *21*, 2047–2057.

Wildsmith, E., Schelar, E., Peterson, K., & Manlove, J. (2010). *Sexually transmitted diseases among young adults: Prevalence, perceived risk, and risk-taking behaviors* (Research Brief). Washington, DC: Child Trends.

Wilkerson, J. M., Ross, M. W., & Brooks, A. K. (2009). Social construction influencing sociosexual identity development of collegiate gay and bisexual men. *Sexuality Research & Social Policy*, *6*(2), 71–87.

Willand, V. J., & Pollard, P. (2003). Likelihood of acquaintance rape as a function of males' sexual expectations, disappointment, and adherence to rape-conducive attitudes. *Journal of Social and Personal Relationships*, *20*, 637–661.

Willetts, M. C., Sprecher, S., & Beck, F. D. (2004). Overview of sexual practices and attitudes within relational contexts. In J. H. Harvey, A. Wenzel, & S. Sprecher (Eds.), *The handbook of sexuality in close relationships* (pp. 57–85). Mahwah, NJ: Erlbaum.

William T. Grant Foundation Commission on Work, Family, and Citizenship. (1988). *The forgotten half: Non-college bound youth in America*. Washington, DC: William T. Grant Foundation.

Williams, J. E., & Holmes, K. A. (1981). *The second sexual assault: Rape and public attitudes*. Westport, CT: Greenwood.

Williams, S. L., & Frieze, I. H. (2005). Courtship behaviors, relationship violence, and breakup persistence in college men and women. *Psychology of Women Quarterly*, *29*, 248–257.

Williamson, G. M., & Silverman, J. G. (2001). Violence against female partners: Direct and interactive effects of family history, communal orientation, and peer-related variables. *Journal of Social and Personal Relationships*, *18*(4), 535–549.

Willis, C. E. (1992). The effect of sex role stereotype, victim and defendant race, and prior relationships on rape culpability attributions. *Sex Roles*, *26*, 213–226.

Willness, C. R., Steel, P., & Lee, K. (2007). A meta-analysis of the antecedents and consequences of workplace sexual harassment. *Personnel Psychology*, *60*, 127–162.

Wilson, A. E., Calhoun, K. S., & Bernat, J. A. (1999). Risk recognition and trauma-related symptoms among sexually revictimized women. *Journal of Consulting and Clinical Psychology*, *67*, 705–710.

Wilson, G., & Rahman, Q. (2005). *Born gay? The psychobiology of sex orientation*. London, England: Peter Owen.

Wilson, K., Mattingly, B. A., Clark, E. M., Weidler, D. J., & Bequette, A. W. (2011). The gray area: Exploring attitudes toward infidelity and the development of the Perceptions of Dating Infidelity Scale. *Journal of Social Psychology*, *151*(1), 63–86.

Wilson, M., & Daly, M. (1985). Competitiveness, risk-taking, and violence: The young male syndrome. *Ethology and Sociobiology*, *6*, 59–73.

Wilson, W. C. (1975). The distribution of selected sexual attitudes and behaviors among the adult population of the United States. *The Journal of Sex Research*, *11*, 46–64.

Wingood, G., & DiClemente, R. (1998). Relationship characteristics associated with non-condom use among young adult African-American women: Implications for HIV prevention. *Journal of Black Psychology*, *19*, 190–203.

Wingood, G. M., DiClemente, R. J., & Raj, A. (2000). Adverse consequences of intimate partner abuse among women in non-urban domestic violence shelters. *American Journal of Preventive Medicine*, *19*, 270–275.

Wink, P. (1991). Two faces of narcissism. *Journal of Personality and Social Psychology*, *61*, 590–597.

Wolf-Wendel, L. E., Toma, J. D., & Morphew, C. C. (2001). How much difference is too much difference? Perceptions of gay men and lesbians in intercollegiate athletics. *Journal of College Student Development*, *42*, 465–479.

Working Group for a New View of Women's Sexual Problems. (2001). A new view of women's sexual problems. *Women & Therapy*, *24*(1/2), 1–8.

Worthington, R. L., Savoy, H. B., Dillon, F. R., & Vernaglia, E. R. (2002). Heterosexual identity development: A multidimensional model of individual and social identity. *The Counseling Psychologist*, *30*, 496–531.

Wright, L. W., Jr., Adams, H. E., & Bernat, J. (1999). Development and validation of the Homophobia Scale. *Journal of Psychopathology and Behavioral Assessment*, *21*, 337–347.

Wyatt, G. E. (1992). The sociocultural context of African American and white American women's rape. *Journal of Social Issues*, *48*, 77–91.

Wyatt, G. E., Guthrie, D., & Notgrass, C. M. (1992). Differential effects of women's child sexual abuse and subsequent sexual victimization. *Journal of Consulting and Clinical Psychology*, *60*, 167.

Xia, Y. R., & Zhou, Z. G. (2003). The transition of courtship, mate selection, and marriage in China. In R. R. Hamon & B. B. Ingoldsby (Eds.), *Mate selection across cultures* (pp. 231–246). Thousand Oaks, CA: Sage.

Xu, X., & Whyte, M. K. (1990). Love matches and arranged marriages: A Chinese replication. *Journal of Marriage and the Family*, *52*, 709–722.

Yamagishi, T., & Yamagishi, M. (1994). Trust and commitment in the United States and Japan. *Motivation and Emotion*, *18*, 129–166.

Yarab, P. E., Allgeier, E. R., & Sensibaugh, C. C. (1999). Looking deeper: Extradyadic behaviors, jealousy, and perceived unfaithfulness in hypothetical dating relationships. *Personal Relationships*, *6*, 305–316.

Yarab, P. E., Sensibaugh, C. C., & Allgeier, E. R. (1998). More than just sex: Gender differences in the incidence of self-defined unfaithful behavior in heterosexual dating relationships. *Journal of Psychology & Human Sexuality*, *10*, 45–57.

Yeater, E. A., Treat, T. A., Viken, R. J., & McFall, R. M. (2010). Cognitive processes underlying women's risk judgments: Associations with sexual victimization history and rape myth acceptance. *Journal of Consulting and Clinical Psychology*, *78*, 375–386.

Yoder, J. D., & Kahn, A. S. (1992). Toward a feminist understanding of women and power. *Psychology of Women Quarterly*, *16*, 381–388.

Yost, M. R., & Zurbriggen, E. L. (2006). Gender differences in the enactment of sociosexuality: An examination of implicit social motives, sexual fantasies, coercive sexual attitudes, and aggressive sexual behavior. *The Journal of Sex Research*, *43*(2), 163–173.

Zawacki, T., Abbey, A., Buck, P. O., McAuslan, P., & Clinton-Sherrod, A. M. (2003). Perpetrators of alcohol-involved sexual assaults: How do they differ from other sexual assault perpetrators and non-perpetrators? *Aggressive Behavior*, *29*, 366–380.

Zilbergeld, B. (1999). *The new male sexuality* (rev. ed.). New York, NY: Bantam Books. (Original work published 1978)

Zoucha- Jensen, J. M., & Coyne, A. (1993). The effects of resistance strategies on rape. *American Journal of Public Health*, *83*, 1633–1634.

Zuckerman, M. (1979). Sensation seeking and risk taking. In C. E. Izard (Ed.), *Emotions in personality and psychopathology* (pp. 163–197). New York, NY: Plenum.

Zuckerman, M. (1994). Impulsive unsocialized sensation seeking: The biological foundations of basic dimension of personality. In J. E. Bates & T. D. Wachs (Eds.), *Temperament: Individual differences at the interface of biology and behavior* (pp. 219–258). Washington, DC: American Psychological Association.

Zuckerman, M., & Kuhlman, D. M. (2000). Personality and risk-taking: Common biosocial factors. *Journal of Personality*, *68*(6), 999–1029.

Zweig, J. M., Lindberg, L. D., & McGinley, K. A. (2001). Adolescent health risk profiles: The co-occurence of health risks among females and males. *Journal of Youth and Adolescence*, *30*(6), 707–728.

ABOUT THE EDITOR

RICHARD D. MCANULTY, PhD, is Associate Professor of Psychology at the University of North Carolina at Charlotte. He has taught college courses, including human sexuality, for over 20 years. His research interests broadly encompass human sexuality and its problems. Previously published books include *The Psychology of Sexual Orientation, Behavior, and Identity: A Handbook* (1994) (edited with Louis Diamant; Greenwood), the three-volume *Sex and Sexuality* (2006) (edited with Michele Burnette; Praeger), and *Exploring Human Sexuality: Making Healthy Decisions* (2000, 2004) (with Michele Burnette; Allyn & Bacon). He has served on the board of several journals, including the *Journal of Sex Research.*

ABOUT THE CONTRIBUTORS

SARAH E. AINSWORTH graduated with a BA in German from the University of Florida in 2007. After completing postbaccalaureate studies in psychology at the University of Florida, she enrolled in the social psychology doctoral program at Florida State University in 2009. She is currently working with Dr. Roy Baumeister as her main adviser, and her research interests include self-control, free will, and sexuality.

ROY F. BAUMEISTER, PhD, is the Eppes Eminent Professor of Psychology at Florida State University. He has over 450 research publications on topics that include self and identity, self-control, the need to belong and interpersonal rejection, sexuality, aggression, and violence. His books include *The Cultural Animal: Human Nature, Meaning, and Social Life*, *The Social Dimension of Sex*, *Evil: Inside Human Violence and Cruelty*, and *Meanings of Life*.

JOSEPH G. BENJAMIN is a member of the Adolescent Community Health Research Group at DePaul University. His professional background includes extensive work within community-based HIV services organizations on the study, development, and training of various counseling interventions for individuals living with HIV, placing an emphasis on young adults and young men who have sex with men of color.

ANTHONY G. BONITA, MA, is a graduate student in the clinical psychology PhD program at Western Michigan University. He earned his BA in psychology from Loyola College in Maryland, and his MA in clinical psychology from Western Michigan University. His research interests include sexual coercion in college and the online sexual activities of men and women with a range of sexual interests, and he is investigating a treatment for depression and its effect on sexual desire. Anthony has also taught an upper-level course on human sexuality, the psychology of aging, and introduction to psychology. He is a member of the Society for the Scientific Study of Sexuality (SSSS) and has presented research at their national conference.

ANDREA BRADFORD, PhD, is an Instructor in the Department of Gynecologic Oncology and Reproductive Medicine at the University of Texas M. D. Anderson Cancer Center. Her research interests include women's sexuality in the context of chronic illness and treatment of sexual dysfunctions. She is a member of the American Psychological Association, the International Society for the Study of Women's Sexual Health, and the International Academy of Sex Research.

CHARLES A. BURGESS, BA, is a doctoral student in clinical health psychology at University of North Carolina at Charlotte. His primary research interests focus on transition-aged youth with emotional and behavioral disorders, particularly within the context of secondary prevention and early intervention. Other research interests include program evaluation, clinical assessment, and substance abuse prevention and treatment.

KAREN S. CALHOUN, PhD is Professor Emerita of Psychology at the University of Georgia. She is a Fellow of the American Psychological Association and past president of the Society of Clinical Psychology as well as the Southeastern Psychological Association. She has been associate editor of the *Journal of Consulting and Clinical Psychology* and the *Psychology of Women Quarterly*. Her research into the consequences, causes, and prevention of sexual assault has been funded by the NIMH, the CDC, and the National Institute of Justice. She is cochair of the University of Georgia Violence Research Study Group, and winner of the Creative Research Medal and the William A. Owens Award for Creative Research.

ARNIE CANN, PhD, is a Professor in the Psychology Department and the Interdisciplinary Health Doctoral Program at the University of North Carolina–Charlotte. His research has examined relationship issues ranging from responses to infidelity to the impact of sense of humor on relationship satisfaction. Current research is looking at humor as a factor in supporting psychological health and well-being, and at the positive changes that can result from the challenges associated with facing significant life stressors.

KATIE M. EDWARDS, PhD, is an Assistant Professor in the Department of Psychology at the University of New Hampshire. Her area of research focuses broadly on sexual assault and dating violence among adolescents and young adults. Specific research interests include predictors and correlates of interpersonal victimization and perpetration experiences, women's leaving processes in abusive relationships, interpersonal trauma recovery, and ethics of interpersonal trauma research. The ultimate goal of her work is to utilize research data to design efficacious programming and treatment efforts at the individual level and advocate for legislative policy and social change at the institutional and societal levels.

VIRGINIA GIL-RIVAS, PhD, is an Associate Professor of Psychology and Director of the Health Psychology PhD Program at the University of North Carolina at Charlotte. She has received funding from NIH to conduct research on factors contributing to psychosocial adjustment and health among youths and adults exposed to trauma. She has authored numerous journal articles and book chapters, and recently she coedited the book *Helping Families and Communities Recover from Disaster: Lessons Learned from Hurricane Katrina and Its Aftermath* (published by the American Psychological Association).

MASON G. HABER, PhD, is an Assistant Professor of Psychology at the University of North Carolina at Charlotte. His research focuses on coordination of services and other supports for youth facing challenges in transitioning to adulthood, including youth with serious mental health conditions, youth with disabilities, and youth who are residentially unstable or homeless. He has served as a program consultant or evaluator for programs serving transitioning youth in several states in educational, juvenile justice, and behavioral health service systems. His recent publications include a review of models of coordinating care for youth in the criminal justice and mental health settings, and a study of outcomes of youth enrolled at sites in a national demonstration of programs for transitioning youth, the Partnerships for Youth Transition initiative.

GARY W. HARPER, PhD, MPH, is a Professor in the Department of Psychology and Director of the Master of Public Health Program at DePaul University. . His research is focused on multisystemic explorations of the sexual health promotion needs of young people who experience varying degrees of societal oppression and marginalization, with a focus on homeless youth, urban African American and Latina female youth, African American and

Latino gay/bisexual male youth, youth living with HIV, and rural youth in Kenya. For more than 20 years he has worked collaboratively with community agencies and community members to develop and evaluate a range of culturally and developmentally appropriate sexual health promotion/HIV prevention programs for young people, in both the United States and in Kenya.

MICHAEL R. KAUTH, PhD, is Codirector and Associate Director for Education of the Department of Veterans Affairs South Central Mental Illness Research, Education, and Clinical Center (MIRECC) at the Michael E. DeBakey VA Medical Center, Houston, Texas, and Associate Professor in the Menninger Department of Psychiatry and Behavioral Sciences, Baylor College of Medicine. His scholarly interests include models of sexual orientation, evolutionary psychology, dissemination and implementation of educational interventions, and health psychology related to HIV disease. He is the author of *True Nature: A Theory of Sexual Attraction* (2000) and the editor of *Handbook of the Evolution of Human Sexuality* (2006). He is past president of the Mid-continent Region of the Society for the Scientific Study of Sexuality and a member of the American Psychological Association.

PEGGY J. KLEINPLATZ, PhD, is a clinical psychologist, AASECT-certified sex therapist, sex therapy supervisor, and sex educator. She is a Professor in the Faculty of Medicine and Clinical Professor in the School of Psychology, University of Ottawa, Canada. Kleinplatz has been teaching human sexuality since 1983 and was awarded the Prix d'Excellence by the University of Ottawa in 2000. She also teaches sex therapy at the affiliated Saint Paul University's Institute of Pastoral Studies. Her work focuses on optimal sexuality, eroticism, and transformation. Kleinplatz is the editor of *New Directions in Sex Therapy: Innovations and Alternatives* (Routledge, 2001, 2nd edition, 2012).

DIANA LEMOS, MPH, is a doctoral student in community psychology at DePaul University in Chicago, Illinois. Her primary research interests include understanding the factors and mechanisms responsible for urban adolescent healthy development and psychosocial adjustment, with a particular emphasis on micro- and macrolevel processes that impact risk. Additional research interests include primary and secondary HIV, STI prevention, and the relationship between mentoring relationships and psychosocial adjustment.

DAVID P. MCANULTY, PhD, is Associate Professor of Psychology at Abilene Christian University. His research interests include the psychology of religion and the influence of spirituality and religiosity on behavior. Prior to his academic appointment, he spent 22 years in clinical practice with specific specializations in marriage and relationships, as well as in health psychology.

EMILY R. MOUILSO, MS, is a doctoral student in clinical psychology at the University of Georgia, Athens. Her research, under the supervision of Dr. Karen Calhoun, centers on understanding the factors and mechanisms responsible for sexual assault perpetration and victimization, with a particular emphasis on personality. Additional research interests include prevention of sexual assault and the relationship between sexual aggression and general aggression.

DANIEL PERLMAN, PhD, received his doctorate in psychology from the Claremont Graduate University (1971) and has been on faculty at the University of Manitoba (1970–83), the University of British Columbia (1983–2007), and the University of North Carolina at Greensboro (2007–present). His scholarly activities have focused on close relationships, especially loneliness. An advocate of interdisciplinarity, his own training was in social psychology, with its emphasis on individual and interpersonal processes, and family sociology. He is coauthor of the text *Intimate Relationships* (McGraw-Hill) and coeditor of the *Cambridge Handbook of Personal Relationships*. In recent years he has published on the history of relationship research, the beginnings of relationships, interpersonal aspects of sexuality, the maintenance of relationships, the problematic aspects of relationships, and the ways relationships foster well-being. He has served as editor or coeditor of four journals including the *Journal of Social and Personal Relationships* and *Personal Relationships*. He has been actively involved as an elected officer in the International Society for the Study of Personal Relationships (ISSPR), the Society for the Psychological Study of Social Issues (SPSSI), and the Canadian Psychological Association.

PAMELA C. REGAN, PhD, is Professor of Psychology at California State University–Los Angeles. She received her doctorate in psychology from the University of Minnesota and her undergraduate degree in English from Williams College. Her research interest is in the area of interpersonal relationships, with an emphasis on passionate love, sexual attraction, and mate preference. She has published more than 100 journal articles, book chapters, and reviews (and has given over 75 professional presentations) on the dynamics of sex, love, and human mating, and she is the author of *Close Relationships* (Routledge/Taylor & Francis, 2010) and *The Mating Game: A Primer on Love, Sex, and Marriage* (Sage, 2008), and the coauthor (with Ellen Berscheid) of *The Psychology of Interpersonal Relationships* (Pearson, 2005) and *Lust: What We Know about Human Sexual Desire* (Sage, 1999). In 2007, she was honored with the Outstanding Professor Award for excellence in instructional and professional achievement.

SUSAN SPRECHER, PhD, is a Distinguished Professor in the Department of Sociology and Anthropology, at Illinois State University, with a joint appointment in Psychology. She received her doctorate degree from the University of Wisconsin–Madison. Her research, which has spanned over 30 years, has focused on a number of issues about close relationships and sexuality. She was the editor of the journal *Personal Relationships* (2002–6) and has coedited several books or handbooks, most recently, *The Handbook of Sexuality and Close Relationships* (2004; Lawrence Erlbaum), *The Handbook of Relationship Initiation* (2008; Taylor & Francis), *The Science of Compassionate Love* (2009; Blackwell-Wiley), and *The Encyclopedia of Human Relationships* (2009; Sage). She has been actively involved in various positions in the International Association for Relationship Research.

JESSICA VELCOFF, PhD, completed her doctoral degree in community psychology at DePaul University. Her primary research and practice focus is on sexual health. She has worked both domestically and in Kenya on HIV and other STI prevention projects. She has experience in prevention intervention development and evaluation and in research using both qualitative and quantitative methods, and is currently working for the Chicago Women's AIDS Project as an independent consultant.

MICHAEL W. WIEDERMAN, PhD, is a Professor of Psychology at Columbia College, an all-women's college in Columbia, South Carolina. His primary teaching and research interests include human sexuality, gender, evolutionary psychology, and body image. He served as the assistant editor and book review editor for *The Journal of Sex Research*, wrote *Understanding Sexuality Research* (2000; Wadsworth), and coedited *The Handbook for Conducting Research on Human Sexuality* (with B. E. Whitley Jr., 2001; Psychology Press).

LESTER W. WRIGHT JR., PhD, is an Associate Professor of Psychology and directs the Clinical Studies Laboratory at Western Michigan University. He earned his BA in psychology from Florida International University, and his MS and PhD from University of Georgia. He completed his clinical internship at University of Mississippi Medical School/Jackson Veterans Affairs Hospital Consortium and did a one-year postdoctoral fellowship in the Department of Psychiatry at University Hospitals of Cleveland/Case Western Reserve University. His areas of interest are in human sexual behavior and criminal behavior. His current research focuses on deviant sexual behavior, sexual scripts, homophobia, hypermasculinity, empathy in sex offenders, the effects of mood disorders on sexual functioning, and negative and positive gender roles. He is the past president of the Western Michigan Psychological Association.

INDEX

ABOUT THE SERIES EDITOR

JUDY KURIANSKY, PhD, is a licensed clinical psychologist, and adjunct faculty in the Department of Clinical Psychology at Columbia University Teachers College and the Department of Psychiatry at Columbia University College of Physicians and Surgeons, as well as a visiting professor at Peking University Health Sciences Center and Honorary Professor in the Department of Psychiatry of the University of Hong Kong. A Diplomate of the American Board of Sexology, and Fellow of the American Academy of Clinical Sexology, she was awarded the AACS Medal of Sexology for Lifetime Achievement. Dr. Judy is a pioneer of sex diagnosis, dating back to being on the DSM III committee; sex therapy evaluation, including of early Masters and Johnson therapy; and call-in advice about sex on the radio and TV. A cofounder of the Society for Sex Therapy and Research, and past board member of the American Association of Sex Educators, Counselors and Therapists (AASECT), she has authored hundreds of article in professional journals, including the *Journal of Marital and Sex Therapy* and SIECUS reports, and mass-market articles including in *Cosmopolitan* and *Family Circle* magazines. She has written sex advice columns worldwide, including for the *South China Morning Post*, *Singapore Straits Times*, *Sankei Sinbun* newspaper, and the *New York Daily News*. She has developed and led hundreds of workshops about sexuality around the world from China and Japan to India, Israel, Iran, Austria, and Argentina, including on an integration of Eastern and Western techniques for safe sex and for relationship enhancement.